DAX Cookbook

Over 120 recipes to enhance your business with analytics, reporting, and business intelligence

Greg Deckler

BIRMINGHAM - MUMBAI

D1211149

DAX Cookbook

Copyright © 2020 Packt Publishing

Commissioning Editor: Sunith Shetty
Acquisition Editor: Reshma Raman
Content Development Editor: Athikho Sapuni Rishana
Senior Editor: David Sugarman
Technical Editor: Manikandan Kurup
Copy Editor: Safis Editing
Project Coordinator: Aishwarya Mohan
Proofreader: Safis Editing
Indexer: Rekha Nair
Production Designer: Aparna Bhagat

First published: March 2020

Production reference: 1180320

Published by Packt Publishing Ltd.
Livery Place
35 Livery Street
Birmingham
B3 2PB, UK.

ISBN 978-1-83921-707-4

www.packt.com

To my son, Rocket, who thinks it's a big deal that I have my own side panel when he searches my name.

To Charles Sterling, for getting me started with being a Microsoft MVP.

To my friends and family that I ignored because this book took up all my free time.

– Greg Deckler

Packt.com

Subscribe to our online digital library for full access to over 7,000 books and videos, as well as industry leading tools to help you plan your personal development and advance your career. For more information, please visit our website.

Why subscribe?

- Spend less time learning and more time coding with practical eBooks and Videos from over 4,000 industry professionals

- Improve your learning with Skill Plans built especially for you

- Get a free eBook or video every month

- Fully searchable for easy access to vital information

- Copy and paste, print, and bookmark content

Did you know that Packt offers eBook versions of every book published, with PDF and ePub files available? You can upgrade to the eBook version at www.packt.com and as a print book customer, you are entitled to a discount on the eBook copy. Get in touch with us at customercare@packtpub.com for more details.

At www.packt.com, you can also read a collection of free technical articles, sign up for a range of free newsletters, and receive exclusive discounts and offers on Packt books and eBooks.

Contributors

About the author

Greg Deckler is Vice President of the Microsoft Practice at Fusion Alliance and has been a professional technology systems consultant for over 25 years. Internationally recognized as an expert in Power BI, Greg Deckler is a Microsoft MVP for Data Platform and a superuser within the Power BI community with over 100,000 messages read, more than 11,000 replies, over 2,300 answers, and more than 75 entries in the Quick Measures Gallery. Greg founded the **Columbus Azure ML and Power BI User Group (CAMLPUG)** and presents at numerous conferences and events, including SQL Saturday, DogFood, and the Dynamic Communities User Group/Power Platform Summit.

About the reviewers

Bill Anton is an expert in Analysis Services and an experienced data warehouse practitioner. In 2013, he founded Opifex Solutions, a consulting firm with deep expertise in enterprise-scale architecture, design, and performance optimization of analysis services and Power BI solutions. He loves eating and spends most of his free time convincing his beloved wife to adopt more golden retrievers.

Denis Trunin has a master's degree in computer science from Moscow State Technical University, Russia. He has worked with Microsoft Dynamics 365 Finance and Operations (formerly known as Dynamics AX) as a technical consultant for more than 18 years. He is very passionate about Power BI as it has tight integration with the Dynamics 365 product line. He has also been involved in several Power BI implementation projects. Denis lives in Australia with his wife and two kids.

Packt is searching for authors like you

If you're interested in becoming an author for Packt, please visit authors.packtpub.com and apply today. We have worked with thousands of developers and tech professionals, just like you, to help them share their insight with the global tech community. You can make a general application, apply for a specific hot topic that we are recruiting an author for, or submit your own idea.

Table of Contents

Preface

DAX provides an extra edge by extracting key information from the data that is already present in your model. Filled with examples of practical, real-world calculations geared toward business metrics and **key performance indicators (KPIs)**, this cookbook features solutions that you can use for your own business analysis needs.

You'll learn how to write various DAX expressions and functions in order to understand how DAX queries work. This book also contains sections on dates, time, and duration to help you deal with working days, time zones, and shifts. You'll then discover how to manipulate text and numbers in order to create dynamic titles and ranks and deal with measure totals. Later, you'll explore common business metrics for finance, customers, employees, and projects. This book will also show you how to implement common industry metrics such as days of supply, mean time between failures, order cycle time, and overall equipment effectiveness. In the concluding chapters, you'll learn how to apply statistical formulas for covariance, kurtosis, and skewness. Finally, you'll explore advanced DAX patterns for interpolation, inverse aggregators, inverse slicers, and even forecasting with a deseasonalized correlation coefficient.

By the end of this book, you'll have the skills you need to use DAX's functionality and flexibility in business intelligence and data analytics.

Who this book is for

Business users, BI developers, data analysts, and SQL users who are looking for solutions to the challenges faced while solving analytical operations using DAX techniques and patterns will find this book useful. Basic knowledge of the DAX language and Microsoft services is mandatory.

What this book covers

Chapter 1, *Thinking in DAX*, introduces the basic concepts of DAX as a language, including how to think in DAX, where DAX can be used and basic elements such as data model elements, data types, and operators. Also covered are best practices for writing DAX and demonstrating key concepts such as context. Finally, some common DAX calculation patterns are presented with a focus on specific groups of functions.

Chapter 2, *Dealing with Dates and Calendars*, is all about working with calendars and dates. Many useful DAX calculations will be presented that allow the reader to manipulate date and calendar information to derive data that's useful in a business context. This includes dealing with the built-in DAX time intelligence functions but also how to deal with dates when the standard DAX time intelligence functions do not apply. Finally, special attention is paid to dealing with working days and week calculations as they are not covered in standard time intelligence.

Chapter 3, *Tangling with Time and Duration*, is all about working with time and duration. Time and duration are challenging subjects in DAX because duration data types are not supported. While there are numerous date functions, there are few, if any, time functions. In addition, DAX time intelligence really does not deal with time but rather with dates. The chapter provides recipes for many different variations in the concept of time that are useful for most if not all businesses.

Chapter 4, *Transforming Text and Numbers*, focuses on creating general DAX calculations that deal with text and numbers. This includes common patterns such as running and rolling totals for numbers and the concatenation of text. In addition, more uncommon patterns are presented that deal with measure totals, formatting text, and counting the number of items in a list.

Chapter 5, *Figuring Financial Rates and Revenues*, focuses on business financial metrics and how to use DAX to calculate important financial KPIs. All businesses, even non-profits, have financials that must be tracked and measured. This chapter also presents common KPIs that are important to most if not all businesses. Standard AP/AR KPIs are presented along with more uncommon patterns, such as dealing with currency exchange rates.

Chapter 6, *Computing Customer KPIs*, focuses on business customer metrics and how to use DAX to calculate important customer KPIs. All businesses have customers, and there are common customer metrics that most businesses find important. This chapter provides patterns for calculating the customer metrics important to most if not all businesses.

Chapter 7, *Evaluating Employment Measures*, focuses on business employee metrics and how to use DAX to calculate important employee KPIs. All businesses and organizations have employees, and it is important for any organization to have happy, satisfied employees. This chapter provides calculations and patterns for measuring employee health and happiness.

Chapter 8, *Processing Project Performance*, focuses on business project metrics and how to use DAX to calculate important project KPIs. Almost all businesses undertake projects. It is important to track key project metrics to ensure that expected outcomes are being met. This chapter presents numerous KPIs that help ensure that everyone understands the status of projects within the business.

Chapter 9, *Calculating Common Industry Metrics*, focuses on business metrics used in industries such as manufacturing, healthcare, and other industry sectors. The chapter also covers how to use DAX to calculate important industry KPIs.

Chapter 10, *Using Uncommon DAX Patterns*, presents a number of more uncommon DAX patterns that are useful in a wide array of scenarios. These patterns provide the reader with a more in-depth understanding of how to create complex DAX calculations that can solve many different problems. This includes overcoming DAX's inherent limitations regarding looping and recursion, dealing with hierarchies, and even using measures when you are not normally allowed to.

Chapter 11, *Solving Statistical and Mathematical Formulas*, presents a number of advanced DAX calculations for statistical measures and other mathematical formulas. Many of these calculations are very complex and push the limits of DAX coding, but can be incredibly useful in a wide variety of businesses and situations.

Chapter 12, *Applying Advanced DAX Patterns*, presents a number of advanced DAX calculations that demonstrate how to create complex and truly stunning DAX calculations. These DAX calculations push the limits of DAX coding to solve vexing problems as well as complex code for displaying graphics.

Chapter 13, *Debugging and Optimizing DAX*, presents provides guidance around how to handle errors in DAX as well as how to debug DAX calculations and optimize DAX formulas. There are various techniques for debugging DAX calculations. In addition, there are a number of useful techniques for optimizing DAX calculations.

To get the most out of this book

You will need Power BI Desktop and some familiarity with basic operations such as how to create tables, measures, and columns. In addition, it is important that you have some basic data modeling abilities for creating relationships between tables. Finally, you should at least have a rudimentary understanding of DAX as well as some familiarity with the Desktop interface for things such as Sort By columns and formatting options for visuals. All code examples were tested on the latest version of the Power BI Desktop available at the time of writing (February 2020). Older versions of the Power BI Desktop may not have all of the DAX functions used in this book.

If you are using the digital version of this book, we advise you to type the code yourself or access the code via the GitHub repository (the link is in the next section). Doing so will help you avoid any potential errors related to copy/pasting of code.

Download the example code files

You can download the example code files for this book from your account at `www.packt.com`. If you purchased this book elsewhere, you can visit `www.packtpub.com/support` and register to have the files emailed directly to you.

You can download the code files by following these steps:

1. Log in or register at `www.packt.com`.
2. Select the **Support** tab.
3. Click on **Code Downloads**.
4. Enter the name of the book in the **Search** box and follow the onscreen instructions.

Once the file is downloaded, please make sure that you unzip or extract the folder using the latest version of:

- WinRAR/7-Zip for Windows
- Zipeg/iZip/UnRarX for Mac
- 7-Zip/PeaZip for Linux

The code bundle for the book is also hosted on GitHub at https://github.com/PacktPublishing/DAX-Cookbook. In case there's an update to the code, it will be updated on the existing GitHub repository.

We also have other code bundles from our rich catalog of books and videos available at https://github.com/PacktPublishing/. Check them out!

Download the color images

We also provide a PDF file that has color images of the screenshots/diagrams used in this book. You can download it here: https://static.packt-cdn.com/downloads/9781839217074_ColorImages.pdf.

Conventions used

There are a number of text conventions used throughout this book.

CodeInText: Indicates code words in text, database table names, folder names, filenames, file extensions, pathnames, dummy URLs, user input, and Twitter handles. Here is an example: "Mount the downloaded WebStorm-10*.dmg disk image file as another disk in your system."

A block of code is set as follows:

```
Unix2UTC =
    VAR __UnixEpoch = 'R03_Table'[UnixTime]
    VAR __Time = DIVIDE(__UnixEpoch, (60*60*24))
    VAR __SourceBaseDate = DATE(1970, 1, 1)
RETURN (__SourceBaseDate + __Time)
```

Bold: Indicates a new term, an important word, or words that you see onscreen. For example, words in menus or dialog boxes appear in the text like this. Here is an example: "For both visualizations, turn on **Data labels** and set the **Display units** to **None**."

 Warnings or important notes appear like this.

 Tips and tricks appear like this.

Sections

In this book, you will find several headings that appear frequently (*Getting ready, How to do it..., How it works..., There's more...,* and *See also*).

To give clear instructions on how to complete a recipe, use these sections as follows:

Getting ready

This section tells you what to expect in the recipe and describes how to set up any software or any preliminary settings required for the recipe.

How to do it...

This section contains the steps required to follow the recipe.

How it works...

This section usually consists of a detailed explanation of what happened in the previous section.

There's more...

This section consists of additional information about the recipe in order to make you more knowledgeable about the recipe.

See also

This section provides helpful links to other useful information for the recipe.

Get in touch

Feedback from our readers is always welcome.

General feedback: If you have questions about any aspect of this book, mention the book title in the subject of your message and email us at customercare@packtpub.com.

Errata: Although we have taken every care to ensure the accuracy of our content, mistakes do happen. If you have found a mistake in this book, we would be grateful if you would report this to us. Please visit www.packtpub.com/support/errata, selecting your book, clicking on the Errata Submission Form link, and entering the details.

Piracy: If you come across any illegal copies of our works in any form on the Internet, we would be grateful if you would provide us with the location address or website name. Please contact us at copyright@packt.com with a link to the material.

If you are interested in becoming an author: If there is a topic that you have expertise in and you are interested in either writing or contributing to a book, please visit authors.packtpub.com.

Reviews

Please leave a review. Once you have read and used this book, why not leave a review on the site that you purchased it from? Potential readers can then see and use your unbiased opinion to make purchase decisions, we at Packt can understand what you think about our products, and our authors can see your feedback on their book. Thank you!

For more information about Packt, please visit packt.com.

Thinking in DAX

Many moons ago, when learning to write Perl code, I read a blog article about hashes and Perl. While that blog article has been lost to time and the ever-morphing internet, the crux of the article was that if you weren't thinking in hashes, unordered key-value pairs, then you weren't truly thinking in Perl. The theory here was that hashes were the fundamental, native, internal data structure for Perl, and so it was critical that you understood how hashes worked in order to write fast, efficient Perl code.

While I have moved far beyond Perl code in my career, the lesson of that blog article stuck in my mind as I learned new technologies. I have found it incredibly useful to understand the inner workings of new languages and how those languages *think*. Thus, this chapter is all about teaching you how to *think* the way DAX *thinks*. In other words, teaching you how to understand the base inner workings of DAX so that you can write fast, efficient, reliable, and supportable DAX code.

The recipes included in this chapter are as follows:

- Using DAX in Excel, Power BI, and SQL
- Writing good DAX
- Using variables
- Confronting context
- Grouping and summarizing
- Filtering and unfiltering
- Exploiting relationships
- Implementing iterators
- Using conditional logic

Technical requirements

The following are required to complete all of the recipes in this chapter:

- Microsoft Excel (first recipe)
- Power BI Desktop (all recipes)
- SQL Server Management Studio (first recipe)
- **Data files:** https://github.com/PacktPublishing/DAX-Cookbook/tree/master/Chapter01

Using DAX in Excel, Power BI, and SQL

DAX is the native formula and query language for Microsoft Power Pivot (Excel), Power BI Desktop, and **SQL Server Analysis Services (SSAS)** tabular models. Thus, DAX can be used in any of these programs.

Getting ready

Ensure that you have Power Pivot for Excel, Power BI Desktop, or an SSAS tabular cube.

How to do it...

Depending upon the program being used, where DAX is entered varies somewhat. Use the following instructions according to the program you are using.

Excel

Perform the following steps to enter DAX in Excel:

1. Open Excel and create a data model using the **Power Pivot** tab in the ribbon and then click **Add to Data Model**. You must have a data model created before you can enter DAX.
2. To create a measure in Excel, select the **Power Pivot** tab from the ribbon, and then choose **Measures** followed by **New Measure.** A new window called **Measure** will appear where you can enter a DAX formula in the **Formula** area.

3. To create a new calculated column in Excel, select the **Power Pivot** tab from the ribbon and then **Manage**. In the **Power Pivot** window, select **Design** from the ribbon and then **Add** in the **Columns** section. A formula bar will appear just below the ribbon and your cursor will become active in the formula bar.

Power BI

Perform the following steps to enter DAX in Power BI Desktop:

1. Open Power BI Desktop.
2. In Power BI Desktop, select the **Modeling** tab from the ribbon and then choose **New Measure** | **New Column** or **New Table**.

The formula bar will appear just below the ribbon and your cursor will become active in the formula bar.

SQL Server

Perform the following steps to enter DAX in SQL Server:

1. Open SQL Server Management Studio.
2. In SQL Server Management Studio, connect to a deployed tabular Analysis Server data model.
3. Right-click the database in the deployed tabular model and choose **New Query** and then **MDX.**
4. When writing your DAX query, ensure that you begin your query with the EVALUATE keyword.

See also

For more details regarding this recipe, refer to the following links:

- **Data Analysis Expressions (DAX)** in Power Pivot: https://support.office.com/en-us/article/Data-Analysis-Expressions-DAX-in-Power-Pivot-BAB3FBE3-2385-485A-980B-5F64D3B0F730
- DAX basics in Power BI Desktop: https://docs.microsoft.com/en-us/power-bi/desktop-quickstart-learn-dax-basics

- Getting started with the DAX queries for SQL Server Analysis Services: `https://www.mssqltips.com/sqlservertip/4068/getting-started-with-the-dax-queries-for-sql-server-analysis-services`

Writing good DAX

While the term *good* can be subjective, writing good DAX code is very much like writing code in other programming languages; the code should be readable and easy to understand. In this recipe, we will learn how to properly format DAX as well as how to use comments.

Getting ready

To prepare for this recipe, perform the following steps:

1. Open Power BI Desktop.
2. Create a table using the following formula:

   ```
   R02_Table = GENERATESERIES(1,30,1)
   ```

3. Create a column in that table using the following formula:

   ```
   Column = ROUNDUP('R02_Table'[Value]/11,0)
   ```

How to do it...

Let's assume that you have a measure formula that looks something like the following:

```
Bad DAX =
SUMX(FILTER(SUMMARIZE('R02_Table',[Column],"Value",SUM([Value])),[Column]=2
||[Column]=3),[Value])
```

While the preceding formula is syntactically correct and will work, it is difficult to read and understand the intent of the calculation. There are a number of best practices that can be followed to make the code more readable, including the following:

1. Use single-line comments (//) or comment blocks (/*...*/) to document the calculation being made.
2. Use *Alt+Enter* and *Tab* to separate and indent nested functions and multiple arguments.

3. Always use the full, canonical syntax when referring to a column, enclosing the table name portion in single quotes.
4. Use spaces to provide visual separation between elements, including parentheses and operators.
5. When creating data elements within a calculation, such as columns, clearly name these elements distinctly in order to avoid confusion.

Following these simple best practices, we can rewrite the measure as follows:

```
Good DAX =
/* Creates a filtered sum for a certain business purpose
 *
 * Gregory J. Deckler
 * gdeckler@fusionalliance.com
 * 10/7/2019
 */
SUMX (
    FILTER (
        SUMMARIZE (
            'R02_Table',
            'R02_Table'[Column],
            "__Value",
            SUM ( 'R02_Table'[Value] )
        ) ,                                  // End SUMMARIZE
        'R02_Table'[Column] = 2
        ||
        'R02_Table'[Column] = 3
    ) ,                                      // End FILTER
    [__Value]
)                                            // End SUMX
```

It is best practice to use single quotes for referencing table names. The issue is consistency. If you have spaces in your table names, then you need single quotes. If you do not, you can get away with not having single quotes, but it will burn you eventually. So, it is better to always use single quotes, and this has the added benefit of you always knowing that these are tables being referenced when you see single quotes.

How it works...

The comment block at the top of the function provides useful information regarding the purpose of the measure as well as a description regarding its operation. In addition, this comment block includes information about the author, including contact information and when the calculation was created. This information assists someone else reviewing the code or the author if revisiting the code at a later date. A space and asterisk have been added to lines within the comment block to visually cue the reader that the entire comment section belongs together. In addition to the comment block, inline comments have been used to call out where functions end. This makes it much easier to read the code instead of hunting for beginning and end parentheses.

Each function has been placed on its own, separate line by using the *Alt+Enter* key combination. In addition, each argument for each function is also on its own line, except for the SUM function, since this only has a single argument. The *Tab* key has been used to indent the nested functions, clearly denoting the nesting hierarchy. In addition, the *Tab* key has been used to indent function arguments underneath each function, visually keeping coding elements together.

The full, canonical name of columns has been used in order to remove any ambiguity and improve readability. Someone looking at the code immediately understands what column and table is being referenced in the code. These table names have been prefixed and suffixed with single quotes. While not required for table names without spaces, for consistency, they should always be used.

Spaces inserted after beginning parentheses and before end parentheses, as well as before and after the equals sign, provide visual separation between elements and make things easier to read.

Finally, the creation of the column in the SUMMARIZE statement has been created with the name prefixed by two underscore characters, unlike the original formula, where this column is the same name as a column from the original table. While DAX can generally figure out which column is being referenced, having duplicate names is confusing for the reviewer and can create actual confusion and problems in complex DAX formulas.

There's more...

Inline or single-line comments can also be executed by using -- instead of // at the beginning of the comment. You can also use *Ctrl+/* to automatically comment out or comment in a line using the // style of comment.

Instead of using *Alt+Enter* and *Tab*, you can use *Shift+Enter* to move to a new line and indent all at once. In addition, you can use *Ctrl+]* to indent and *Ctrl+[* to outdent instead of using *Tab* and *Shift+Tab*.

See also

For more details regarding this recipe, refer to the following links:

- Rules for DAX formatting: `https://www.sqlbi.com/articles/rules-for-dax-code-formatting/`
- DAX Formatter: `https://www.daxformatter.com/`
- DAX formula bar keyboard shortcuts in Power BI Desktop: `https://xxlbi.com/blog/dax-formula-bar-keyboard-shortcuts-in-power-bi-desktop/`
- The *Using variables* recipe

Using variables

While DAX functions can be nearly infinitely nested, using variables can avoid doing the same calculation multiple times and also improves overall code readability. Using variables can help you break complex calculations down into smaller, more consumable pieces that can be individually verified step by step.

Getting ready

To prepare for this recipe, perform the following steps:

1. Create a table using the following formula:

```
R3_Table = GENERATESERIES(1,30,1)
```

2. Create a column in that table using the following formula:

```
Column = ROUNDUP('R3_Table'[Value]/11,0)
```

How to do it...

Variables are created by using the VAR statement with the following syntax:

```
VAR <name> = <expression>
```

<name> is the name of the variable. Variable names must begin with the letters a-z or A-Z. The only other supported characters within variable names are the characters 0-9. Existing table names and certain keywords are not permitted as variable names.

DAX calculations that use a VAR statement must also use a RETURN statement.

By following these principles, we can write a DAX measure as follows:

```
Variable DAX =
/*
 * This measure summarizes the table, Table, grouping by [Column] and
summing [Column1]. This
 * summarized table is then filtered to values 2 and 3 in [Column] and then
sums up [Column1]
 *
 * Gregory J. Deckler
 * gdeckler@fusionalliance.com
 * 10/7/2019
 */
VAR __summarizedTable =                  // Summarize table by [Column],
summing [Value]
    SUMMARIZE(
        'R03_Table',
        'R03_Table'[Column],
        "__Value",
        SUM( 'R03_Table'[Value] )
    )
VAR __filteredTable =                     // Filter summarized table for 2
and 3
    FILTER(
        __summarizedTable,                // Here we use our
__summarizedTable variable
        [Column] = 2
        ||
        [Column] = 3
    )
VAR __sum =                               // Sum [__Value]
    SUMX(
        __filteredTable,                  // Here we use our __filteredTable
variable
        [__Value]
```

```
    )
RETURN                                // If result is < 400, return the
sum, otherwise -1
    IF (
        __sum < 400,                  // We avoid having to do the same
calculation twice
        __sum,
        -1
    )
```

How it works...

The code creates three variables, __summarizedTable, __filteredTable, and __sum.
The __summarizedTable variable creates a table in memory using the SUMMARIZE
function to return a table summarized by [Column] and by summing the [Value] column.
This variable takes on the value of the table as shown:

Column	__Value
1	66
2	187
3	212

The __filteredTable variable uses the FILTER function to filter the table represented by
the __summarizedTable variable to just the values 2 and 3 in the [Column] column. This
variable takes on the value of the table as shown:

Column	__Value
2	187
3	212

The __sum variable uses the SUMX function to sum the [__Value] column of the two
remaining rows in the table, taking on a value of 187 + 212, or 399.

The RETURN statement uses an IF statement. This IF statement checks to see whether the
__sum variable is less than 400. If the variable is less than 400, the value stored in the __sum
variable is returned. Otherwise, the value -1 is returned.

Variables can only be referenced within the DAX calculation in which they are created. As
shown in both __filteredTable and __sum, variables can refer to previously created
variables within the same DAX calculation.

There's more...

You can nest variables. For example, this recipe could be written as follows:

```
Nested Variable DAX =
/*
 * This measure summarizes the table, Table, grouping by [Column] and
summing [Column1]. This
 * summarized table is then filtered to values 2 and 3 in [Column] and then
sums up [Column1]
 *
 * Gregory J. Deckler
 * gdeckler@fusionalliance.com
 * 10/7/2019
 */
VAR __sum =                                      // Sum [__Value]
    SUMX(
        VAR __filteredTable =
            FILTER(                              // Filter summarized
table for 2 and 3
                VAR __summarizedTable =          // Summarize table by
[Column], summing [Value]
                    SUMMARIZE(
                        'R03_Table',
                        'R03_Table'[Column],
                        "__Value",
                        SUM( 'R03_Table'[Value] )
                    )
                RETURN __summarizedTable         // Return the summarized
table
                ,
                [Column] = 2
                ||
                [Column] = 3
            )
        RETURN __filteredTable                   // Return the filtered
table
        ,
        [__Value]
    )
RETURN                                           // If result is < 400,
return the sum, otherwise -1
    IF(
        __sum < 400,
        __sum,
        -1
    )
```

See also

For more details regarding this recipe, refer to the following links:

- VAR: `https://docs.microsoft.com/en-us/dax/var-dax`
- Using variables in Power BI – a detailed example: `https://blog.enterprisedna.co/2019/09/09/using-variables-in-dax-a-detailed-example/`
- Using DAX variables in iterators: `https://www.kasperonbi.com/using-dax-variables-in-iterators/`
- Using variables within DAX: `https://powerbi.tips/2017/05/using-variables-within-dax/`
- Variables in DAX: `https://www.sqlbi.com/articles/variables-in-dax/`
- Using variables in DAX: `https://exceleratorbi.com.au/using-variables-dax/`
- Power BI Quick Measure, Runge Kutta: `https://community.powerbi.com/t5/Quick-Measures-Gallery/Runge-Kutta/m-p/411280`

Confronting context

There is perhaps no more important subject to understanding DAX than context. Context is essential to DAX and is also something that is relatively unique to the language. In fact, context is so fundamental to DAX that a DAX calculation cannot return a result without context. Thus, understanding context is crucial to understanding DAX as it is context that provides much of the unbridled power of the DAX language. Conversely, context also contributes significantly to the learning curve for the DAX language.

Official Microsoft documentation cites three types of context:

- Row context
- Query context
- Filter context

Most other sources essentially ignore the concept of query context, and the Microsoft documentation is somewhat vague regarding this concept. The best analysis is that the combination of row and filter creates the final query context for DAX to retrieve the required data from the underlying data model for the requisite calculation. Users essentially only ever explicitly define row and filter context for DAX, and DAX itself implicitly creates query context from the row and filter context. Thus, we will focus on row and filter context in this recipe.

Getting ready

To prepare for this recipe, perform the following steps:

1. Create a table using the following formula:

```
R04_Table = GENERATESERIES(DATE(2020,1,1),DATE(2022,12,31))
```

2. Create a measure in that table using the following formula:

```
CountOfDays = COUNT([Value])
```

How to do it...

To demonstrate row context at work, create the following three columns in the R04_Table **table**:

```
Year = [value].[Year]
Month = [value].[Month]
Weekday = FORMAT([Value],"dddd")
```

To demonstrate filter context, perform the following steps:

1. Create a **Report** page and place a **Matrix** visualization on the page.
2. Within the **Matrix** visualization selected, place the following columns and measures from the R04_Table table in the indicated fields for the matrix visualization:

Column/Measure	Field
Month	Rows
Year	Columns
CountOfDays	Values

3. Note that the matrix displays the following information:

Month	2020	2021	2022	Total
April	30	30	30	90
August	31	31	31	93
December	31	31	31	93
February	29	28	28	85
January	31	31	31	93

July	31	31	31	**93**
June	30	30	30	**90**
March	31	31	31	**93**
May	31	31	31	**93**
November	30	30	30	**90**
October	31	31	31	**93**
September	30	30	30	**90**
Total	**366**	**365**	**365**	**1096**

4. Place a **Slicer** visualization on the same page and place the `Weekday` column from the `R04_Table` table in the **Field** for the slicer.
5. Select `Saturday` from the slicer. The **Matrix** visualization now displays the following:

Month	2020	2021	2022	Total
April	4	4	5	**13**
August	5	4	4	13
December	4	4	5	13
February	5	4	4	13
January	4	5	5	14
July	4	5	5	14
June	4	4	4	12
March	4	4	4	12
May	5	5	4	**14**
November	4	4	4	12
October	5	5	5	15
September	4	4	4	12
Total	**52**	**52**	**53**	**157**

How it works...

With regard to row context, DAX automatically applies row context to any calculated column. Therefore, the three columns created, `Year`, `Month`, and `Weekday`, all have row context applied. This is why there is a single value returned despite the fact that we have no aggregation function applied. Thus, within row context, references to columns such as `[Value]`, when not referenced from within an aggregation function, always return a single value, the value of the referenced column in that row. This is really as complex as row context gets, with the exception that it is possible to create row context outside of tables and calculated columns. To create row context within measures, we can use certain DAX functions such as `ADDCOLUMN`.

Filter context is somewhat trickier. Filter context is created by the combination of visuals and the fields within those visuals, as well as explicit filters created using the **Filters** pane in Power BI Desktop or directly within a DAX calculation when using a filters clause. In *step 3*, the matrix rows and columns define the context for the `CountOfDays` measure. Thus, for each cell, excluding the `Total` cells, we get the number of days in each month for each year. This is why the cell intersecting February and 2020 has 29, and 2020 is a leap year. The `Total` column removes the filter context for the individual columns but not the individual rows, and so we get the total number of days for all three years, **2020**, **2021**, and **2022**, for each month. Conversely, the `Total` row removes the filter context for the individual rows but not for the individual columns, and so we get the total number of days in each year. Finally, the cell on the right in the bottom row removes the filter context for both the individual rows and individual columns, and so we get the total number of day in all three years. Therefore, the filter context for this cell is effectively no filters or all data referenced by the matrix visualization.

Adding the slicer and selecting an individual weekday adds additional filter context to the matrix since the default in Power BI Desktop is to cross-filter visualizations. Thus, in addition to the filter context of the individual rows and columns in the matrix, the cells also encapsulate the filter context of the slicer, and so we are presented with the number of `Saturdays` in each month of each year with their corresponding totals in the `Totals` row and column. Selecting a different weekday from the slicer, or a combination of weekdays, will present their corresponding counts in the matrix visualization.

There's more...

Create a new column in the `R04_Table` table with the following formula:

```
Days = COUNT([Value])
```

You may be surprised to see the number **1096** in this column for every row of the table. This is the count of days in all three years of the table. You may have expected to see **1** for each row in this column. This result is driven by the exception mentioned earlier when dealing with column references in row context. The aggregation function effectively switches the calculation from row context to filter context and, since there is no filter context, the final query context is all rows within the table.

See also

For more details regarding this recipe, refer to the following links:

- DAX overview – context: `https://docs.microsoft.com/en-us/dax/dax-overview#context`
- The most important DAX concept: `https://powerdax.com/important-dax-concept/`
- Understanding evaluation contexts in DAX: `https://www.microsoftpressstore.com/articles/article.aspx?p=2449191`

Grouping and summarizing

Grouping and summarizing information is a powerful feature of Excel pivot tables and Power BI table and matrix visualizations. However, it is often necessary to group and summarize information in DAX as well. Grouping and summarizing in DAX can be accomplished through the use of two functions, SUMMARIZE and GROUPBY. In this recipe, we will create new tables that summarize information by using the SUMMARIZE and GROUPBY functions.

Getting ready

To prepare for this recipe, perform the following steps:

1. Create a table using the following formula:

```
R05_Table = GENERATESERIES(DATE(2020,1,1),DATE(2020,12,31))
```

2. Create a column in that table using the following formula:

```
Month = [Value].[Month]
```

3. Create another column in that table using the following formula:

```
Weekday = FORMAT([Value], "dddd")
```

How to do it...

The SUMMARIZE function has the following syntax:

```
SUMMARIZE(<table>, <groupBy_columnName>[, <groupBy_columnName>]...[, <name>, <expression>]...)
```

To use the SUMMARIZE function to return the number of weekdays in each month as well as the first day when each weekday occurs in each month, create a new table with the following formula:

```
R05_summarizedTable =
    SUMMARIZE(
        'R05_Table', // This is the table to summarize
        [Month], // This is the column by which we want to group values
        [Weekday], // This is a second column by which we want to group
values
        "# of Days", // Create a column called "# of Days"
        COUNTROWS('R05_Table'), // Return the count of rows for "# of Days"
        "First Date", // Create a second column called "First Date"
        MINX('R05_Table','R05_Table'[Value]) // Return first date weekday
occurs in the month in "First Date"
    )
```

An excerpt of the table returned by this formula is as follows:

Month	# of Days	Weekday	First Date
January	5	Wednesday	1/1/2020 12:00:00 AM
February	4	Wednesday	2/5/2020 12:00:00 AM
March	4	Wednesday	3/4/2020 12:00:00 AM
April	5	Wednesday	4/1/2020 12:00:00 AM
May	4	Wednesday	5/6/2020 12:00:00 AM
June	4	Wednesday	6/3/2020 12:00:00 AM
July	5	Wednesday	7/1/2020 12:00:00 AM

August	4	Wednesday	8/5/2020 12:00:00 AM
September	5	Wednesday	9/2/2020 12:00:00 AM
October	4	Wednesday	10/7/2020 12:00:00 AM
November	4	Wednesday	11/4/2020 12:00:00 AM
December	5	Wednesday	12/2/2020 12:00:00 AM
January	5	Thursday	1/2/2020 12:00:00 AM
February	4	Thursday	2/6/2020 12:00:00 AM

We can also use the GROUPBY function to return the same information in a table. The GROUPBY function has the following format:

```
GROUPBY (<table>, [<groupBy_columnName1>], [<name>, <expression>]... )
```

To do this, create a new table with the following formula:

```
R05_groupedTable =
    GROUPBY (
        'R05_Table', // This is the table to group
        [Month], // This is the column to group by
        [Weekday], // This is a second column by which we want to group
values
        "# of Days", // Create a new column in this table called "# of
Days"
        COUNTX(CURRENTGROUP(),'R05_Table'[Value]), // Return the count of
values for "# of Days"
        "First Date", // Create a second column called "First Date"
        MINX(CURRENTGROUP(),'R05_Table'[Value]) // Return first date
weekday occurs in the month in "First Date"
    )
```

This formula returns a table that is identical to our SUMMARIZE formula, except that the order of the rows differs slightly.

How it works...

Looking at the SUMMARIZE formula, the first parameter is the table that we want to summarize, and the next two columns are the columns according to which we want to group our data. Note that you can group by one, two, three, or nearly any number of columns.

The next four parameters are name/expression pairs. DAX understands where these pairs start when you stop referring to column names in the table and enter a text value for a parameter denoted by double quotes. These name/expression pairs specify a column name as the first part of the pair and a DAX expression to evaluate as the second portion of the pair. We first create a column called # of Days, and the value to be returned in this column is the count of the rows from our groupings. In other words, we get the number of each weekday in each month as our value. For the second column called First Date, we return the minimum date from our groupings. In other words, we get the first date of each weekday within each month as our value.

Looking at our GROUPBY formula, the first parameter is the table that we want to group. The next two columns are the columns according to which we want to group our data. This works in the same way as the SUMMARIZE function in that you can group by one, two, three, or nearly any number of columns.

Again, with the next four parameters, these are similar to the SUMMARIZE function in that they are name/expression pairs. This works exactly like the SUMMARIZE function except that instead of referring to the original table, you must refer to a special DAX function that can only be used within a GROUPBY function – the CURRENTGROUP function. In other words, you are referring to the current row of the Cartesian product created by your grouping columns.

There's more...

OK, so the most obvious question is likely something related to why there are two extremely similar functions that essentially do precisely the same thing. The answer is that while they are similar and do similar things, the way in which these functions go about what they do is fairly different. The order of the resulting table rows returned by these functions provides a hint that they are operating somewhat differently within the bowels of DAX.

Without going into excruciating detail regarding the internals of DAX calculations, the best way to describe the differences is to understand that within name/expression pairs of a SUMMARIZE function, the expression portion must always refer to an actual table name within the data model, while within the name/expression pairs of a GROUPBY function, the expression portion must always refer to CURRENTGROUP. This means that if you were to nest two SUMMARIZE functions, you could not refer to the table or columns created by the first SUMMARIZE function within the second (nested) SUMMARIZE function.

However, with GROUPBY, it would be possible to refer to a column created by the first GROUPBY function within the second (nested) GROUPBY function. This can be fairly powerful under the right circumstances. Conversely, because the SUMMARIZE expressions do not need to refer to CURRENTGROUP, this provides a certain flexibility that is not possible when using GROUPBY. For example, if you were to change the last parameter of each formula, within SUMMARIZE, as shown in the following line of code:

```
DAY(MINX('R05_Table',[Value]))
```

This would work and you would return just the day of the first date of the weekday within each month instead of the full date. However, you would receive an error in the GROUPBY formula because the specified expression does not aggregate over the current group.

See also

For more details regarding this recipe, refer to the following links:

- SUMMARIZE: https://docs.microsoft.com/en-us/dax/summarize-function-dax
- GROUPBY: https://docs.microsoft.com/en-us/dax/groupby-function-dax
- Nested grouping using GROUPBY **versus** SUMMARIZE: https://www.sqlbi.com/articles/nested-grouping-using-groupby-vs-summarize/

Filtering and unfiltering

Filtering is a critical concept in DAX because filters provide the main context under which DAX calculations evaluate. In addition, unlike when working with Excel, you cannot specify exact cells or ranges within DAX. Instead, if you want to use particular rows and columns of information within a table, you must filter that table down to the particular rows and columns desired for your calculation. The primary DAX function that allows you to filter rows in a table is the FILTER function.

Conversely, DAX allows you to remove, ignore, and change filter context within calculations. This is powerful and useful in many situations, such as in Power BI, where slicers, page, or report filters may need to be overridden within certain calculations and visualizations. DAX functions that allow the removal or editing of filter behavior include the following:

- ALL
- ALLCROSSFILTERED

- ALLEXCEPT
- ALLNOBLANKROW
- ALLSELECTED
- KEEPFILTERS
- REMOVEFILTERS

Getting ready

To prepare for this recipe, perform the following steps:

1. Create a table using the following formula:

    ```
    R06_Table = GENERATESERIES(DATE(2020,1,1),DATE(2022,12,31))
    ```

2. Create a column in that table using the following formula:

    ```
    Year = [Value].[Year]
    ```

3. Create a second column in that table using the following formula:

    ```
    Month = [Value].[Month]
    ```

4. Create a third column in that table using the following formula:

    ```
    Weekday = FORMAT([Value], "dddd")
    ```

How to do it...

To implement this recipe, perform the following steps:

1. Create the following measures:

    ```
    Days = COUNTROWS('R06_Table')

    January Days = COUNTROWS(FILTER('R06_Table',[Month] = "January"))

    January Wednesday Days = COUNTROWS(FILTER('R06_Table',[Month] =
    "January" && [Weekday] = "Wednesday"))

    All Days = COUNTROWS(ALL('R06_Table'))

    Weekday Days = CALCULATE(COUNTROWS('R06_Table'),
    ```

```
    ALLEXCEPT('R06_Table','R06_Table'[Weekday]))

All Years January Days = CALCULATE([January
Days],REMOVEFILTERS('R06_Table'[Year]))

January Days? =
CALCULATE (
    CALCULATE (
        COUNTROWS('R06_Table'),
        'R06_Table'[Month] = "January"
    ) ,
    'R06_Table'[Month] = "February"
)

January Days! =
CALCULATE (
    CALCULATE (
        COUNTROWS('R06_Table'),
        KEEPFILTERS (
            'R06_Table'[Month] = "January"
            || 'R06_Table'[Month] = "February"
        )
    ) ,
    'R06_Table'[Month] = "January"
    || 'R06_Table'[Month] = "March"
)
```

2. Place each of these measures in a **Card** visualization on a page.
3. Add three slicers to this page for the `Year`, `Month`, and `Weekday` columns from the `R06_Table` table.

How it works...

With all of the slicers set to **All**, the values for each of these measures is as follows:

Measure	Value	Explanation
Days	1096	This measure counts all of the rows in the table (366 + 365 + 365).
January Days	93	This measure only counts days in the table with a month of January (31 + 31 + 31).
January Wednesday Days	13	This measure only counts days in January that are Wednesdays (5 + 4 + 4).

All Days	1096	This measure always counts all of the rows in the table (366 + 365 + 365).
Weekday Days	1096	This measure counts all of the rows in the table unless there is a weekday filter (366 + 365 + 365).
All Years January Days	93	This measure counts days in January, ignoring filters for Year, but not other filters.
January Days?	93	This measure only counts days in January.
January Days!	93	This measure only counts days in January.

For January Days?, it may appear odd that this measure calculates the number of days in January for the three years of dates listed in the table since the outer CALCULATE function clearly specifies a filter of February. However, the default behavior of CALCULATE is to use the innermost filter value when the same column is specified within nested CALCULATE statements.

Given the default behavior of the CALCULATE function, it may seem even more odd that the January Days! measure also returns the number of days in January. The reason for this is the KEEPFILTERS function. The KEEPFILTERS function changes the default behavior of the CALCULATE function by adding another filter. The calculation now becomes the intersection of the two filters instead of a complete override. Thus, since the only value that is in common between the two filters is January, only the count of the days in January is returned!

There's more...

Use the **Year** slicer to only choose **2020**. The values for the measures become the following:

Measure	Value	Explanation
Days	366	This measure is being filtered by the **Year** slicer and 2020 is a leap year.
January Days	31	This measure is being filtered by the **Year** slicer and January has 31 days.
January Wednesday Days	5	This measure is being filtered by the **Year** slicer and January 2020 has five Wednesdays.
All Days	1096	The ALL function overrides the filter from the **Year** slicer, so this is a count of all rows in the table.
Weekday Days	1096	The ALLEXCEPT function overrides the filter from the **Year** slicer, so this is a count of all rows in the table.

All Years January Days	93	The REMOVEFILTERS function removes the **Year** slicer filter from the calculation, so this is the number of days in January for the three years.
January Days?	93	This measure only counts days in January and is filtered by the **Year** slicer.
January Days!	93	This measure only counts days in January and is filtered by the **Year** slicer.

Leave the **Year** slicer set to **2020** and now use the **Month** slicer to only choose **February**. The values for the measures become the following:

Measure	Value	Explanation
Days	29	This measure is being filtered by the **Year** slicer and the **Month** slicer and 2020 is a leap year.
January Days	(Blank)	This measure is being filtered by the **Year** slicer and the **Month** slicer, but also has a filter within the calculation of January. Since February and January have no intersecting days, the ultimate value is blank (null).
January Wednesday Days	5	This measure is being filtered by the **Year** slicer and the **Month** slicer, but also has a filter within the calculation of January and Wednesday. Since February and January have no intersecting days, the ultimate value is blank (null).
All Days	1096	The ALL function overrides the filter from the **Year** and **Month** slicers, so this is a count of all rows in the table.
Weekday Days	1096	The ALLEXCEPT function overrides the filter from the **Year** and **Month** slicers, so this is a count of all rows in the table.
All Years January Days	(Blank)	The REMOVEFILTERS function removes the **Year** slicer filter from the calculation, but not the **Month** slicer filter. Since February and January have no intersecting days, the ultimate value is blank (null).
January Days?	31	Since the **Month** slicer and internal filters all refer to the same column, the default behavior for the CALCULATE function is to override all filters on that column with the innermost filter, which is January Days. However, the **Year** slicer refers to a different column, so the filter on the Year column is also enforced.

January Days!	31	KEEPFILTERS modifies the behavior of the CALCULATE function, such that this is the intersection of all of the filters on the Month column, which still only leaves January. However, the **Year** slicer refers to a different column, so the filter on the Year column is also enforced. The **Month** slicer is effectively ignored. You can test this by switching the **Month** slicer to November, December, or another value.

Leave the **Year** slicer set to **2020** and the **Month** slicer set to **February**. Now, change the **Weekday** slicer to only choose **Friday**. The values for the measures become the following:

Measure	Value	Explanation
Days	29	This measure is being filtered by the **Year** slicer, **Month** slicer, and **Weekday** slicer, and there are only four Fridays in January 2020.
January Days	(Blank)	This measure is being filtered by the **Year** slicer and the **Month** slicer, but also has a filter within the calculation of January. Since February and January have no intersecting days, the ultimate value is blank (null).
January Wednesday Days	5	This measure is being filtered by the **Year** slicer, **Month** slicer, and **Weekday** slicer, but also has a filter within the calculation of January and Wednesday. Since February and January have no intersecting days, the ultimate value is blank (null). This measure would also be blank if you selected January in the **Month** slicer instead of February since there are no Fridays that are also Wednesdays!
All Days	1096	The ALL function overrides the filter from the **Year**, **Month**, and **Weekday** slicers, so this is a count of all rows in the table.
Weekday Days	1096	The ALLEXCEPT function overrides the filter from the **Year** and **Month** slicers, but not the **Weekday** slicer, so this is a count of all Fridays for all years and months in the table.
All Years January Days	(Blank)	The REMOVEFILTERS function removes the **Year** slicer filter from the calculation, but not the **Month** slicer filter. Since February and January have no intersecting days, the ultimate value is blank (null).

January Days?	5	Since the **Month** slicer and internal filters all refer to the same column, the default behavior for the CALCULATE function is to override all filters on that column with the innermost filter. However, the **Year** and **Weekday** slicers refer to different columns, so the filters on the Year and Weekday columns are also enforced.
January Days!	5	KEEPFILTERS modifies the behavior of the CALCULATE function such that this is the intersection of all of the filters on the Month column, which still only leaves January. However, the **Year** and **Weekday** slicers refer to different columns, so the filters on the Year and Weekday columns are also enforced.

See also

For more details regarding this recipe, refer to the following link:

- Filter functions: https://docs.microsoft.com/en-us/dax/filter-functions-dax

Exploiting relationships

Relationships connect tables together within a data model by defining an affiliation between a column in one table and a column in a second table. Creating a relationship between two columns in a table ties the two tables together such that it is expected that values from a column in the first table will be found in the other column in the second table. These table relationships can be exploited by DAX calculations as DAX intrinsically understands these relationships within the data model.

Getting ready

To prepare for this recipe, perform the following steps:

1. Create a table using the following formula:

   ```
   R07_TableA = GENERATESERIES(DATE(2020,1,1),DATE(2020,12,31))
   ```

2. Create a column in this table using the following formula:

   ```
   Month = [value].[Month]
   ```

3. Create a second table called R07_TableB using an **Enter Data** query with the following data:

Month	Date
January	1/1/2020
February	2/1/2020
March	3/1/2020
April	4/1/2020
May	5/1/2020
June	6/1/2020
July	7/1/2020
August	8/1/2020
September	9/1/2020
October	10/1/2020
November	11/1/2020
December	12/1/2020

4. Ensure that the Date column is formatted as Date/Time.
5. Create a relationship between the Month column in the R07_TableB table and the Month column in the R07_TableA table. Make sure that the cross-filter direction of this relationship is set to Both.
6. Create a measure using the following formula:

```
R07_CountOfDays = COUNTROWS('R07_TableA')
```

How to do it...

To demonstrate how relationships work, perform the following steps:

1. On a **Report** page, create a **Table** visualization and place the Month column from the R07_TableB table as a field in the visual.
2. While that visualization is still selected, place the R07_CountOfDays measure in the visual.
3. Create a second **Table** visual and place the Month column from the R07_TableA table as a field in the visual.
4. With this second visualization still selected, drag the Date column from the R07_TableA table into the visual and change its default aggregation to Count.

The first **Table** visualization lists the months in alphabetical order, while the R07_CountOfDays measure displays the number of days in each month. The second **Table** visualization also lists the months in alphabetical order and the second column displays **1** for all rows.

How it works...

For the first visualization, placing the Month column from R07_TableB in the visualization creates filter context on the R07_TableA table. Thus, when the R07_CountOfDays measure is calculated in this context, this filter context from the relationship applies to the calculation. Thus, we get the number of rows in R07_TableA that are related to the relevant context. In short, the number of rows in R07_TableA that have the same month as our month values from R07_TableB are displayed.

The second visualization functions in the same way, except that since we placed the Month column from R07_TableA in the visualization and are counting the values in R07_TableB, a **1** is displayed because there is only a single matching row in R07_TableB that matches each distinct Month value in R07_TableA.

There's more...

To explore relationships and how they affect filter context, perform the following steps:

1. Create a second relationship between the Value column in R07_TableA and the Date column in R07_TableB.
2. Ensure that the relationship direction is Both and note that the line is dotted. The dotted line indicates that this relationship is inactive. This is because data models can only have a single active filter pathway between tables.
3. Create the following measure:

```
R07_CountOfDays2 =
CALCULATE([R07_CountOfDays],USERELATIONSHIP(R07_TableA[Value],R07_T
ableB[Date]))
```

4. Place this measure in the first **Table** visualization created.

Note that adding this measure, R07_CountOfDays2, to the first table visualization lists the value of **1** for each month. In addition, an extra row is added to the visualization that has no value for the Month column and lists a value of **354** for the R07_CountOfDays2 measure.

The way that the R07_CountOfDays2 measure works is that we have explicitly overridden the default filter context by the CALCULATE function to explicitly define our filter context and then used the USERELATIONSHIP DAX function to define that filter context. Essentially, we have explicitly told DAX to use the inactive relationship we created as its filter context between the two tables. Thus, only a single row in R07_TableA matches each date value in R07_TableB. However, we have **354** (366 days in 2020 minus 12 matching rows) rows in R07_TableA that do not match any value in R07_TableB, and so this shows up in our table visualization. This actually demonstrates a powerful feature of DAX in helping us find bad data.

See also

For more details regarding this recipe, refer to the following links:

- COUNTROWS: https://docs.microsoft.com/en-us/dax/countrows-function-dax
- CALCULATE: https://docs.microsoft.com/en-us/dax/calculate-function-dax
- USERELATIONSHIP: https://docs.microsoft.com/en-us/dax/userelationship-function-dax

Implementing iterators

In DAX, iterators are functions that evaluate an expression for every row of a table and then aggregate the result. These functions are called iterators because the functions iterate over each row of a table. Within DAX, iterator functions end with an X character and include the following functions:

- AVERAGEX
- COUNTAX
- COUNTX
- GEOMEANX
- MAXX
- MEDIANX

- MINX
- PRODUCTX
- STDEVX.P
- STDEVX.S
- SUMX
- VARX.P
- VARX.S

Each of these iterator functions performs exactly the same calculation as their non-X equivalent aggregation functions, except that the X functions perform their aggregation over a table specified as the first parameter of the function.

All of these iterator functions have the following general form:

```
<function>(<table>, <expression>)
```

Here, `<function>` is the name of the iterator function. Each iterator function takes a table as its first parameter as well as a DAX expression as its second parameter. The expression is evaluated for each row of the table and then the aggregation function aggregates the results of each of those evaluations.

Getting ready

To prepare for this recipe, perform the following steps:

1. Create a table using the following formula:

   ```
   R08_Table = GENERATESERIES(DATE(2020,1,1),DATE(2022,12,31))
   ```

2. Create a column in that table using the following formula:

   ```
   Year = [Value].[Year]
   ```

3. Create a second column in that table using the following formula:

   ```
   MonthNo = FORMAT([Value].[MonthNo],"00")
   ```

4. Create a third column in that table using the following formula:

   ```
   Weeknum = FORMAT(WEEKNUM([Value],1),"00")
   ```

How to do it...

To implement this recipe, perform the following steps:

1. Create the following three measures:

```
Count = COUNTX('R08_Table',[Value])
Max = MAXX(R08_Table,[Year] & [MonthNo] & [Weeknum])
Min = MINX(R08_Table,[Year] & [MonthNo] & [Weeknum])
```

2. Place each of these measures in its own **Card** visualization and note the values returned by each:

   - Count: 1096
   - Max: 20221253
   - Min: 20200101

How it works...

For the `Count` measure, the first parameter is again our table, R08_Table, which has a row for every day of the years 2020, 2021, and 2022. For each row, the expression simply evaluates to the value of the date in our `Value` column. The iterator then simply counts how many values have been returned as its aggregation, in this case, 1,096 days. That is 366 values for 2020, a leap year, and then 365 for both 2021 and 2022.

For the `Max` measure, the first parameter is again our table, R08_Table, which has a row for every day of the years 2020, 2021, and 2022. For each row in the table, the expression concatenates the `Year`, `MonthNo`, and `Weeknum` columns using the ampersand (`&`) concatenation operator. Once all of the values are calculated, the `MAXX` function then performs the aggregation step to return the maximum value calculated, in this case, 20221253, the last week of December in the year 2022.

The `Min` measure works in an identical fashion to the `Max` measure, except that the `MINX` function returns the minimum value calculated, in this case, 20200101, the first week of January in the year 2020.

There's more...

The first parameter to iterate functions does not have to be simply a table reference; it can actually be any DAX expression that returns a table. To demonstrate this, create the following measure:

```
Product = PRODUCTX(DISTINCT('R08_Table'[MonthNo]), [MonthNo]+0)
```

Place this measure in a **Card** visualization and note that the value displayed is 479M, or 479 million.

In this measure, we use the DISTINCT function to return only the unique values from the MonthNo column of our table, R08_Table. This returns the numbers 1-12. As our expression, we add 0 to the MonthNo column for each row in order to convert the expression to a numeric value from text. The PRODUCTX function then multiplies each of these unique values together. If you calculate the factorial of 12 (12!) on a calculator, the value is indeed 479,001,600, or roughly 479 million.

See also

For more details regarding this recipe, refer to the following links:

- AVERAGEX: https://docs.microsoft.com/en-us/dax/averagex-function-dax
- COUNTAX: https://docs.microsoft.com/en-us/dax/countax-function-dax
- COUNTX: https://docs.microsoft.com/en-us/dax/countx-function-dax
- GEOMEANX: https://docs.microsoft.com/en-us/dax/geomeanx-function-dax
- MAXX: https://docs.microsoft.com/en-us/dax/maxx-function-dax
- MEDIANX: https://docs.microsoft.com/en-us/dax/meadianx-function-dax
- MINX: https://docs.microsoft.com/en-us/dax/minx-function-dax
- PRODUCTX: https://docs.microsoft.com/en-us/dax/productx-function-dax
- STDEVX.P: https://docs.microsoft.com/en-us/dax/stdevx-p-function-dax
- STDEVX.S: https://docs.microsoft.com/en-us/dax/stdevx-s-function-dax
- SUMX: https://docs.microsoft.com/en-us/dax/sumx-function-dax
- VAR.P: https://docs.microsoft.com/en-us/dax/varx-p-function-dax
- VAR.S: https://docs.microsoft.com/en-us/dax/varx-s-function-dax
- Optimizing nested iterators in DAX: https://www.sqlbi.com/articles/optimizing-nested-iterators-in-dax/

Using conditional logic

Conditional logic is an important concept for programming in general, and DAX is no different. There are many circumstances where we want to present different values for a measure or column based upon a series of conditions or circumstances; for example, if a particular day is a workday or weekend, or if a value is even or odd. In this recipe, we will learn how to use conditional logic in DAX to create a custom column that calculates the quarter for a nonstandard fiscal year that runs from June to May instead of from January to December using two different conditional logic DAX functions, IF and SWITCH.

Getting ready

To prepare for this recipe, perform the following steps:

1. Create a table using the following formula:

```
R09_Table = GENERATESERIES(DATE(2020,1,1),DATE(2020,12,31))
```

2. Create a column in that table using the following formula:

```
MonthNo = [Value].[MonthNo]
```

How to do it...

The first conditional logic function that most people use is the IF function. The IF function has the following format:

```
IF(<condition> , <value to return if true> , <value to return if false)
```

Complex conditional logic can be created by nesting IF functions. For example, in the true or false value to return, another IF statement can be inserted. To create our custom quarter calculation, we will actually need three nested IF functions. Create a new column in R09_Table with the following formula:

```
QuarterNo =
    IF('R09_Table'[MonthNo] < 4,
        "Q3", // If the month is 1-3 then this is Q3
        IF('R09_Table'[MonthNo] < 7,
            "Q4", // If the month is 3-6 then this is Q4
            IF('R09_Table'[MonthNo] < 10,
                "Q1", // If the month is 7-9 then this is Q1
                "Q2" // If no other condition is met, then the month is
```

```
10-12, Q2
            ) // End 3rd IF
        ) // End 2nd IF
    ) // End 1st IF
```

IF statements work perfectly fine for conditional logic, but, as you can see, nesting can become somewhat difficult to format and read. A preferred way to do conditional logic is to instead use the SWITCH statement for easier formatting and readability. The SWITCH statement has the following format:

```
SWITCH(<expression> , <value> , <result> [ , <value> , <result>]...[ ,
<else>])
```

An equivalent SWITCH statement can be written by creating a new column with the following formula:

```
QuarterNo1 =
 SWITCH(
 'R09_Table'[MonthNo], // Check the [MonthNo] column
 1,"Q3", // If the [MonthNo] is 1, then return Q3
 2,"Q3", // If the [MonthNo] is 2, then return Q3
 3,"Q3", // If the [MonthNo] is 3, then return Q3
 4,"Q4", // If the [MonthNo] is 4, then return Q4
 5,"Q4", // If the [MonthNo] is 5, then return Q4
 6,"Q4", // If the [MonthNo] is 6, then return Q4
 7,"Q1", // If the [MonthNo] is 7, then return Q1
 8,"Q1", // If the [MonthNo] is 8, then return Q1
 9,"Q1", // If the [MonthNo] is 9, then return Q1
 "Q2" // Else if none of the other conditions are met, Q2
 )
```

How it works...

Looking at the IF formula, the formula starts with a condition, [MonthNo] < 4, for the first parameter. If this condition is true, then the next parameter is returned, in this case Q3. However, if the statement is not true, then another IF statement is evaluated and the pattern continues. It is important to understand that IF conditions are evaluated in order. In other words, the first IF statement is evaluated first and must be evaluated as either true or false before either returning a value or executing the next IF statement. This is why we do not need to worry about month numbers 1, 2, and 3 when evaluating [MonthNo] < 7 in the second IF statement. We can be certain that if this expression evaluates to true, then [MonthNo] must be 4, 5, or 6, and not 1, 2, or 3, because these latter numbers have already been excluded.

For the SWITCH statement, the first parameter is the value to evaluate, in this case [MonthNo]. The subsequent parameters come in pairs, the first value of this pair being the potential value of the expression in the first parameter, and the second being the value to return if the expression in the first parameter equals the paired value. At the end is a catch-all else value, the value to return if no other conditions are met. As you can see, the SWITCH statement, while more verbose, is much easier to read and understand.

There's more...

There is a trick for the SWITCH statement that makes this function even more valuable and also less verbose to write. This trick is the TRUE expression trick, where the first parameter for the SWITCH statement is the TRUE function. When using the SWITCH statement in this way, the first parameter of the value/result parameter pairs is actually a conditional statement that, if true, returns the corresponding result parameter. To demonstrate how this works, create a column with the following formula:

```
QuarterNo2 =
SWITCH(
TRUE(), // First parameter is the function TRUE, which always returns TRUE
'R09_Table'[MonthNo] < 4,"Q3", // If the [MonthNo] is 1-3, then Q3
'R09_Table'[MonthNo] < 7,"Q4", // If the [MonthNo] is 4-6, then Q4
'R09_Table'[MonthNo] < 10,"Q1", // If the [MonthNo] is 7-9, then Q1
"Q2" // Else, Q2
)
```

This version of the SWITCH statement looks very much like our IF statement, but is far easier to read and understand. The first parameter is the TRUE function, which turns on the special mode of the SWITCH statement where the first parameter of the value/result parameter pairs is a conditional statement. If the statement is true, for example [MonthNo] < 4, then the corresponding result is returned, Q3.

Finally, it is worth noting that any conditional logic statement can use AND and OR logic. In DAX, && is used for AND and | | is used for OR. For example, our preceding SWITCH statement could alternatively be written as follows:

```
QuarterNo3 =
 SWITCH(
 TRUE(),
 [MonthNo] = 1 || [MonthNo] = 2 || [MonthNo] = 3,"Q3", // If the [MonthNo]
is 1, 2 or 3, Q3
 [MonthNo] = 4 || [MonthNo] = 5 || [MonthNo] = 6,"Q4", // If the [MonthNo]
is 4, 5 or 6, Q4
 [MonthNo] = 7 || [MonthNo] = 8 || [MonthNo] = 9,"Q1", // If the [MonthNo]
is 7, 8 or 9, Q1
 "Q2" // Else, Q2
 )
```

See also

For more details regarding this recipe, refer to the following links:

- IF: https://docs.microsoft.com/en-us/dax/if-function-dax

- SWITCH: https://docs.microsoft.com/en-us/dax/switch-function-dax

- Making the "Case" for SWITCH(): https://powerpivotpro.com/2012/06/dax-making-the-case-for-switch/

- DAX – the diabolical genius of "SWITCH TRUE": https://powerpivotpro.com/2015/03/the-diabolical-genius-of-switch-true/

- DAX IF & Switch Statement Performance – Does Order Matter?: https://joyfulcraftsmen.com/blog/dax-if-switch-statement-performance-does-order-matter/

Dealing with Dates and Calendars 2

It is a rare business scenario and data model that does not have something related to dates at its core. So much of the business world deals with dates. People work on certain dates and not others. Deadlines are due on specific days. Bonuses and key performance indicators are dependent upon what week, month, or quarter sales occur. This chapter is all about working with dates, weeks, months, quarters, and years.

This chapter comprises the following recipes:

- Using time intelligence
- Creating quarters
- Calculating leap years
- Determining day and working day numbers in a year
- Determining date of the day number of a year
- Finding week start and end dates
- Finding working days for weeks, months, quarters, and years
- Constructing a sequential week number
- Computing rolling weeks
- Replacing Excel's NETWORKDAYS function
- Working with date intervals
- Exploiting alternatives to DAX's time intelligence

Technical requirements

The following are required to complete all of the recipes in this chapter:

- Power BI Desktop
- A GitHub repository: `https://github.com/PacktPublishing/DAX-Cookbook/tree/master/Chapter02`

Using time intelligence

Time intelligence in DAX is somewhat of a misnomer. Time intelligence actually does not deal with time in the sense of hours, minutes, seconds, and so on. Instead, time intelligence would be better off being called **date intelligence** or **calendar intelligence**, because the time intelligence functions in DAX really deal with dates. Hence, if you are looking for calculations involving time in the sense of hours, minutes, and seconds, proceed to the next chapter. Otherwise, this recipe will demonstrate how to use the time intelligence functions in DAX to perform calculations related to things such as year-over-year, month-over-month, and quarter-to-date.

Getting ready

To prepare for this recipe, perform the following steps:

1. Create a table using the following formula:

   ```
   R01_Calendar = CALENDAR(DATE(2015,1,1),DATE(2022,12,31))
   ```

2. Create a table called `R01_Sales` by importing the `Sales.csv` file from the GitHub repository: `https://github.com/PacktPublishing/DAX-Cookbook/tree/master/Chapter02`.

3. Create a column in the `R01_Sales` table using the following formula:

   ```
   Year = YEAR([Date])
   ```

4. Create another column in the `R01_Sales` table using the following formula:

   ```
   Month = FORMAT([Date],"mmmm")
   ```

5. Create a third column in the `R01_Sales` table using the following formula:

```
Month Sort = MONTH([Date])
```

6. Set the `Sort by` column for `Month` to `Month Sort`.
7. Create a bidirectional relationship between the `Date` column in the `R01_Sales` table and the `Date` column in the `R01_Calendar` table.

How to do it...

To implement this recipe, perform the following steps:

1. Create the following measures:

```
Opening Balance =
OPENINGBALANCEMONTH(SUM('R01_Sales'[Value]),'R01_Calendar'[Date])

Closing Balance =
CLOSINGBALANCEMONTH(SUM('R01_Sales'[Value]),'R01_Calendar'[Date])

Month to Date =
TOTALMTD(SUM('R01_Sales'[Value]),'R01_Calendar'[Date])

Previous Month =
TOTALMTD(SUM('R01_Sales'[Value]),PREVIOUSMONTH('R01_Calendar'[Date]
))

Year to Date =
TOTALYTD(SUM('R01_Sales'[Value]),'R01_Calendar'[Date])

Previous Year =
TOTALYTD(SUM('R01_Sales'[Value]),PREVIOUSYEAR('R01_Calendar'[Date])
)
```

2. Create a **Table** visualization and place the `Date` column from the `R01_Sales` table, as well as all of the measures created in *Step 1*, in the **Values** field for this visualization.
3. Create a **Matrix** visualization and place the `Year` column from the `R01_Sales` table in the **Rows** field.
4. In the same **Matrix** visualization, place the `Month` column from the `R01_Sales` table in the **Rows** field underneath the `Year` column.
5. In the same **Matrix** visualization, place all of the measures created in *Step 1* in the **Values** field.

How it works...

For the `Opening Balance` measure, note that all values for January 2017 are blank. This is because there is no ending value for the month previous to January 2017. For February 2017, note that the value of the `Opening Value` measure is `155.00`. In the data, `155.00` is the value of January 31, 2017. Also, note the value for January 2018 dates. The value is `136.92`. Note that in the data, this is the value (rounded up to two decimals) of December 31, 2017. Thus, the `OPENINGBALANCEMONTH` function essentially lists the final value as computed by the expression specified in the first parameter, in this case, `SUM([Value])`, for the previous month.

The `Closing Balance` measure utilizes the `CLOSINGBALANCEMONTH` function. This works similarly to the `OPENINGBALANCEMONTH` function except that it lists the final value for the month as computed by the expression specified in the first parameter, in this case, `SUM([Value])`.

The `Month to Date` measure utilizes the `TOTALMTD` function. At the day level, you can see that this measure is summing up the current day as well as any previous days in the month since we have specified the computational expression to use `SUM([Value)`. In the **Matrix** visualization, the value of `1,710.00` is displayed for the `Month to Date` measure. This value of `1,710.00` corresponds to the `Month to Date` measure value for the date January 31, 2017. Thus, we can see that the `TOTALMTD` function computes the value of the specified expression for all days in the current month in context that are on or before the current date in context.

The `Previous Month` measure also uses the `TOTALMTD` function with the same calculation expression, `SUM([Value])`, but, for the dates, specifies the `PREVIOUSMONTH` function. January 2017 dates are blank because there is no previous month's data. However, the February dates all read `1,710.00`, which is the value for `Month to Date` for January 31, 2017. Hence, using the `PREVIOUSMONTH` function as the dates clause causes all dates within the previous month, and only those dates, to be included in the calculation of the specified expression. This may or may not be what you intended! For example, what you might have intended was for this measure in February to show the total for the same number of days in January. If this was indeed the intention, then we could have used the DAX function, `PARALLELPERIOD`, to achieve this.

The `Year to Date` measure uses the `TOTALYTD` function. This function works in an identical manner to the `TOTALMTD` function, except at the year granularity. Similarly, `Previous Year` makes use of the `PREVIOUSYEAR` function, which works identically to the `PREVIOUSMONTH` function except at the year level of granularity.

There's more...

Perhaps the biggest mistake people make when attempting to use DAX's time intelligence functions is to not utilize a related date table for the dates parameter of the functions. Not utilizing a related table of dates can cause unexpected results. To see how things can go awry, perform the following steps:

1. Create the following measure:

```
Opening Balance 2 =
OPENINGBALANCEMONTH(SUM([Value]),'R01_Sales'[Date])
```

2. Place the `Opening Balance 2` measure in both the **Table** visualization and the **Matrix** visualization created earlier.
3. Delete the relationship between the `R01_Sales` and `R01_Calendar` tables.

Note that the `Opening Balance 2` measure values are all blank in the **Matrix** table, but are correct in the **Table** visualization. As already stated, you can get unexpected results when not using a related date table.

See also

For more details, refer to the following link:

- Time-intelligence functions: `https://docs.microsoft.com/en-us/dax/time-intelligence-functions-dax`

Creating quarters

You may consider it somewhat silly to have a recipe for determining the quarter of a date since quarter is included in the default hierarchy for a date. However, many organizations do not adhere to a standard calendar quarter. For example, Microsoft's fiscal calendar runs from June to May. Other organizations start and stop their quarters on specific dates of the year. This quarter calculation can be used with standard quarterly calendars as well as non-standard quarterly calendars. It is easily modified to fit just about any custom quarterly schedule you can imagine. The quarter table that we will create in this recipe has the following quarters:

- Q1: August 15 – November 14
- Q2: November 15 – February 14

- Q3: February 15 – May 14
- Q4: May 15 – August 14

Getting ready

To prepare for this recipe, perform the following steps:

1. Create a table using the following formula:

```
R02_Calendar = CALENDAR(DATE(2018,1,1),DATE(2022,12,31))
```

How to do it...

To implement this recipe, perform the following steps:

1. Create a column in the R02_Calendar table using the following formula:

```
QuarterNonStandard =
VAR __Q1StartMonth = 8               // Starting Q1 month
number
VAR __Q1StartDay = 15                // Starting day number of
Q1
VAR __Q2StartMonth = 11              // Starting Q2 month
number
VAR __Q2StartDay = 15                // Starting day number of
Q2
VAR __Q3StartMonth = 2               // Starting Q3 month
number
VAR __Q3StartDay = 15                // Starting day number of
Q3
VAR __Q4StartMonth = 5               // Starting Q4 month
number
VAR __Q4StartDay = 15                // Starting day number of
Q4
VAR __Year = YEAR('R02_Calendar'[Date])
VAR __date = 'R02_Calendar'[Date]
//
// Do not modify below this line
//
VAR __QuarterMonths =
    {   __Q1StartMonth,
        __Q2StartMonth,
        __Q3StartMonth,
        __Q4StartMonth
```

```
        }
VAR __MaxQuarterStartMonth = MAXX(__QuarterMonths,[Value])
VAR __Quarter =
    SWITCH(
        TRUE(),
        __Q1StartMonth = __MaxQuarterStartMonth &&
            (
                __date >= DATE(__Year,__Q1StartMonth,__Q1StartDay)
||
                __date < DATE(__Year,__Q2StartMonth,__Q2StartDay)
            ),"Q1",
        __Q2StartMonth = __MaxQuarterStartMonth &&
            (
                __date >= DATE(__Year,__Q2StartMonth,__Q2StartDay)
||
                __date < DATE(__Year,__Q3StartMonth,__Q3StartDay)
            ),"Q2",
        __Q3StartMonth = __MaxQuarterStartMonth &&
            (
                __date >= DATE(__Year,__Q3StartMonth,__Q3StartDay)
||
                __date < DATE(__Year,__Q4StartMonth,__Q4StartDay)
            ),"Q3",
        __Q4StartMonth = __MaxQuarterStartMonth &&
            (
                __date >= DATE(__Year,__Q4StartMonth,__Q4StartDay)
||
                __date < DATE(__Year,__Q1StartMonth,__Q1StartDay)
            ),"Q4",
        __date >= DATE(__Year,__Q1StartMonth,__Q1StartDay) &&
            __date < DATE(__Year,__Q2StartMonth,__Q2StartDay),"Q1",
        __date >= DATE(__Year,__Q2StartMonth,__Q2StartDay) &&
            __date < DATE(__Year,__Q3StartMonth,__Q3StartDay),"Q2",
        __date >= DATE(__Year,__Q3StartMonth,__Q3StartDay) &&
            __date < DATE(__Year,__Q4StartMonth,__Q4StartDay),"Q3",
        __date >= DATE(__Year,__Q4StartMonth,__Q4StartDay) &&
            __date < DATE(__Year,__Q1StartMonth,__Q1StartDay),"Q4",
        "Error"
    )
RETURN __Quarter
```

How it works...

The first eight lines are designed for the user to define the starting numeric months and days on which their quarters begin. The ninth line grabs the year from the current date and the tenth line simply gets the date from the current row. These ten variables are then used throughout the remainder of the DAX calculation to determine to which quarter a date belongs.

Following along with the calculation, the next step is to create a table called __QuarterMonths. The DAX table constructor is used along with the starting month variables __Q1StartMonth, __Q2StartMonth, __Q3StartMonth, and __Q4StartMonth. On the next line, we calculate the maximum value of these starting months using the MAXX iterator function. It may not seem like it, but this is the real magic of this recipe. We need to know which quarter might roll over between years. In the example, that quarter is Q2, since part of Q2 is in one year (November and December) and part is in the next year (January and February).

The first four conditions of the SWITCH statement are designed to catch the condition where a quarter rolls over from one year to the next. The only quarter that can possibly roll over from one year to the next is the quarter with the highest number for its starting month. Thus, this is the first check of each of these first four conditions. If this statement is true, then we know that the quarter might roll over from one year to the next, and so we check whether the date is greater than or equal to the starting date of the current quarter or less than the starting date of the next quarter. We use the DATE function to construct these dates from the variables set at the start of the recipe. We must have one of these statements for each quarter, since we have no idea where an organization might begin or end their quarters.

Once we account for the odd case of a quarter rolling over from one year to the next, the next four conditional statements are fairly straightforward. We can again construct dates using the DATE function for the starting and ending of quarters and simply check whether the current date under consideration is greater than or equal to the current quarter start date and less than the next quarter's start date. Again, we need one of these for each quarter.

Although the last condition for Q4 could have been replaced by the catch-all else condition of the SWITCH statement, it was instead decided to make the SWITCH statement conditions all inclusive and return an error if one of the conditions is not met. In other words, instead of checking explicitly for Q4, we could have had the last value for the SWITCH statement simply be Q4 instead of Error, the thought being that if none of the other conditions are met, the value must be Q4.

However, because this recipe is specifically designed for the user to enter their own values, it was determined safer to identify any odd condition as an error rather than masking it with a potentially incorrect Q4 value.

The really nifty part is that this recipe also works for standard calendar quarters!

There's more...

First, to convert this DAX calculation from a column to a measure, simply edit these two lines as follows:

```
VAR __Year = YEAR(MAX('R02_Calendar'[Date]))
VAR __date = MAX('R02_Calendar'[Date])
```

Second, a company may have a really obscure method of assigning quarters, such as the first Monday in October, or the first working day in October. Since this technique only relies upon assigning numeric months and days for quarter starting dates, this recipe can be combined with other recipes in this book, such as those for finding the first working day of a month.

See also

For more details regarding the functions in this recipe, refer to the following links:

- DATE: https://docs.microsoft.com/en-us/dax/date-function-dax
- Table constructor: https://docs.microsoft.com/en-us/dax/table-constructor
- MAXX: https://docs.microsoft.com/en-us/dax/maxx-function-dax
- SWITCH: https://docs.microsoft.com/en-us/dax/switch-function-dax

Calculating leap years

A leap year is defined as a year that is evenly divisible by 4, but not evenly divisible by 100 unless that year is also evenly divisible by 400. Confused? This is why this recipe exists! This recipe calculates whether or not a year is a leap year and the number of days in a year.

Getting ready

To prepare for this recipe, perform the following steps:

1. Create a table using the following formula:

```
R03_Years = GENERATESERIES(1899,3000,1)
```

How to do it...

To implement this recipe, perform the following steps:

1. Create the following columns in the R03_Years table:

```
IsLeapYear =
VAR __Year = INT('R03_Years'[Value])
VAR __Div4 = IF(MOD(__Year,4)=0,TRUE(),FALSE())
VAR __Div100 = IF(MOD(__Year,100)=0,TRUE(),FALSE())
VAR __Div400 = IF(MOD(__Year,400)=0,TRUE(),FALSE())
VAR __IsLeapYear =
    SWITCH(TRUE(),
        __Div4 && NOT(__Div100),TRUE(),
        __Div4 && __Div100 && __Div400,TRUE(),
        FALSE()
    )
RETURN __IsLeapYear
```

How it works...

The preceding formula uses MOD, which returns the modulus or remainder of a division operation. A modulus of 0 means that there is no remainder or that the numerator was evenly divisible by the denominator. We store these remainders in the variables __Div4, __Div100, and __Div400. We can then use these values to determine whether the year is a leap year by using a simple SWITCH statement that defines the rules.

There's more...

First, to convert this calculation from a column to a measure, simply edit the first line as follows:

```
VAR __Year = INT(MAX('R03_Years'[Value]))
```

Second, returning the number of days in a year requires only a slight modification. Create this additional column in the `R03_Years` table:

```
DaysInYear =
VAR __Year = INT('R03_Years'[Value])
VAR __Div4 = IF(MOD(__Year,4)=0,TRUE(),FALSE())
VAR __Div100 = IF(MOD(__Year,100)=0,TRUE(),FALSE())
VAR __Div400 = IF(MOD(__Year,400)=0,TRUE(),FALSE())
VAR __IsLeapYear =
    SWITCH(TRUE(),
        __Div4 && NOT(__Div100),TRUE(),
        __Div4 && __Div100 && __Div400,TRUE(),
        FALSE()
    )
RETURN
    IF(__IsLeapYear,366,365)
```

See also

For more details regarding the functions in this recipe, refer to the following links:

- Method to determine whether a year is a leap year: https://docs.microsoft.com/en-us/office/troubleshoot/excel/determine-a-leap-year
- MOD: https://docs.microsoft.com/en-us/dax/mod-function-dax
- SWITCH: https://docs.microsoft.com/en-us/dax/switch-function-dax

Determining day and working day numbers in a year

There are many business scenarios where you need to know the sequential day number of the year or the sequential working day number of the year. For example, February 1 would be the 32nd day of the year (since January has 31 days). This recipe provides calculations for finding this sequential day number within a year as well as the sequential working day number within a year (excludes weekends).

Getting ready

To prepare for this recipe, perform the following steps:

1. Create a table using the following formula:

```
R04_Calendar = CALENDAR(DATE(2018,1,1),DATE(2022,12,31))
```

How to do it...

To implement this recipe, create the following columns in the R04_Calendar table:

```
DayNoOfYear =
    DATEDIFF(
        DATE(YEAR('R04_Calendar'[Date]), 1, 1 ),
        'R04_Calendar'[Date],
        DAY
    ) + 1

WorkingDayNoOfYear =
VAR __Date = 'R04_Calendar'[Date]
VAR __Year = YEAR(__Date)
VAR __Calendar =
    FILTER(
        ALL('R04_Calendar'),
        YEAR('R04_Calendar'[Date]) = __Year
    )
VAR __Calendar1 =
    ADDCOLUMNS(
        __Calendar,
        "__WeekDay",
        WEEKDAY([Date],2)
    )
VAR __Calendar2 =
    FILTER(
        __Calendar1,
        [__WeekDay]<6
    )
VAR __Calendar3 =
    ADDCOLUMNS(
        __Calendar2,
        "__WorkingDayNoOfYear",
        COUNTROWS(
            FILTER(
                __Calendar2,
                [Date]<__Date
```

```
            )
        ) + 1
    )
RETURN
    MAXX(
        FILTER(
            __Calendar3,
            'R04_Calendar'[Date] = __Date
        ),
        [__WorkingDayNoOfYear]
    )
```

How it works...

DayNoOfYear is a fairly straightforward calculation. We simply use the DATEDIFF function to return the number of DAY intervals between our current working date and January 1 of the same year. We then simply need to add 1 to this number so that January 1 does not end up being zero. DATEDIFF can return differences between dates in the following increments:

- SECOND
- MINUTE
- HOUR
- DAY
- WEEK
- MONTH
- QUARTER
- YEAR

WorkingDayNoOfYear is relatively more complex than DayNoOfYear. We begin by getting the current date and the year of that date and storing those values in the variables, __Date and __Year. Next, we create a variable that stores a temporary table called __Calendar, which contains all dates within our date table filtered to our current working year. We then use the ADDCOLUMNS function to add a __Weekday column to the __Calendar table using the WEEKDAY function and return the resulting table in the __Calendar1 variable. It should be noted that the second parameter for the WEEKDAY function can be 1, 2, or 3.

This translates into the following return values:

- 1: The week begins on Sunday (1) and ends on Saturday (7).
- 2: The week begins on Monday (1) and ends on Sunday (7).
- 3: The week begins on Monday (0) and ends on Sunday (6).

Once we have our __Weekday column in __Calendar1, we can then use FILTER
on __Calendar1 to only include weekdays (__Weekday values less than 6) and return the
result in the __Calendar2 variable. We can then create our final temporary table,
__Calendar3, by using __Calendar2 and adding a column using ADDCOLUMNS to create a
__WorkingDayNoOfYear column. This column is created by counting the number of rows
(+ 1) in the table where the Date is less than our current working date (__Date). It may
seem like an odd construct to be adding a column to a table variable while, at the same
time, basing the value of the column on counting a filtered subset of that same table
variable, but this is perfectly legal in DAX!

Once we have the final __Calendar3 table, we can return the desired value by filtering this
table down to the current date we are working with and wrapping an iterative aggregation
function around the result. In this instance, we chose MAXX, but we could just as easily have
chosen MINX, SUMX, or AVERAGEX, since we are filtering down to only a single value.

There's more...

A shorter formula for DayNoOfYear exists that demonstrates a useful trick for dates but can
somewhat obfuscate what is going on and therefore be harder to read and decipher. To use
this technique, create a new column in the R04_Calendar table with the following formula:

```
DayNoOfYear2 =
    ('R04_Calendar'[Date] - DATE(YEAR('R04_Calendar'[Date]), 1, 1 )) * 1 +
1
```

Instead of using DATEDIFF, we can simply subtract the dates from one another to get the
number of days. This is because a date is really just a decimal number where the whole
number portion is the number of days since December 30, 1898. The decimal portion is the
time component as a fraction of the day.

Since we are dealing with pure dates where the time is essentially midnight (12:00:00 AM),
we do not have to worry about the time component because 0 – 0 = 0. Thus, when we
subtract dates, we get back the number of days between the two dates.

However, because we are subtracting dates, DAX believes that we want a date returned from the calculation. If we did not take steps to compensate, we would end up with a date that was, however, many days returned from the subtraction away from December 30, 1899 which is most definitely not what we want!

To avoid getting back an obscure date, we can wrap our date subtraction in parentheses and multiply by 1. Multiplying by 1 forces DAX to understand that we desire a number from our calculation instead of a date. We then just need to add 1 to the result of this calculation for the same reason as in `DayNoOfYear`.

See also

For more details regarding the functions in this recipe, refer to the following links:

- DATEDIFF: https://docs.microsoft.com/en-us/dax/datediff-function-dax
- WEEKDAY: https://docs.microsoft.com/en-us/dax/weekday-function-dax
- ADDCOLUMNS: https://docs.microsoft.com/en-us/dax/addcolumns-function-dax
- Dates prior to 1900 in DAX: https://community.powerbi.com/t5/Community-Blog/Dates-Prior-to-1900-in-DAX/ba-p/15306
- Using DAX with DateTime values: https://www.sqlbi.com/blog/alberto/2019/03/25/using-dax-with-datetime-values/

Determining date of the day number of a year

This recipe comes in handy if you know the day number of a year and wish to determine the actual date of that day.

Getting ready

To prepare for this recipe, perform the following steps:

1. Create a table using the following formula:

```
R05_Calendar = CALENDAR(DATE(2018,1,1),DATE(2022,12,31))
```

2. In this table, create the following column:

```
DayNoOfYear = ('R05_Calendar'[Date] -
DATE(YEAR('R05_Calendar'[Date]), 1, 1 )) * 1 + 1
```

How to do it...

To implement this recipe, perform the following steps:

1. Create a column in the R05_Calendar table with the following formula:

```
DateOfYear =
VAR __Year = YEAR('R05_Calendar'[Date])
VAR __DayNoOfYear = 'R05_Calendar'[DayNoOfYear]
VAR __Calendar =
    ADDCOLUMNS (
        CALENDAR(DATE(__Year,1,1),DATE(__Year,12,31))
        ,"__DayNoOfYear",
        DATEDIFF(DATE(__Year,1,1),[Date],DAY)+1
    )
VAR __DateOfYear =
    MAXX (
        FILTER (
            __Calendar,
            [__DayNoOfYear]=__DayNoOfYear
        ),
        [Date]
    )
RETURN
    IF (
        ISBLANK(__DateOfYear),
        BLANK(),
        __DateOfYear
    )
```

How it works...

We begin by setting a year and our working day number of the year in the variables __Year and __DayNoOfYear, respectively. We then create a variable to hold a temporary __Calendar table and add a column to this table, __DayNoOfYear, which holds the sequential day number of the year. With this table, we can then essentially *lookup* our desired date by filtering the table down to the single row that equals our current working __DayNoOfYear.

Finally, we perform a quick check to ensure that we matched a row. If so, we return our __DateOfYear variable, otherwise we return blank (BLANK).

There's more...

To convert this recipe from a column to a measure, simply edit these lines as follows:

```
VAR __Year = YEAR(MAX('R05_Calendar'[Date]))
VAR __DayNoOfYear = MAX('R05_Calendar'[DayNoOfYear])
```

When calculating __DateOfYear, we could use any iterative aggregation function such as MINX, SUMX, or AVERAGEX instead of MAXX since we are filtering down to a single value.

See also

For more details regarding the functions in this recipe, refer to the following links:

- CALENDAR: https://docs.microsoft.com/en-us/dax/calendar-function-dax
- DATEDIFF: https://docs.microsoft.com/en-us/dax/datediff-function-dax
- ISBLANK: https://docs.microsoft.com/en-us/dax/isblank-function-dax
- BLANK: https://docs.microsoft.com/en-us/dax/blank-function-dax

Finding week start and end dates

Many organizations have the concept of week starting and week ending, especially when dealing with time tracking or reporting. This recipe provides a way to calculate the week start and end dates for any date within a calendar year.

Getting ready

To prepare for this recipe, perform the following steps:

1. Create a table using the following formula:

```
R06_Calendar = CALENDAR(DATE(2018,1,1),DATE(2022,12,31))
```

2. Create a column in this table using the following formula:

```
Weekday = FORMAT([Date],"dddd")
```

The `Weekday` column is simply for reference and checking; it is not a required part of the recipe.

How to do it...

To implement this recipe, perform the following steps:

1. Create the following column in the `R06_Calendar` table:

```
WeekStarting =
VAR __WeekDay = 1  // 1 = Sunday, 2 = Monday ... 7 = Saturday
VAR __Date = 'R06_Calendar'[Date]
//
// Do not modify below this line except RETURN line
//
VAR __WeekNum = WEEKNUM(__Date)
VAR __Year = YEAR(__Date)
VAR __Calendar =
    ADDCOLUMNS(
        CALENDAR(
            DATE(__Year - 1 ,1 , 1),
            DATE(__Year ,12 , 31)
        ),
        "__WeekNum",WEEKNUM([Date]),
        "__WeekDay",WEEKDAY([Date])
    )
VAR __WeekDate =
    MINX(
        FILTER(
            __Calendar,
            YEAR([Date]) = __Year &&
                [__WeekNum]=__WeekNum &&
                    [__WeekDay] = __WeekDay
        ),
        [Date]
    )
VAR __WeekDate1 =
    IF(
        ISBLANK(__WeekDate),
        MINX(
            FILTER(
                __Calendar,
```

```
                         YEAR([Date]) = __Year - 1 &&
                             [__WeekNum] = MAXX(__Calendar,[__WeekNum]) &&
                             [__WeekDay] = __WeekDay
                    ),
                    [Date]
            ),
            __WeekDate
        )
RETURN
//
// Modify the return format as desired
//
// Example: "W" & __WeekNum & " Week Starting " & __WeekDate1
__WeekDate1
```

2. **Create this additional column in the** R06_Calendar **table:**

```
WeekEnding =
VAR __WeekDay = 7  // 1 = Sunday, 2 = Monday ... 7 = Saturday
VAR __Date = 'R06_Calendar'[Date]
//
// Do not modify below this line except RETURN line
//
VAR __WeekNum = WEEKNUM(__Date)
VAR __Year = YEAR(__Date)
VAR __Calendar =
    ADDCOLUMNS(
        CALENDAR(
            DATE(__Year ,1 , 1),
            DATE(__Year + 1 ,12 , 31)
        ),
        "__WeekNum",WEEKNUM([Date]),
        "__WeekDay",WEEKDAY([Date])
    )
VAR __WeekDate =
    MINX(
        FILTER(
            __Calendar,
            YEAR([Date]) = __Year &&
                [__WeekNum]=__WeekNum &&
                    [__WeekDay] = __WeekDay
        ),
        [Date]
    )
VAR __WeekDate1 =
    IF(
        ISBLANK(__WeekDate),
        MINX(
```

```
                         FILTER(
                             __Calendar,
                             YEAR([Date]) = __Year + 1 &&
                                 [__WeekNum] = MINX(__Calendar,[__WeekNum]) &&
                                     [__WeekDay] = __WeekDay
                         ),
                         [Date]
                     ),
                     __WeekDate
                 )
         RETURN
         //
         // Modify the return format as desired
         //
         // Example: "W" & __WeekNum & " Week Ending" & __WeekDate1
         __WeekDate1
```

How it works...

Both `WeekStarting` and `WeekEnding` employ the same pattern, with only minor differences. The first line where the `__WeekDay` variable is set, is designed to be edited by the user. This sets the day on which a week begins or ends. This can vary by organization, as some organizations start their weeks on Sunday, while others start their weeks on Monday or even other days of the week. The next line sets the current working date and stores this in the `__Date` variable. We use this variable to get the week number and year of this date and store these values in the variables `__WeekNum` and `__Year`, respectively.

Next, we create a variable to house a temporary calendar table in the `__Calendar` variable. We start with a calendar table created by the CALENDAR function. For `WeekStarting`, we want this table to include all dates in the current working year as well as the previous year, since weeks may start in the previous year. For `WeekEnding`, we want all dates in the current working year as well as the subsequent year, since weeks may end in the next year. We use the ADDCOLUMNS function to add the week number and the weekday using the WEEKNUM and WEEKDAY functions.

Now that we have a temporary calendar table, we can use this table to attempt to look up the date in the same year and week number as our current working date. This date will have a weekday that corresponds with the weekday that starts or ends our week (`__WeekDay`). This is done by using FILTER to filter down to a single value and wrapping this filter clause with an iterative aggregator such as MINX. We store this date in the `__WeekDate` variable.

Because a week may start or end in the previous year or subsequent year, we must add a check to account for this. We do this in the __WeekDate1 variable. We begin by checking whether our __WeekDate variable is blank by using the ISBLANK function. If __WeekDate is blank, then we know that the week does not start or end in the current working year and we need to check the previous or subsequent year. If __WeekDate is not blank, we simply return its value to __WeekDate1.

The RETURN line can be modified to return whatever format is desired, including just returning the raw date from the __WeekDate1 variable.

There's more...

To convert these columns to measures, simply edit the following line for each column:

```
VAR __Date = MAX('R06_Calendar'[Date])
```

See also

For more details regarding the functions in this recipe, refer to the following links:

- CALENDAR: https://docs.microsoft.com/en-us/dax/calendar-function-dax
- ADDCOLUMNS: https://docs.microsoft.com/en-us/dax/addcolumns-function-dax
- FILTER: https://docs.microsoft.com/en-us/dax/filter-function-dax
- MINX: https://docs.microsoft.com/en-us/dax/minx-function-dax
- ISBLANK: https://docs.microsoft.com/en-us/dax/isblank-function-dax

Finding working days for weeks, months, quarters, and years

Finding the first and last days of a month in DAX is fairly straightforward. The starting day of a month is always 1 and DAX includes a handy EOMONTH function to return the last day of a month. Similarly, finding the first and last days of a year is extremely straightforward considering that years always begin on January 1 and end on December 31. Nevertheless, things become trickier when attempting to find the first and last day of a week and become much, much trickier when trying to identify the first working day of a week, month, or year.

However, since most businesses have the concept of a work week that includes work days and non-work days, it is often important to be able to identify the first and last working days of weeks, months, and years. Luckily, this recipe shows exactly how to accomplish finding the first and last working days of weeks, months, and years.

Getting ready

To prepare for this recipe, perform the following steps:

1. Create a table using the following formula:

```
R07_Calendar = CALENDAR(DATE(2018,1,1),DATE(2022,12,31))
```

2. Create a column in this table using the following formula:

```
Weekday = FORMAT([Date],"dddd")
```

3. Create another column in this table using the following formula:

```
WeekNum = WEEKNUM([Date])
```

The `Weekday` and `WeekNum` columns are simply for reference and checking; they are not a necessary part of the recipe.

How to do it...

To implement this recipe, perform the following steps:

1. Create the following columns in the R07_Calendar table:

```
First Working Day of Week =
    VAR __Date = 'R07_Calendar'[Date]
    VAR __Calendar =
        FILTER(
            ADDCOLUMNS(
                CALENDAR(__Date - 5 ,__Date + 5),
                "__WeekNum",WEEKNUM('R07_Calendar'[Date]),
                "__WeekDay",WEEKDAY('R07_Calendar'[Date], 2)
            ),
            [__WeekDay] = 1
        )
    VAR __WorkingDay = MINX(__Calendar,'R07_Calendar'[Date])
    RETURN __WorkingDay
```

```
First Working Day of Month =
    VAR __Date = 'R07_Calendar'[Date]
    VAR __Month = MONTH(__Date)
    VAR __Year = YEAR(__Date)
    VAR __Calendar =
        FILTER(
            ADDCOLUMNS(
                CALENDAR(
                    DATE(__Year, __Month, 1),
                    DATE(__Year, __Month, DAY(EOMONTH(__Month,0)))
                ),
                "__Month",MONTH('R07_Calendar'[Date]),
                "__WeekDay",WEEKDAY('R07_Calendar'[Date], 2)
            ),
            [__WeekDay] < 6
        )
    VAR __WorkingDay = MINX(__Calendar,'R07_Calendar'[Date])
RETURN __WorkingDay
```

2. Create the following additional columns in the R07_Calendar **table:**

```
First Working Day of Quarter =
    VAR __Date = 'R07_Calendar'[Date]
    VAR __Quarter = ROUNDUP(MONTH([Date])/3,0)
    VAR __Year = YEAR(__Date)
    VAR __Calendar =
        FILTER(
            ADDCOLUMNS(
                CALENDAR(
                    DATE(__Year, 1, 1),
                    DATE(__Year, 12, 31)
                ),
    "__Quarter",ROUNDUP(MONTH('R07_Calendar'[Date])/3,0),
                "__WeekDay",WEEKDAY('R07_Calendar'[Date], 2)
            ),
            [__Quarter] = __Quarter &&
            [__WeekDay] < 6
        )
    VAR __WorkingDay = MINX(__Calendar,'R07_Calendar'[Date])
RETURN __WorkingDay

First Working Day of Year =
    VAR __Date = 'R07_Calendar'[Date]
    VAR __Year = YEAR(__Date)
    VAR __Calendar =
        FILTER(
            ADDCOLUMNS(
                CALENDAR(
```

```
                    DATE(__Year, 1, 1),
                    DATE(__Year, 12, 31)
                ),
                "__WeekDay",WEEKDAY('R07_Calendar'[Date], 2)
            ),
            [__WeekDay] < 6
        )
    VAR __WorkingDay = MINX(__Calendar,'R07_Calendar'[Date])
    RETURN __WorkingDay
```

How it works...

All of these formulas work in the same way. The first few lines get the working date along with any relevant information we may require, such as the month, quarter, or year for that date. We then construct a calendar table with the narrowest possible definition initially and then filter this table to a relevant set, which always only contains working days (not Saturday or Sunday). We can then simply get the minimum value in this table and return it as our first working day value.

There's more...

To convert any of these columns to measures, we simply need to replace the first line with the following:

```
VAR __Date = MAX([Date])
```

For all of these calculations except `First Working Day of Week`, if we want to know the last working day of the period in question, we simply need to edit the line above the `RETURN` line to use `MAXX` instead of `MINX`.

To find the last working day of a week, we use this formula:

```
Last Working Day of Week =
    VAR __Date = 'R07_Calendar'[Date]
    VAR __Calendar =
        FILTER(
            ADDCOLUMNS(
                CALENDAR(__Date - 5 ,__Date + 5),
                "__WeekNum",WEEKNUM('R07_Calendar'[Date]),
                "__WeekDay",WEEKDAY('R07_Calendar'[Date], 2)
            ),
            [__WeekDay] = 5
        )
```

```
    VAR __WorkingDay = MAXX(__Calendar,'R07_Calendar'[Date])
RETURN __WorkingDay
```

Here, we have changed the weekday number that we are filtering on from a 1 (Monday) to a 5 (Friday) and are using a `MAXX` function instead of a `MINX` function in our calculation for the `__WorkingDay` variable.

There is a variation for finding the first and last working days of weeks. The formulas presented span years, such that, if a week starts or ends in a previous or subsequent year, the formula returns the date in that previous or subsequent year. If it is instead desired to only include the start and end working days for a week within the same year, use this variation for `First Working Day of Week`:

```
First Working Day of Week 2 =
    VAR __Date = 'R07_Calendar'[Date]
    VAR __WeekNum = WEEKNUM(__Date)
    VAR __Calendar =
        FILTER(
            ADDCOLUMNS(
                CALENDAR(__Date - 5 ,__Date + 5),
                "__WeekNum",WEEKNUM('R07_Calendar'[Date]),
                "__WeekDay",WEEKDAY('R07_Calendar'[Date], 2)
            ),
            [__WeekNum] = __WeekNum &&
                [__WeekDay] < 6
        )
    VAR __WorkingDay = MINX(__Calendar,'R07_Calendar'[Date])
RETURN __WorkingDay
```

For the same variation for `Last Working Day of Week`, simply replace the `MINX` function in this variation with the `MAXX` function in the line immediately above the `RETURN` line.

Finally, if you are using non-standard calendar quarters, simply edit the calculation for the `__Quarter` variable and the `__Quarter` column to correspond with your custom quarter calculation. Refer to the *Creating quarters* recipe in this chapter.

See also

For more details regarding the functions in this recipe, refer to the following links:

- ADDCOLUMNS: https://docs.microsoft.com/en-us/dax/addcolumns-function-dax
- FILTER: https://docs.microsoft.com/en-us/dax/filter-function-dax
- CALENDAR: https://docs.microsoft.com/en-us/dax/calendar-function-dax

- WEEKDAY: https://docs.microsoft.com/en-us/dax/weekday-function-dax
- ROUNDUP: https://docs.microsoft.com/en-us/dax/roundup-function-dax

Constructing a sequential week number

While perhaps not obviously useful on its own, there are many circumstances where having a sequential number across weeks, months, quarters, and years can facilitate other calculations. This recipe demonstrates how to construct a sequential week number across years.

Getting ready

To prepare for this recipe, perform the following steps:

1. Create a table using the following formula:

```
R08_Calendar = CALENDAR(DATE(2018,1,1),DATE(2022,12,31))
```

How to do it...

To implement this recipe, perform the following steps:

1. Create the following column in the `R08_Calendar` table:

```
SequentialWeek =
    VAR __Date = 'R08_Calendar'[Date] // The working date, edit if
column is not Date
    VAR __Year = YEAR(__Date) // Get the working date
    VAR __Calendar = // Create calendar table with year and weeknum
        ADDCOLUMNS (
            ALL('R08_Calendar'), // Edit table name to match
            "__Year",
            YEAR('R08_Calendar'[Date]), // Edit table and column to
match
            "__WeekNum",
            WEEKNUM('R08_Calendar'[Date]) // Edit table and column
to match
        )
    VAR __FirstYear = MINX(__Calendar,[__Year]) // Determine the
first year in our table
    VAR __WeekNum = // Get the current working week number
```

```
        MAXX(
            FILTER(
                __Calendar,
                [Date] = __Date
            ),
            [__WeekNum]
        )
    VAR __MaxWeeks = // Create a table of years and their max week
numbers
        GROUPBY(
            __Calendar,
            [__Year],
            "__MaxWeek",
            MAXX(
                CURRENTGROUP(),
                [__WeekNum]
            )
        )
    VAR __Start = // Use __MaxWeeks table to get starting point for
week number
        SUMX(
            FILTER(
                __MaxWeeks,
                [__Year]<__Year
            ),
            [__MaxWeek]
        )
    VAR __Sequential =
        IF(
            __Year=__FirstYear,
            __WeekNum, // If first year, then just the week number
            __Start + __WeekNum // Otherwise, __Start + current
week number
        )
    RETURN __Sequential
```

How it works...

We start by getting our current working date and the year of that date. We then construct a calendar table, adding the year and week number as columns and return that to a variable named __Calendar. We use this __Calendar variable to find our first year, which is the starting year for our sequential week number. We store this year in the __FirstYear variable.

We now need to know the week number of our current working date within the year that it occurs. We do this by simply filtering our __Calendar variable down to our working date and grabbing the week number out of the __WeekNum column. We will use this later when calculating the sequential week number for weeks that occur after our first year (__FirstYear).

The next step is to find the starting week number for weeks that occur after our first year. We do this by first constructing a table called __MaxWeeks, grouping our __Calendar table by year (__Year) and placing the maximum week number for each year in a column called __MaxWeek. Once we have this table, we simply need to get the sum of these __MaxWeek values for every year that is less than our current working year. So, for example, if 2018 and 2019 each have 53 weeks, the starting point for the first week of 2020 is 53 + 53, or 106.

The last step is fairly straightforward. If our current working date is in the first year (__FirstYear), then our sequential number is simply the week number for that date in that year. However, for dates after our first year, we need to add our starting week (__Start) to our current week number (__WeekNum).

There's more...

One drawback to the SequentialWeek recipe is that it does not account for weeks at the end of a year that do not contain a full seven days. For example, if we look at the end of 2018, we see that there are only two days in week 53 and that the first day of 2019 starts at week 54. Luckily, with a bit of extra code, we can fix this so that our sequential week counter always accounts for full seven-day weeks! To create this version of the recipe, create the SequentialWeek2 column in the R08_Calendar table using the code found in the R08_SequentialWeek2.txt file located in the GitHub repository. This code is almost exactly the same as before, except for the creation of three new variables, __Calendar1, __SubtractTable, and __Subtract, as well as a small change in the calculation of our __Sequential variable.

The goal here is to figure out how many of the years preceding our current working year do not have a full seven days in the last week of the year. We do this by first adding a column called __MaxWeek to our __Calendar table that stores the maximum week number in that year and storing this new table in the __Calendar1 variable. Because we are adding a column, we can use the row context and the EARLIER function to first filter our __Calendar table for all rows where the __Year column equals the __Year column of our current row. We then simply get the maximum value for the __WeekNum column within this filtered context.

Once we have this new column in our calendar table, now __Calendar1, we create a new table, __SubtractTable, that holds a table of years less than our current working year along with a column, __NumWeekDays, that holds the number of days in the last week of each of those years. Breaking the __SubtractTable calculation down, we apply FILTER to our __Calendar1 table such that we only filter the rows in the table where the years are less than our current working year and the week number equals our maximum week number for that year. We then group (GROUPBY) this filtered table by year and add in a count of the days within each group.

We can now simply count the rows in this new __SubtractTable variable that have __NumWeekDays less than seven to determine how many week numbers to subtract from our final sequential week number. We store this value in a variable called __Subtract and use this in our final __Sequential calculation for dates that are not in our first year (__FirstYear).

See also

For more details regarding the functions in this recipe, refer to the following links:

- ADDCOLUMNS: https://docs.microsoft.com/en-us/dax/addcolumns-function-dax
- FILTER: https://docs.microsoft.com/en-us/dax/filter-function-dax
- GROUPBY: https://docs.microsoft.com/en-us/dax/groupby-function-dax
- EARLIER: https://docs.microsoft.com/en-us/dax/earlier-function-dax

Computing rolling weeks

There are a number of business analysis calculations, such as forecasting, that often require an analysis of a sliding scale of the data from previous (complete) date periods. For example, it is fairly common that the last 3 complete months' worth of data is used to forecast the current month. In other words, if today's date is April 6, 2020, then the dates desired would be from January 1, 2020 to March 31, 2020. These sliding scales must be able to cross year boundaries as well as ensure that the date ranges calculated are exact. Being off by even a single day can sometimes greatly affect forecasts.

While Power BI has a DAX rolling average quick measure, this measure only works with days, months, quarters, and years. The reason is that DAX's time intelligence generally does not support weeks, and for good reason. Dealing with weeks tends to get tricky. This recipe demonstrates how to compute calculations that utilize rolling weeks but be warned; this is probably the most complex recipe in this chapter!

Getting ready

To prepare for this recipe, perform the following steps:

1. Create a table called `R09_Sales` by importing the `Sales.csv` file from the GitHub repository here: `https://github.com/PacktPublishing/DAX-Cookbook/tree/master/Chapter02`.

How to do it...

To implement this recipe, perform the following steps:

1. Create the following measure:

```
Rolling Week Average =
    VAR __Date = MAX('R09_Sales'[Date])
    VAR __Sales = ALL('R09_Sales')
    VAR __WeeksBack = 4
    VAR __WeeksForward = 0
    VAR __RollingWeekStartDate = __Date - 7 * __WeeksBack
    VAR __RollingWeekEndDate = (__Date + 7 * __WeeksForward) - 1
RETURN
    AVERAGEX(
        FILTER(
            __Sales,
            [Date] >= __RollingWeekStartDate &&
                [Date] <= __RollingWeekEndDate
        ),
        [Value]
    )
```

2. Create a **Line Chart** visualization and place the `Date` column from the `R09_Sales` table in the **Axis** field and the `Rolling Week Average` measure in the **Values** field.

How it works...

We begin by initializing the date we are working with, __Date, and the table where we will be averaging values, __Sales. We then set how many weeks backward and forward that we want to include in our averages for any particular day and store these in the variables __WeeksBack and __WeeksForward, respectively.

We can use these variables to calculate the start and end dates of our rolling weeks in the __RollingWeekStartDate and __RollingWeekEndDate variables. In the case of __RollingWeekStartDate, we simply need to use date subtraction to subtract the number of __WeeksBack variable by 7 (seven days in a week). For __RollingWeekEndDate, it is a similar calculation except that we are adding days and we subtract 1 in order to not include the current date.

Once we have the dates to include, we FILTER the table to only include dates within and including our __RollingWeekStartDate and __RollingWeekEndDate variables and use AVERAGEX to average the Value column.

There's more...

Now, there are a couple of issues associated with our rolling week average calculation. First, this calculation does not look very complex at all despite the warning at the beginning of this recipe! Second, and most importantly, this really is not a rolling four week average; it is more like a rolling 28 day average. Fear not. This initial calculation is simply an example to explain the concept of rolling averages. In short, the entire crux of the issue is to calculate the start and end dates for our rolling window of dates and use those to filter our table such that only the values within that date range are included in our calculation.

What we really want, however, is to include the last four full weeks of values for any particular date. To do this, we will need some help from our *Finding week start and end dates* recipe. We can use that recipe to adjust our calculation for __RollingWeekStartDate and __RollingWeekEndDate . To do this, create a measure from the code located in the R09_RollingWeekAverage2.txt file in the GitHub repository.

OK. You were warned that this was complex! So, let's break this calculation down. The first four lines are largely the same except, since we are only interested in full weeks, we set our __WeeksForward variable to -1 to ensure that the last full week, and not the current week, is included in the final range of dates.

The majority of the remainder of the calculation is dominated by the creation of a calendar table variable, `__Calendar`. This variable contains a calendar that will be used by the subsequent steps in the calculation and is central to the entire solution. The creation of this variable begins with the creation of a calendar table that contains a range of date values based on our `__WeeksBack` and `__WeeksForward` variables. To this table we then add two columns, `__WeekStarting` and `__WeekEnding`, based on our *Finding week start and end dates* recipe. For a full explanation of these two columns, refer to the *Finding week start and end dates* recipe. There are no real changes required other than those required to fit them into the formula as essentially nested `VAR` statements. You should observe that any formula for computing these two columns could be inserted, such as finding the first and last working days of a week.

Once we have our calendar table with our `__WeekStarting` and `__WeekEnding` columns, we can now create the dates whose `__WeekStarting` and `__WeekEnding` dates we wish to look up. These variables are `__LookupDateStart` and `__LookupDateEnd`, which are essentially the same calculation we used earlier in our original formula for `Rolling Week Average` when computing `__RollingWeekStartDate` and `__RollingWeekEndDate`. This time, when computing `__RollingWeekStartDate` and `__RollingWeekEndDate`, we use the `__LookupDateStart` and `__LookupDateEnd` variables to find the corresponding dates in our `__Calendar` table and return either the `__WeekStarting` or `__WeekEnding` dates, respectively.

Once we have our `__RollingWeekStartDate` and `__RollingWeekEndDate` values, the remainder of our formula is the same as before.

See also

For more details regarding the functions in this recipe, refer to the following links:

- ADDCOLUMNS: https://docs.microsoft.com/en-us/dax/addcolumns-function-dax
- FILTER: https://docs.microsoft.com/en-us/dax/filter-function-dax
- CALENDAR: https://docs.microsoft.com/en-us/dax/calendar-function-dax
- AVERAGEX: https://docs.microsoft.com/en-us/dax/averagex-function-dax

Replacing Excel's NETWORKDAYS function

Excel has a NETWORKDAYS function that calculates the number of days between two dates minus weekends and holidays. While DAX has a DATEDIFF function that calculates the number of days between two dates, the DATEDIFF function does not account for subtracting weekends and holidays. This recipe is a recreation of Excel's NETWORKDAYS function in DAX.

Getting ready

To prepare for this recipe, perform the following steps:

1. Use an **Enter Data** query to create a table called R10_Table with the following columns and rows:

Created Date	Finished Date
11/17/2019	12/29/2019
12/15/2019	1/13/2020
1/12/2020	3/30/2020

2. Ensure that both columns are set to have a data type of Date.
3. Create the following column in the R10_Table table:

```
Number of Days = DATEDIFF([Created Dated],[Finished Date],DAY)
```

4. Place all three columns from the R10_Table table in a **Table** visualization on a **Report** page.
5. Set the Created Date and Finished Date fields in this **Table** visualization to be their actual dates, not their date hierarchies.

How to do it...

To implement this recipe, perform the following steps:

1. Create a new measure with the following formula:

```
NetWorkDays =
    VAR __Date1 = MAX('R10_Table'[Created Date])
    VAR __Date2 = MAX('R10_Table'[Finished Date])
```

```
            VAR __Date1a = MINX( { __Date1, __Date2 },[Value])
            VAR __Date2a = MAXX( { __Date1, __Date2 },[Value])
            VAR __Calendar =
                ADDCOLUMNS(
                    CALENDAR(__Date1a, __Date2a),
                    "__WeekDay",
                    WEEKDAY([Date],2)
                )
        RETURN
            COUNTX(
                FILTER(
                    __Calendar,
                    [__WeekDay] < 6
                ),
                [Date]
            )
```

2. Place the `NetWorkDays` measure in the **Table** visualization created earlier.

How it works...

This recipe is fairly straightforward. The first four lines simply ensure that we construct our calendar table in such a way that the earliest date comes first. We then construct a calendar table, `__Calendar`, that holds our two dates as well as all of the dates between those two dates. We add a column, `__WeekDay`, which stores the number of the week day (1-7). By using the 2 as our second parameter for the `WEEKDAY` function, Saturday = 6 and Sunday = 7. We then simply need to filter this table where the `__WeekDay` column is not 6 or 7 and return the count of the days (rows) remaining.

There's more...

We can modify our `NetWorkDays` calculation to account for holidays as well. To do this, observe the following steps:

1. Create the following table using an **Enter Data** query:

Date
12/24/2019
12/25/2019
1/1/2019

2. Ensure that the `Date` column is flagged as having a data type of `Date`.

3. Create a new measure with the following formula:

```
NetWorkDays2 =
    VAR __Date1 = MAX('R10_Table'[Created Date])
    VAR __Date2 = MAX('R10_Table'[Finished Date])
    VAR __Date1a = MINX( { __Date1, __Date2 },[Value])
    VAR __Date2a = MAXX( { __Date1, __Date2 },[Value])
    VAR __Calendar =
        ADDCOLUMNS (
            EXCEPT (
                CALENDAR(__Date1a, __Date2a),
                'R10_Holidays'
            ),
            "__WeekDay",
            WEEKDAY([Date],2)
        )
RETURN
    COUNTX (
        FILTER (
            __Calendar,
            [__WeekDay] < 6
        ),
        [Date]
    )
```

4. Place this `NetWorkDays2` measure in the **Table** visualization created earlier.

The small change to the formula to account for holidays is to use the `EXCEPT` function to remove the dates in the `R10_Holidays` table from the calendar table that we create, `__Calendar`.

See also

For more details regarding the functions in this recipe, refer to the following links:

- CALENDAR: https://docs.microsoft.com/en-us/dax/calendar-function-dax
- WEEKDAY: https://docs.microsoft.com/en-us/dax/weekday-function-dax
- FILTER: https://docs.microsoft.com/en-us/dax/filter-function-dax
- COUNTX: https://docs.microsoft.com/en-us/dax/countx-function-dax
- EARLIER: https://docs.microsoft.com/en-us/dax/earlier-function-dax

Working with date intervals

There are many scenarios involving dates where you have two or more sets of dates as items or transactions move through a process. It is often desirable to know how many items or transactions are in one state or another at any given time. Unfortunately, this is something that is not straightforward to present in a report given that, with just the raw data, it is difficult, if not impossible, to depict how and when items and transactions transitioned from one state to another.

This recipe presents a simple scenario where help tickets are opened on one date and then closed. This recipe demonstrates how to see how many tickets are in process (open) at different date intervals, such as by year, month, and day.

Getting ready

To prepare for this recipe, perform the following steps:

1. Use an **Enter Data** query to create a table called R11_Table with the following columns and rows:

Ticket Number	Opened Date	Closed Date
1	1/4/2020	4/15/2020
2	2/8/2020	2/15/2020
3	1/14/2020	2/3/2020
4	2/4/2020	3/12/2020
5	1/29/2020	1/29/2020
6	2/18/2020	2/19/2020
7	1/5/2020	2/24/2020
8	1/5/2020	3/2/2020
9	3/3/2020	3/15/2020
10	3/6/2020	4/13/2020
11	4/1/2020	

2. Ensure that both the Opened Date and Closed Date columns are set to have a data type of Date.

3. Create a table with the following formula:

```
R11_Calendar = CALENDAR(DATE(2020, 1, 1), DATE(2020, 12, 31))
```

4. Ensure that there is no relationship between these two tables.
5. On a **Report** page, create a **Clustered Column Chart** with the **Date** field from the R11_Calendar table in the **Axis** field.
6. Ensure that the **Date** field is set to use the **Date** hierarchy and remove the **Quarter** level of the hierarchy.

How to do it...

To implement this recipe, perform the following steps:

1. Create the following measure:

```
Open Tickets =
    VAR __Tickets =
        ADDCOLUMNS (
            'R11_Table',
            "__EffectiveDate",
            IF (
                ISBLANK ('R11_Table'[Closed Date]),
                TODAY (),
                'R11_Table'[Closed Date]
            )
        )
    VAR __Table =
    SELECTCOLUMNS (
        FILTER (
            GENERATE (
                __Tickets,
                'R11_Calendar'
            ),
            AND (
                [Date] >= [Opened Date] &&
                    [Date] <= [__EffectiveDate],
                NOT ([Opened Date]=[__EffectiveDate])
            )
        ),
        "ID",[Ticket Number],
        "Date",[Date]
    )
    RETURN
```

```
COUNTROWS(
    GROUPBY(
        __Table,
        [ID]
    )
)
```

2. Place this measure in the **Value** field of the **Clustered Column** visualization created earlier.
3. Select the **Clustered Column** visualization and use the forked arrow drill-down icon to drill from the **Year** level to the **Month** level of the hierarchy.

How it works...

We start by creating a variable called __Tickets that holds all of our table information with the added column of __EffectiveDate. This __EffectiveDate column simply holds either the closed date of the ticket or today's date if there is no Closed Date. We use the TODAY function to insert today's current date. In this way, we can observe the status of tickets through to the present.

Next, we create a table of all tickets across all days that those tickets are open, storing this in a variable called __Table. To do this, first we generate the Cartesian product of our __Tickets table and our unrelated R10_Calendar table using the GENERATE function. The GENERATE function creates a Cartesian product between each row in the first table and the table that results from evaluating the second table in the context of the current row from the first table. Since we have no relationship between our tables, *if there is no other context involved,* then all rows from our R10_Calendar table would be included for each row of our __Tickets table.

We then need to filter this table such that it only includes rows where the Date falls inclusively between the ticket's opened date and its effective date (ostensibly when the ticket is considered closed). However, we do not want to include tickets that were opened and closed on the same day, so we include an additional clause to filter out those tickets where the value of Opened Date column equals the __EffectiveDate column. Finally, to complete the calculation of __Table, we also filter out our columns to just an ID column and our Date column, since these are the only two columns from the Cartesian product of our two tables that we actually need.

We then simply need to return the count of rows in our __Table variable once it is grouped by ID. This essentially allows us to simply count distinct ticket numbers included in our table.

Now, the real magic of this calculation is when we place this measure within the content of an axis that holds our `Date` column from the `R11_Calendar` table. This is because the axis provides a filter context for the `R11_Calendar` table that is honored by our `GENERATE` function when creating our `__Table`. Thus, within the context of each year, month, or day column in our axis, we are only creating the Cartesian product of our `__Tickets` table with the dates that are in context for the specific column in our axis. This, coupled with our `FILTER` statement, ensures that only tickets open within the context of the column are displayed!

See also

For more details regarding the functions in this recipe, refer to the following links:

- ADDCOLUMNS: https://docs.microsoft.com/en-us/dax/addcolumns-function-dax
- ISBLANK: https://docs.microsoft.com/en-us/dax/isblank-function-dax
- TODAY: https://docs.microsoft.com/en-us/dax/weekday-function-dax
- SELECTCOLUMNS: https://docs.microsoft.com/en-us/dax/selectcolumns-function-dax
- FILTER: https://docs.microsoft.com/en-us/dax/filter-function-dax
- GENERATE: https://docs.microsoft.com/en-us/dax/generate-function-dax
- AND: https://docs.microsoft.com/en-us/dax/and-function-dax
- GROUPBY: https://docs.microsoft.com/en-us/dax/groupby-function-dax
- COUNTROWS: https://docs.microsoft.com/en-us/dax/countrows-function-dax

Exploiting alternatives to DAX's time intelligence

The problem with DAX's time intelligence functions, other than the fact that they are ill-named, is that, well, they really are not all that intelligent. You see, all of these functions proceed from the same basic assumption that everything works on the basis of a standard calendar year. However, this is not the case for many businesses, including Microsoft! Thus, this underlying assumption of a standard calendar year makes any DAX time intelligence functions dealing with quarters particularly useless. In addition, many of the time intelligence functions are not supported in DirectQuery mode, which, again, makes them entirely useless in such scenarios.

But fear not, as I have mentioned, the vast majority of DAX's time intelligence functions are really not all that intelligent. In fact, they are really simple shorthand for date filtering calculations you could otherwise perform using non-time intelligent DAX functions. This recipe will demonstrate how to emulate DAX's time intelligence functions through the use of standard, non-time intelligent DAX functions.

Getting ready

To prepare for this recipe, perform the following steps:

1. Create a table called `R01_Sales` by importing the `Sales.csv` file from the GitHub repository here: `https://github.com/PacktPublishing/DAX-Cookbook/tree/master/Chapter02`.

2. Create a column in the `R01_Sales` table using the following formula:

   ```
   Year = YEAR([Date])
   ```

3. Create another column in the `R01_Sales` table using the following formula:

   ```
   Month = FORMAT([Date],"mmmm")
   ```

How to do it...

To implement this recipe, perform the following steps:

1. Create the following measures:

   ```
   R12 Opening Balance =
       VAR __Date = MAX('R12_Sales'[Date])
       VAR __Year = YEAR(__Date)
       VAR __Month = MONTH(__Date)
       VAR __LookupYear = IF(__Month = 1 , __Year - 1 , __Year)
       VAR __LookupMonth = IF(__Month = 1 , 12 , __Month - 1)
       VAR __Table =
           FILTER(
               ALL('R12_Sales'),
               YEAR('R12_Sales'[Date]) = __LookupYear &&
                   MONTH('R12_Sales'[Date]) = __LookupMonth &&
                       NOT(ISBLANK('R12_Sales'[Value]))
           )
       VAR __MaxDate = MAXX(__Table,[Date])
   RETURN
       SUMX(
   ```

```
        FILTER(
            __Table,
            [Date] = __MaxDate
        ),
        [Value]
    )

R12 Closing Balance =
VAR __Date = MAX('R12_Sales'[Date])
VAR __Year = YEAR(__Date)
VAR __Month = MONTH(__Date)
VAR __Table =
    FILTER(
        ALL('R12_Sales'),
        YEAR('R12_Sales'[Date]) = __Year &&
            MONTH('R12_Sales'[Date]) = __Month &&
                NOT(ISBLANK('R12_Sales'[Value]))
    )
VAR __MaxDate = MAXX(__Table,[Date])
RETURN
    SUMX(
        FILTER(
            __Table,
            [Date] = __MaxDate
        ),
        [Value]
    )
```

2. Create these additional two measures:

```
R12 Month to Date =
    VAR __Date = MAX('R12_Sales'[Date])
    VAR __Year = YEAR(__Date)
    VAR __Month = MONTH(__Date)
    VAR __Table =
        FILTER(
            ALL('R12_Sales'),
            YEAR('R12_Sales'[Date]) = __Year &&
                MONTH('R12_Sales'[Date]) = __Month &&
                    NOT(ISBLANK('R12_Sales'[Value]))
        )
RETURN
    SUMX(
        FILTER(
            __Table,
            [Date] <= __Date
        ),
        [Value]
```

```
    )

R12 Previous Month =
    VAR __Date = MAX('R12_Sales'[Date])
    VAR __Year = YEAR(__Date)
    VAR __Month = MONTH(__Date)
    VAR __LookupYear = IF(__Month = 1 , __Year - 1 , __Year)
    VAR __LookupMonth = IF(__Month = 1 , 12 , __Month - 1)
    VAR __Table = ALL('R12_Sales')
    VAR __LastMonth =
        FILTER(
            __Table,
            YEAR([Date]) = __LookupYear &&
                MONTH([Date]) = __LookupMonth &&
                    NOT(ISBLANK([Value]))
        )
    VAR __LastDayLastMonth = DAY(MAXX(__LastMonth,[Date]))
    VAR __ThisMonth =
        FILTER(
            __Table,
            YEAR([Date]) = __Year &&
                MONTH([Date]) = __Month &&
                    NOT(ISBLANK([Value]))
        )
    VAR __Rows = COUNTROWS(__ThisMonth)
    VAR __CurrentRow =
        COUNTROWS(
            FILTER(
                __ThisMonth,
                [Date] <= __Date
            )
        )
    VAR __LookupDay = INT(__LastDayLastMonth * __CurrentRow/__Rows)
RETURN
    SUMX(
        FILTER(
            __LastMonth,
            DAY([Date]) <= __LookupDay
        ),
        [Value]
    )
```

3. Create these final two measures:

```
R12 Year to Date =
    VAR __Date = MAX('R12_Sales'[Date])
    VAR __Year = YEAR(__Date)
    VAR __Table =
        FILTER(
            ALL('R12_Sales'),
            YEAR('R12_Sales'[Date]) = __Year &&
                NOT(ISBLANK('R12_Sales'[Value]))
        )
RETURN
    SUMX(
        FILTER(
            __Table,
            [Date] <= __Date
        ),
        [Value]
    )


R12 Previous Year =
    VAR __Date = MAX('R12_Sales'[Date])
    VAR __Year = YEAR(__Date)
    VAR __Month = MONTH(__Date)
    VAR __Day = DAY(__Date)
    VAR __LookupYear = __Year - 1
    VAR __LookupDate = DATE(__Year - 1 , __Month , __Day)
    VAR __Table = ALL('R12_Sales')
    VAR __LastYear =
        FILTER(
            __Table,
            YEAR('R12_Sales'[Date]) = __LookupYear &&
                NOT(ISBLANK('R12_Sales'[Value]))
        )
RETURN
    SUMX(
        FILTER(
            __LastYear,
            [Date] <= __LookupDate
        ),
        [Value]
    )
```

How it works...

Let's start with the R12 Opening Balance measure. To make this measure work in the same way as the OPENINGBALANCEMONTH function, we want the last non-blank value for the previous month. We can achieve this by first getting our working date and the year and month for that date and storing these values in the variables __Date, __Year, and __Month respectively. We can then use these variables to calculate the previous month. If the month is January (month number 1), we need December (month number 12) of last year. We store this year and month in the variables __LookupYear and __LookupMonth, respectively. We can now create a table, __Table, with the relevant dates from last month. We then compute the maximum date in that range of values, __MaxDate, and finally simply return the value for that __MaxDate from our __Table table.

The R12 Closing Balance measure works almost identically to the R12 Opening Balance measure, except that, when we compute our __Table table, we do so for the current month instead of the previous month.

The R12 Month to Date measure is identical to the R12 Closing Balance measure, except that we are looking for all dates in the current month that are less than our current working date instead of the last date in the month.

The R12 Previous Month measure is the most complex although it begins in a similar manner to R12 Opening Balance and R12 Closing Balance. The differences lie in the fact that we create tables for both last month and our current month, __LastMonth and __ThisMonth, respectively. We also compute the last day in the __LastMonth table in the __LastDayLastMonth variable. The __Rows variable determines the number of days in the current month by using COUNTROWS to count the number of rows in the __ThisMonth variable.

We also determine how many rows in the __ThisMonth table we have that are less than or equal to our current working date, __CurrentRows. We then calculate __LookupDay as the day in the last month that represents the same percentage of the month as our current working date is to the maximum days in the current month. In this way, our RETURN statement returns the same percentage of last month as to where we are in the current month. This makes for a much smarter previous month calculation because, for example, if we are on the 26th day of February, this represents 92.86% of the month of February (26 / 28 = 92.86). The equivalent day in January then is the 29th day of January (92.86% * 31 = 28.79 = 29).

The `R12 Year to Date` measure is identical to the `R12 Month to Date` measure, except that, since we are looking for all previous dates in the year, we remove the filter clause that filters our table down to the current month.

The `R12 Previous Year` measure works similarly to the `R12 Previous Month` measure, except that it is more simple in that we are simply looking for all dates in the previous year that are less than or equal to our current working date last year.

There's more...

It should now be obvious that DAX's time intelligence functions are simply shorthand for date filtering operations that we can accomplish through base DAX functions. Therefore, any DAX time intelligence function can be duplicated via DAX code that does not utilize DAX's time intelligence functions. By doing things *the hard way*, we actually gain more control over exactly how our date filtering calculations work as well as make them supportable in more circumstances, such as when using DirectQuery. For example, we can use similar patterns to this recipe and our own non-standard quarters (refer to the *Creating quarters* recipe in this chapter) to replace DAX functions such as CLOSINGBALANCEQUARTER, OPENINGBALANCEQUARTER, ENDOFQUARTER, PREVIOUSQUARTER, and STARTOFQUARTER.

See also

For more details regarding the functions in this recipe, refer to the following links:

- Time-intelligence functions: https://docs.microsoft.com/en-us/dax/time-intelligence-functions-dax
- ISBLANK: https://docs.microsoft.com/en-us/dax/isblank-function-dax
- FILTER: https://docs.microsoft.com/en-us/dax/filter-function-dax
- COUNTROWS: https://docs.microsoft.com/en-us/dax/countrows-function-dax

3
Tangling with Time and Duration

Time and duration have always gotten short shrift when it comes to DAX. Even though there are over 30 DAX functions classified as *time intelligence*, very few of them actually have anything to do with time in terms of hours, minutes, and seconds. And it wasn't until recently that you could actually aggregate durations but have the result displayed in the HH:mm:ss format. But despite DAX's lack of focus and effort on time and duration, time and duration can actually be just as important to a business and that business' analytics as calendar dates—sometimes even more so.

This chapter is all about demonstrating how to perform proper DAX calculations and analysis with time and duration, filling in some of the *holes* as it were in the DAX function library for *actual* time intelligence.

The following recipes will be covered in this chapter:

- Constructing timetables
- Computing an hour breakdown
- Converting Unix into UTC and back
- Adding and subtracting time
- Determining network duration
- Calculating shifts
- Aggregating duration
- Transforming milliseconds into duration
- Tinkering with time zones
- Converting duration into seconds
- Creating a last-refreshed timestamp

Technical requirements

The following are required to complete all of the recipes in this chapter:

- Power BI Desktop
- **GitHub repository:** https://github.com/PacktPublishing/DAX-Cookbook/tree/master/Chapter03

Constructing timetables

Just as having a date table can be extremely useful for various data models and DAX calculations, timetables can be equally useful. However, while DAX has various functions for easily creating date tables such as CALENDAR and CALENDARAUTO, no such equivalent exists for timetables. This recipe fixes that enables you to create timetables with ease!

Getting ready

Just open Power BI Desktop and you are all set.

How to do it...

To implement this recipe, do the following:

1. Create a new table with the following formula:

```
R01_12-Hour_Clock =
    VAR __hours =
        SELECTCOLUMNS(
            GENERATESERIES(1 , 12 , 1),
            "Hour",
            [Value]
        )
    VAR __minutes =
        SELECTCOLUMNS(
            GENERATESERIES(0 , 59 , 1),
            "Minutes",
            [Value]
        )
    VAR __seconds =
        SELECTCOLUMNS(
            GENERATESERIES(0 , 59 , 1),
```

```
                    "Seconds",
                    [Value]
            )
        VAR __period =
            SELECTCOLUMNS (
                { ("AM"),("PM") },
                "AM/PM",
                [Value]
            )
        VAR __hoursMinutes = GENERATEALL(__hours, __minutes)
        VAR __hoursMinutesSeconds =
    GENERATEALL(__hoursMinutes,__seconds)
        VAR __hoursMinutesSecondsAMPM =
    GENERATEALL(__hoursMinutesSeconds,__period)
        VAR __final =
            SELECTCOLUMNS (
                ADDCOLUMNS (
                    __hoursMinutesSecondsAMPM,
                    "Time",
                    TIMEVALUE (
                        FORMAT([Hour],"00") & ":" &
                            FORMAT([Minutes],"00") & ":" &
                                FORMAT([Seconds],"00") & " " & [AM/PM]
                    )
                ),
                "Time",
                [Time]
            )
    RETURN
        __final
```

2. In the R01_12-Hour_Clock table, ensure that the Time column is set to have a data type of Time.

How it works...

We start by creating four single-column tables and storing these columns in the variables: __hours, __minutes, __seconds, and __period. With the first three tables, we use the GENERATESERIES function to create the rows in our table and then use the SELECTCOLUMNS function to essentially rename our column. For the fourth variable, __period, we use the DAX table constructor to create a two-row table and again use SELECTCOLUMNS to rename the column.

It is important that we give each column a unique name because the next step is creating the Cartesian product of all of these tables using the GENERATEALL function. If the column names were not unique, GENERATEALL would generate an error.

Once we have the Cartesian product of all of our tables, we essentially have a table in memory called __hoursMinutesSecondsAMPM that has four columns and has every possible combination of hours, minutes, seconds, and A.M./P.M. in a day for a 12-hour clock. To create the final table that we will return, __final, we add a column using TIMEVALUE to convert the concatenation of each of our four columns. These columns are concatenated along with separators of colons (:) and spaces as appropriate. Finally, we select only our Time column to return using SELECTCOLUMNS once again. Hence, our final table only has a single column called Time.

There's more...

First, if you need the leading zeros for hours, you will need to make the Time column a text data type and modify the calculation of the __final variable slightly, as follows:

```
VAR __final =
ADDCOLUMNS (
__hoursMinutesSecondsAMPM,
"Time",
 TIMEVALUE (
 FORMAT([Hour],"00") & ":" &
 FORMAT([Minutes],"00") & ":" &
 FORMAT([Seconds],"00") & " " & [AM/PM]
 )
 )
```

Also, you may have a system that keeps data in a 24-hour format. If this is the case, you could create a 24-hour timetable by using the formula for the 12-hour timetable and setting the format for the Time column to 13:30:55 (HH:mm:ss). However, if you need this 24-hour time as a text data type instead of a time data type, you can create a 24-hour timetable using the following formula:

```
R01_24-Hour_Clock =
    VAR __hours =
        SELECTCOLUMNS (
            GENERATESERIES(0, 23 , 1),
            "Hour",
            [Value]
        )
    VAR __minutes =
```

```
    SELECTCOLUMNS(
        GENERATESERIES(0, 59 , 1),
        "Minutes",
        [Value]
    )
VAR __seconds =
    SELECTCOLUMNS(
        GENERATESERIES(0, 59 , 1),
        "Seconds",
        [Value])
VAR __hoursMinutes = GENERATEALL(__hours, __minutes)
VAR __hoursMinutesSeconds = GENERATEALL(__hoursMinutes,__seconds)
VAR __final =
    SELECTCOLUMNS(
        ADDCOLUMNS(
            __hoursMinutesSeconds,
            "Time",
            FORMAT([Hour],"00") &
                ":" & FORMAT([Minutes],"00") &
                    ":" & FORMAT([Seconds],"00")
        ),
        "Time",
        [Time]
    )
RETURN
    __final
```

See also

For more information, refer to the following links:

- GENERATESERIES: https://docs.microsoft.com/en-us/dax/generateseries-function-dax

- GENERATEALL: https://docs.microsoft.com/en-us/dax/generateall-function-dax

- SELECTCOLUMNS: https://docs.microsoft.com/en-us/dax/selectcolumns-function-dax

- ADDCOLUMNS: https://docs.microsoft.com/en-us/dax/addcolumns-function-dax

- FORMAT: https://docs.microsoft.com/en-us/dax/format-function-dax

- DAX table constructor: https://docs.microsoft.com/en-us/dax/table-constructor

Computing an hour breakdown

In the case of an event that starts and stops on the same day, it is sometimes useful to understand how many minutes within each hour of the day that event consumed. This recipe demonstrates how to break down an event into the minutes consumed during each hour that an event spans.

Getting ready

To prepare for this recipe, do the following:

1. Open Power BI Desktop.
2. Create a table called R02_Table using an **Enter Data** query with the following data:

ID	Date	Start	End
1	1/1/2019	8:00:00 AM	9:24:00 AM
1	1/2/2019	5:24:00 AM	9:14:00 PM
2	1/1/2019	9:59:00 AM	4:13:00 PM
2	1/2/2019	3:31:00 AM	12:01:00 PM
3	1/1/2019	8:24:00 AM	8:55:00 AM

3. Create a second table called R02_Hours using the following formula:

```
R02_Hours =
    VAR __Hours =
            SELECTCOLUMNS (
                GENERATESERIES (1 , 12 , 1),
                "Hour",
                [Value] & ":00:00 "
            )
    VAR __Period =
        SELECTCOLUMNS (
            { ("AM"),("PM") },
            "AM/PM",
            [Value]
        )
    VAR __HoursAMPM = GENERATEALL (__Hours, __Period)
    VAR __Final =
        SELECTCOLUMNS (
            ADDCOLUMNS (
                __HoursAMPM,
```

```
            "Time",
            TIMEVALUE([Hour] & [AM/PM])
        ),
        "Time",
        [Time]
    )
RETURN
    __final
```

4. Ensure that these two tables are not related to one another in any way.

How to do it...

To implement this recipe, do the following:

1. Create the following two measures:

```
Hour Breakdown =
    VAR __Hour = HOUR(MAX('R02_Hours'[Time]))
    VAR __StartHour = HOUR(MIN('R02_Table'[Start]))
    VAR __StartMinutes = MINUTE(MIN('R02_Table'[Start]))
    VAR __EndHour = HOUR(MAX('R02_Table'[End]))
    VAR __EndMinutes = MINUTE(MAX('R02_Table'[End]))
    VAR __Table = GENERATESERIES(__StartHour,__EndHour,1)
    VAR __Table1 = ADDCOLUMNS(__Table,"__minutes",
        SWITCH(TRUE(),
            __StartHour < __EndHour &&
                [Value] <> __EndHour &&
                    [Value] <> __StartHour, 60 ,
            __StartHour < __EndHour &&
                [Value] = __EndHour, __EndMinutes ,
            __StartHour < __EndHour &&
                [Value] = __StartHour, 60 - __StartMinutes ,
            __EndMinutes - __StartMinutes
        )
    )
    VAR __Final = FILTER(__Table1, [__minutes]>0)
RETURN
    SUMX(FILTER(__Final, [Value] = __Hour), [__minutes])
```

2. Create a **Matrix** visualization and place the Date column from the R02_Table table into the Rows field for the **Matrix** visualization.

3. Also, place the Time column from the R02_Hours table into the **Rows** field underneath the Date column from the R02_Table table to form an ad hoc hierarchy.

4. Place the ID column from the R02_Table table into the **Columns** field for the **Matrix** visualization.

5. Place the Hour Breakdown measure into the **Values** field for the **Matrix** visualization.

6. In the Format pane for the **Matrix** visualization, expand Subtotals and turn off Row subtotals and Column subtotals.

How it works...

We start by figuring out which hour of the day we are working with and store this value in a variable called __Hour. Next, we determine the hour and minute of our start time, __StartHour and __StartMinutes, as well as the hour and minute of our end time, __EndHour and __EndMinutes.

Next, we use GENERATESERIES to create a table of hours inclusive of our starting hour and ending hour and store this in a variable called __Table. We then add a column to this table using ADDCOLUMNS that determines how many minutes within each hour the event consumed. This is done by a complex SWITCH statement.

The SWITCH statement has three conditions as well as a default value. The first condition is if the start hour is less than the end hour and the hour in the table is neither the start hour or the end hour, then we know that this hour was completely consumed by the event and hence we assign a value for the minutes of 60, the full hour. The second condition is the case where the start hour is less than the end hour and the value we are working with in our table is equal to the end hour of the event. In this case, we can simply assign the __EndMinutes computed earlier. The third condition is similar to the second except that for this condition to be true, we are working with our start hour. In this case, we assign 60 minutes minus our __StartMinutes. If none of these conditions are true, then we know that the start and end hours are the same and hence we simply subtract __EndMinutes from __StartMinutes.

We filter our table to remove any rows with no minutes and for our final RETURN statement, we essentially look up our current working hour, __Hour, within the table and return the value of the __minutes column computed by our SWITCH statement.

There's more...

There is a reason we turned off the row and column totals in the matrix. The reason is that, given the complex nature of this calculation, the totals end up being wrong. If the totals are needed, however, turn the row and column totals on and create the following measure:

```
Hour Breakdown Total =
    VAR __Table = SUMMARIZE('R02_Table',[Date],[ID])
    VAR __Table1 = GENERATE(__Table,'R02_Hours')
    VAR __Table2 = ADDCOLUMNS(__Table1,"__Duration",[Hour Breakdown])
RETURN
    IF(
        HASONEVALUE('R02_Hours'[Time]) &&
            HASONEVALUE('R02_Table'[ID]),
        [Hour Breakdown],
        SUMX(__Table2,[__Duration])
    )
```

Place the `Hour Breakdown Total` measure into the matrix visualization created earlier in the recipe and note that both the individual rows as well as the row and column totals are correct while the row and column totals for the `Hour Breakdown` measure are incorrect.

See also

For more information, refer to the following links:

- GENERATESERIES: https://docs.microsoft.com/en-us/dax/generateseries-function-dax
- GENERATEALL: https://docs.microsoft.com/en-us/dax/generateall-function-dax
- SELECTCOLUMNS: https://docs.microsoft.com/en-us/dax/selectcolumns-function-dax
- ADDCOLUMNS: https://docs.microsoft.com/en-us/dax/addcolumns-function-dax
- TIMEVALUE: https://docs.microsoft.com/en-us/dax/timevalue-function-dax

Converting Unix into UTC and back

Unix uses a system of timekeeping called Unix epoch, which is the number of seconds that have elapsed since January 1, 1970 at midnight, not counting leap seconds. This recipe demonstrates how to convert this Unix epoch into a much more readable **Coordinated Universal Time (UTC)** date/timestamp.

Getting ready

To prepare for this recipe, do the following:

1. Open Power BI Desktop.
2. Use an **Enter Data** query to create a table called R03_Table with the following data:

UnixTime
0
1400000000
1500000000
1600000000
-1400000000
-1500000000
-1600000000

3. Ensure that the data type for this column is set to Whole Number.

How to do it...

To implement this recipe, do the following:

1. Add a column to the R03_Table table using the following formula:

```
Unix2UTC =
    VAR __UnixEpoch = 'R03_Table'[UnixTime]
    VAR __Time = DIVIDE(__UnixEpoch, (60*60*24))
    VAR __SourceBaseDate = DATE(1970, 1, 1)
RETURN (__SourceBaseDate + __Time)
```

2. Ensure that the data type for this column is set to Date/Time.

How it works...

This recipe relies on the fact that date/time values in DAX are stored as decimal numbers where the integer portion (left of the decimal point) represents the number of days while the decimal portion represents fractions of a day. Hence, for example, 1 second would be stored in DAX as *1/86,400 = 1.157407407e-5 (0.00001157407407)*, where 86,400 is the number of seconds in a day.

We can exploit the way DAX stores date/time values as well as our knowledge that Unix epoch timestamps are the number of seconds since 1/1/1970 at midnight. First, since a Unix epoch is expressed in seconds, we can essentially convert this into a DAX date/time value by dividing the Unix epoch time by 86,400 (60 seconds in a minute * 60 minutes in an hour * 24 hours in a day). Then, to arrive at a DAX date/timestamp, we simply add this number to a DAX date value for 1/1/1970.

There's more...

We can also convert from the standard date and time format into Unix epoch time. To see how this works, create a second column in the R03_Table table using the following formula:

```
UTC2Unix =
    VAR __UTC = 'R03_Table'[Unix2UTC]
    VAR __SourceBaseDate = DATE(1970, 1, 1)
RETURN (__UTC - __SourceBaseDate) * 60 * 60 * 24
```

See also

For more information, refer to the following links:

- DATE: https://docs.microsoft.com/en-us/dax/date-function-dax
- DIVIDE: https://docs.microsoft.com/en-us/dax/divide-function-dax

Adding and subtracting time

While the DAX DATEDIFF function supports hours, minutes, and seconds for finding the number of hours, minutes, and seconds between two DAX date/time values, the DAX DATEADD function only supports year, quarter month, and day. This recipe demonstrates how to add and subtract hours, minutes, and seconds to and from a DAX time value.

Getting ready

To prepare for this recipe, do the following:

1. Create a table called R04_Table using the following formula:

```
R04_Table =
    VAR __Hours =
            SELECTCOLUMNS (
                GENERATESERIES (1 , 12 , 1),
                "Hour",
                [Value] & ":00:00 "
            )
    VAR __Period =
        SELECTCOLUMNS (
            { ("AM"),("PM") },
            "AM/PM",
            [Value]
        )
    VAR __HoursAMPM = GENERATEALL (__Hours, __Period)
    VAR __Final =
        SELECTCOLUMNS (
            ADDCOLUMNS (
                __HoursAMPM,
                "Time",
                TIMEVALUE ([Hour] & [AM/PM])
            ),
            "Time",
            CONVERT (TODAY () & " " & [Time], DATETIME)
        )
    RETURN
        __Final
```

2. Ensure that the data type for the Time column is set to Date/Time.

How to do it...

To implement this recipe, do the following:

1. Create the following measures:

```
AddHours =
    VAR __Time = MAX ('R04_Table'[Time])
    VAR __Add = 10
RETURN
    __Time + __Add/24
```

```
AddMinutes =
    VAR __Time = MAX([Time])
    VAR __Add = 10
RETURN
    __Time + __Add/24/60

AddSeconds =
    VAR __Time = MAX([Time])
    VAR __Add = 10
RETURN
    __Time + __Add/24/60/60
```

2. Create a **Table** visualization and place the `Time` column from the `R04_Table` table into this visual as well as the three measures, `AddHours`, `AddMinutes`, and `AddSeconds`.

How it works...

This recipe relies on the fact that date/time values in DAX are stored as decimal numbers where the integer portion (left of the decimal point) represents the number of days while the decimal portion represents fractions of a day. Hence, for example, 1 second would be stored in DAX as *1 / 86,400 = 1.157407407e-5 (0.00001157407407)*, where 86,400 is the number of seconds in a day.

Hence, to add hours, we simply need to multiply the number of hours to add by *1/24 = 0.041666667*. To add minutes, we simply multiply the number of minutes to add by *1/24/60 = 0.00069444444*. To add seconds, we simply multiply the number of seconds to add by *1/24/60/60 = 0.00001157407407*.

There's more...

We can also use this same basic formula to subtract hours, minutes, and seconds. To see how this works, do the following:

1. Create a measure using the following formula:

```
AddHours 2 =
    VAR __Time = MAX([Time])
    VAR __Add = -10
RETURN
    __Time + __Add/24
```

2. Add this measure to the **Table** visualization created earlier.

We can also combine these formulas into a single calculation to add hours, minutes, and seconds within a single calculation. To see this in action, do the following:

1. Create a measure using the following formula:

```
AddHoursMinutesSeconds =
    VAR __Time = MAX([Time])
    VAR __AddHours = 10
    VAR __AddMinutes = 10
    VAR __AddSeconds = 10
RETURN
    __Time + __AddHours/24 + __AddMinutes/24/60 +
__AddSeconds/24/60/60
```

2. Add this measure to the **Table** visualization created earlier.

See also

For more information, refer to the following links:

- GENERATESERIES: https://docs.microsoft.com/en-us/dax/generateseries-function-dax
- GENERATEALL: https://docs.microsoft.com/en-us/dax/generateall-function-dax
- SELECTCOLUMNS: https://docs.microsoft.com/en-us/dax/selectcolumns-function-dax
- ADDCOLUMNS: https://docs.microsoft.com/en-us/dax/addcolumns-function-dax
- CONVERT: https://docs.microsoft.com/en-us/dax/convert-function-dax

Determining network duration

While DAX's DATEDIFF function supports finding the number of hours, minutes, or seconds between two DAX date/time values, this function does not take into account working hours. This recipe demonstrates how to determine the number of minutes between two DAX date/time values taking into account the working hours in a day.

Getting ready

To prepare for this recipe, do the following:

1. In Power BI Desktop, use an **Enter Data** query to create a table called `R05_Table` with the following data:

Start	End
8/2/2019 16:00	8/6/2019 7:30
7/26/2019 17:30	7/30/2019 8:00
7/26/2019 17:30	7/29/2019 8:00
7/27/2019 17:30	7/30/2019 8:00
8/6/2019 10:00	8/6/2019 16:00
8/6/2019 16:00	8/7/2019 8:30

2. Ensure that both the `Start` and `End` columns are set to `Data type` of `Date/Time`.

How to do it...

To implement this recipe, do the following:

1. Create a column in the `R05_Table` table using the following formula:

```
Net Work Duration =
    VAR __startTime = TIMEVALUE("7:30 AM")
    VAR __endTime = TIMEVALUE("6:00 PM")
    VAR __Start = 'R05_Table'[Start]
    VAR __End = 'R05_Table'[End]
    VAR __WeekdayStart = WEEKDAY(__Start , 2)
    VAR __WeekdayEnd = WEEKDAY(__End , 2)
    VAR __NetWorkDays =
        COUNTX(
            FILTER(
                ADDCOLUMNS(
                    CALENDAR(__Start,__End),
                    "WeekDay",
                    WEEKDAY([Date],2)
                ),
                [WeekDay]<6
            ),
            [Date]
        )
```

```
        VAR __fullDayMinutes = DATEDIFF(__startTime , __endTime ,
MINUTE)
        VAR __fullDays =
            SWITCH(TRUE(),
                __WeekdayStart > 5 && __WeekdayEnd > 5 , __NetWorkDays,
                __WeekdayStart > 5 || __WeekdayEnd > 5 , __NetWorkDays
- 1,
                __NetWorkDays < 2 , 0,
                __NetWorkDays - 2
            )
        VAR __fullDaysDuration = __fullDays * __fullDayMinutes
        VAR __startDayTime = TIME( HOUR(__Start) , MINUTE(__Start) ,
SECOND(__Start) )
        VAR __startDayDuration = DATEDIFF(__startDayTime , __endTime ,
MINUTE)
        VAR __endDayTime = TIME( HOUR(__End) , MINUTE(__End) ,
SECOND(__End) )
        VAR __endDayDuration = DATEDIFF(__startTime , __endDayTime ,
MINUTE)
        RETURN
            IF(
                __NetWorkDays = 1,
                DATEDIFF(__Start , __End , MINUTE),
                __fullDaysDuration + __startDayDuration + __endDayDuration
            )
```

How it works...

We start by using DAX's TIMEVALUE function to specify the start and end times of our workday and storing these values in the __startTime and __endTime variables respectively. Next, we get the values for our start and end times and store these in the __Start and __End variables respectively. Then, we determine the weekday for our start and end times using DAX's WEEKDAY function using 2 for the second parameter so that 1 = Monday and 7 = Sunday. We store these values in the __WeekdayStart and __WeekdayEnd variables.

With our base calculations out of the way, we generate a calendar table using DAX's calendar function and for the date range use our __Start and __End variables. To this calendar table, we add a column using the ADDCOLUMNS function that stores the weekday for each date. Finally, we filter this table to remove Saturdays (6) and Sundays (7) and then count how many working days we have using COUNTX. This value is stored in the __NetWorkDays variable.

The next variable we calculate is the number of minutes in a full day, __fullDayMinutes. __fullDayMinutes is the number of minutes between our start time, __startTime, and our end time, __endTime. We use DATEDIFF to calculate this number and this represents the number of minutes in a full workday, in this case, 630 minutes.

We now need to calculate how many full workdays there are between our start time, __startTime, and our end time, __endTime. We do this using a SWITCH statement with several conditions. For the first condition, if neither our start time or end time fall on a Saturday or Sunday, then the number of workdays is simply the value of __NetWorkDays. If either our start time or end time fall on a Saturday or Sunday, then we subtract one from __NetWorkDays. These two conditions account for either the start time or end time or both starting on a weekend. Hence, for subsequent conditions, we are assured that we are only dealing with circumstances where the start or end dates fall on weekdays (workdays).

Hence, with this in mind, we check whether __NetWorkDays is less than two. This would mean that we have no full workdays in between our start and end dates so we return 0. Finally, if none of these conditions are true, then we know that neither our start time or end time fall on a weekend and that we have __NetWorkDays minus 2 full workdays between our start and end dates. The minus 2 accounts for removing our start and end dates since the portion of work during those days will be calculated separately.

We can now calculate the total minutes for the full workdays that fall between our start and end dates by multiplying the number of our full workdays, __fullDays, by the total minutes in a full workday, __fullDayMinutes. We store this value in the __fullDaysDuration variable.

We now need to determine the amount of time in minutes that occurred on our actual start day and end day. We do this by using the DATEDIFF function to return the number of minutes between our start time and the end of the workday as well as the time between our end time and the start of the workday. These values are stored in the __startDayDuration and __endDayDuration variables respectively.

For the value that we RETURN, if __NetWorkDays is 1, then we simply take the minutes elapsed between our start and end times since our event started and ended on the same day. Otherwise, we return the minutes for our full workdays, __fullDaysDuration, plus the minutes elapsed on our start day, __startDayDuration, plus the minutes elapsed on our end day, __endDayDuration.

See also

For more information, refer to the following links:

- TIMEVALUE: https://docs.microsoft.com/en-us/dax/timevalue-function-dax
- WEEKDAY: https://docs.microsoft.com/en-us/dax/weekday-function-dax
- COUNTX: https://docs.microsoft.com/en-us/dax/countx-function-dax
- FILTER: https://docs.microsoft.com/en-us/dax/filter-function-dax
- ADDCOLUMNS: https://docs.microsoft.com/en-us/dax/addcolumns-function-dax
- CALENDAR: https://docs.microsoft.com/en-us/dax/calendar-function-dax
- DATEDIFF: https://docs.microsoft.com/en-us/dax/datediff-function-dax
- SWITCH: https://docs.microsoft.com/en-us/dax/switch-function-dax
- TIME: https://docs.microsoft.com/en-us/dax/time-function-dax
- HOUR: https://docs.microsoft.com/en-us/dax/hour-function-dax
- MINUTE: https://docs.microsoft.com/en-us/dax/minute-function-dax
- SECOND: https://docs.microsoft.com/en-us/dax/second-function-dax

Calculating shifts

Many organizations have the concept of shifts. Essentially, a 24-hour day is typically split up into 3 equal shifts of 8 hours each. It is often important for organizations to understand during what shift an event occurred. This recipe uses DAX to calculate the correct shift for each hour of the day.

Getting ready

To prepare for this recipe, do the following:

1. Create a table called R06_Table using the following formula:

```
R06_Table =
    VAR __Hours =
        SELECTCOLUMNS(
            GENERATESERIES(1 , 12 , 1),
            "Hour",
            [Value] & ":00:00 "
        )
```

```
VAR __Period =
    SELECTCOLUMNS(
        { ("AM"),("PM") },
        "AM/PM",
        [Value]
    )
VAR __HoursAMPM = GENERATEALL(__Hours,__Period)
VAR __Final =
    SELECTCOLUMNS(
        ADDCOLUMNS(
            __HoursAMPM,
            "Time",
            TIMEVALUE([Hour] & [AM/PM])
        ),
        "Time",
        [Time]
    )
RETURN
    __Final
```

2. Ensure that the data type for the `Time` column is set to `Date/Time`.

How to do it...

To implement this recipe, do the following:

1. Create a column in the `R06_Table` table using the following formula:

```
Shift =
    VAR __1stBegin = 9
    VAR __2ndBegin = 17
    VAR __3rdBegin = 1
    VAR __Time = TIMEVALUE('R06_Table'[Time])
    VAR __Hour = HOUR(__Time)
RETURN
    SWITCH(TRUE(),
        __Hour >= __1stBegin && __Hour < __2ndBegin,"First",
        __Hour >= __2ndBegin || __Hour < __3rdBegin,"Second",
        "Third"
    )
```

How it works...

We start by specifying the hour of the day when our three shifts begin, __1stBegin, __2ndBegin, and __3rdBegin. We then get the value of the hour we are working with and store this in the __Time variable. We can then use this information to return the correct shift for the hour by using a SWITCH statement.

See also

For more information, refer to the following links:

- GENERATESERIES: https://docs.microsoft.com/en-us/dax/generateseries-function-dax
- GENERATEALL: https://docs.microsoft.com/en-us/dax/generateall-function-dax
- SELECTCOLUMNS: https://docs.microsoft.com/en-us/dax/selectcolumns-function-dax
- ADDCOLUMNS: https://docs.microsoft.com/en-us/dax/addcolumns-function-dax
- CONVERT: https://docs.microsoft.com/en-us/dax/convert-function-dax
- TIMEVALUE: https://docs.microsoft.com/en-us/dax/timevalue-function-dax
- HOUR: https://docs.microsoft.com/en-us/dax/hour-function-dax

Aggregating duration

Because DAX has no base data type for duration, adding durations has always been a little problematic, especially when attempting to display the end result in the HH:mm:ss format. This recipe allows you to aggregate durations and display them in an actual duration format (HH:mm:ss) within a column chart!

 I will be forever grateful to Konstantinos Ioannou for first teaching me about DAX's VAR statement when I created an early version of this calculation. In addition, I would be remiss if I did not mention Chelsie Eiden, an intern that worked for Microsoft and added the crucial feature that allows custom display formatting for fields while preserving their underlying data type.

Getting ready

To prepare for this recipe, do the following:

1. Open Power BI Desktop and use an **Enter Data** query to create a table called R07_Table with the following data:

Duration	ID	Group
60	1	1
121	2	1
3600	3	1
3670	4	2
12	5	2
4589	6	2
5678	7	3
360573	8	3
36778	9	3

2. Ensure that all of the columns in the table are set to Whole Number.

How to do it...

To implement this recipe, do the following:

1. Create a measure using the following formula:

```
R07_Duration =
    VAR __Duration = SUM('R07_Table'[Duration])
    VAR __Hours = INT ( __Duration / 3600)
    VAR __HoursRemainder = MOD( __Duration - ( __Hours * 3600
),3600 )
    VAR __Minutes = INT ( __HoursRemainder / 60)
    VAR __Seconds = ROUNDUP(MOD ( __HoursRemainder, 60 ),0)
RETURN
    __Hours * 10000 + __Minutes * 100 + __Seconds
```

2. Create a **Clustered column chart** visualization and place the ID column in the **Axis** field and the R07_Duration measure in the **Value** field for the visualization.

3. Create a second **Clustered column chart** visualization and place the `Group` column in the **Axis** field and the `R07_Duration` measure in the **Value** field for the visualization.

4. For both visualizations, turn on **Data labels** and set the **Display units** to **None**.

5. Switch the **Model** view and click on the `R07_Duration` measure.

6. In the **Properties** pane, expand the **Formatting** section, set the **Format** to **Custom,** and enter `00:00:00` as the **Custom format**.

How it works...

In this case, our `Duration` column is expressed in the number of seconds. We aggregate these seconds using the `SUM` function and store the value in a variable called `__Duration`. We can now calculate the hours by dividing `__Duration` by `3600` seconds in an hour. We use the `INT` function to return just the integer portion of this division. We store this value in the `__Hours` variable.

Now that we know how many hours are represented in our `__Duration` variable, we can compute the remainder of the duration in seconds without those hours. We do this by subtracting `__Hours` multiplied by `3600` seconds in an hour from our initial `__Duration` variable and then finding the remainder of this value divided by `3600` seconds in an hour. We use the `MOD` function to return the remainder of the division operation and store this value in the `__HoursRemainder` variable.

Once we have our `__HoursRemainder` variable calculated, if we divide `__HoursRemainder` by `60` minutes in an hour and take the integer portion using `INT`, this provides us with the number of minutes, `__Minutes`. Taking the remainder of this division using `MOD` gives us the number of seconds, `__Seconds`.

We now need to return `__Hours`, `__Minutes`, and `__Seconds` as a number with each component in its proper *place*. So, if we know that we are going to be using the format of HH:mm:ss, then the seconds start in the ones place, minutes start in the hundredths place, and the hours start in the ten thousandths place (ignore the colons). Hence, we multiply `__Hours` by 10,000, `__Minutes` by 100, and `__Seconds` by nothing. Hence, if we have 2 hours, 3 minutes, and 5 seconds, the return value would be 20,305 (20,000 + 300 + 5).

The magic then comes when we apply the custom display formatting developed by Chelsie Eiden. We specify a custom format of `00:00:00`. The specification of 00 means to use a leading zero to pad our number if it is a single digit. Hence, for our example of 2 hours, 3 minutes, and 5 seconds, that results in the number 20,305, which is displayed as 02:03:05—or 2 hours, 3 minutes, and 5 seconds!

See also

For more details, refer to the following links:

- INT: https://docs.microsoft.com/en-us/dax/int-function-dax
- SUM: https://docs.microsoft.com/en-us/dax/sum-function-dax
- MOD: https://docs.microsoft.com/en-us/dax/mod-function-dax
- ROUNDUP: https://docs.microsoft.com/en-us/dax/roundup-function-dax

Transforming milliseconds into duration

Some source systems have millisecond precision. However, measuring things in milliseconds tends to result in large numbers that are more easily consumed in a duration format such as HH:mm:ss:000 (hours, minutes, seconds, and milliseconds). This DAX recipe demonstrates how to transform durations stored in milliseconds into a more readable duration format of HH:mm:ss:000.

Getting ready

To prepare for this recipe, do the following:

1. Open Power BI Desktop and use an **Enter Data** query to create a table called R08_Table with the following data:

Milliseconds	ID	Group
25920	1	1
44999	2	1
12550	3	2
2456	4	2
175	5	3
1244999	6	3

2. Ensure that all of the columns in the table are set to Whole Number.

How to do it...

To implement this recipe, do the following:

1. Create a measure using the following formula:

```
R08_Duration =
    VAR __Duration = SUM('R08_Table'[Milliseconds])
    VAR __Hours = INT ( __Duration / 3600000)
    VAR __HoursRemainder = __Duration - __Hours * 3600000
    VAR __Minutes =
        INT (
            MOD (
                __HoursRemainder,
                3600000
            ) / 60000
        )
    VAR __Seconds =
        INT (
            MOD (
                MOD (
                    __HoursRemainder - (__Minutes * 60000)
                    ,60000
                ),
                60000
            ) / 1000
        )
    VAR __Milliseconds =
        ROUNDUP (
            MOD (
                MOD (
                    MOD (
                        __HoursRemainder,
                        3600000
                    ),
                    60000
                ),
                1000
            ),
            0
        )
    RETURN
        __Hours * 10000000 + __Minutes * 100000 + __Seconds * 1000 +
    __Milliseconds
```

2. Create a **Clustered column chart** visualization and place the ID column in the **Axis** field and the R08_Duration measure in the **Value** field for the visualization.

3. Create a second **Clustered column chart** visualization and place the Group column in the **Axis** field and the R08_Duration measure in the **Value** field for the visualization.

4. For both visualizations, turn on **Data labels** and set the **Display units** to **None**.

5. Switch the **Model** view and click on the R08_Duration measure.

6. In the **Properties** pane, expand the **Formatting** section, set the **Format** to **Custom**, and enter 00:00:00 as the **Custom format**.

How it works...

In this case, our Duration column is expressed in the number of milliseconds. We aggregate these milliseconds using the SUM function and store the value in a variable called __Duration. We can now calculate the hours by dividing __Duration by 3600000 milliseconds in an hour. We use the INT function to return just the integer portion of this division. We store this value in the __Hours variable.

Now that we know how many hours are represented in __Duration, we can compute the remainder of the duration in milliseconds without those hours. We do this by subtracting __Hours multiplied by 3600000 milliseconds in an hour from our initial __Duration variable and then finding the remainder of this value divided by 3600000 milliseconds in an hour. We subtract this number of hours multiplied by 3600000 milliseconds in an hour and store this value in the __HoursRemainder variable.

Once we have our __HoursRemainder variable calculated, if we take the remainder of dividing __HoursRemainder by the 3600000 milliseconds that are in an hour and take the integer portion using INT, and then divide that remainder by 60000 milliseconds in a minute, this provides us with the number of minutes, __Minutes. We can calculate the number of seconds and milliseconds, __Seconds and __Milliseconds, respectively, via similar math.

We now need to return our __Hours, __Minutes, __Seconds, and __Milliseconds as a number with each component in its proper "place." So, if we know that we are going to be using a format of HH:mm:ss:000, then the milliseconds start in the ones place, seconds start in the thousandths place, minutes start in the hundred thousandths place, and the hours start in the 10 millionths place (ignore the colons). Hence, we multiply __Hours by 10 million, __Minutes by one hundred thousand, __Seconds by one thousand, and __Milliseconds by nothing. Hence, if we have 2 hours, 3 minutes, 5 seconds, and 23 milliseconds, the return value would be 20,305,023 (20,000,000 + 300,000 + 5,000 + 23).

The magic then comes when we apply the custom display formatting developed by Chelsie Eiden. We specify a custom format of 00:00:00:000. The specification of 00 means to use a leading zero to pad our number if it is a single digit. Hence, for our example of 2 hours, 3 minutes, 5 seconds, and 23 milliseconds, that results in the number 20,305,023, which is displayed as 02:03:05:023—or 2 hours, 3 minutes, 5 seconds, and 23 milliseconds!

See also

For more information, refer to the following links:

- INT: https://docs.microsoft.com/en-us/dax/int-function-dax
- SUM: https://docs.microsoft.com/en-us/dax/sum-function-dax
- MOD: https://docs.microsoft.com/en-us/dax/mod-function-dax
- ROUNDUP: https://docs.microsoft.com/en-us/dax/roundup-function-dax

Tinkering with time zones

Ah, time zones. Such a simple concept that has caused so much havoc in the world of software development through the years! There are no functions in DAX that really address time zones, but it is often a requirement to convert date and timestamps in one time zone into date and timestamps in a different time zone. This can be especially true when dealing with log files as a data source. This recipe demonstrates how to convert date and timestamps in one time zone into date and timestamps in a different time zone.

Getting ready

To prepare for this recipe, do the following:

1. Open Power BI Desktop and create a table called R09_Timezones by importing the Timezones.csv file from GitHub here: https://github.com/PacktPublishing/DAX-Cookbook/tree/master/Chapter03.

2. Use an **Enter Data** query to create a table called R09_Table with the following data:

Time	Timezone
1:00:00 PM	EST

3. Ensure that the data type for the Time column is set to Time.

4. Create a relationship between the Timezone column in the R09_Table table and the Abbr. column in the R09_Timezones table.

How to do it...

To implement this recipe, do the following:

1. Create a column in the R09_Timezones table with the following formula:

```
DAX UTC Offset = [UTC Offset] / 24
```

2. Create a measure using the following formula:

```
TZ Convert =
    VAR __DestTZ = "ACWST"
    VAR __SourceTime = MAX('R09_Table'[Time])
    VAR __SourceTZ = MAX('R09_Table'[Timezone])
    VAR __SourceOffset =
        LOOKUPVALUE(
            'R09_Timezones'[DAX UTC Offset],
            'R09_Timezones'[Abbr.],
            __SourceTZ
        )
    VAR __DestOffset =
        LOOKUPVALUE(
            'R09_Timezones'[DAX UTC Offset],
            'R09_Timezones'[Abbr.],
            __DestTZ
        )
```

```
            VAR __UTCTime = __SourceTime + -1 * __SourceOffset
    RETURN
    IF(
        ISBLANK(__SourceTime),
        BLANK(),
        __UTCTime + __DestOffset
    )
```

3. Create a **Table** visualization and place the `Time` and `Timezone` columns from the `R09_Table` table as well as the `TZ Convert` measure in the **Value** field for this visualization.

How it works...

To work with time zones, we first need to agree upon a standard list of time zones. This is our `Timezones.csv` file. This can actually be problematic as time zones are sometimes listed by country and, at other times, by abbreviations. Even worse, there can be multiple, duplicate time zone abbreviations with different offsets. In addition, time zone offsets are generally expressed in the hours and minutes (HH:mm) format based upon UTC. To make the calculations easier, the `Timezones.csv` file lists only unique time zone abbreviations and specifies offsets in a form that is more compatible with DAX. Hence, if a time zone offset is -8 hours and 45 minutes (8:45), this is expressed in the time zone table as -8.75 (minus eight hours and .75 of an hour (45/60)). Since we have expressed our offset in this manner, we can simply divide this number by 24 to arrive at a fraction of a day, which is how DAX stores times internally. This is our `DAX UTC Offset` column in the `R09_Timezones` table.

Once we have this column in place, we can use this column in our measure, `TZ Convert`. The `TZ Convert` measure first specifies our target or destination time zone—in this case, **Australian Central Western Standard Time (ACWST)**. We also get our current working time, `__SourceTime`, and our current working time zone, `__SourceTZ`. We now use the `LOOKUPVALUE` function to look up `DAX UTC Offset` in the `R09_Timezones` table for both our source and destination time zones and store these values in the `__SourceOffset` and `__DestOffset` variables respectively. In this particular case, **Eastern Standard Time (EST)** has an offset of -5 hours (-.208333) from UTC while ACWST has an offset of 8.75 hours (.3645833).

The next step is to convert our source timestamp from the source time into UTC time. Because offsets are expressed in the difference *from* UTC *to* the specified time zone, we need to multiply the source offset, __SourceOffset, by -1 and add the result to our source timestamp, __SourceTime. -1 is necessary since we are going *from* the source time zone *to* UTC! We store the resulting value in the __UTCTime variable. After that, we can return our final calculation, which is to simply add our destination offset, __DestOffset, to __UTCTime. In this case, we do not need -1 because we are going *from* UTC *to* our destination time zone.

See also

For more information, refer to the following links:

- LOOKUPVALUE: https://docs.microsoft.com/en-us/dax/lookupvalue-function-dax
- ISBLANK: https://docs.microsoft.com/en-us/dax/isblank-function-dax
- BLANK: https://docs.microsoft.com/en-us/dax/blank-function-dax

Converting duration into seconds

Unlike Power Query, DAX has no base data type for duration in the form of HH:mm:ss. However, there are many systems that store durations in the format HH:mm:ss (hours, minutes, and seconds) or d.HH:mm:ss (days, hours, minutes, and seconds). This recipe demonstrates how to convert a duration in the form of HH:mm:ss into the number of seconds using DAX.

Getting ready

To prepare for this recipe, do the following:

1. Open Power BI Desktop and use an **Enter Data** query to create a table called R10_Table with the following data but *do not click the* **Load** *button*:

Duration
01:01:01
01:30:30

2. Click the **Edit** button.

3. Remove the **Changed type** step in the **Query Settings** and then click **Close & Apply**.

How to do it...

To implement this recipe, do the following:

1. Create a column in the R10_Table table with the following formula:

```
Duration2Seconds =
    VAR __Duration = 'R10_Table'[Duration]
    VAR __Sub = SUBSTITUTE(__Duration , ":" , "|")
    VAR __Hours = VALUE(PATHITEM(__Sub , 1)) * 3600
    VAR __Minutes = VALUE(PATHITEM(__Sub , 2)) * 60
    VAR __Seconds = VALUE(PATHITEM(__Sub , 3)) * 1
RETURN __Hours + __Minutes + __Seconds
```

How it works...

We use the SUBSTITUTE function to replace the colons (:) in our duration text value with the pipe character (|). This allows us to extract the __Hours, __Minutes, and __Seconds using the PATHITEM function. By replacing the colons with pipes, the PATHITEM function can extract each element by specifying where in the hierarchy the element exists. In this case, our hours are in the first element, 1; minutes are in the second element, 2; and seconds are in the third element, 3. Because we are converting this into the number of seconds, we simply need to multiply each of these elements by the number of seconds in an hour and a minute and then add these values together.

There's more...

Because Power Query supports a base data type for duration, we can leverage this to perform this calculation in a different manner by doing the following:

1. Edit the query for R10_Table.

2. Copy the Duration column and paste it into a new column, which will automatically be named Duration.1.

3. Right-click the Duration.1 column and choose **Change Type** and then Duration.

4. Click **Close & Apply**.
5. Create a new column in the R10_Table table using the following formula:

```
Duration2Seconds2 =
    'R10_Table'[Duration.1] * 24 * 60 * 60
```

In this case, when we specify a data type of Duration in Power Query, this imports Duration2Seconds2 into our model as fractions of a day. Hence, to arrive at the number of seconds, we simply need to multiply the value by 86,400 (24*60*60).

See also

For more information, refer to the following links:

- SUBSTITUTE: https://docs.microsoft.com/en-us/dax/substitute-function-dax
- PATHITEM: https://docs.microsoft.com/en-us/dax/pathitem-function-dax

Creating a last-refreshed timestamp

This recipe demonstrates how to create a last-refreshed timestamp for your reports.

Getting ready

Open Power BI Desktop and you are all set!

How to do it...

To implement this recipe, do the following:

1. Use an **Enter Data** query to create a table called R11_Table with the following information:

UTC Offset
-5

2. Create a column in the `R11_Table` table using the following formula:

```
Last Refreshed = UTCNOW() + 'R11_Table'[UTC Offset] / 24
```

3. Create a **Card** visualization and place the `Last Refreshed` column into the **Fields** field for this visualization.

How it works...

By creating a table and adding a column to this table that includes the DAX `UTCNOW` function, this column will be recalculated each time the model is refreshed. It is important that you enter the `UTC Offset` for the time zone where you will be using the report. In addition, this offset should be entered in hours and fractions of an hour. In other words, if the `UTC Offset` is 8 hours and 30 minutes, this should be entered as `8.5`. If the `UTC Offset` is 8 hours and 45 minutes, this should be entered as `8.75`.

See also

For more information, refer to the following link:

- UTCNOW: `https://docs.microsoft.com/en-us/dax/utcnow-function-dax`

4
Transforming Text and Numbers

All or nearly all data models include data in the form of text and numbers. However, it is also often necessary to transform this text and number data into something useful for reporting purposes or even clean up this data for various reasons. This chapter is all about working with text and numeric data, providing useful recipes whose techniques can be applied in a variety of situations.

The following is the list of recipes that we will cover in this chapter:

- Crafting a dynamic slicer title
- Creating a greeting
- Counting a list of items
- Ranking columns and measures
- Totaling measures
- Converting from Cartesian to polar and back
- Computing percentages
- Calculating mode for single and multiple columns
- Extracting text
- Detecting prime numbers

Technical requirements

The following are required to complete all of the recipes in this chapter:

- Power BI Desktop
- GitHub repository: https://github.com/PacktPublishing/DAX-Cookbook/tree/master/Chapter04

Crafting a dynamic slicer title

It is often helpful to provide users with visual cues that inform them of what they are viewing on a report. This can be very important with slicers so that users do not become confused about exactly what the report is displaying. Because slicers can come in a variety of forms, including drop-down lists, the slicer selections can, in effect, become hidden from report viewers. If the report viewer is not paying close attention, the viewer may misinterpret the information displayed on the report because the viewer does not realize that the information on the report has been filtered by slicers or other report filters.

This recipe provides a handy method of creating a dynamic title that can be displayed in a card visual in order to inform the report viewer of any filtering occurring on the page.

Getting ready

To prepare for this recipe, perform the following steps:

1. Open Power BI Desktop.
2. Use an **Enter Data** query to create a table called `R01_Table` with the following information:

Country	Advertiser	Brand
C1	A1	B1
C1	A1	B2
C1	A2	B3
C1	A2	B4
C2	A1	B1
C2	A1	B5
C2	A2	B6
C2	A2	B3
C2	A2	B7
C2	A3	B8

How to do it...

To implement this recipe, perform the following steps:

1. Create the following measure:

```
Dynamic Slicer Title =
VAR __ALLTEXT = "all"
VAR __NONETEXT = "no"
VAR __DIRECTFILTERPRETEXT = "You have chosen "
VAR __POSTTEXT = " brand(s)."
VAR __CONCATENATE_TEXT = ", "
VAR __LASTCONCATENATE_TEXT = " and "
VAR __SIMPLEMULTIPLETEXT = "Multiple"
VAR __TOOMANY_MAX = 4
VAR __TOTAL_ROWS = COUNTROWS(DISTINCT(ALL('R01_Table'[Brand])))
VAR __CURRENT_ROWS = COUNTROWS(DISTINCT('R01_Table'[Brand]))
VAR __MAINTEXT =
    SWITCH(
        TRUE(),
        __CURRENT_ROWS = __TOTAL_ROWS,__ALLTEXT,
        __CURRENT_ROWS = 0 ,__NONETEXT,
        __CURRENT_ROWS = 1 , MAX('R01_Table'[Brand]),
        __CURRENT_ROWS < __TOOMANY_MAX,
            CONCATENATEX(
                TOPN(__CURRENT_ROWS -
1,DISTINCT('R01_Table'[Brand])),
                [Brand],
                __CONCATENATE_TEXT
            ) &
                __LASTCONCATENATE_TEXT &
LASTNONBLANK(DISTINCT('R01_Table'[Brand]),TRUE()),
            __SIMPLEMULTIPLETEXT
    )
VAR __PRETEXT = __DIRECTFILTERPRETEXT
RETURN __PRETEXT & __MAINTEXT & __POSTTEXT
```

2. On a **Report** page, create a **Slicer** visualization and place the Brand column from R01_Table in the **Field** area of the visualization.
3. On the same **Report** page, create a **Card** visualization and place the Dynamic Slicer Title measure in the **Fields** area of the visualization.

Experiment by choosing different items, including multiple items in the slicer, and observe how the text within the card visualization changes.

How it works...

The first seven VAR statements simply store components of the text that we will display. The __TOOMANY_MAX variable stores the maximum number of items that will be displayed. We need this since, otherwise, the text output can become too long to display within a visualization. The next variable, __TOTAL_ROWS, is the count of how many total distinct items we have in our base table. The variable after that, __CURRENT_ROWS, is the count of how many current distinct items we have chosen in our slicer.

The next variable, __MAINTEXT, is more complex and the heart of our dynamic slicer title. The value of this variable is determined by a SWITCH statement with various conditions. The first condition we check is whether the current rows equal the total rows in our base table and, if so, __MAINTEXT gets the value for all items, __ALLTEXT. The second condition checks whether there are no rows left and, in this case, __MAINTEXT gets the value for no items, __NONETEXT. The third condition checks whether there is only a single row and, in this case, __MAINTEXT simply takes on the value of the single item we have selected in our slicer. The next condition checks to make sure that we have not reached the maximum individual items that we will display. If this is not the case, then we use CONCATENATEX to concatenate all of the slicer items together, separated by __CONCATENATE_TEXT, except for the last item. We tack the last item onto the text by concatenating the __LASTCONCATENATE_TEXT variable, coupled with using LASTNONBLANK to grab the last selected item. Finally, if none of the previous conditions are met, we know that we have too many items to display individually, and so __MAINTEXT gets the value stored by the __SIMPLEMULTIPLETEXT variable.

In this simple dynamic title slicer, we set a variable called __PRETEXT to the value stored in the __DIRECTFILTERPRETEXT variable, and finally return the concatenation of our __PRETEXT, __MAINTEXT, and __POSTTEXT variables.

There's more...

We can get very fancy with our dynamic title measure. The following measure provides a variety of output options that can be changed simply by adjusting variables such as __USEPERCENT and even displays different output depending upon whether items are filtered directly or cross-filtered (filtered via another column). To create this measure, create the Dynamic Slicer Title1 measure using the code in R01_DynamicSlicerTitle1.txt, which is located in the GitHub repository.

See also

For more details regarding functions in this recipe, refer to the following links:

- COUNTROWS: https://docs.microsoft.com/en-us/dax/countrows-function-dax
- DISTINCT: https://docs.microsoft.com/en-us/dax/distinct-function-dax
- CONCATENATEX: https://docs.microsoft.com/en-us/dax/concatenatex-function-dax
- LASTNONBLANK: https://docs.microsoft.com/en-us/dax/lastnonblank-function-dax
- TOPN: https://docs.microsoft.com/en-us/dax/topn-function-dax
- ISFILTERED: https://docs.microsoft.com/en-us/dax/isfiltered-function-dax
- ISCROSSFILTERD: https://docs.microsoft.com/en-us/dax/iscrossfiltered-function-dax

Creating a greeting

It is often nice to add elements of personalization to reports and dashboards. This recipe provides a way to add some relatively simple personalization that greets the user viewing the report in a mildly intelligent manner by taking into account the current time of the day as well as the identity of the individual viewing the report.

Getting ready

Just open Power BI Desktop and you are all set.

How to do it...

To implement this recipe, perform the following steps:

1. Create the following measure:

```
Greeting =
    VAR __User = USERNAME()
    VAR __Hour = HOUR(NOW())
    VAR __Prefix =
        SWITCH(
            TRUE(),
```

```
                        __Hour < 12 , "Good morning ",
                        __Hour >= 12 && __Hour < 17 , "Good afternoon ",
                        "Good evening "
                )
        RETURN
                CONCATENATE(__Prefix , __User)
```

2. Create a **Card** visualization and place the Greeting measure in the **Fields** area for the **Card** visualization.

How it works...

The key to this recipe is the USERNAME DAX function. This function retrieves the user that is logged on to Power BI. On premises, this may appear in the domain/account format, while online, this will appear as your email address. The results of this function are stored in the __User variable.

Next, we retrieve the current hour of the day using the HOUR and NOW DAX functions. NOW retrieves the current date and time, while HOUR provides us with the integer value from 0-23, representing the hour of the current time.

We can now use a relatively simple SWITCH statement to determine whether the current time is in the morning, afternoon, or evening, and store a pleasant greeting in the __Prefix variable.

Finally, we simply use the DAX CONCATENATE function to RETURN the __Prefix and __User variables as a single string value.

There's more...

We can create a variation of this greeting to display someone's actual name or even nickname. To do this, observe the following steps:

1. Use an **Enter Data** query to create a table called R02_Table with the following columns and data:

ID	User
FA\gdeckler	Greg Deckler
gdeckler@fusionalliance.com	Greg Deckler
	Unknown

2. Replace the data in the table with information for your own user account or add additional rows with your own user account information.

3. Create the following measure:

```
Greeting1 =
    VAR __User = USERNAME()
    VAR __Display = LOOKUPVALUE('R02_Table'[User] , 'R02_Table'[ID]
, __User)
    VAR __Hour = HOUR(NOW())
    VAR __Prefix =
        SWITCH(
            TRUE(),
            __Hour < 12,"Good morning ",
            __Hour >= 12 && __Hour < 17,"Good afternoon ",
            "Good evening "
        )
RETURN CONCATENATE(__Prefix , __Display)
```

4. Create a **Card** visualization and place the `Greeting1` measure in the **Fields** area for the **Card** visualization.

See also

For more details regarding functions in this recipe, refer to the following links:

- USERNAME: https://docs.microsoft.com/en-us/dax/username-function-dax
- HOUR: https://docs.microsoft.com/en-us/dax/hour-function-dax
- NOW: https://docs.microsoft.com/en-us/dax/now-function-dax
- SWITCH: https://docs.microsoft.com/en-us/dax/switch-function-dax
- CONCATENATE: https://docs.microsoft.com/en-us/dax/concatenate-function-dax

Counting a list of items

While, often, Power Query will be used to break a list of items up into individual columns or even individual rows, there are times when the raw information is required within the data model. In such cases, it is sometimes more important to understand how many items are in the list rather than the actual list items themselves. This recipe provides a convenient method of quickly determining the number of items in a list of items.

Getting ready

To prepare for this recipe, perform the following steps:

1. Open Power BI Desktop.
2. Use an **Enter Data** query to create a table called `R03_Table` with the following data:

List
One
One, Two
One, Two, Three
One, One, One, Two, Two, Three

How to do it...

To implement this recipe, perform the following steps:

1. Create the following column in the `R03_Table` table:

```
CountOfItems =
    VAR __List = 'R03_Table'[List]
    VAR __Length = LEN( __List )
    VAR __Length2 = LEN( SUBSTITUTE( __List , "," , "" ) )
RETURN
    __Length - __Length2 + 1
```

How it works...

We start by retrieving our list from the column list and storing its value in the __List variable. Next, we retrieve the total length of our list using the LEN function and store this in the __Length variable. The next line where we calculate the __Length2 variable is where the magic happens. We use the SUBSTITUTE function to replace the delimiter in our list, in this case a comma, with nothing (double quotes side by side). We then determine the length of this modified string using the LEN function once again.

Once we have these two lengths, the number of items in our list is simply the length of our original list, __Length, minus the length of our modified list where we substituted nothing for our delimiters, __Length2. Given that we have substituted nothing for each of our delimiters, our modified string length, __Length2, is shorter than our original string length, __Length, by exactly the number of delimiters in our list, __List. We need to add 1 to this number to determine the number of items in the list since the number of delimiters in our list is always one less than the number of items in our list.

There's more...

First, in order to turn this calculation into a measure, simply replace the first line of the CountOfItems calculation with the following:

```
VAR __List = MAX('R03_Table'[List])
```

Second, this recipe can work with any delimiter between values. Simply replace the middle parameter of the SUBSTITUTE function with the delimiter used within your list.

Third, you may run into a situation where you have a multi-character delimiter such as the following table, R03_Table1, where the delimiter is a double quote followed by a comma followed by a space followed by another double quote:

List
"One, Two"
"One, Two", "One, Two"
"One, Two", "One, Two", "One Two Three"
"One, Two", "One, Two", "One Two Three", "One, Two, Three"

In this circumstance, the same recipe can be used with minor modifications as follows:

```
CountOfItems =
    VAR __List = 'R03_Table1'[List]
    VAR __Length = LEN( __List )
    VAR __Delimiter = """, """
    VAR __LenDelimiter = LEN(__Delimiter)
    VAR __Length2 = LEN( SUBSTITUTE( __List , __Delimiter , "" ) )
    VAR __Count = DIVIDE(__Length - __Length2 , __LenDelimiter, 1)
RETURN
    __Count + 1
```

See also

For more details regarding functions in this recipe, refer to the following links:

- LEN: https://docs.microsoft.com/en-us/dax/len-function-dax
- SUBSTITUTE: https://docs.microsoft.com/en-us/dax/substitute-function-dax
- DIVIDE: https://docs.microsoft.com/en-us/dax/divide-function-dax

Ranking columns and measures

Ranking columns and measures can prove challenging when first learning DAX. It is easy to arrive at seemingly nonsensical ranks or ranks that are all 1. This recipe demonstrates how to properly use DAX's RANKX function to rank items when dealing with calculated columns as well as measures.

Getting ready

To prepare for this recipe, perform the following steps:

1. Open Power BI Desktop.
2. Use an **Enter Data** query to create a table called R04_Table with the following data:

Item	Category1	Category2	Value
Item 1	Green	Blue	100
Item 2	Blue	Green	200
Item 3	Green	Blue	300
Item 4	Blue	Green	400
Item 5	Red	Blue	500
Item 6	Red	Green	600
Item 7	Red	Blue	700
Item 8	Red	Green	800

How to do it...

To implement this recipe, perform the following steps:

1. Create the following columns in the R04_Table table:

```
ColumnRank = RANKX('R04_Table',[Value])

ColumnRank2 =
RANKX(
    FILTER(
        'R04_Table',
        'R04_Table'[Category1] = EARLIER('R04_Table'[Category1])
    ),
    'R04_Table'[Value]
)

ColumnRank3 =
RANKX(
    FILTER(
        'R04_Table',
        'R04_Table'[Category1] = EARLIER('R04_Table'[Category1]) &&
            'R04_Table'[Category2] =
EARLIER('R04_Table'[Category2])
    ),
    'R04_Table'[Value]
)
```

How it works...

The first column, ColumnRank, is extremely simple. This calculation simply uses DAX's RANKX function to rank the rows according to the Value column.

The second column, ColumnRank2, is slightly more complex. The goal of this column is to rank the rows based upon the Value column, but within all related rows based upon the Category1 column; in other words, for two or more rows, having the same value for Category1, which ranks higher based upon the Value column. Thus, if two rows both have a Green for the Category1 column, which row has the higher Value? The DAX FILTER function is used to restrict the ranking performed by RANKX to only those rows in which the Category1 column is the same as the current row's Category1 column. This is done by using the EARLIER function, which essentially returns the current row's Category1 value.

The third column, ColumnRank3, is similar to ColumnRank2, but ranks rows based upon both Category1 and Category2. Thus, for multiple rows having the same Category1 and the same Category2, which row has the higher Value?

It is important to understand this because RANKX is an iterative function. Within a calculated column, the RANKX function supplants strict row context, such that all rows within the table are within the context of RANKX when calculating the rank of any particular row within the table.

There's more...

We can also use DAX's RANKX function to create rankings based on measures. To demonstrate how this works, perform the following steps:

1. Create the following measures:

   ```
   Average = AVERAGE([Value])

   Rank = RANKX(ALL('R04_Table'),[Average])

   Rank2 = RANKX(ALL('R04_Table'[Category1]),[Average])

   Rank3 =
   RANKX(ALL('R04_Table'[Category1],'R04_Table'[Category2]),[Average])
   ```

2. Create a **Table** visualization and place the Item column, as well as the Average and Rank measures, in the **Values** area for visualization.
3. Create a second **Table** visualization and place the Category1 columns, as well as the Average, Rank, and Rank2 measures, in the **Values** area for visualization.
4. Create a third **Table** visualization and place the Category1 and Category2 columns, as well as the Average, Rank, Rank2, and Rank3 measures, in the **Values** area for the visualization.

These measures and tables emulate the functionality of ColumnRank, ColumnRank2, and ColumnRank3 just with measures instead of columns. The base measure, Average, is the measure by which we rank the rows within our table visualizations.

For the `Rank` measure, it is imperative that the `ALL` function, or a similar function, such as `ALLSELECTED`, be used. This is because the filter context of the visualization pre-filters the rows available to `RANKX` within the base table. Thus, without the use of `ALL`, the only row within the base table available for the `RANKX` function to iterate over would be those rows defined by the filter context of the visualization. In the case of the `Rank` measure used within the table containing the `Item` column, this would mean that without the `ALL` function to expand the filter context, all of the ranks would be 1 because only the current row would be available to the `RANKX` function to iterate over.

Similarly, with the `Rank2` measure, because our second visualization groups rows by the `Category1` column, we must use the column form of the `ALL` function to specify that all values of `Category1` should be included when computing the rank. The same is true for the `Rank3` measure, except that because both `Category1` and `Category2` are included in our third visualization, we must specify that all values of `Category1` and `Category2` be included when computing rank.

A failure to include the proper context for `RANKX` results in unexpected (incorrect) results in our second and third visualizations for `Rank` in the second visualization, and for both `Rank` and `Rank1` in our third visualization.

See also

For more details regarding functions in this recipe, refer to the following links:

- RANKX: https://docs.microsoft.com/en-us/dax/rankx-function-dax
- FILTER: https://docs.microsoft.com/en-us/dax/filter-function-dax
- ALL: https://docs.microsoft.com/en-us/dax/all-function-dax

Totaling measures

Measure totals have been a problem since the dawn of placing DAX measures in table and matrix visualizations. The issue strikes at the core of the DAX language itself – context. The problem arises because the context in a total line for a table or matrix is effectively all rows. However, evaluating a DAX calculation in the context of all rows can often produce very different results than anticipated, which, for most users, would be the total of the numbers displayed in the rows of the table. However, DAX does not even consider the actual numbers displayed in rows of a table or matrix visualization when calculating the total line for a table or matrix visualization.

To be clear, DAX is doing exactly what it was programmed to do. The problem is that what it is doing is not in line with the expectations of users conditioned by decades of experience with Excel and every other known system in existence since the beginning of computer science, where total lines are the actual total of the rows displayed. This is called the **Measures Total Problem**, and I absolutely shudder to think how many Power BI reports are floating around out there with users blissfully unaware that their total values are not what they think they are, the total of all of the rows displayed.

This recipe demonstrates a simple scenario where the total lines for a measure are not what the user would expect.

 Note that I did not say the word *incorrect* because, technically, the calculation is correct. Luckily, this recipe also shows how to essentially transform any measure that exhibits this *Measures Total Problem* into a measure that displays a result that is more in line with a normal user's expectations.

Getting ready

To demonstrate the *Measures Total Problem* for yourself, perform the following steps:

1. Open Power BI Desktop.
2. Use an **Enter Data** query to create a table called R05_Table with the following data:

Item	Category1	Category2	Value
Item 1	Blue	Green	100
Item 2	Blue	Green	200
Item 3	Green	Blue	300
Item 4	Green	Blue	400
Item 5	Red	Green	500
Item 6	Red	Green	600
Item 7	Red	Blue	700
Item 8	Red	Blue	800

3. Create the following measure:

```
Sum = SUM('R05_Table'[Value]) - 50
```

4. Create a **Table** visualization and place the Item and Value columns from the R05_Table table, as well as the measure, Sum, in the **Values** area for the visualization.

Note that, for each row, the Value displayed corresponds with the Value for each item. In addition, for each row, the Sum measure displays 50 less than Value. However, note that the total line for the table visualization displays **3,600** in the Values column and **3,550** (50 less than the total of Value) in the Sum column. This is almost certainly not what we humans have come to expect from information presented in the format of a table. Our expectation is that the total line for the Sum column should display 3,200 (50 * 8 = 400 less than the total sum of the Value column in the table).

The reason for this lack of adherence to convention is context, specifically, the filter context. Within rows of a table or matrix visualization, the measure is evaluated within a filter context that corresponds to the filtered rows from the base table. By placing the item column in our visualization, we end up with each row in the table corresponding to a single row in our base table. However, within the total line for the table, the context is all rows within our base table. Thus, when the Sum measure is evaluated, it sums all of the values in the Value column and then subtracts 50 from that total. This is why, in the total line, the value of our Sum measure is only 50 less than the total sum of the Value column.

If you have any doubts about how fundamental context is to DAX, remove those doubts from your mind immediately. Context is so fundamental to DAX that it causes DAX to defy hundreds, if not thousands, of years' worth of defined convention for how humans expect tables to present data!

How to do it...

Clearly, we need to *fix* the total line for our measure. To demonstrate how this is done, perform the following steps:

1. Create the following measure:

```
SumTotal =
    IF(
        HASONEVALUE('R05_Table'[Item]),
        [Sum],
        VAR __Table =
```

```
        SUMMARIZE('R05_Table','R05_Table'[Item],"__value",[Sum])
                RETURN
                    SUMX(__Table,[__value])
        )
```

2. Place the `SumTotal` measure in the **Table** visualization created previously.

Note that the row values for the `SumTotal` measure agree with those for the `Sum` measure, but that the total row in the table displays **3,200** for `SumTotal`, which is what we would expect.

How it works...

The key to this recipe is the true/false statement for our `IF` function. The `HASONEVALUE` function checks to see whether we have a single value for the `Item` column. If so, we simply return the value from our `SUM` function. If not, we use the `SUMMARIZE` function to group our base table in exactly the same manner as our table visualization and then use an analogous iterative aggregator, in this case `SUMX`, to iteratively aggregate the values in our summarized table.

What this means is that in order to ensure that our measure totals are correct, we must tailor the calculation of the total line to how the measure is used within the context of each visualization. If you are thinking that this severely impacts the self-service aspect of measures, you would be correct.

This recipe has been specifically crafted around performance, and so we start with an `IF` statement that essentially checks to see whether we should display our measure calculated for a single-row or for a total-row. Because of this structure, we never calculate the summarized table or use the iterative aggregator unless we are in a total row, which happens relatively infrequently within the vast majority of table and matrix visualizations.

Also, it is important to stress that the iterative aggregator used within the *total* version of our measure must correspond to the aggregation function used within the single-row version of our measure. Thus, if we had used the `AVERAGE` function in our original `Sum` measure, we would need to use the corresponding `AVERAGEX` function in our `SumTotal` measures.

Finally, you may question why we use two measures, one for single-rows and one that accounts for returning either the single-row aggregate or the total line aggregate versus combining the two measures into a single measure. This can be argued from a variety of perspectives, but the most important aspect is the fact that the single-row version of the measure should stand on its own because it is correct for all instances where a single-row is displayed within a visualization. You may use that measure in a variety of visualizations with different summarizations or groupings of items. Thus, coding best practices dictate that the code should be written on one occasion, versus being written multiple times within multiple measures. In the event that a change is required to the base, a single-row version of the measure, it is best to only have to edit the code once versus searching for all instances of the code within multiple measures.

There's more...

To demonstrate how you must tailor this recipe depending upon the context in which the measure is used within visualizations, perform the following steps:

1. Create the following measures:

```
SumTotal 2 =
    IF(
        HASONEVALUE('R05_Table'[Category1]),
        [Sum],
        VAR __Table =
SUMMARIZE('R05_Table','R05_Table'[Category1],"__value",[Sum])
            RETURN
                SUMX(__Table,[__value])
    )

SumTotal 3 =
    IF(
        HASONEVALUE('R05_Table'[Category2]),
        [Sum],
        VAR __Table =
SUMMARIZE('R05_Table','R05_Table'[Category2],"__value",[Sum])
            RETURN
                SUMX(__Table,[__value])
    )

SumTotal 4 =
    IF(
        HASONEVALUE('R05_Table'[Category1]) &&
HASONEVALUE('R05_Table'[Category2]),
        [Sum],
```

```
        VAR __Table =
SUMMARIZE('R05_Table','R05_Table'[Category1],'R05_Table'[Category2]
,"__value",[Sum])
            RETURN
                SUMX(__Table,[__value])
    )
```

2. Create a second **Table** visualization and place the `Category1` column, as well as the `Sum` and `SumTotal 2` measures, in the **Values** area for the visualization.
3. Create a third **Table** visualization and place the `Category2` column, as well as the `Sum` and `SumTotal 3` measures, in the **Values** area for the visualization.
4. Create a fourth **Table** visualization and place the `Category1` and `Category2` columns, as well as the `Sum` and `SumTotal 4` measures, in the **Values** area for the visualization.
5. Create a **Matrix** visualization and place the `Category1` and `Category2` columns in the **Rows** area of the visualization, as well as the `Sum` and `SumTotal 4` measures, in the **Values** area for the visualization.

Note that the total lines for the `SumTotal 2`, `SumTotal 3`, and `SumTotal 4` measures are correct within their respective visualizations, but that the total line for the `Sum` measure is incorrect. Also note that the `HASONEVALUE` and `SUMMARIZE` statements for `SumTotal 2`, `SumTotal 3`, and `SumTotal 4` correspond with how information is grouped within the visualizations in which they are used.

See also

For more details regarding functions in this recipe, refer to the following links:

- `SUMMARIZE`: https://docs.microsoft.com/en-us/dax/summarize-function-dax
- `HASONEVALUE`: https://docs.microsoft.com/en-us/dax/hasonevalue-function-dax
- `ISINSCOPE`: https://docs.microsoft.com/en-us/dax/isinscope-function-dax

Converting from Cartesian to polar and back

The Cartesian and polar coordinate systems are both used to uniquely determine the position of something within an area or space. This area or space is most often projected as two-dimensional. Within a two-dimensional space, the Cartesian coordinate system expresses points as numbers along infinite perpendicular axes denoted as the x axis and the y axis. Conversely, the polar coordinate system expresses points as a distance and an angle. This recipe demonstrates how to convert between these two coordinate systems.

Getting ready

To prepare for this recipe, perform the following steps:

1. Open Power BI Desktop.
2. Use an **Enter Data** query to create a table called `R06_Table` with the following data:

x	y
1	1
2	2
-1	-1
0	0
1	0
0	1
-1	0
0	-1
8	5
9	5

How to do it...

To implement this recipe, perform the following steps:

1. Create the following columns in the `R06_Table` table:

```
r =
    VAR __x = 'R06_Table'[x]
    VAR __y = 'R06_Table'[y]
RETURN
```

```
        SQRT( POWER( __x , 2 ) + POWER( __y , 2 ) )

    theta =
        VAR __x = 'R06_Table'[x]
        VAR __y = 'R06_Table'[y]
    RETURN
        SWITCH(TRUE(),
            __x > 0 , ATAN( __y / __x ) ,
            __x < 0 && __y >= 0 , ATAN( __y / __x ) + PI() ,
            __x < 0 && __y < 0 , ATAN( __y / __x ) - PI() ,
            __x = 0 && __y > 0 , PI() / 2 ,
            __x = 0 && __y < 0 , -1 * PI() / 2 ,
            0
        )
```

How it works...

To convert from Cartesian coordinates (x and y) to polar coordinates, we need to compute the distance from the pole, in this case, coordinates 0, 0, to the reference point provided by the x and y coordinates with which we are working. This distance is called the **radial coordinate**, radial distance, or simply radius, and is often simply denoted as r. Thus, our first calculation is to calculate r and this is simply an implementation of using the Pythagorean theorem to calculate the hypotenuse of a right triangle with two known sides.

The second part of the polar coordinate system is called the angular coordinate, polar angle, or azimuth. The polar angle is often denoted by the Greek symbol for theta. This angle is expressed in either degrees or radians. 2π radians = 360 degrees. To compute this angle, we generally take the arctangent, or inverse tangent, of our x, y style coordinate. However, we need to account for the quadrant in which our reference point lies. In addition, we must also account for the way in which the DAX function for arctangent, ATAN, operates. The DAX function, ATAN, returns values in radians in the range of -π/2 and π/2. Thus, the SWITCH statement for our theta column simply has a list of conditions for calculating the value of theta. The first condition simply checks whether x is greater than 0 and, if so, the calculation for theta is straightforward. The second condition is for calculating theta when the reference point lies in the upper-left quadrant. The third condition takes care of the reference point being in the lower-left quadrant. The next two conditions account for the angle being 90 degrees or -90 degrees.

There's more...

First, in order to convert these column calculations to measures, simply replace the first two lines of each formula with the following:

```
VAR __x = MAX('R06_Table'[x])
VAR __y = MAX('R06_Table'[y])
```

Second, if given polar coordinates in radians and radius, we can convert these to Cartesian coordinates using the following column formulas:

```
x' =
    VAR __r = 'R06_Table'[r]
    VAR __theta = 'R06_Table'[theta]
RETURN
    ROUND( __r * COS( __theta ) , 2)

y' =
    VAR __r = 'R06_Table'[r]
    VAR __theta = 'R06_Table'[theta]
RETURN
    ROUND( __r * SIN( __theta ) , 2)
```

Finally, the angular portion of polar coordinates is generally expressed in either radians or degrees. We can convert our theta column to degrees using DAX's DEGREES function, as in the following column formula:

```
Degrees =
    VAR __theta = 'R06_Table'[theta]
RETURN
    DEGREES(__theta)
```

We can also convert degrees to radians using DAX's RADIANS function, as in the following column formula:

```
theta' =
    VAR __degrees = 'R06_Table'[Degrees]
RETURN
    RADIANS( __degrees )
```

See also

For more details regarding functions in this recipe, refer to the following links:

- SQRT: https://docs.microsoft.com/en-us/dax/sqrt-function-dax
- POWER: https://docs.microsoft.com/en-us/dax/power-function-dax
- SWITCH: https://docs.microsoft.com/en-us/dax/switch-function-dax
- ATAN: https://docs.microsoft.com/en-us/dax/atan-function-dax
- PI: https://docs.microsoft.com/en-us/dax/pi-function-dax
- COS: https://docs.microsoft.com/en-us/dax/cos-function-dax
- SIN: https://docs.microsoft.com/en-us/dax/sin-function-dax
- DEGREES: https://docs.microsoft.com/en-us/dax/degree-function-dax
- RADIANS: https://docs.microsoft.com/en-us/dax/radians-function-dax

Computing percentages

Power BI Desktop has a handy feature for showing percentages when numeric measures or column aggregations are placed in the **Values** area of visualizations. This feature allows you to right-click the measure or column and choose **Show value as** and then **Percent of grand total**, **Percent of column total**, and **Percent of row total**, depending on the type of visual. This is a nice, easy method to compute and display these percentages. However, not all places where DAX is used has such a convenient shortcut. Therefore, this recipe demonstrates how to compute these percentages using just plain old DAX.

Getting ready

To prepare for this recipe, perform the following steps:

1. Open Power BI Desktop.
2. Use an **Enter Data** query to create a table called R07_Table with the following data:

Item	Category1	Category2	Value
Item 1	Blue	Green	100
Item 2	Blue	Green	200
Item 3	Green	Blue	300
Item 4	Green	Blue	400

Item 5	Red	Green	500
Item 6	Red	Green	600
Item 7	Red	Blue	700
Item 8	Red	Blue	800

3. Create a **Matrix** visualization and, using the R07_Table table, place the Category1 column in the **Rows** area of the visual, the Category2 column in the **Columns** area of the visual, and the Value column in the **Values** area for the visualization.

4. Right-click the Value column and choose **Show value as** and then **Percent of Grand Total**.

5. Create a second **Matrix** visualization and, using the R07_Table table, place the Category1 column in the **Rows** area of the visual, the Category2 column in the **Columns** area of the visual, and the Value column in the **Values** area for the visualization.

6. Right-click the Value column and choose **Show value as** and then **Percent of Column Total**.

7. Create a third **Matrix** visualization and, using the R07_Table table, place the Category1 column in the **Rows** area of the visual, the Category2 column in the **Columns** area of the visual, and the Value column in the **Values** area for the visualization.

8. Right-click the Value column and choose **Show value as** and then **Percent of Row Total**.

We will use these matrix visualizations to check our math!

How to do it...

To demonstrate how to calculate your own equivalent percentages using DAX, perform the following steps:

1. Create the following measures:

```
PercentageGT =
    DIVIDE(
        SUM('R07_Table'[Value]),
        SUMX(ALL(R07_Table),[Value])
    )

PercentageCT =
```

```
            DIVIDE(
                SUM('R07_Table'[Value]),
                SUMX(
                    CALCULATETABLE(
                        'R07_Table',
                        ALL(R07_Table[Category1])
                    ),
                    [Value]
                )
            )

    PercentageRT =
        DIVIDE(
            SUM('R07_Table'[Value]),
            SUMX(
                CALCULATETABLE(
                    'R07_Table',
                    ALL(R07_Table[Category2])
                ),
                [Value]
            )
        )
```

2. Create a fourth **Matrix** visualization and, using the R07_Table table, place the Category1 column in the **Rows** area of the visual, the Category2 column in the **Columns** area of the visual, and the PercentageGT measure in the **Values** area for the visualization.

3. Format the PercentageGT measure as a percentage.

4. Create a fifth **Matrix** visualization and, using the R07_Table table, place the Category1 column in the **Rows** area of the visual, the Category2 column in the **Columns** area of the visual, and the PercentageCT measure in the **Values** area for the visualization.

5. Format the PercentageCT measure as a percentage.

6. Create a sixth **Matrix** visualization and, using the R07_Table table, place the Category1 column in the **Rows** area of the visual, the Category2 column in the **Columns** area of the visual, and the PercentageRT measure in the **Values** area for the visualization.

7. Format the PercentageRT measure as a percentage.

How it works...

The first measure, `PercentageGT`, is fairly straightforward. In order to compute the appropriate percentage of the grand total, we simply need to divide our chosen aggregate, in this case `SUM`, in its current context and divide that number by the same chosen aggregate computed against all values in the table. We accomplish this second part (the denominator) by using the iterator equivalent to our chosen aggregation, in this case `SUMX`, and using the `ALL` function to place all rows within the base table within the context of our computation.

The second measure, `PercentageCT`, functions along the same lines as `PercentageGT` except that for our denominator, we want all of the values from our base table that belong with our current column in our matrix (`Category2`), effectively ignoring the context provided by the rows in our matrix (`Category1`). To accomplish this, we use the `CALCULATETABLE` function. The `CALCULATETABLE` function allows us to maintain our overall filter context but replace specific column contexts within that filter context with a new context for the specified columns. Hence, in our example, by specifying to use `ALL` of `Category1` within our table, we remove all other filter contexts for `Category1` (such as the context provided by the rows in the matrix) and replace that context with the context of `ALL` of `Category1`. This replaces the context for `Category1`, but maintains our current, existing context for `Category2` within the column of the matrix.

The third measure, `PercentageRT`, is identical to `PercentageCT`, except that we want to replace the filter context on the `Category2` column since we want to ignore the context provided by the columns in our matrix in the calculation of our denominator.

See also

For more details regarding functions in this recipe, refer to the following links:

- DIVIDE: https://docs.microsoft.com/en-us/dax/divide-function-dax
- CALCULATETABLE: https://docs.microsoft.com/en-us/dax/calculatetable-function-dax
- ALL: https://docs.microsoft.com/en-us/dax/all-function-dax

Calculating mode for single and multiple columns

Mode is a common mathematical concept defined as the most frequently occurring value in a series. Excel has a built-in function called MODE for calculating the mode of a series of values. However, DAX has no such equivalent function. This recipe demonstrates how to calculate the mode of a series of values using DAX.

Getting ready

To prepare for this recipe, perform the following steps:

1. Open Power BI Desktop.
2. Use an **Enter Data** query to create a table called R08_Table1 with the following data:

Method
A
B
C
A
B
C
A
A
A
B
B
C

How to do it...

To implement this recipe, perform the following steps:

1. Create the following measure:

```
Mode =
    VAR __Table =
        SUMMARIZE (
            'R08_Table1',
            'R08_Table1'[Method],
            "__Count", COUNT('R08_Table1'[Method])
        )
    VAR __Table2 =
        FILTER(__Table , [__Count] = MAXX( __Table , [__Count] ) )
    VAR __Mode =
        IF (
            COUNTROWS( __Table2 ) = 1,
            MAXX( __Table2 , [Method] ),
            CONCATENATEX( __Table2 , [Method] , "," )
        )
    RETURN
        __Mode
```

2. Create a **Card** visualization and place the Mode measure in the **Fields** area for the **Card** visualization.

How it works...

Overall, the recipe for mode is relatively straightforward. We start by creating a table that uses the DAX SUMMARIZE function to group the rows in our data table by the column for which we are attempting to find the mode. In this case, the column is called Method. Within the same function, we create a column called __Count that stores the count of the original rows in the data table for each value in the column for which we are finding the mode. We store this table in a variable called __Table.

The next step is to simply filter our __Table to only contain the rows that have the highest number within the __Count column. This value, or values, of __Count is our mode. We store this filtered table in the __Table2 variable. We can finally calculate the __Mode variable and return either the single value using MAXX or, if there are ties, multiple values using CONCATENATEX.

There's more...

We can use the same basic technique to calculate the mode of multiple columns. To see how this works, perform the following steps:

1. Use another **Enter Data** query to create a table called R08_Table2 with the following data:

Index	M1	M2	M3	M4
0	AAA3	AAA3	AAA3	AAA3
1	BBB3	CCC3		CCC3
2				DDD2

2. Create the following measure:

```
MMode =
    VAR __Table =
        UNION(
            UNION(
                UNION(
SUMMARIZE('R08_Table2','R08_Table2'[Index],"__Methods",MAX('R08_Tab
le2'[M1])),
SUMMARIZE('R08_Table2','R08_Table2'[Index],"__Methods",MAX('R08_Tab
le2'[M2]))
                ),
SUMMARIZE('R08_Table2','R08_Table2'[Index],"__Methods",MAX('R08_Tab
le2'[M3]))
            ),
SUMMARIZE('R08_Table2','R08_Table2'[Index],"__Methods",MAX('R08_Tab
le2'[M4]))
        )
    VAR __Table1 =
        FILTER(
            GROUPBY(__Table,[Index],[__Methods],"__Count",
COUNTX(CURRENTGROUP(), [__Methods])),
            [__Methods]<>""
        )
    VAR __Table2 = FILTER(__Table1,[__Count] =
MAXX(__Table1,[__Count]))
    VAR __Mode =
        IF(
            COUNTROWS( __Table2 ) = 1,
            MAXX( __Table2 , [__Methods] ),
            CONCATENATEX( __Table2 , [__Methods] , ",")
        )
RETURN __Mode
```

3. Create a **Card** visualization and place the MMode measure in the **Fields** area for the **Card** visualization.

This technique is extremely similar to our Mode measure. The primary difference is the use of the UNION statements. These UNION statements require some sort of unique row identifier, in this case, our Index column. We use SUMMARIZE to group our table rows by the Index column with the value for our columns, M1, M2, M3, and M4. Each of these SUMMARIZE statements returns a two-column table that lists each index value coupled with each value from the columns M1, M2, M3, and M4. Thus, the first SUMMARIZE statement would return a table along the lines of the following:

Index	__Methods
0	AAA3
1	BBB3
2	

We use UNION to combine all of these tables together so that we have essentially in-pivoted our columns M1, M2, M3, and M4 into a single column called __Methods. Thus, at this point, we are essentially performing the same calculation as our original Mode measure!

You should note that this same technique of un-pivoting columns using DAX can be used to calculate any multicolumn aggregation, including SUM, AVERAGE, MIN, MAX, COUNT, and even PRODUCT.

See also

For more details regarding functions in this recipe, refer to the following links:

- SUMMARIZE: https://docs.microsoft.com/en-us/dax/summarize-function-dax
- FILTER: https://docs.microsoft.com/en-us/dax/filter-function-dax
- COUNTROWS: https://docs.microsoft.com/en-us/dax/countrows-function-dax
- MAXX: https://docs.microsoft.com/en-us/dax/maxx-function-dax
- CONCATENATEX: https://docs.microsoft.com/en-us/dax/concatenatex-function-dax
- UNION: https://docs.microsoft.com/en-us/dax/union-function-dax
- GROUPBY: https://docs.microsoft.com/en-us/dax/groupby-function-dax

Extracting text

We often have to deal with data that is less than pristine. For example, we may encounter a multi-value text column in which we are not able to easily split the information out because the multiple values within the column are in a random order and of varying length. This recipe demonstrates how to use the text-parsing functions within DAX to extract information from such complex strings.

Getting ready

To prepare for this recipe, perform the following steps:

1. Open Power BI Desktop.
2. Use an **Enter Data** query to create a table called `R09_Table` with the following data:

Column1
Color: Red; Name: abc; Number: 123
Name: de; Number: 4567; Color: Blue
number: 89; color: Green; name: fghi

How to do it...

To implement this recipe, perform the following steps:

1. Create the following columns:

```
Color =
    VAR __find = "Color: "
    VAR __pos = SEARCH(__find,'R09_Table'[Column1],,BLANK())
    VAR __semipos = SEARCH(";",'R09_Table'[Column1],__pos,BLANK())
    VAR __semipos1 =
IF(ISBLANK(__semipos),LEN('R09_Table'[Column1]) + 1,__semipos)
    VAR __len = LEN(__find)
    VAR __start = __pos + __len
RETURN
    IF(
        ISBLANK(__pos),
        BLANK(),
        MID('R09_Table'[Column1],__start, __semipos1 - __start)
    )
```

```
Name =
    VAR __find = "Name: "
    VAR __pos = SEARCH(__find,'R09_Table'[Column1])
    VAR __semipos = SEARCH(";",'R09_Table'[Column1],__pos,BLANK())
    VAR __semipos1 =
IF(ISBLANK(__semipos),LEN('R09_Table'[Column1]) + 1,__semipos)
    VAR __len = LEN(__find)
    VAR __start = __pos + __len
RETURN
    IF(
        ISBLANK(__pos),
        BLANK(),
        MID('R09_Table'[Column1],__start, __semipos1 - __start)
    )


Number =
    VAR __find = "Number: "
    VAR __pos = SEARCH(__find,'R09_Table'[Column1])
    VAR __semipos = SEARCH(";",'R09_Table'[Column1],__pos,BLANK())
    VAR __semipos1 =
IF(ISBLANK(__semipos),LEN('R09_Table'[Column1]) + 1,__semipos)
    VAR __len = LEN(__find)
    VAR __start = __pos + __len
RETURN
    IF(
        ISBLANK(__pos),
        BLANK(),
        MID('R09_Table'[Column1],__start, __semipos1 - __start)
    )
```

How it works...

All of these columns work identically. We start by creating a variable, __find, that defines the starting text identifier for the information we are trying to extract from the string. We then use the SEARCH function to return the starting position of that string within our text (Column1). In the event that the text is not found, we return BLANK. The value returned is stored within the __pos variable.

We can then use SEARCH again to find the end of our information within the text string, in this case denoted by a semicolon (;). This time, we utilize the third parameter of the SEARCH function to start searching for the text at our __pos variable. This ensures that we find the next ending separator. We again return BLANK if nothing is found and we store the result in the __semipos variable. Since the last value within our string has no final ending semicolon, we do a quick check to see whether the value returned to __semipos is BLANK. If so, we know that we are at the end of the string, so we return the full length of the string using the LEN function plus 1, since positions within a string start at 0. We store this possibly revised value in the __semipos1 variable.

Next, we determine the length of the starting text we are trying to find using the LEN function and store this in the __len variable. We need this since SEARCH returns the starting position of text for which we are searching. Since we are trying to extract the text between our starting search text and our ending search text, we do not want any extra characters that are part of our starting search text included in our end result. We can now calculate the actual starting position of the text we are attempting to extract by adding this __len to our __pos variable. We store this starting position in the __start variable.

Finally, our final string can be returned by checking to see whether __pos is blank and, if so, then our text was not found, so we return BLANK. Otherwise, we use the MID function to return our final text. MID uses a starting position, in this case __start, and the number of characters after the starting position to return, which is simply the position of our ending search text, __semipos1, minus our starting position, __start.

There's more...

The SEARCH DAX function is a case-insensitive function. To conduct case-sensitive searches, use FIND instead. DAX also has the functions RIGHT and LEFT for extracting text characters from the beginning or end of strings.

See also

For more details regarding functions in this recipe, refer to the following links:

- SEARCH: https://docs.microsoft.com/en-us/dax/search-function-dax
- BLANK: https://docs.microsoft.com/en-us/dax/blank-function-dax
- ISBLANK: https://docs.microsoft.com/en-us/dax/isblank-function-dax
- LEN: https://docs.microsoft.com/en-us/dax/len-function-dax

- MID:: https://docs.microsoft.com/en-us/dax/mid-function-dax
- FIND: https://docs.microsoft.com/en-us/dax/find-function-dax
- RIGHT: https://docs.microsoft.com/en-us/dax/right-function-dax
- LEFT: https://docs.microsoft.com/en-us/dax/left-function-dax

Detecting prime numbers

Prime numbers, whole numbers greater than 1 that cannot be divided evenly by any number other than themselves and 1, have been studied for millennia. Prime numbers continue to be of the utmost importance today, particularly in the field of computer cryptography. This recipe demonstrates how to determine whether a given number is prime.

Getting ready

To prepare for this recipe, perform the following steps:

1. Open Power BI Desktop.
2. Create a new table with the following formula:

```
R10_Table = GENERATESERIES(1 , 1000 , 1)
```

How to do it...

To implement this recipe, perform the following steps:

1. Create the following column in the R10_Table table:

```
IsPrime =
    VAR __num = 'R10_Table'[Value]
    VAR __max = INT(SQRT(__num))
    VAR __table = GENERATESERIES(2 , __max , 1)
    VAR __table1 = ADDCOLUMNS(__table,"__mod",MOD(__num , [Value]))
RETURN
    SWITCH(
        TRUE(),
        __num = 1, FALSE(),
        ISBLANK(COUNTROWS(FILTER(__table1,[__mod] = 0))),TRUE(),
        FALSE()
    )
```

How it works...

We start by storing our working number in the __num variable. Next, we calculate the maximum number that we will need to check as a divisor. This maximum number is the square root of our working number. We use the SQRT DAX function to find the square root of our working number and round this to the integer portion using INT. Any number larger than the square root of our number cannot possibly be an even divisor of our working number. This greatly reduces the number of divisors that we will need to check. We store this maximum number in the __max variable.

We then create a table from the number 2 to our __max variable in increments of 1 and add a column to this table that is the MOD function of our working number and the values in this table. The MOD function returns the remainder of a division operation, meaning, if the remainder of a division operation is 0, then the numerator is evenly divisible by the denominator. We store this final table in the __table1 variable.

For our RETURN statement, we use a SWITCH statement to first check whether the working number is 1. If so, we return FALSE, since 1 cannot be a prime number by definition. Our next check is to count all of the rows in our __table1 variable whose __mod column is 0. If there are no such rows, then COUNTROWS will return BLANK. We check to see whether the result of the COUNTROWS function is blank (ISBLANK) and, if so, we return TRUE, meaning that the working number is a prime number! Otherwise, we return FALSE, meaning the number is not a prime number.

There's more...

To turn this calculated column into a measure, replace the first row of the formula with the following:

```
VAR __num = MAX('R10_Table'[Value])
```

See also

For more details regarding functions in this recipe, refer to the following links:

- INT: https://docs.microsoft.com/en-us/dax/int-function-dax
- SQRT: https://docs.microsoft.com/en-us/dax/sqrt-function-dax
- BLANK: https://docs.microsoft.com/en-us/dax/blank-function-dax
- ISBLANK: https://docs.microsoft.com/en-us/dax/isblank-function-dax
- GENERATESERIES: https://docs.microsoft.com/en-us/dax/generateseries-function-dax
- ADDCOLUMNS: https://docs.microsoft.com/en-us/dax/addcolumns-function-dax
- SWITCH: https://docs.microsoft.com/en-us/dax/switch-function-dax
- COUNTROWS: https://docs.microsoft.com/en-us/dax/countrows-function-dax
- FILTER: https://docs.microsoft.com/en-us/dax/filter-function-dax
- TRUE: https://docs.microsoft.com/en-us/dax/true-function-dax
- FALSE: https://docs.microsoft.com/en-us/dax/false-function-dax

5
Figuring Financial Rates and Revenues

It is rare for a business to not closely track and regularly report on financial metrics. Financial metrics are perhaps the best measure of the health of a business or organization. While many financial metrics have relatively simple math behind them, calculating these metrics based on raw financial data and at varying levels within the organization can sometimes prove challenging. This chapter is all about demonstrating how to calculate common financial metrics or KPIs. We will provide useful recipes whose techniques can be applied in a variety of situations.

In this chapter, we will cover the following recipes:

- Computing gross margin, revenue, and cost
- Building a revenue growth rate
- Generating an accounts payable turnover ratio
- Fashioning the market share and relative market share
- Determining compound interest
- Working with periodic revenue (reverse **year-to-date (YTD)**)
- Comparing budgets and actuals
- Crafting currency exchange rates
- Assessing days sales outstanding

Technical requirements

The following are required to complete all of the recipes in this chapter:

- Power BI Desktop
- This book's GitHub repository: `https://github.com/PacktPublishing/DAX-Cookbook/tree/master/Chapter05`

Computing gross margin, revenue, and cost

Gross margin is an important financial metric that represents the percentage of revenue retained after direct costs are incurred. However, there are times when businesses understand their costs and desired gross margin and thus need to determine how much revenue they should be making for their goods and services. Conversely, there are also times where businesses understand how much revenue they can make, as well as their desired gross margin, and thus need to understand their maximum cost. The latter scenario is fairly common in the services sector when attempting to understand the maximum hourly cost of a resource for a given revenue and gross margin.

The formula for gross margin is as follows:

$$GrossMargin = \frac{(Revenue - Cost)}{Revenue}$$

This recipe demonstrates how to calculate gross margin when given a certain revenue and cost. In addition, this recipe demonstrates how to calculate the revenue for a given cost and gross margin. Finally, we will show you how to calculate the cost of a given revenue and gross margin.

Getting ready

To prepare for this recipe, do the following:

1. Open Power BI Desktop.
2. Create a table called `R01_Revenue` using the following formula:

```
R01_Revenue = GENERATESERIES(1,1000,1)
```

3. Create a table called R01_Cost using the following formula:

```
R01_Cost = GENERATESERIES(1,1000,1)
```

4. Create a table called R01_GrossMargin using the following formula:

```
R01_GrossMargin = GENERATESERIES(.01,1,.01)
```

5. Create a **Slicer** visualization using the Value column of the R01_Revenue table and rename the column in the **Field** area of the visualization from Value to Revenue.

6. Create a **Slicer** visualization using the Value column of the R01_Cost table and rename the column in the **Field** area of the visualization from Value to Cost.

7. Create a **Slicer** visualization using the Value column of the R01_GrossMargin table and rename the column in the **Field** of the visualization area from Value to Gross Margin.

How to do it...

To implement this recipe, do the following:

1. Create the following measures:

```
GM % =
    DIVIDE(
        ( SELECTEDVALUE('R01_Revenue'[Value]) -
SELECTEDVALUE('R01_Cost'[Value]) ),
        SELECTEDVALUE('R01_Revenue'[Value]),
        BLANK()
    )

Revenue =
    DIVIDE(
        SELECTEDVALUE('R01_Cost'[Value]),
        ( 1 - SELECTEDVALUE('R01_GrossMargin'[Value])),
        BLANK()
    )

Cost =
    SELECTEDVALUE('R01_Revenue'[Value]) * (1 -
SELECTEDVALUE('R01_GrossMargin'[Value]))
```

2. Format GM % as a percentage.

3. On the **Report** page, create a **Card** visualization and place the GM % measure in the **Fields** area for the visualization.

4. Choose **100** from the **Revenue** slicer and **60** from the **Cost** slicer. Note that the **GM %** card visualization displays **40.00%**. Thus, for a revenue of $100 and a cost of $60, the gross margin percentage is 40%.

5. On the same **Report** page, create a second **Card** visualization and place the Revenue measure in the **Fields** area for the visualization.

6. Leave the **Revenue** and **Cost** slicers set to **100** and **60**, respectively, and choose **40.00%** from the **Gross Margin** slicer.

7. Note that the **Revenue** card visualization displays **100**. Thus, for a cost of $60 and a desired gross margin % of 40%, the revenue needs to be $100.

8. On the same **Report** page, create a third **Card** visualization and place the Cost measure in the **Fields** area for the visualization. Note that this card visualization displays **60**, indicating that for a revenue of $100 and a desired gross margin of 40%, the cost needs to be $60. Change the **Gross Margin** slicer to **55.00%** and notice that the **Cost** card visualization value changes to **45**.

How it works...

The percentage gross margin is given by the following formula:

$$PercentGrossMargin = (Revenue - Cost) \div Revenue$$

Using a bit of algebra, we can solve this equation for *Revenue* using the following formula:

$$Revenue = Cost \div (1 - PercentGrossMargin)$$

We can use a bit more algebra to solve either of these equations for *Cost*:

$$Cost = Revenue \times (1 - PercentGrossMargin)$$

Each of the measures, that is, GM %, Revenue, and Cost, implements these formulas and uses the SELECTEDVALUE DAX function to get the values that were selected in the respective slicers. We use the DIVIDE function with the third alternative result parameter to return BLANK in the event that nothing is selected in the slicers and to avoid division by zero errors.

See also

For more details regarding the functions in this recipe, please refer to the following links:

- **Gross Margin Definition:** https://www.investopedia.com/terms/g/grossmargin.asp
- SELECTEDVALUE: https://docs.microsoft.com/en-us/dax/selectedvalue-function-dax
- DIVIDE: https://docs.microsoft.com/en-us/dax/divide-function-dax
- BLANK: https://docs.microsoft.com/en-us/dax/blank-function-dax

Building a revenue growth rate

How fast a company is growing or shrinking is a critical factor in any business analysis. The revenue growth rate is a direct way of measuring growth based on the revenue generated by the sale of goods and services. The revenue growth rate compares the revenue generated by business between two equal-length periods, such as this year and the previous year, this quarter and the previous quarter, or this month and the previous month.

This recipe demonstrates how to create a revenue growth rate metric and display this metric in a visualization.

Getting ready

To prepare for this recipe, do the following:

1. Open Power BI Desktop.
2. Use an **Enter Data** query to create a table called R02_Table that contains the following information:

YearMonth	Revenue	Year	MonthNum
201901	100	2019	1
201902	200	2019	2
201903	300	2019	3
201904	400	2019	4
201905	500	2019	5
201906	600	2019	6
201907	700	2019	7

201908	800	2019	8
201909	900	2019	9
201910	1,000	2019	10
201911	1,100	2019	11
201912	1,200	2019	12
202001	1,300	2020	1
202002	1,400	2020	2
202003	1,500	2020	3

How to do it...

To implement this recipe, do the following:

1. Create the following measure:

```
Revenue Growth Rate =
    VAR __ThisMonth = MAX('R02_Table'[MonthNum])
    VAR __ThisMonthYear = MAX('R02_Table'[Year])
    VAR __ThisMonthRevenue = SUM('R02_Table'[Revenue])
    VAR __LastMonth = IF(__ThisMonth = 1 ,12 ,__ThisMonth - 1)
    VAR __LastMonthYear = IF(__ThisMonth = 1, __ThisMonthYear - 1 ,
__ThisMonthYear)
    VAR __LastMonthRevenue =
        SUMX(
            FILTER(
                ALL('R02_Table'),
                'R02_Table'[MonthNum] = __LastMonth &&
'R02_Table'[Year] = __LastMonthYear
            ),
            'R02_Table'[Revenue])
RETURN
    DIVIDE(
        __ThisMonthRevenue - __LastMonthRevenue,
        __LastMonthRevenue,
        0
    )
```

2. Format the `Revenue Growth Rate` measure as a percentage.
3. Create a **Line** chart visualization.

4. Put the `YearMonth` column from the `R02_Table` table into the **Axis** area and the `Revenue Growth Rate` measure into the **Values** area of this line chart visualization.

5. Format the X axis so that it's `Categorical` and not `Continuous`.

6. Ensure that the **Line** chart visualization is sorted by `YearMonth`.

How it works...

In this recipe, we compared the revenue growth rate from one month to the next. As shown by the data, the revenue per month is growing by a steady amount of 100 per month. However, after an initial jump, this steady growth represents a declining percentage of the overall revenue for the company, indicating that the growth is slowing down over time.

We start by simply getting the values for the current month, `__ThisMonth`, current year, `__ThisMonthYear`, and the revenue, `__ThisMonthRevenue`. Then, we need to find these same values for the previous month so that we can compare these values. For `__LastMonth`, we simply check if the current month is December (`12`) and if so, we set this variable to January (`1`); otherwise, we simply subtract `1` from our month number, `__ThisMonth`, to get the previous month number. Similarly, for `__LastMonthYear`, we check if the current month is January (`1`) and if so, we set this to our current year, `__ThisMonthYear`, minus one since our previous month would be December of last year. Otherwise, we know that the year is the same as our current month, `__ThisMonthYear`.

Calculating the previous month's revenue, `__LastMonthRevenue`, is slightly trickier. Since this measure is used within a visualization that only has a single month in the context at any one time, we must use `ALL` to override this context and include all the rows of the table within our calculation context. Then, we `FILTER` all of these rows down to only the row(s) that we desire, which in this case is the row that has a value in the `MonthNum` column equal to our previously calculated `__LastMonth` and a value in the `Year` column equal to our previously calculated `__LastMonthYear`. Then, we can use the `SUMX` function to sum the `Revenue` column values across these rows (in this case, just a single row) to arrive at a value for the previous month's revenue, `__LastMonthRevenue`.

Finally, we simply need to return the comparison between our current month revenue, `__ThisMonthRevenue`, and last month's revenue, `__LastMonthRevenue`, as a percentage. We do this using the `DIVIDE` function, which divides the difference between this month's and last month's revenue by last month's revenue. This provides a percentage increase or decrease for our current month compared to the previous month.

See also

For more details regarding the functions in this recipe, please refer to the following links:

- **Growth Rates:** https://www.investopedia.com/terms/g/growthrates.asp
- MAX: https://docs.microsoft.com/en-us/dax/max-function-dax
- SUM: https://docs.microsoft.com/en-us/dax/sum-function-dax
- IF: https://docs.microsoft.com/en-us/dax/if-function-dax
- ALL: https://docs.microsoft.com/en-us/dax/all-function-dax
- FILTER: https://docs.microsoft.com/en-us/dax/filter-function-dax
- SUMX: https://docs.microsoft.com/en-us/dax/sumx-function-dax
- DIVIDE: https://docs.microsoft.com/en-us/dax/divide-function-dax

Generating an accounts payable turnover ratio

The accounts payable turnover ratio is a financial measure that indicates how many times a business can pay off the balance of its purchases over a given length of time. A business that has a higher accounts payable turnover ratio indicates that the business has a higher liquidity value (the availability of liquid assets, such as cash) than a business with a lower accounts payable turnover. Businesses with high liquidity are more attractive to creditors, as well as vendors.

This recipe demonstrates how to calculate the accounts payable turnover ratio for a business.

Getting ready

To prepare for this recipe, do the following:

1. Open Power BI Desktop.
2. Use an **Enter Data** query to create a table called R03_Table that contains the following information:

Date	Category	Amount
1/1/2019	Accounts Payable	15,000,000
12/31/2019	Accounts Payable	20,000,000

1/1/2020	Accounts Payable	20,000,000
12/31/2020	Accounts Payable	40,000,000
12/31/2019	Purchases	110,000,000
12/31/2020	Purchases	100,000,000

This table represents a business that started in 2019 with an accounts payable balance of $15 million and ended the same year with an accounts payable balance of $20 million. During that year, the business made $110 million worth of purchases. Similarly, the business started 2020 with an accounts payable balance of $20 million and ended 2020 with an accounts payable balance of $40 million. The total purchases during 2020 came to $100 million.

How to do it...

To implement this recipe, do the following:

1. Create the following measure:

```
AP Turnover Ratio =
    VAR __Purchases =
        SUMX (
            FILTER('R03_Table',[Category] = "Purchases"),
            'R03_Table'[Amount]
        )
    VAR __OpeningAP =
        SUMX (
            FILTER(
                'R03_Table',
                'R03_Table'[Date] = MIN('R03_Table'[Date]) &&
                    'R03_Table'[Category] = "Accounts Payable"),
            [Amount]
        )
    VAR __ClosingAP =
        SUMX (
            FILTER(
                'R03_Table',
                'R03_Table'[Date] = MAX('R03_Table'[Date]) &&
                    'R03_Table'[Category] = "Accounts Payable"),
            [Amount]
        )
    VAR __AverageAP = DIVIDE(__OpeningAP + __ClosingAP ,2 ,0)
    RETURN
        DIVIDE(__Purchases, __AverageAP, 0)
```

2. In the R03_Table table, create a column with the following formula:

    ```
    Year = YEAR([Date])
    ```

3. Create a **Table** visualization and place the Year column from
    the R03_Table table, as well as the AP Turnover Ratio measure, into the
    Values area for the visualization.

For 2019, the AP Turnover Ratio value is 6.29, while in 2020, the value is 3.33, indicating that the business had almost twice the liquidity in 2019 compared to 2020.

How it works...

The accounts payable turnover ratio is calculated using the following formula:

$$Accounts\ Payable\ Turnover\ Ratio = Purchases \div Average\ Accounts\ Payable$$

To get the total purchases for the year, we simply need to sum the rows in the table that have a categorization of Purchases. We do this using the SUMX DAX function. With this, we filter our base table, R03_Table, where the Category column has a value of Purchases, and then sum the Amount column.

In order to calculate the average accounts payable for the year, we need to find our opening and closing balances for the year. We calculate the opening balance, __OpeningAP, by filtering our base table, R03_Table, where the Category column has a value of Accounts Payable and the Date column has the minimum date within the current context. Since this is a measure, we need to use aggregation (in this case, provided by SUMX), but since we are returning a single row, we could have used a different aggregation function, such as MAXX or MINX. Similarly, we calculate the closing balance, __ClosingAP, by filtering our base table, R03_Table, where the Category column has a value of Accounts Payable and the Date column has the maximum date within the current context.

To arrive at the average between the opening and closing accounts payable balances, __AverageAP, we simply need to DIVIDE the sum of our __OpeningAP and __ClosingAP balances by 2.

Once we have calculated our `__Purchases` and `__AverageAP` variables, we can employ our accounts payable turnover ratio formula and simply divide `__Purchases` by `__AverageAP`.

See also

For more details regarding the functions in this recipe, please refer to the following links:

- Accounts Payable Turnover Ratio Definition: `https://www.investopedia.com/terms/a/accountspayableturnoverratio.asp`
- MAX: `https://docs.microsoft.com/en-us/dax/max-function-dax`
- MIN: `https://docs.microsoft.com/en-us/dax/min-function-dax`
- FILTER: `https://docs.microsoft.com/en-us/dax/filter-function-dax`
- SUMX: `https://docs.microsoft.com/en-us/dax/sumx-function-dax`
- DIVIDE: `https://docs.microsoft.com/en-us/dax/divide-function-dax`

Fashioning the market share and relative market share

The market share is the percentage of an economic market or industry that's accounted for by a specific business. The market share can be based on units or revenue. The relative market share compares a business' market share with that of the largest competitor within the market or industry. Both of these metrics are important financial measures for businesses since a market or industry is generally viewed as an equity pie divided between businesses that operate (the sale of goods and services) within that market or industry. Businesses with a larger market share have greater potential profit than those with less market share. In addition, businesses that are increasing their market share are effectively winning in the market by taking market share from their competitors.

This recipe demonstrates how to calculate the market share and relative market share for businesses within a market or industry. In addition, this recipe shows how to calculate the overall competitiveness of a market or industry.

Getting ready

To prepare for this recipe, do the following:

1. Open Power BI Desktop.
2. Use an **Enter Data** query to create a table called `R04_Table` that contains the following information:

Brand	Unit Sales
A	40,000
B	30,000
C	20,000
D	6,000
E	4,000

This data table represents a market with only five businesses operating within that market and lists the number of units sold by each business within an operating period such as a month, quarter, or year.

How to do it...

To implement this recipe, do the following:

1. Create a column in the `R04_Table` table with the following formula:

```
Unit Market Share = 'R04_Table'[Unit Sales] /
SUMX(ALL('R04_Table'),'R04_Table'[Unit Sales])
```

2. Create a second column in the `R04_Table` table with the following formula:

```
Relative Market Share =
    VAR __LargestCompetitor = MAX('R04_Table'[Unit Market Share])
    VAR __SecondLargestCompetitor =
        IF(
            COUNTROWS(
                FILTER(
                    ALL('R04_Table'),
                    'R04_Table'[Unit Market Share] =
__LargestCompetitor
                )
            ) > 1,
            __LargestCompetitor,
            MAXX(
```

```
                    FILTER(
                        ALL('R04_Table'),
                        'R04_Table'[Unit Market Share] <>
        __LargestCompetitor
                    ),
                    'R04_Table'[Unit Market Share])
            )
    RETURN
        IF(
            [Unit Market Share] = __LargestCompetitor,
            __LargestCompetitor / __SecondLargestCompetitor,
            [Unit Market Share] / __LargestCompetitor
        )
```

3. Format both the Unit Market Share column and the Relative Market Share column as percentages.

How it works...

Market share is simply the amount of market owned by a specific business compared to the total market. Thus, when calculating Unit Market Share, we simply need to take the Unit Sales value of the current business and divide this number by the sum of all of the Unit Sales values. Since we are creating a calculated column and therefore have a row context, the current business' unit sales are simply the Unit Sales values column from the current row. We divide this number by the sum of all of the Unit Sales within the table. To do this, we use the ALL function to break down the row context and return all of the rows of the table. By doing this, we can use the SUMX function to sum the Unit Sales column across these rows.

To calculate Relative Market Share, we must compare each business with its largest competitor. For the largest competitor in the market, its largest competitor is the second-largest competitor in the market. To find the largest competitor's unit sales, __LargestCompetitor, we simply need to take the maximum value of the Unit Market Share column. Note that the MAX function breaks the row context and returns the largest value within the specified column.

To find the second-largest competitor's unit sales, `__SecondLargestCompetitor`, we need to check if there are two largest competitors that are equal in size. We do this using an `IF` statement, whose condition is to return all of the rows in the table that equal `__LargestCompetitor`. The `ALL` function is necessary to break the row context. If there is more than 1 row, then we have two equal largest competitors and simply return `__LargestCompetitor` as our value for `__SecondLargestCompetitor`. If there are no coequal largest competitors, then we filter all of the rows in the table where the `Unit Market Share` column equals the largest competitor's `Unit Market Share`. Then, we find the maximum remaining value for `Unit Market Share` using the `MAXX` function.

Now that we have calculated `__LargestCompetitor` and `__SecondLargestCompetitor`, we can return `Relative Market Share` by checking if the current `Unit Market Share` equals our calculated value for `__LargestCompetitor`. If so, then this row represents our largest competitor within the market, so we divide `__LargestCompetitor` by `__SecondLargestCompetitor`. In all other cases, we simply divide the row's market share, `Unit Market Share`, by `__LargestCompetitor`.

There's more...

We can use our `Unit Market Share` column to compute how competitive a market is. The competitiveness of a market is determined by how many businesses operate within that market and their percentage market shares relative to one another. We can determine the competitiveness of a market by computing the Herfindahl–Hirschman Index.
The Herfindahl–Hirschman Index is computed by summing the squares of the individual market shares for competitors within a market. To compute the Herfindahl–Hirschman Index, do the following:

1. Create a column in the `R04_Table` table with the following formula:

```
HHI = POWER('R04_Table'[Unit Market Share],2)
```

2. Format the `HHI` column as a percentage.
3. On a **Report** page, create a **Card** visualization and place the `HHI` column into the **Fields** area for the visualization.
4. Ensure that the default aggregation for the `HHI` column is set to `Sum`.

In our example, the **Card** visualization displays **29.52%**. A Herfindahl–Hirschman Index greater than 25% indicates a high market concentration.

See also

For more details regarding the functions in this recipe, please refer to the following links:

- **Market share:** https://www.investopedia.com/terms/m/marketshare.asp
- **Relative market share:** https://en.wikipedia.org/wiki/Relative_market_share
- **Market concentration:** https://en.wikipedia.org/wiki/Market_concentration
- **Herfindahl–Hirschman Index:** https://www.investopedia.com/terms/h/hhi.asp
- SUMX: https://docs.microsoft.com/en-us/dax/sumx-function-dax
- MAX: https://docs.microsoft.com/en-us/dax/max-function-dax
- COUNTROWS: https://docs.microsoft.com/en-us/dax/countrows-function-dax
- MAXX: https://docs.microsoft.com/en-us/dax/maxx-function-dax
- FILTER: https://docs.microsoft.com/en-us/dax/filter-function-dax
- ALL: https://docs.microsoft.com/en-us/dax/all-function-dax
- IF: https://docs.microsoft.com/en-us/dax/if-function-dax
- POWER: https://docs.microsoft.com/en-us/dax/power-function-dax

Determining compound interest

Simple interest is the interest that is calculated on the initial principal amount. Conversely, compound interest is the interest calculated that is calculated on the initial principal, plus the accumulated interest for all previous periods. Thus, with simple interest, the amount of interest for each period is the same, while for compound interest, the interest changes for each period.

Getting ready

To prepare for this recipe, do the following:

1. Open Power BI Desktop.
2. Use a **Bank** query to create a table called R05_Table.

How to do it...

To implement this recipe, do the following:

1. Create the following measures:

```
Principal = 100000
Interest Rate = .05
Periods = 10
Compound Interest = [Principal] * ( POWER(1 + [Interest
Rate],[Periods]) - 1 )
```

2. On a **Report** page, create a **Card** visualization and place the `Compound Interest` measure into the **Fields** area for the visualization.

How it works...

In this example, we are computing the compounded interest for an original principal amount of $100,000 with an interest rate of 5% over 10 periods of time. Thus, this could represent a 5% interest rate compounded annually over 10 years. The `Principal` measure represents the amount of our original principal, while the `Interest Rate` measure represents our interest rate. Finally, the `Periods` measure represents the number of periods over which interest is compounded.

We can compute the amount of compound interest for a given original principal amount, interest rate, and the number of compounding periods by implementing the formula for compound interest in DAX. The formula for compound interest is as follows:

$$Principal \times [(1 + InterestRate)^{NumberofPeriods} - 1]$$

Our `Compound Interest` measure implements this formula using the POWER DAX function, as well as basic DAX math operators. In our example, the interest that's earned on a $100,000 investment with an interest rate of 5% compounded annually over 10 years is $62,890, as shown by our **Card** visualization.

There's more...

We can compare the difference between simple interest and compound interest by doing the following:

1. Create a measure using the following formula:

   ```
   Simple Interest = [Principal] * [Interest Rate] * [Periods]
   ```

2. On the same **Report** page, create a **Card** visualization and place the `Simple Interest` measure into the **Fields** area for the visualization.

Observe that the simple interest that's earned over the same period is only $50,000.

See also

For more details regarding the functions in this recipe, please refer to the following links:

- Compound Interest: `https://www.investopedia.com/terms/c/compoundinterest.asp`
- POWER: `https://docs.microsoft.com/en-us/dax/power-function-dax`

Working with periodic revenue (reverse YTD)

Tracking revenue per month is extremely common for many businesses and organizations. Often, this revenue tracking takes the form of either simply tracking the revenue for each month or tracking the accumulated revenue for each month since the beginning of the year. Various business systems track or report revenue in different ways. Some systems provide revenue that's already been accumulated since the beginning of the year. This recipe demonstrates how to reverse engineer the accumulated revenue and the revenue year to date into the individual periodic revenue for each month.

Getting ready

To prepare for this recipe, do the following:

1. Open Power BI Desktop.
2. Use an **Enter Data** query to create a table called `R06_Table` that contains the following information:

Year	Month	Revenue YTD
2019	10	110,000,000
2019	11	122,000,000
2019	12	130,000,000
2020	1	12,000,000
2020	2	19,000,000
2020	3	31,000,000
2020	4	42,000,000

How to do it...

To implement this recipe, do the following:

1. Create a new column in the `R06_Table` table using the following formula:

```
Periodic Revenue =
    VAR __Month = 'R06_Table'[Month]
    VAR __Year = 'R06_Table'[Year]
    VAR __Revenue = 'R06_Table'[Revenue YTD]
    VAR __LastMonthRevenue =
        CALCULATE (
            SUM ('R06_Table'[Revenue YTD]),
            FILTER (
                ALL ('R06_Table'),
                'R06_Table'[Month]= __Month - 1
                    && 'R06_Table'[Year] = __Year
            )
        )
    RETURN
        __Revenue - __LastMonthRevenue
```

How it works...

The first three lines simply get the current row values from the Month, Year, and Revenue YTD columns and store these values in the __Month, __Year, and __Revenue variables, respectively. In order to calculate the current month's revenue, we need to compare the current Revenue YTD value with last month's Revenue YTD value. We do this by using ALL to break the row context and get all of the rows in our table. Then, we use FILTER to filter down to the single row whose Year column equals our current row's Year column, __Year, as well as whose Month column equals our current row's Month column, __Month, minus one. We could use any aggregation on this single row, but for multiple rows, we would most likely want to use the SUM function.

Once we have the Revenue YTD value for the current row, __Revenue, as well as the Revenue YTD value for the previous month, __LastMonthRevenue, the revenue for the current month is simply the difference between these two values.

There's more...

To convert the column formula into a measure, simply replace the first three lines of code with the following:

```
VAR __Month = MAX('R06_Table'[Month])
VAR __Year = MAX('R06_Table'[Year])
VAR __Revenue = MAX('R06_Table'[Revenue YTD])
```

We can also demonstrate how to calculate the YTD revenue for a month if we're given the periodic revenue for each month. To do this, create a column in the R06_Table table using the following formula:

```
YTD Revenue =
    SUMX(
        FILTER(
            ALL('R06_Table'),
            'R06_Table'[Year] = EARLIER('R06_Table'[Year]) &&
                'R06_Table'[Month] <= EARLIER('R06_Table'[Month])
        ),
        [Periodic Revenue]
    )
```

This formula demonstrates a different method of referring to the current row's Month and Year column values, as well as a different method of calculating the sum of the returned rows from our FILTER function. In this case, we use the EARLIER function to reference the current row's Month and Year column values and use the SUMX function instead of the CALCULATE and SUM functions.

See also

For more details regarding the functions in this recipe, please refer to the following links:

- SUMX: https://docs.microsoft.com/en-us/dax/sumx-function-dax
- MAX: https://docs.microsoft.com/en-us/dax/max-function-dax
- CALCULATE: https://docs.microsoft.com/en-us/dax/calculate-function-dax
- SUM: https://docs.microsoft.com/en-us/dax/sum-function-dax
- FILTER: https://docs.microsoft.com/en-us/dax/filter-function-dax
- ALL: https://docs.microsoft.com/en-us/dax/all-function-dax

Comparing budgets and actuals

Budgets and actuals for businesses are generally reported at two different calendar scales. For example, budgets are often presented at the month or year scale, while actuals are generally presented on the day scale. Because of these two different scales, it can be difficult to track daily revenue versus budget to determine whether a particular month or year is on track to meet or exceed the budget for that month or year.

This recipe demonstrates how to rationalize and compare revenue figures that are provided at two different time scales by demonstrating how to compare actual revenue provided at a daily scale with budget numbers provided at a monthly scale.

Getting ready

To prepare for this recipe, do the following:

1. Open Power BI Desktop.

2. Use an **Enter Data** query to create a table called R07_Budget that contains the following information:

Month	Date	Budget
January	1/1/2019	3,100,000
February	2/1/2019	2,800,000
March	3/1/2019	3,200,000
April	4/1/2019	3,000,000
May	5/1/2019	3,100,000
June	6/1/2019	2,900,000
July	7/1/2019	2,900,000
August	8/1/2019	2,800,000
September	9/1/2019	3,000,000
October	10/1/2019	3,200,000
November	11/1/2019	2,800,000
December	12/1/2019	2,500,000

3. Use an **Enter Data** query to create a table called R07_Revenue that contains the following information:

Date	Revenue
1/1/2019	100,000
1/2/2019	110,000
1/3/2019	110,000
1/4/2019	110,000
1/5/2019	115,000
1/6/2019	115,000
1/7/2019	115,000
1/8/2019	110,000
1/9/2019	110,000
1/10/2019	110,000
1/11/2019	100,000
1/12/2019	100,000
1/13/2019	100,000
1/14/2019	110,000
1/15/2019	110,000

1/16/2019	110,000
1/17/2019	115,000
1/18/2019	115,000
1/19/2019	115,000
1/20/2019	110,000
1/21/2019	110,000
1/22/2019	110,000
1/23/2019	100,000
1/24/2019	100,000
1/25/2019	100,000
1/26/2019	95,000
1/27/2019	95,000
1/28/2019	95,000
1/29/2019	90,000
1/30/2019	90,000
1/31/2019	90,000
2/1/2019	90,000
2/1/2019	90,000
2/2/2019	90,000
2/3/2019	90,000
2/4/2019	90,000
2/5/2019	95,000
2/6/2019	95,000
2/7/2019	95,000
2/8/2019	95,000
2/9/2019	95,000
2/10/2019	100,000
2/11/2019	100,000
2/12/2019	110,000
2/13/2019	110,000
2/14/2019	115,000

4. Ensure that there is no relationship between these tables.

How to do it...

To implement this recipe, do the following:

1. Create the following measures:

```
Running Monthly Revenue =
    VAR __Date = MAX('R07_Revenue'[Date])
    VAR __Month = MONTH(__Date)
    VAR __Year = YEAR(__Date)
RETURN
    SUMX(
        FILTER(
            ALL('R07_Revenue'),
            MONTH([Date]) = __Month &&
                YEAR([Date]) = __Year &&
                    [Date] <= __Date
        ),
        'R07_Revenue'[Revenue]
    )


Running Monthly Budget Per Day =
    VAR __Date = MAX('R07_Revenue'[Date])
    VAR __Month = MONTH(__Date)
    VAR __Year = YEAR(__Date)
    VAR __Day = DAY(__Date)
    VAR __Budget =
        SUMX(
            FILTER(
                'R07_Budget',
                MONTH([Date]) = __Month &&
                    YEAR([Date]) = __Year
            ),
            [Budget]
        )
    VAR __Days = DAY(EOMONTH(DATE(__Year,__Month,1),0))
RETURN
    __Budget * __Day / __Days
```

2. On a **Report** page, create a **Clustered column chart** visualization and place the Date column from the R07_Revenue table into the **Axis** area and place the Running Monthly Revenue and Running Monthly Budget Per Day measures in the **Value** area.

How it works...

We want to judge whether or not we are tracking the monthly budget on a daily basis. Therefore, we need to compare the running total of the monthly revenue with the running total of our monthly budget at the day level.

We start by calculating a monthly running total for our revenue, `Running Monthly Revenue`. This formula starts by simply getting the current date out of our `Date` column in the `R07_Revenue` table and storing this value in the `__Date` variable. We can then use this `__Date` variable to calculate the `MONTH`, `__Month`, `YEAR`, and `__Year` values of that date. Using these variable values, we can compute the running total of revenue for a month by using the `ALL` function to return all of the rows in the `R07_Revenue` table and then use the `FILTER` function to filter these rows to only the rows that have a `YEAR` value that equals our current year, `__Year`, have a `MONTH` value that equals our current month, `__Month`, and have a value in the `Date` column that is less than or equal to our current date, `__Date`. Then, we can use the `SUMX` function to sum the values in the `Revenue` column to iterate over these filtered rows.

For comparison purposes, we also need a running budget figure for each day, `Running Monthly Budget Per Day`, which is similar to the formula for `Running Monthly Revenue`. We start by simply getting the current date of our `Date` column in the `R07_Revenue` table and storing this value in the `__Date` variable. Then, we can use this `__Date` variable to calculate the `MONTH`, `__Month`, `YEAR`, and `__Year` values of that date and the `DAY` value, `__Day`, of that date. Then, we can use the `__Month` and `__Year` variables to extract the corresponding budget, `__Budget`, for the current month and year from the `R07_Budget` table using the `FILTER` and `SUMX` functions.

Finally, we need to calculate the number of days in the current month, `__Days`. We can do this by using the `DAY`, `EOMONTH`, and `DATE` DAX functions in conjunction with one another. The explanation of this calculation is that we create a DAX date by using the `DATE` function and specifying our `__Year`, `__Month`, and the first day of the month, `1`. The `EOMONTH` function returns the last date of the month given a date and an offset specified in the number of months; in this case, `0`. Thus, `EOMONTH` effectively returns the last date of the current month and we use the `DAY` function to get the value of that `DAY`, such as 31 for January.

Now, we can return our budget, `__Budget`, multiplied by a percentage of the current day versus the total days in the month to spread our monthly budget evenly over the number of days in each month.

There's more...

We can modify these measures slightly to track revenue versus budget for the entire year. To see how this works, do the following:

1. Create the following measures:

```
Running Yearly Revenue =
    VAR __Date = MAX('R07_Revenue'[Date])
    VAR __Year = YEAR(__Date)
RETURN
    SUMX(
        FILTER(
            ALL('R07_Revenue'),
            YEAR([Date]) = __Year &&
                [Date] <= __Date
        ),
        'R07_Revenue'[Revenue]
    )

Running Yearly Budget Per Day =
    VAR __Date = MAX('R07_Revenue'[Date])
    VAR __Month = MONTH(__Date)
    VAR __Year = YEAR(__Date)
    VAR __Day = DATEDIFF(DATE(__Year,1,1),__Date,DAY) + 1
    VAR __Budget = SUM([Budget])
    VAR __Days = DATEDIFF(DATE(__Year,1,1),DATE(__Year,12,31),DAY)
+ 1
RETURN
    __Budget * __Day / __Days
```

2. On a **Report** page, create a **Clustered column chart** visualization and place the `Date` column from the `R07_Revenue` table into the **Axis** area and place the `Running Yearly Revenue` and `Running Yearly Budget Per Day` measures in the **Value** area.

The only change we've made to the `Running Yearly Revenue` measure with respect to the `Running Monthly Revenue` measure is that we remove any references to the month. For the `Running Yearly Budget Per Day` measure, the differences lie in how we calculate the current day of the year, `__Day`, and the total days in the year, `__Days`, using `DATEDIFF`.

We can also use our measure calculations to return a percentage that indicates how much our running revenue is above or below our running budget per day. To see how this works, do the following:

1. Create the following measure:

```
Percent of Budget = [Running Monthly Revenue] / [Running Monthly
Budget Per Day]
```

2. On a **Report** page, create a **Line chart** visualization and place the Date column from the R07_Revenue table into the **Axis** area. Then, place the Percent of Budget measure into the **Value** area.

See also

For more details regarding the functions in this recipe, please refer to the following links:

- MAX: https://docs.microsoft.com/en-us/dax/max-function-dax
- MONTH: https://docs.microsoft.com/en-us/dax/month-function-dax
- YEAR: https://docs.microsoft.com/en-us/dax/year-function-dax
- DAY: https://docs.microsoft.com/en-us/dax/day-function-dax
- SUMX: https://docs.microsoft.com/en-us/dax/sumx-function-dax
- FILTER: https://docs.microsoft.com/en-us/dax/filter-function-dax
- ALL: https://docs.microsoft.com/en-us/dax/all-function-dax
- EOMONTH: https://docs.microsoft.com/en-us/dax/eomonth-function-dax
- DATE: https://docs.microsoft.com/en-us/dax/date-function-dax
- DATEDIFF: https://docs.microsoft.com/en-us/dax/datediff-function-dax

Crafting currency exchange rates

Many organizations conduct business globally. In such circumstances, goods and services may be transacted in multiple currencies around the globe. However, organizations will often desire revenue figures to be reported using a single currency. When this happens, organizations must use currency exchange rates to convert transactions conducted in one or more currencies into a single currency for reporting purposes.

This recipe demonstrates how to convert revenue numbers in multiple currencies and report on this revenue in a single reporting currency using currency exchange rates that change over time.

Getting ready

To prepare for this recipe, do the following:

1. Open Power BI Desktop.
2. Use an **Enter Data** query to create a table called `R08_Currencies` that contains the following information:

Currency
GBP
EUR
USD

3. Use an **Enter Data** query to create a table called `R08_Rates` that contains the following information:

From	To	Date	Rate
USD	EUR	12/3/2019	0.90258
USD	GBP	12/3/2019	0.77062
EUR	USD	12/3/2019	1.10781
EUR	GBP	12/3/2019	0.85373
GBP	USD	12/3/2019	1.29746
GBP	EUR	12/3/2019	1.17109
USD	EUR	12/15/2019	0.90138
USD	GBP	12/15/2019	0.76851
EUR	USD	12/15/2019	1.10654
EUR	GBP	12/15/2019	0.85117
GBP	USD	12/15/2019	1.29296
GBP	EUR	12/15/2019	1.17109
USD	EUR	12/27/2019	0.90361
USD	GBP	12/27/2019	0.77332

EUR	USD	12/27/2019	1.10929
EUR	GBP	12/27/2019	0.85639
GBP	USD	12/27/2019	1.30102
GBP	EUR	12/27/2019	1.17109

4. Use an **Enter Data** query to create a table called `R08_Sales` that contains the following information:

Date	Currency	Amount
12/3/2019	USD	100
12/4/2019	EUR	100
12/5/2019	GBP	100
12/15/2019	USD	200
12/22/2019	EUR	200
12/24/2019	GBP	200
12/27/2019	USD	300
12/28/2019	EUR	300
12/29/2019	GBP	300

5. Ensure that there are no relationships between these three tables.

It is important to note that currency exchange rates are not purely reciprocal. In other words, it is not necessarily correct that if the currency exchange rate between USD and EUR is .9 then the exchange rate between EUR and USD is 1 + (1 - .9) or 1.1. Exchange rates are actually slightly different when selling a currency or buying a currency between the same conversion currency. This is the reason why our currency exchange rate table requires two rows per currency exchange pair: one for converting from a given currency to a different given currency and the reverse.

How to do it...

To implement this recipe, do the following:

1. Create the following measures:

```
Reporting Amount =
    VAR __ReportingCurrency =
SELECTEDVALUE('R08_Currencies'[Currency])
```

```
VAR __SalesCurrency = MAX('R08_Sales'[Currency])
VAR __SalesDate = MAX('R08_Sales'[Date])
VAR __SalesAmount = SUM('R08_Sales'[Amount])
VAR __ExchangeRateDate =
    MAXX(
        FILTER(
            'R08_Rates',
                'R08_Rates'[Date] <= __SalesDate &&
                    'R08_Rates'[From] = __SalesCurrency &&
                        'R08_Rates'[To] = __ReportingCurrency
        ),
        'R08_Rates'[Date]
    )
VAR __ExchangeRate =
    IF(__SalesCurrency = __ReportingCurrency,
        1,
        MAXX(
            FILTER(
                'R08_Rates',
                'R08_Rates'[Date] = __ExchangeRateDate &&
                    'R08_Rates'[From] = __SalesCurrency &&
                        'R08_Rates'[To] = __ReportingCurrency
            ),
            'R08_Rates'[Rate]
        )
    )
RETURN
    __ExchangeRate * __SalesAmount

Reporting Amount Total =
    IF(HASONEVALUE('R08_Sales'[Date]),
        [Reporting Amount],
        SUMX(
            SUMMARIZE(
                'R08_Sales',
                'R08_Sales'[Date],
                'R08_Sales'[Currency],
                "__Reporting Amount",
                [Reporting Amount]
            ),
            [__Reporting Amount]
        )
    )
```

2. On a **Report** page, create a **Slicer** visualization and place the `Currency` column from the `R08_Currencies` table into the **Field** area of the visualization.

3. On the same **Report** page, create a **Table** visualization and place the `Date`, `Currency`, and `Amount` columns from the `R08_Sales` table, as well as the `Reporting Amount Total` measure, into the **Values** area of the visualization.

4. Use the **Slicer** visualization to change the reporting currency. Note how the `Reporting Amount Total` measure values change in the table visualization.

How it works...

The `Reporting Amount` measure begins by getting the currency selected in the slicer and storing this value in the `__ReportingCurrency` variable. Next, we get the current `Currency` and `Date` and store these values in `__SalesCurrency` and `__SalesDate`, respectively. Then, we get the sum of the amount of sales in `R08_Sales` and store that in the `__SalesAmount` variable. Now, we want to determine the date in our `R08_Rates` table so that we can use it as the effective date for our rate conversion, `__ExchangeRateDate`. To do this, we filter the `R08_Rates` table for all the values that have a `To` column value equal to our `__ReportingCurrency` variable, a `From` column value equal to our `__SalesCurrency` variable, and a `Date` column value that is less than or equal to our `__SalesDate` variable.

Then, we take the maximum value of the `Date` column for this filtered table using `MAXX` since we desire the most current exchange rate for each given sale. Once we know `__ExchangeRateDate`, we can use the same technique to calculate `__ExchangeRate`. However, first, we check to see whether `__SalesCurrency` and `__ReportingCurrency` are equal. If so, then `__ExchangeRate` should be 1. Otherwise, we calculate `__ExchangeRate` by essentially looking up the specified value in our `R08_Rates` table for the specified `__ReportingCurrency`, `__SalesCurrency`, and `__ExchangeRateDate` variables. Finally, we can `RETURN` our `__SalesAmount` multiplied by `__ExchangeRate` to return the `__SalesAmount` variable, which was converted into `__ReportingCurrency`.

The `Reporting Amount Total` measure addresses the common issue of measure totals in tables. The `Reporting Amount Total` measure uses `HASONVALUE` to determine whether the measurement context is an individual row within the table visualization or a total row. If it's an individual row, then the value to be displayed is simply the `Reporting Amount` measure. However, if the context is a total row, then the calculation summarizes the `R08_Sales` table by `Date` and `Currency`, adds `Reporting Amount` as the `__Reporting Amount` column, and then uses `SUMX` to sum the `__Reporting Amount` column.

See also

For more details regarding the functions in this recipe, please refer to the following links:

- Currency Converter: `https://www1.oanda.com/currency/converter/`
- MAX: `https://docs.microsoft.com/en-us/dax/max-function-dax`
- SUM: `https://docs.microsoft.com/en-us/dax/sum-function-dax`
- SELECTEDVALUE: `https://docs.microsoft.com/en-us/dax/selectedvalue-function-dax`
- MAXX: `https://docs.microsoft.com/en-us/dax/maxx-function-dax`
- FILTER: `https://docs.microsoft.com/en-us/dax/filter-function-dax`
- IF: `https://docs.microsoft.com/en-us/dax/if-function-dax`
- SUMX: `https://docs.microsoft.com/en-us/dax/sumx-function-dax`
- SUMMARIZE: `https://docs.microsoft.com/en-us/dax/summarize-function-dax`
- HASONEVALUE: `https://docs.microsoft.com/en-us/dax/hasonevalue-function-dax`

Assessing days sales outstanding

Days sales outstanding measures the average number of days required to collect the payment for sales made on credit. Thus, days sales outstanding is an indicator of the cash flow for an organization. A high days sales outstanding figure indicates that a business is taking longer to collect payment for sales compared to a business with a low days outstanding figure. Days sales outstanding is often calculated at the monthly, quarterly, and yearly calendar scales.

This recipe demonstrates how to calculate days sales outstanding for an organization.

Getting ready

To prepare for this recipe, do the following:

1. Open Power BI Desktop.

2. Use an **Enter Data** query to create a table called R09_Table that contains the following information:

Year	Quarter	Month	Category	Value
2020	Q1	1	Accounts Receivable	15,000
2020	Q1	1	Net Credit Sales	30,000
2020	Q1	2	Accounts Receivable	10,000
2020	Q1	2	Net Credit Sales	30,000
2020	Q1	3	Accounts Receivable	25,000
2020	Q1	3	Net Credit Sales	60,000
2020	Q2	4	Accounts Receivable	20,000
2020	Q2	4	Net Credit Sales	40,000
2020	Q2	5	Accounts Receivable	15,000
2020	Q2	5	Net Credit Sales	20,000
2020	Q2	6	Accounts Receivable	60,000
2020	Q2	6	Net Credit Sales	100,000
2020	Q3	7	Accounts Receivable	20,000
2020	Q3	7	Net Credit Sales	100,000
2020	Q3	8	Accounts Receivable	50,000
2020	Q3	8	Net Credit Sales	100,000
2020	Q3	9	Accounts Receivable	40,000
2020	Q3	9	Net Credit Sales	80,000
2020	Q4	10	Accounts Receivable	30,000
2020	Q4	10	Net Credit Sales	60,000
2020	Q4	11	Accounts Receivable	15,000
2020	Q4	11	Net Credit Sales	30,000
2020	Q4	12	Accounts Receivable	20,000
2020	Q4	12	Net Credit Sales	30,000

How to do it...

To implement this recipe, do the following:

1. Create the following measure:

```
Days Sales Outstanding (Month) =
    VAR __Year = MAX('R09_Table'[Year])
    VAR __Month = MAX('R09_Table'[Month])
    VAR __BeginDate = DATE(__Year , __Month , 1)
    VAR __EndDate = EOMONTH(__BeginDate, 0)
    VAR __Days = DATEDIFF(__BeginDate, __EndDate, DAY) + 1
    VAR __AR =
        SUMX(
            FILTER(
                'R09_Table',
                'R09_Table'[Category] = "Accounts Receivable"
            ),
            'R09_Table'[Value]
        )
    VAR __Credit =
        SUMX(
            FILTER(
                'R09_Table',
                'R09_Table'[Category] = "Net Credit Sales"
            ),
            'R09_Table'[Value]
        )
RETURN
    DIVIDE(__AR, __Credit, 0) * __Days
```

2. On a **Report** page, create a **Matrix** visualization and add the `Month` column from the `R09_Table` table to the **Rows** area of the visualization, as well as the `Days Sales Outstanding (Month)` measure, to the **Values** area of the visualization.

How it works...

The formula for days sales outstanding is as follows:

$$AccountsReceivable \div TotalCreditSales \times NumberOfDays$$

It is important to note that *AccountsReceivable* is the balance of the accounts receivable at the end of the reporting period. Conversely, *TotalCreditSales* is the total of all credit sales made within the reporting period. Finally, *NumberofDays* is the total number of days within the reporting period.

To implement days sales outstanding in DAX at the month scale, we start by retrieving the current values for the `Year` and `Month` columns from the `R09_Table` table within the current context. These become our working values for `__Year` and `__Month`, respectively.

Since we need to know the number of days within the reporting period, we can do this by creating `__BeginDate` using the `DATE` function and providing the parameters of our working `__Year` and `__Month` and the first day of every month, `1`. Then, we can get our `__EndDate` by using the `EOMONTH` function, where we specify a starting date of `__BeginDate` and the number of months offset to `0`. To get the number of days within the reporting period, we simply need to use `DATEDIFF` to return the difference between `__BeginDate` and `__EndDate` at the granularity of `DAY` and then add `1`.

Next, we need to calculate our accounts receivable, `__AR`. Since our visualization is at the lowest granularity of our source table, `R09_Table`, we simply need to use `FILTER` to extract the row with a `Category` column equal to `Accounts Receivable` and return an aggregation of the row. In this case, we use `SUMX`. We use an identical pattern to return our total credit sales, `__Credit`, except that we filter rows for `Net Credit Sales` instead of `Accounts Receivable`.

Finally, we simply need to implement the formula for days sales outstanding in our `RETURN` statement.

There's more...

As denoted by its name, the `Days Sales Outstanding (Month)` measure only works at the month scale for computing the correct values for days sales outstanding. This formula does not work at the quarter and year scales. To construct a days sales outstanding formula that works at the monthly, quarterly, and yearly scales, do the following:

1. Create a measure using the following formula:

```
Days Sales Outstanding =
    VAR __Year = MAX('R09_Table'[Year])
    VAR __Month = MAX('R09_Table'[Month])
    VAR __Quarter = MAX('R09_Table'[Quarter])
    VAR __BeginDate =
        SWITCH(TRUE(),
```

```
                ISINSCOPE('R09_Table'[Month]), DATE(__Year , __Month ,
1),
                ISINSCOPE('R09_Table'[Quarter]),
                    SWITCH(__Quarter,
                        "Q1", DATE(__Year, 1, 1),
                        "Q2", DATE(__Year, 4, 1),
                        "Q3", DATE(__Year, 7, 1),
                        "Q4", DATE(__Year, 10, 1)
                    ),
                ISINSCOPE('R09_Table'[Quarter]),DATE(__Year, 1, 1),
                DATE(MIN('R09_Table'[Year]),1,1)
        )
    VAR __EndDate =
        SWITCH(TRUE(),
            ISINSCOPE('R09_Table'[Month]), EOMONTH(__BeginDate, 0),
            ISINSCOPE('R09_Table'[Quarter]), EOMONTH(DATE(__Year,
__Month, 1), 0),
            DATE(__Year, 12, 31)
        )
    VAR __Days = DATEDIFF(__BeginDate, __EndDate, DAY) + 1
    VAR __AR =
        SUMX(
            FILTER(
                'R09_Table',
                'R09_Table'[Category] = "Accounts Receivable" &&
                    'R09_Table'[Year] = __Year &&
                        'R09_Table'[Month] = __Month
            ),
            'R09_Table'[Value]
        )
    VAR __Credit =
        SUMX(
            FILTER(
                'R09_Table',
                'R09_Table'[Category] = "Net Credit Sales"
            ),
            'R09_Table'[Value]
        )
RETURN
    DIVIDE(__AR, __Credit, 0) * __Days
```

2. On a **Report** page, create a **Matrix** visualization and add the `Year`, `Quarter`, and `Month` columns from the `R09_Table` table to the **Rows** area of the visualization. Ensure that `Year` is at the top, `Quarter` is second, and `Month` is last. Now, add the `Days Sales Outstanding (Month)` and `Days Sales Outstanding` measures to the **Values** area of the visualization.

3. Right-click the **Year 2020** in the visualization and choose **Expand** and then **All.**

This version of the formula changes how `__BeginDate`, `__EndDate`, and `__AR` are calculated. For `__BeginDate`, we use a `SWITCH` statement with the `TRUE` DAX function as its first parameter. This version of the `SWITCH` statement means that our conditions are DAX expressions that return either `TRUE` or `FALSE`. For the first condition, we check to see whether the `Month` column is currently in scope using the `ISINSCOPE` function. If so, we use the same formula as before for calculating `__BeginDate`. Next, we check to see if the `Quarter` column `ISINSCOPE`. If so, we use a second `SWITCH` statement based on the `Quarter` column and return the appropriate starting date for each quarter. Then, we check whether the `Year` column `ISINSCOPE` and if so, we return the beginning date of that year. Finally, if the `Month`, `Quarter`, or `Year` columns are not in scope, then we know that we are in a total row within the matrix and we default to returning the beginning date of the entire minimum year within the current context.

The order for the `SWITCH` statement is important when using `ISINSCOPE`. It is important to remember that when at the `Month` granularity level of the matrix visualization, the `Year`, `Quarter`, and `Month` columns are all in the scope of the `ISINSCOPE` function. However, at the `Quarter` granularity level, only the `Quarter` and `Year` columns are in the scope of the `ISINSCOPE` function, while when at the `Year` granularity level, only the `Year` column is in the scope of the `ISINSCOPE` function. Thus, it is imperative that we check whether the `Month` column `ISINSCOPE`, then check whether the `Quarter` column `ISINSCOPE`, and finally check whether the `Year` column `ISINSCOPE`. If we were to reverse these checks, then all of the rows in our matrix would get a `__BeginDate` value at the beginning of the year.

Calculating __EndDate is similar to calculating __BeginDate. We use a SWITCH statement with the TRUE DAX function as its first parameter. If the Month column ISINSCOPE, we use the same calculation to determine the end date of the month as our previous formula. If the Quarter column ISINSCOPE, we can use the EOMONTH function coupled with a DATE value derived from our __Year and __Month and the first day of every month, 1. This works because our __Month variable uses the MAX aggregation and thus we are assured that we are in the last month of our quarter! Finally, we can default to the last day of the current working year provided by __Year since our calculation for this variable also uses the MAX function. This assures us that we are calculating the last day of the last year within the current context.

Finally, our __AR calculation changes slightly since we only want the current accounts receivable for the latest date within context, and since we are using the MAX aggregation for both __Year and __Month, we can use the FILTER function to filter down to the correct row in our table.

See also

For more details regarding the functions in this recipe, please refer to the following links:

- **Days Sales Outstanding Definition:** https://www.investopedia.com/terms/d/dso.asp
- MAX: https://docs.microsoft.com/en-us/dax/max-function-dax
- EOMONTH: https://docs.microsoft.com/en-us/dax/eomonth-function-dax
- DATE: https://docs.microsoft.com/en-us/dax/date-function-dax
- DATEDIFF: https://docs.microsoft.com/en-us/dax/datediff-function-dax
- SUMX: https://docs.microsoft.com/en-us/dax/sumx-function-dax
- FILTER: https://docs.microsoft.com/en-us/dax/filter-function-dax
- SWITCH: https://docs.microsoft.com/en-us/dax/switch-function-dax
- ISINSCOPE: https://docs.microsoft.com/en-us/dax/isinscope-function-dax

Computing Customer KPIs 6

Customers are critical to most businesses. Without customers to buy goods and services, for-profit businesses would quickly go bankrupt and close their doors. Even charities and not-for-profit businesses, in essence, have customers in the form of donors that provide funding for the organization. Thus, it makes sense that most businesses would like to become smarter about metrics that assist with such things as tracking customer behavior, analyzing the most effective methods of acquiring customers, and identifying the most valuable customers. This chapter is all about customer metrics and KPIs. Many useful recipes are included to assist in analyzing the process by which new customers are acquired, when customers leave, which customers are advocates for the business, and how much it costs to acquire customers.

The following is the list of recipes that we will cover in this chapter:

- Crafting a funnel drop-off rate
- Finding new and returning customers
- Identifying lost and recovered customers
- Creating a Net Promoter Score
- Analyzing customer churn rate
- Calculating the customer lifetime value
- Computing the customer acquisition cost

Technical requirements

The following are required to complete all of the recipes in this chapter:

- Power BI Desktop
- **GitHub repository:** https://github.com/PacktPublishing/DAX-Cookbook/tree/master/Chapter06

Crafting a funnel drop-off rate

The funnel drop-off rate is a metric often used in e-commerce, particularly with a web-based purchasing process involving a shopping cart. During this process, there are generally multiple steps involved for a customer to ultimately purchase a product. For example, the customer must add the desired products to their shopping cart. Then the customer must visit the shopping cart and check out. The check-out process involves steps to enter payment information and potentially other information such as a shipping address. Finally, the customer must confirm the purchase. At any point along this conversion process, the customer may end the purchase and discontinue the process. Analyzing the funnel drop-off rate can help identify steps in the process that are causing customers to discontinue engagement and are thus areas of focus for improvement.

This recipe demonstrates how to calculate a funnel drop-off rate with respect to an e-commerce purchasing process involving a shopping cart and payment. However, the same techniques can be used to analyze any multi-step customer engagement process.

Getting ready

To prepare for this recipe, do the following:

1. Open Power BI Desktop.
2. Create a table called `R01_Table` using the following formula:

```
R01_Table =
UNION(
    ADDCOLUMNS(
        GENERATESERIES(1,10000,1),
        "Page",
        "Product",
        "Step",
        1
    ),
    ADDCOLUMNS(
        GENERATESERIES(1,7000,1),
        "Page",
        "Add to Shopping Cart",
        "Step",
        2
    ),
    ADDCOLUMNS(
        GENERATESERIES(1,2000,1),
        "Page",
```

```
        "Payment",
         "Step",
        3
    ),
    ADDCOLUMNS (
        GENERATESERIES(1,1200,1),
        "Page",
        "Confirmation",
        "Step",
        4
    )
)
```

How to do it...

To craft a funnel drop-off rate, do the following:

1. Create the following measure:

```
Drop Off Rate =
    VAR __CurrentStep = MAX([Step])
    VAR __PreviousStep = __CurrentStep - 1
    VAR __CurrentCount = COUNTROWS('R01_Table')
    VAR __PreviousCount =
        IF(
            __CurrentStep = 1 ,
            0 ,
            COUNTROWS(FILTER(ALL('R01_Table'),[Step] =
__PreviousStep ))
        )
RETURN
    DIVIDE(__CurrentCount - __PreviousCount, __PreviousCount, 0)
```

2. Format Drop Off Rate as a percentage.
3. On a report page, create a **Funnel** visualization and place the Page column from R01_Table into the **Group** area of the visualization.
4. In the same visualization, place the Page column from R01_Table into the **Values** area of the visualization and ensure that the summarization is set to Count.
5. In the same visualization, place the Drop Off Rate measure into the **Tooltips** area of the visualization.

How it works...

This recipe computes a simple percentage of the number of customers in the current step of the process versus the number of customers in the previous step of the process. To accomplish this, the first line gets the current step of the process in context and stores this value in the __CurrentStep variable. The next line computes the previous step of the process and stores this in the __PreviousStep variable. Note that in this recipe, the steps have been numbered and thus it is simple to compute the identity of the previous step. In more complex data models, this computation may need to have increased complexity and involve an IF, SWITCH, or even LOOKUPVALUE DAX function.

Once the current and previous steps are identified, the number of customers that made it to the current step of the process are computed using the COUNTROWS DAX function and stored in the __CurrentCount variable. The number of customers in the previous process, __PreviousCount, is computed by first checking to see whether __CurrentStep is 1. In this case, there is no previous step of the process, so __PreviousCount is set to 0. Otherwise, the number of customers in the previous step can be computed by using FILTER combined with ALL to filter all of the rows in the table that are identified as the previous step and then using COUNTROWS to determine the number of customers.

Once the counts of customers are computed, the DIVIDE function is used to calculate a simple percentage of the customers in the previous step that did not make it to the current step.

There's more...

The terms **funnel drop-off rate** and **funnel abandonment rate** are often used interchangeably. In addition, this metric can be calculated in one of two ways. One method, as demonstrated previously, is to compute the percentage of customers in a step that does not make it to the next step. Another method is to compute the percentage of customers at the beginning of the process that does not make it to each step along the process. The following measure demonstrates how to calculate this second version of the funnel drop-off rate:

```
Abandonment Rate =
    VAR __CurrentStep = MAX([Step])
    VAR __PreviousStep = 1
    VAR __CurrentCount = COUNTROWS('R01_Table')
    VAR __PreviousCount =
        COUNTROWS(FILTER(ALL('R01_Table'),[Step] = __PreviousStep ))
RETURN
    DIVIDE(__CurrentCount - __PreviousCount, __PreviousCount, 0)
```

See also

For more details on the functions in this recipe, refer to the following links:

- **Funnel drop-off/abandonment rate:** https://www.rohankapooronline.com/2008/01/funnel-drop-offabandonment-rate.html
- MAX: https://docs.microsoft.com/en-us/dax/max-function-dax
- COUNTROWS: https://docs.microsoft.com/en-us/dax/countrows-function-dax
- DIVIDE: https://docs.microsoft.com/en-us/dax/divide-function-dax
- FILTER: https://docs.microsoft.com/en-us/dax/filter-function-dax
- ALL: https://docs.microsoft.com/en-us/dax/all-function-dax

Finding new and returning customers

The number of new and returning customers can be important business metrics. New customers are defined as customers making purchases in a specified time period that have never purchased in prior time periods, and returning customers are defined as customers making purchases in a specified time period that have purchased in previous time periods. Understanding how many customers return to make subsequent purchases helps a business understand whether or not they have a customer loyalty issue. This is highly important because retaining customers is generally considered far easier than attracting new customers. In addition, tracking new customers can be an important measure of how well a business is marketing its products and services.

This recipe demonstrates how to calculate new and returning customers using DAX.

Getting ready

To prepare for this recipe, do the following:

1. Open Power BI Desktop.
2. Use an **Enter Data** query to create a table called R02_Table with the following data:

Date	Customer
3/1/2015	1
12/1/2016	1
6/1/2017	2

8/1/2017	2
9/1/2017	2
1/1/2018	3
3/1/2018	3
1/1/2019	4
3/1/2019	5
8/1/2019	4
9/1/2019	3
9/1/2019	2
9/1/2019	5
9/1/2019	4
9/1/2019	6
9/1/2019	6

3. Create the following columns in `R02_Table`:

```
Month Name = FORMAT([Date],"mmmm")
Year = YEAR([Date])
Month = MONTH([Date])
```

4. Create the following measure:

```
Customers = COUNTROWS(VALUES('R02_Table'[Customer]))
```

5. On a **Report** page, create a matrix visualization with the `Month Name` column as `Rows`, the `Year` column as `Columns`, and the `Customers` measure as `Values`.

6. Set the `Sort by` column for the `Month Name` column to the `Month` column.

How to do it...

Finding new and returning customers can be done as follows:

1. Create the following measures:

```
Returning Customers =
    VAR __Month = MAX('R02_Table'[Month])
    VAR __Year = MAX('R02_Table'[Year])
    VAR __PreviousCustomers =
        DISTINCT(
            SELECTCOLUMNS(
```

```
                    FILTER(
                        ALL('R02_Table'),
                        [Date] < DATE(__Year,__Month,1)
                    ),
                    "__Customer",[Customer]
                )
            )
    VAR __CurrentCustomers =
        DISTINCT(
            SELECTCOLUMNS(
                'R02_Table',
                "__Customer",[Customer]
            )
        )
    VAR __Count =
        COUNTROWS(
            INTERSECT(
                __PreviousCustomers,
                __CurrentCustomers
            )
        )
RETURN
    IF( ISBLANK(__Count), 0, __Count)

New Customers = [Customers] - [Returning Customers]
```

2. On a **Report** page, copy and paste the matrix visualization created earlier and replace the Customers measure in Values with the Returning Customers measure.

3. On the same **Report** page, copy and paste the matrix visualization created earlier and replace the Customers measure in Values with the New Customers measure.

How it works...

The data in the R02_Table fact table represents sample data for something like an e-commerce website where purchases are intermittent as opposed to something like a monthly or yearly subscription service.

For returning customers, the first two lines simply store the values for the month and year within the current context. This context is provided by the rows and columns of the matrix visualization.

The next step is to store the distinct values for all customers in previous months and years in the __PreviousCustomers variable. We do this by changing the context to all rows in our R03_Table fact table using the ALL function. We then use the FILTER function to get all of the rows in the table prior to the current month and year. We then use SELECTCOLUMNS to select the Customer column. Finally, we use the DISTINCT function to return only the unique values. We use an identical process to return current customers in the __CurrentCustomers variable, except that no filtering is necessary since the rows for current customers are already in context.

Once we know the values for all previous customers and current customers, we can compute returning customers and store these in the __ReturningCustomers variable. To do this, we use INTERSECT.

Note that to identify returning customers, you may be tempted to use the EXCEPT DAX function. The EXCEPT DAX function returns the rows in the table specified in the first parameter that are not in the table specified in the second parameter. However, if we used the __CurrentCustomers variable as the first parameter and __PreviousCustomers as the second parameter, we would get both new customers and not returning customers. Conversely, if we used __PreviousCustomers as the first parameter and __CurrentCustomers as the second parameter, we would get a table of non-returning customers.

Once we know the returning customers for a month, we can simply calculate new customers by subtracting the number of returning customers in a month from the total number of customers in a month.

There's more...

If we were to independently create a measure for new customers without already having a returning customers measure, it would look like this:

```
New Customers Alt =
    VAR __Month = MAX('R02_Table'[Month])
    VAR __Year = MAX('R02_Table'[Year])
    VAR __PreviousCustomers =
        DISTINCT(
            SELECTCOLUMNS(
                FILTER(
                    ALL('R02_Table'),
                    [Date] < DATE(__Year,__Month,1)
                ),
```

```
            "__Customer",[Customer]
        )
    )
VAR __CurrentCustomers =
    DISTINCT(
        SELECTCOLUMNS(
            'R02_Table',
            "__Customer",[Customer]
        )
    )
VAR __NewCustomers = EXCEPT(__CurrentCustomers, __PreviousCustomers)
VAR __Count = COUNTROWS(__NewCustomers)
RETURN
    IF( ISBLANK(__Count), 0, __Count)
```

See also

For more details on the functions in this recipe, refer to the following links:

- MAX: https://docs.microsoft.com/en-us/dax/max-function-dax
- COUNTROWS: https://docs.microsoft.com/en-us/dax/countrows-function-dax
- DISTINCT: https://docs.microsoft.com/en-us/dax/distinct-function-dax
- SELECTCOLUMNS: https://docs.microsoft.com/en-us/dax/distinct-function-dax
- FILTER: https://docs.microsoft.com/en-us/dax/filter-function-dax
- ALL: https://docs.microsoft.com/en-us/dax/all-function-dax
- ADDCOLUMNS: https://docs.microsoft.com/en-us/dax/addcolumns-function-dax
- TRUE: https://docs.microsoft.com/en-us/dax/true-function-dax
- ISBLANK: https://docs.microsoft.com/en-us/dax/isblank-function-dax
- IN: https://docs.microsoft.com/en-us/dax/in-function
- INTERSECT: https://docs.microsoft.com/en-us/dax/intersect-function

Identifying lost and recovered customers

The number of lost and recovered customers can be important business metrics. Lost customers are defined as customers who previously made purchases but have made no subsequent purchases within a specified amount of time.

Recovered customers are customers that made a purchase, made no subsequent purchases within a specified range of time, and then subsequently made an additional purchase after being considered lost. Understanding how many customers are lost helps a business understand and measure their customer retention, while tracking recovered customers can be an important measure of a business' customer outreach or marketing program.

This recipe demonstrates how to calculate lost and recovered customers using DAX.

Getting ready

To prepare for this recipe, do the following:

1. Open Power BI Desktop.
2. Use an **Enter Data** query to create a table called `R03_Table` with the following data:

Date	Customer
3/1/2015	1
12/1/2016	1
6/1/2017	2
8/1/2017	2
9/1/2017	2
1/1/2018	3
3/1/2018	3
1/1/2019	4
3/1/2019	5
8/1/2019	4
9/1/2019	3
9/1/2019	2
9/1/2019	5
9/1/2019	4
9/1/2019	6
9/1/2019	6

3. Create the following columns in R03_Table:

```
Month Name = FORMAT([Date],"mmmm")
Year = YEAR([Date])
Month = MONTH([Date])
```

4. Create the following table, R03_Dates:

```
R03_Dates =
    SELECTCOLUMNS(
        GENERATESERIES(
            MIN('R03_Table'[Date]),
            MAX('R03_Table'[Date]),
            1
        ),
        "Date",
        [Value]
    )
```

5. Create the following columns in R03_Dates:

```
Month Name = FORMAT([Date],"mmmm")
Year = YEAR([Date])
Month = MONTH([Date])
```

6. Ensure that the R03_Table and R03_Dates tables are not related to one another.

How to do it...

To implement this recipe, do the following:

1. Create the following measures:

```
Lost Customers =
    VAR __Threshold = 1
    VAR __ThresholdUnit = "YEARS"
    VAR __Month = MAX('R03_Dates'[Month])
    VAR __Year = MAX('R03_Dates'[Year])
    VAR __MonthStart = DATE(__Year, __Month, 1)
    VAR __MonthEnd = MAX('R03_Dates'[Date])
    VAR __PreviousCustomers =
        SUMMARIZE(
            FILTER(
                'R03_Table',
                [Date] < __MonthEnd
            ),
```

```
            [Customer],
            "__LastPurchase",MAX([Date])
        )
    VAR __PreviousCustomers1 =
        ADDCOLUMNS(
            __PreviousCustomers,
            "__LostDate",
            SWITCH(
                __ThresholdUnit,
                "DAYS",[__LastPurchase] + __Threshold,
                "MONTHS",EOMONTH([__LastPurchase],__Threshold),
                "YEARS",DATE(YEAR([__LastPurchase]) +
__Threshold,MONTH([__LastPurchase]),1)
            )
        )
    VAR __LostCustomers =
        DISTINCT(
            SELECTCOLUMNS(
                FILTER(
                    __PreviousCustomers1,
                    MONTH([__LostDate]) = __Month &&
                        YEAR([__LostDate]) = __Year),
                "__Customer",[Customer]
            )
        )
    RETURN
        COUNTROWS(__LostCustomers)
```

2. Create the `Recovered Customers` measure using the code in
   the `R03_RecoveredCustomers.txt` text file located in the GitHub repository.

3. On a **Report** page, create a matrix visualization and place the `Month Name`
   column from `R03_Dates` into the **Rows** area, the `Year` column from `R03_Dates`
   into the **Columns** area, and the `Lost Customers` measure into the **Values** area.

4. On a report page, create a matrix visualization and place the `Month Name`
   column from `R03_Dates` into the **Rows** area, the `Year` column from `R03_Dates`
   into the **Columns** area, and the `Recovered Customers` measure into the **Values**
   area.

How it works...

The data in the R03_Table fact table represents sample data for something like an e-commerce website where purchases are intermittent, as opposed to something like a monthly or yearly subscription service.

For the Lost Customers measure, the first two lines define the number threshold increments, __Threshold, as well as the threshold interval unit, __ThresholdUnit. Together, these define the period of time from a customer's last purchase, after which a customer is considered lost. This recipe supports any number for the value of __Threshold and the values DAYS, MONTHS, or YEARS for the value of __ThresholdUnit.

The next four lines simply collect information with regard to the current context within which the measure is performing its calculation and stores these in the __Month, __Year, __MonthStart, and __MonthEnd variables.

The next calculation is to create a table variable called __PreviousCustomers. This calculation uses FILTER to return the rows within the R03_Table fact table for all purchases made in all previous months. Note that the use of ALL or ALLEXCEPT is not required here because the matrix visualization uses the MonthName and Year columns from the R03_Dates table and the R03_Dates table is not related to R03_Table. The SUMMARIZE function is used to create a unique row for each customer and add the __LastPurchase column, whose value becomes the date of the last purchase date by that customer.

We continue to build upon our __PreviousCustomers table variable by using ADDCOLUMNS to add the __LostDate column and store this revised table in the __PreviousCustomers1 variable. While we could have combined these two steps into a single variable calculation, it is easier to understand, maintain, and modify the code with separate calculations for each step. The __LostDate column calculation is based upon the __ThresholdUnit value specified earlier. If DAYS is specified, we simply need to add the __Threshold variable to the LastPurchase column to arrive at the date upon which the customer is considered lost. If MONTHS is specified, we use the EOMONTH function to add the number of months specified by the __Threshold variable to our LastPurchase date. Finally, if YEARS is specified, we can construct LostDate by using the DATE function and adding the __Threshold variable to the YEAR of our LastPurchase date.

We can now compute a table of values for lost customers, __LostCustomers, by using the FILTER function to return only the rows in __PreviousCustomers1 whose LostDate has the same month, __Month, and year, __Year, as the current context provided by the matrix visualization. We use SELECTCOLUMNS to select only the Customers column and then use DISTINCT to only return unique values. We then simply need to return the number of rows in the __LostCustomers table variable using the COUNTROWS function.

For Recovered Customers, the first portion of the formula is nearly identical to Lost Customers. There is one difference in the calculation of the __PreviousCustomers variable, which is to include the date of a customer's first purchase in the __FirstPurchase column. Similarly, there is a slight difference in the calculation of the __PreviousCustomers1 variable, where we use FILTER to remove the rows for customers whose first purchase, __FirstPurchase, is in the current month under consideration. The calculation for the __LostCustomers variable is identical to the calculation in the Lost Customers measure.

Next, we need to identify the current customers within the month and year in question. We do this using FILTER, SELECTCOLUMNS, and DISTINCT to return a table that contains the unique values of customers who made purchases between the start of the month, __MonthStart, and the end of the month, _MonthEnd.

Once we know the values for all lost customers and current customers, we can compute recovered customers and store these in the __RecoveredCustomers variable. To do this, we use ADDCOLUMNS to add the __IsCurrent column to our __LostCustomers table variable. For the value of the __IsCurrent column, we check to see whether the customer specified in the __Customer column for the current row is in the __CurrentCustomers table. We do this using the IN function. The IN function returns true if the specified value is in a specified column of a table, and false if it is not.

Once we have identified rows in the __LostCustomers table variable that are also in the __CurrentCustomers table variable, we can simply use COUNTROWS to count the rows in __RecoveredCustomers where the __IsCurrent column is true and return this as the value for the measure.

See also

For more details on the functions in this recipe, refer to the following links:

- MAX: https://docs.microsoft.com/en-us/dax/max-function-dax
- MIN: https://docs.microsoft.com/en-us/dax/min-function-dax

- MONTH: https://docs.microsoft.com/en-us/dax/month-function-dax
- YEAR: https://docs.microsoft.com/en-us/dax/year-function-dax
- DATE: https://docs.microsoft.com/en-us/dax/date-function-dax
- SWITCH: https://docs.microsoft.com/en-us/dax/switch-function-dax
- EOMONTH: https://docs.microsoft.com/en-us/dax/eomonth-function-dax
- SUMMARIZE: https://docs.microsoft.com/en-us/dax/summarize-function-dax
- COUNTROWS: https://docs.microsoft.com/en-us/dax/countrows-function-dax
- DISTINCT: https://docs.microsoft.com/en-us/dax/distinct-function-dax
- SELECTCOLUMNS: https://docs.microsoft.com/en-us/dax/distinct-function-dax
- FILTER: https://docs.microsoft.com/en-us/dax/filter-function-dax
- ALL: https://docs.microsoft.com/en-us/dax/all-function-dax
- ADDCOLUMNS: https://docs.microsoft.com/en-us/dax/addcolumns-function-dax
- TRUE: https://docs.microsoft.com/en-us/dax/true-function-dax
- ISBLANK: https://docs.microsoft.com/en-us/dax/isblank-function-dax
- IN: https://docs.microsoft.com/en-us/dax/in-function

Creating a Net Promoter Score

The **Net Promoter Score (NPS)** is a metric that is based on responses to the question, "*How likely is it that you would recommend our company/product/service to a friend or colleague?*" The response to this question is generally scored on a scale from 0 to 10, with 0 being highly unlikely and 10 being very likely. The NPS is a registered trademark of Fred Reichheld, Bain & Company, and Satmetrix.

Responses to the question are categorized into the following groups:

- 0 - 6: Detractors
- 7 - 8: Passives
- 9 - 10: Promoters

The formula used for the NPS subtracts the percentage of detractors from the percentage of promoters and returns a value from -100 to 100.

This recipe demonstrates how to calculate the NPS using DAX.

Getting ready

To prepare for this recipe, do the following:

1. Open Power BI Desktop.
2. Use an **Enter Data** query to create a table called `R04_Table` with the following data:

Response	Score
1	9
2	9
3	6
4	8
5	10
6	9
7	9
8	7
9	9
10	10

How to do it...

Create a measure using the following formula:

```
NPS =
    VAR __TotalResponses = COUNTROWS('R04_Table')
    VAR __Detractors = COUNTROWS(FILTER('R04_Table',[Score] <= 6))
    VAR __Promoters = COUNTROWS(FILTER('R04_Table',[Score] >= 9))
    VAR __PercentDetractors = DIVIDE(__Detractors, __TotalResponses, 0)
    VAR __PercentPromoters = DIVIDE(__Promoters, __TotalResponses, 0)
RETURN
    (__PercentPromoters - __PercentDetractors) * 100
```

How it works...

We start by first counting all of the responses provided by customers in R04_Table by simply using the COUNTROWS function and storing this count in the __TotalResponses variable. Next, we determine the number of detractors by using FILTER to select only the responses where the rating, Score, is less than or equal to 6, using COUNTROWS to count the number of filtered rows and storing this count in the __Detractors variable. Similarly, we calculate the number of promoters, but, this time, we filter the records where Score is greater than or equal to 9 and store this count in the __Promoters variable.

We can now calculate the percentages of detractors and promoters by simply dividing __Detractors and __Promoters by __TotalResponses. We store these calculations in the __PercentDetractors and __PercentPromoters variables respectively. Finally, we subtract __PercentDetractors from __PercentPromoters and multiply the result by 100 to return the NPS.

See also

For more details on the functions in this recipe, refer to the following links:

- COUNTROWS: https://docs.microsoft.com/en-us/dax/countrows-function-dax
- DIVIDE: https://docs.microsoft.com/en-us/dax/divide-function-dax

Analyzing customer churn rate

In concept, the customer churn rate is fairly simple. The basic concept behind the customer churn rate is to measure how many customers leave a business within a given time period. The customer churn rate helps businesses identify whether they are growing or shrinking and whether or not there is some kind of problem within the business. An increasing churn rate can be an indication of something fundamentally wrong within the business or that there is a problem area that needs to be addressed.

The customer churn rate is perhaps most often used with subscription services and has thus received more attention as service and software providers move toward subscription models in the cloud. The churn rate is also an important metric required in the predictive calculation of **customer lifetime value (CLTV)**, which has recently gained wide acceptance within leading Fortune 500 firms (see the *Calculating customer lifetime value* recipe within this chapter). While simple in concept, the calculation of the customer churn rate can become complex as high growth rates and other factors can skew results. Despite this, leading authorities primarily advocate for the use of a simple model when it comes to calculating customer churn rate.

This recipe provides a method for calculating the churn rate based upon a relatively simple methodology. The methodology used is to first calculate the total number of customers at the beginning of a time period. We then calculate the number of lost customers by comparing this figure with the total number of customers at the end of the time period minus any new customers. Keeping things simple allows the calculation to be easily understandable, makes things comparable to outside entities, and provides a clear basis for further analysis.

Getting ready

To prepare for this recipe, do the following:

1. Open Power BI Desktop.
2. Create a table called `R05_Table` using the following formula:

```
R05_Table =
    VAR __Table1 =
        GENERATE(
SELECTCOLUMNS(GENERATESERIES(DATE(2019,1,15),DATE(2019,3,31),30),"D
ate",[Value]),
            SELECTCOLUMNS(GENERATESERIES(1,6,1),"Customer",[Value])
        )
    VAR __Table2 =
        GENERATE(
SELECTCOLUMNS(GENERATESERIES(DATE(2019,1,15),DATE(2019,2,28),30),"D
ate",[Value]),
            SELECTCOLUMNS(GENERATESERIES(7,9,1),"Customer",[Value])
        )
    VAR __Table3 =
        GENERATE(
SELECTCOLUMNS(GENERATESERIES(DATE(2019,1,15),DATE(2019,1,31),30),"D
ate",[Value]),
SELECTCOLUMNS(GENERATESERIES(10,10,1),"Customer",[Value])
```

```
                )
        VAR __Table4 =
            GENERATE (
SELECTCOLUMNS (GENERATESERIES (DATE (2019,2,14),DATE (2019,3,31),30),"D
ate", [Value]),
SELECTCOLUMNS (GENERATESERIES (11,11,1),"Customer",[Value])
                )
        VAR __Table5 =
            GENERATE (
SELECTCOLUMNS (GENERATESERIES (DATE (2019,3,16),DATE (2019,3,31),30),"D
ate", [Value]),
SELECTCOLUMNS (GENERATESERIES (12,13,1),"Customer",[Value])
                )
    RETURN
        UNION (__Table1, __Table2, __Table3, __Table4, __Table5)
```

3. Create columns in `R05_Table` using the following formulas:

```
Month = FORMAT ([Date],"mmmm")
Month Sort = MONTH ([Date])
```

4. Set the `Sort by` column for the `Month` column to the `Month Sort` column.

The data in `R05_Table` is representative of the data for a monthly subscription service and includes customers that fail to renew their monthly subscriptions as well as customers that add new subscriptions. Customers 1-6 start and remain loyal customers during the months of January, February, and March. Customers 7, 8, and 9 drop their subscriptions in March. Customer 10 drops their subscription in February. Customer 11 becomes a new customer in February and continues their subscription in March. Customers 12 and 13 both start new subscriptions in March.

How to do it...

To implement this recipe, do the following:

1. Create a measure using the following formula:

```
Churn Rate =
    VAR __MinDate = MIN ('R05_Table'[Date])
VAR __Year = YEAR(__MinDate)
VAR __Month = MONTH(__MinDate)
VAR __PreviousMonthYear = IF(__Month = 1, __Year - 1 , __Year)
VAR __PreviousMonth = IF(__Month = 1, 12, __Month - 1)
VAR __CustomersStart =
DISTINCT (
```

```
        SELECTCOLUMNS(
        FILTER(
        ALL('R05_Table'),
        MONTH([Date]) = __PreviousMonth &&
        YEAR([Date]) = __PreviousMonthYear
                        ),
                        "__Customer",[Customer]
                )
            )
        VAR __CustomersEnd =
            DISTINCT(
                SELECTCOLUMNS(
                    'R05_Table',
                    "__Customer",[Customer]
                )
            )
        VAR __NewCustomers = EXCEPT(__CustomersEnd, __CustomersStart)
        VAR __CustomersEnd1 = EXCEPT(__CustomersEnd, __NewCustomers)
        VAR __TotalLostCustomers = COUNTROWS(__CustomersStart) -
    COUNTROWS(__CustomersEnd1)
    RETURN
        DIVIDE(__TotalLostCustomers, COUNTROWS(__CustomersStart),
    BLANK())
```

2. On a report page, create a table visualization and place the `Month` column from `R05_Table` as well as the measure `Churn Rate` into the **Values** area of the visualization.

How it works...

We start by getting the minimum date within the current context and storing this date in the `__MinDate` variable. We then use `__MinDate` to calculate the year, `__Year`, and month, `__Month`, of this date. Since we want to calculate the number of customers at the start of the time period in question, in this case each month, we need to calculate the number of customers in the previous month. Thus, we calculate the year of the previous month, `__PreviousMonthYear`, and the previous month, `__PreviousMonth`, using simple `IF` statements to check whether we are at the beginning of the year (January, or a month number of 1). If so, our `__PreviousMonthYear` becomes the current year, `__Year`, minus 1. If not, then the year of the previous month is the same as the year of the current month, `__Year`. Similarly, if we are at the beginning of the year, then the previous month is December, or a month number of 12. Otherwise, the previous month is simply the current month number, `__Month`, minus 1.

Now that the base calculations are complete, we can calculate the total number of customers at the start of the time period in question, __CustomersStart. We do this by calculating the number of customers in the previous month. We first must bring all rows of R05_Table back into context using the ALL function. We then use FILTER to select only the rows in the table whose month equals our __PreviousMonth and whose year equals our __PreviousYear. We then use SELECTCOLUMNS to choose only the Customer column and then use DISTINCT to only return the unique values within that column.

We can now calculate the number of customers at the end of our time period, __CustomersEnd. In our case, this is simply the number of customers that continued their subscription in the current month. Thus, the calculation is identical to __CustomersStart, except that we do not need to filter the base R05_Table table because the rows that we desire are already in context.

Now that we have the customers at the start of our time period, __CustomersStart, and the customers at the end of our time period, __CustomersEnd, we can use these to determine any new customers that subscribed within the time period in question. We can calculate the __NewCustomers variable by returning the rows in __CustomersEnd that are not in __CustomersStart. We do this using the EXCEPT function. Since we do not want to count these customers when calculating the final churn rate, we calculate the __TotalCustomersEnd1 variable and remove these new customers by again using the EXCEPT function.

The number of lost customers within the current time period, __TotalLostCustomers, can now be computed as the difference between the count of total unique customers at the start of the period and the count of the total unique customers at the end of the period excluding new customers. We do this by using COUNTROWS to return the number of rows in the __CustomersStart and __CustomersEnd1 variables respectively.

Finally, in order to arrive at a percentage, we simply divide the count of our lost customers, __TotalLostCustomers, by the row count of __CustomersStart.

There's more...

The customer churn rate is often paired with the customer growth rate in order to provide a more complete picture of the health of a business. To calculate and compare the customer growth rate, do the following:

1. Create the following measure:

```
Growth Rate =
    VAR __MinDate = MIN('R05_Table'[Date])
    VAR __Year = YEAR(__MinDate)
    VAR __Month = MONTH(__MinDate)
    VAR __PreviousMonthYear = IF(__Month = 1, __Year - 1 , __Year)
    VAR __PreviousMonth = IF(__Month = 1, 12, __Month - 1)
    VAR __CustomersStart =
        DISTINCT(
            SELECTCOLUMNS(
                FILTER(
                    ALL('R05_Table'),
                    MONTH([Date]) = __PreviousMonth &&
                        YEAR([Date]) = __PreviousMonthYear
                ),
                "__Customer",[Customer]
            )
        )
    VAR __CustomersEnd =
        DISTINCT(
            SELECTCOLUMNS(
                'R05_Table',
                "__Customer",[Customer]
            )
        )
    VAR __NewCustomers = EXCEPT(__CustomersEnd, __CustomersStart)
    RETURN
        DIVIDE(COUNTROWS(__NewCustomers), COUNTROWS(__CustomersStart),
    BLANK())
```

2. In the same table visualization created previously, place this new measure, Growth Rate, into the **Values** area of the visualization.

From the visualization, we can see that both Churn Rate and Growth Rate were 10% in February. However, in March, we can see that Churn Rate is 30% while Growth Rate is 20%, meaning that the business actually shrank 10% during the month of March.

See also

For more details on the functions in this recipe, refer to the following links:

- MAX: `https://docs.microsoft.com/en-us/dax/max-function-dax`
- MIN: `https://docs.microsoft.com/en-us/dax/min-function-dax`
- MONTH: `https://docs.microsoft.com/en-us/dax/month-function-dax`
- YEAR: `https://docs.microsoft.com/en-us/dax/year-function-dax`
- IF: `https://docs.microsoft.com/en-us/dax/if-function-dax`
- COUNTROWS: `https://docs.microsoft.com/en-us/dax/countrows-function-dax`
- DISTINCT: `https://docs.microsoft.com/en-us/dax/distinct-function-dax`
- SELECTCOLUMNS: `https://docs.microsoft.com/en-us/dax/distinct-function-dax`
- FILTER: `https://docs.microsoft.com/en-us/dax/filter-function-dax`
- ALL: `https://docs.microsoft.com/en-us/dax/all-function-dax`
- EXCEPT: `https://docs.microsoft.com/en-us/dax/except-function-dax`
- COUNTROWS: `https://docs.microsoft.com/en-us/dax/countrows-function-dax`

Calculating the customer lifetime value

The customer lifetime value, variously abbreviated as CLV or CLTV and also called **lifetime customer value (LCV)** as well as **lifetime value (LTV)**, has become an important customer metric for businesses since its introduction in the late 1980s. In concept, the CLV is a predictive measure of the expected revenue or profit for a customer or group of customers over the entire lifespan of their relationship with a business.

While there is no universal methodology by which the CLV is constructed, at least there are not any approved by the **Marketing Accountability Standards Board (MASB)**, this has not stopped the CLV from becoming widely adopted by Fortune 500 firms and other businesses. The reason for this is that the CLV confers a number of benefits including the ability to estimate, analyze, and/or justify customer acquisition/marketing strategies and costs, as well as the ability to segment customers into groups based upon their value to the business.

This recipe provides one methodology for calculating a predictive value for the CLV and demonstrates how this can be used to identify the most valuable customers to a business. Our goal is to create a measure that provides a measure of the CLV for individual customers as well as one that works in the aggregate to provide the average CLV for groups of customers. In addition, we want our CLV measure to work for different time periods of source data. In other words, our measure should be able to handle source data for customer sales over a single year or multiple years and still provide the correct calculation.

Getting ready

To prepare for this recipe, do the following:

1. Open Power BI Desktop.
2. Use an Enter Data query to create a table called R06_Table with the following data:

Date	Customer	Value
3/1/2015	1	500
12/1/2016	1	300
6/1/2017	2	200
8/1/2017	2	600
9/1/2017	2	800
1/1/2018	3	200
3/1/2018	3	250
1/1/2019	4	1200
3/1/2019	5	1100
8/1/2019	4	1500
9/1/2019	3	200
9/1/2019	2	500
9/1/2019	5	1400
9/1/2019	4	1500
9/1/2019	6	600
9/1/2019	6	200

3. Create a measure using the following formula:

```
Yearly Churn Rate = .2
```

In this recipe, we use a static churn rate in our calculation of the CLV. The churn rate can be used to create a predictive measure of the CLV in the absence of sufficient historical data. For an example of calculating the customer churn rate, see the *Analyzing customer churn rate* recipe in this chapter.

How to do it...

To implement this recipe, do the following:

1. Create the following measure:

```
CLTV =
    VAR __Customers = COUNTROWS(VALUES('R06_Table'[Customer]))
    VAR __MaxDate = MAX('R06_Table'[Date])
    VAR __MinDate = MIN('R06_Table'[Date])
    VAR __Years =
        IF(
            (__MaxDate - __MinDate) * 1. > 365,
            YEAR(__MaxDate) - YEAR(__MinDate) + 1,
            1
        )
    VAR __AveragePurchaseFrequency =
            DIVIDE(
                COUNTROWS('R06_Table'),
                __Years,
                BLANK()
            )
    VAR __AveragePurchaseValue = AVERAGE('R06_Table'[Value])
    VAR __AverageCustomerValue = __AveragePurchaseValue *
__AveragePurchaseFrequency
    VAR __AverageCustomerLifespan = 1/[Yearly Churn Rate]
RETURN
    DIVIDE(__AverageCustomerValue * __AverageCustomerLifespan,
__Customers, BLANK())
```

2. On a report page, create a card visualization and place the measure, CLTV, into the **Fields** area of the visualization.

How it works...

We start by getting the current number of customers within the current context and store this number in the __Customers variable. We only want the number of unique customers, so we use the VALUES function to return the unique values from the Customer column in R06_Table and then we use COUNTROWS to count the number of unique values returned.

Next, we want to calculate the average frequency of purchases from our customer or customers. To do this, we first need to calculate the minimum and maximum purchase dates within the context. We store these values in the __MaxDate and __MinDate variables. Next, we calculate the number of years over which purchases were made and store this in the __Years variable. We check whether or not all purchases were made in the same year and if so, set the number of years to 1.

Otherwise, we calculate the number of years between __MaxDate and __MinDate. We can now calculate the average purchase frequency and store this in the __AveragePurchaseFrequency variable. Since each row in the R06_Table source table represents a purchase, we simply need to use COUNTROWS to return the number of rows within the context in R06_Table and then we divide that value by the number of years over which our source data spans. This provides us with the frequency of purchases over the date range spanned in our source data (purchases per year). However, we want the number of purchases within a single year. Thus, we divide our value by the number of years in your source data again. We now have __AveragePurchaseFrequency as the average amount of purchases within one year's time.

We can now calculate the average value of purchases and store this as __AveragePurchaseValue. Next, we can calculate the average customer value per year by multiplying the average value of purchases, __AveragePurchaseValue, by the frequency per year, __AveragePurchaseFrequency. This provides us with the average customer value per year, __AverageCustomerValue.

In order to calculate the lifetime value of a customer, we need to know how many years that customer will be a customer of the business. In the absence of decades of historical information, we can use the customer churn rate to calculate this. In this recipe, we have specified a static churn rate of .2 or 20% per year in the Yearly Churn Rate measure. For an example of how to calculate churn rate, see the *Analyzing customer churn rate* recipe in this chapter. Since the churn rate defines the number of customers lost within a given period of time, in this case per year, then the average customer lifetime, __AverageCustomerLifespan, is simply the reciprocal of the churn rate.

We can now calculate the CLV by multiplying the average customer value per year, `__AverageCustomerValue`, by the average customer lifetime in years, `__AverageCustomerLifespan`, and then dividing this value by the number of customers in the context, `__Customers`.

There's more...

You can also use this metric to analyze the value of individual customers to the organization. To see how this works, do the following:

1. On a report page, create a table visualization.
2. Place the `Customer` column from `R06_Table` into the **Values** area of the table visualization.
3. Set the aggregation for the `Customer` field to `Don't summarize`.
4. Place the `CLTV` measure into the **Values** area for the table visualization.

We can now clearly see that customer 4 has the most potential value for the business, followed by customer 5. Note that the **Total** line for the table matches the value displayed in the previously created card visualization.

See also

For more details on the functions in this recipe, refer to the following links:

- MAX: https://docs.microsoft.com/en-us/dax/max-function-dax
- MIN: https://docs.microsoft.com/en-us/dax/min-function-dax
- YEAR: https://docs.microsoft.com/en-us/dax/year-function-dax
- DIVIDE: https://docs.microsoft.com/en-us/dax/divide-function-dax
- AVERAGE: https://docs.microsoft.com/en-us/dax/average-function-dax

Computing the customer acquisition cost

The **customer acquisition cost**, or **CAC**, is the cost of all activities related to convincing a customer to purchase goods or services from a business for the first time. The CAC is generally computed in the aggregate, meaning the average cost of acquiring new customers within a given period of time. By itself, the CAC can be a useful measure for comparing different types of sales and marketing activities that lead to new customers. However, the CAC is perhaps most useful when used in conjunction with other metrics such as the CLV. See the *Calculating the customer lifetime value* recipe in this chapter.

This recipe provides an example of calculating the CAC for marketing campaigns as well as the total cost of acquiring new customers within a specific range of time.

Getting ready

To prepare for this recipe, do the following:

1. Open Power BI Desktop.
2. Use an Enter Data query to create a table called R07_Table with the following data:

Campaign	# of Clicks	Cost Per Click	New Customers
Click-ad Campaign 1	200	50	20
Click-ad Campaign 2	200	100	20
Click-ad Campaign 3	200	200	20

This table represents data on three different pay-per-click ad campaigns. For each campaign, the number of clicks paid for was 200, and for each campaign 20 new customers were acquired. The cost per click for each campaign varied.

How to do it...

To implement this recipe, do the following:

In R07_Table, create new columns with the following formulas:

```
Total Campaign Cost = 'R07_Table'[# of Clicks] * 'R07_Table'[Cost Per
Click]
CAC = DIVIDE('R07_Table'[Total Campaign Cost],'R07_Table'[New
Customers],BLANK())
```

How it works...

We first use the information in the data to create a total cost for each campaign in the `Total Campaign Cost` column. This is simply the number of clicks paid for, multiplied by the cost per click. We can then use `Total Campaign Cost` to calculate `CAC` by dividing `Total Campaign Cost` by the number of new customers acquired.

We can immediately see that `Click-ad Campaign 1` was far more cost-effective than `Click-ad Campaign 3`.

There's more...

While the simple CAC calculation presented is useful when comparing different marketing campaigns, using only the direct costs of the marketing campaigns does not present a holistic picture of the true CAC. To get a more holistic value for the CAC, we must take indirect costs, such as sales and marketing salaries, commissions, and agency fees, into account. To get a more complete picture of the CAC, do the following:

1. Use an Enter Data query to create a table called `R07_Table2` with the following data:

Item	Yearly Cost
Fully loaded marketing salaries	98000
Fully loaded sales salaries	130000
Agency fees	1000
Creative fees	2000
Sales commissions	30000
Payment processing fees on first time purchases	100

2. Ensure that there is no relationship between `R07_Table` and `R07_Table2`.

3. Create a new measure with the following formula:

```
Total Yearly CAC =
    VAR __NumberOfCampaigns =
COUNTROWS(VALUES(R07_Table[Campaign]))
    VAR __NumberOfAllCampaigns =
COUNTROWS(DISTINCT(ALL(R07_Table[Campaign])))
    VAR __CampaignCosts = SUM('R07_Table'[Total Campaign Cost])
    VAR __OtherCosts = SUM('R07_Table2'[Yearly Cost])
    VAR __NewCustomers = SUM('R07_Table'[New Customers])
RETURN
```

```
DIVIDE(
    DIVIDE(
        __OtherCosts,
        __NumberOfAllCampaigns,
        BLANK()
    ) * __NumberOfCampaigns + __CampaignCosts,
    __NewCustomers,
    BLANK()
)
```

4. On a report page, create a card visualization and place the `Total Yearly CAC` measure into the **Fields** area of the visualization.
5. On the same report page, create a table visualization and place the `Campaign` and `CAC` columns from `R07_Table`, as well as the `Total Yearly CAC` measure, into the **Values** area of the visualization.
6. Change the aggregation for the `CAC` column to be `Average`.

Note that the total line for `Total Yearly CAC` in the table visualization is the same as the value presented in the card visualization. We can clearly see that the direct costs of the marketing campaigns are very small when compared to the other costs involved.

The `Total Year CAC` measure is designed to spread the indirect costs of marketing campaigns across all of the campaigns undertaken within the given timeframe, in this case, one year. This allows the measure to be used when analyzing individual campaigns as well as any grouping of campaigns.

We start by getting the current number of campaigns within the current context, `__NumberOfCampaigns`. Since we are dealing with a column in a table, we can use `VALUES` to return the unique values in the column and then use `COUNTROWS` to return how many unique values exist within that column.

Next, we get the number of unique marketing campaigns run during the entire time period, `__NumberOfAllCampaigns`. We do this by ensuring that all rows are in context through the use of the `ALL` function. We then use `DISTINCT` to return the unique values within the `Campaign` column and again use `COUNTROWS` to get the count of unique values.

We can now compute the costs involved in our marketing campaigns by simply summing the `Total Campaign Cost` column in `R07_Table` to return the total direct costs of our campaigns, `__CampaignCosts`. Similarly, we can compute the indirect costs by summing the `Yearly Cost` column in the `R07_Table2` table, `__OtherCosts`. The other item we need is the total number of new customers acquired, `__NewCustomers`, and this is simply the sum of the `New Customers` column in `R07_Table`.

To arrive at our `Total Year CAC` measure value, we start by dividing `__OtherCosts` by `__NumberOfAllCampaigns`. This spreads our indirect, yearly costs across all of the campaigns run during that time period, or essentially an indirect cost per campaign. We multiply this value by the number of campaigns currently in the context, `__NumberOfCampaigns`, and then add our direct costs, `__CampaignCosts`. We then divide this figure by the number of new customers, `__NewCustomers`.

By performing the calculation in this manner, the measure works for evaluating the CAC for one campaign, all campaigns, or any subset of campaigns.

See also

For more details on the functions in this recipe, refer to the following links:

- SUM: https://docs.microsoft.com/en-us/dax/sum-function-dax
- COUNTOWS: https://docs.microsoft.com/en-us/dax/countrows-function-dax
- VALUES: https://docs.microsoft.com/en-us/dax/values-function-dax
- DIVIDE: https://docs.microsoft.com/en-us/dax/divide-function-dax
- DISTINCT: https://docs.microsoft.com/en-us/dax/distinct-function-dax
- BLANKS: https://docs.microsoft.com/en-us/dax/blank-function-dax

Evaluating Employment Measures

7

Employees are the lifeblood of every business. Without employees, work does not get accomplished, value is not added to goods and services, and customers go wanting. Thus it makes sense that savvy businesses will want to keep track of their employees in terms of employee engagement at work, whether their employees are satisfied with work or not, how often employees leave the company, and perhaps how often employees have unexcused absences. This chapter has many useful recipes to help you analyze employee metrics and KPIs, such as when employees leave or are likely to leave, which employees are advocates for the business, and how much profit employees add to the business.

The following is the list of recipes that we will cover in this chapter:

- Calculating employee turnover rate
- Computing absenteeism
- Evaluating employee engagement
- Determining human capital value added
- Finding full-time equivalent
- Using Kaplan-Meier survival curves

Technical requirements

The following are required to complete all of the recipes in this chapter:

- Power BI Desktop
- GitHub repository: https://github.com/PacktPublishing/DAX-Cookbook/tree/master/Chapter07

After downloading and opening the file for this chapter, go to **File** in the menu and then choose **Options and settings**. Choose **Options**. In the **Options** window under **CURRENT FILE**, choose **Data Load** and check the box under **Time Intelligence** for **Auto date/time**. This option was turned off for reasons of file size. Close the **Options** window.

Calculating employee turnover rate

Employee turnover rate, or **ETR**, is a measure of how many employees leave an organization within a given span of time. ETR is perhaps one of the most important human resources metrics for an organization to track and understand. This is because a high ETR has many negative aspects for business, including the cost of replacement, loss of productivity, and loss of organizational and business knowledge.

To calculate ETR, use the following formula:

$$ETR = EmployeesLeaving \div Average\ Employees \times 100$$

You simply take the number of employees leaving within a given time period divided by the average number of employees during that time period and then multiply by 100.

This recipe demonstrates how to calculate ETR.

Getting ready

To prepare for this recipe, do the following:

1. Open Power BI Desktop.
2. Use an **Enter Data** query to create a table called `R02_Table` with the following data:

Employee	Hire Date	Leave Date
Greg	3/1/2015	1/1/9999
Julie	12/1/2016	1/1/9999
Scott	6/1/2017	1/1/9999
Bob	8/1/2017	1/1/9999
Jimmy	9/1/2017	2/1/2019
John	1/1/2018	1/1/9999

Terry	3/1/2018	1/1/9999
Billy	1/1/2018	12/1/2018
Sam	3/1/2019	1/1/9999
Harry	8/1/2018	1/1/9999
Jerry	9/1/2019	1/1/9999
Rob	9/1/2019	1/1/9999
Sajith	9/1/2019	1/1/9999
Pam	9/1/2019	1/1/9999
Mike	9/1/2019	1/1/9999
Aaron	9/1/2019	1/1/9999

This data represents a typical employee table that contains dates for when an employee was hired by the organization and when they left the organization. Many such systems track leave dates by using a nonsensical date such as 1/1/1900 or 1/1/9999 as the `Leave Date` for employees that are still with the company. Other systems use a blank or null value. The recipe presented here can be easily adjusted to account for these differences between systems.

How to do it...

Calculating ETR can be done as follows:

1. Create the following measure:

```
Annual ETR =
    VAR __Year = 2019
    VAR __StartPeriod = DATE(__Year,1,1)
    VAR __EndPeriod = DATE(__Year,12,31)
    VAR __BeginningEmployees =
        COUNTROWS(
            FILTER(
                'R01_Table',
                'R01_Table'[Hire Date] <= __StartPeriod &&
                    'R01_Table'[Leave Date] > __StartPeriod
            )
        )
    VAR __EndingEmployees =
        COUNTROWS(
            FILTER(
                'R01_Table',
                'R01_Table'[Hire Date] <= __EndPeriod &&
```

```
                                    ('R01_Table'[Leave Date] > __EndPeriod ||
                                        'R01_Table'[Leave Date] = DATE(9999,1,1)
                                    )
                                )
                            )
                VAR __LostEmployees =
                    COUNTROWS(
                        FILTER(
                            'R01_Table',
                            'R01_Table'[Leave Date] >= __StartPeriod &&
                            'R01_Table'[Leave Date] <= __EndPeriod
                        )
                    )
            RETURN
                DIVIDE(
                    __LostEmployees,
                    (__BeginningEmployees + __EndingEmployees) / 2,
                    0
                )
```

2. Format ETR as a percentage.
3. On a report page, create a Card visualization and place the ETR measure in the **Fields** area of the visualization.

How it works...

The formula for ETR requires that we identify a specific time period during which we wish to calculate the ETR. This is necessary in order to define which employees that have left the organization should be counted, as well as to determine the average number of employees during that time. For this recipe, we have simplified things and simply chosen to compute an annual ETR for the year 2019. Thus, we set the __Year variable to the value 2019 in the first line and then calculate the start date of our period, __StartPeriod, and end date of our period, __EndPeriod, to be the first day of 2019 and the last day of 2019 respectively.

We know that we want to calculate the average number of employees during our defined time period. To do this, we will take the average of the number of employees at the beginning of the time period and the number of employees at the end of the time period. To calculate the number of employees at the beginning of the time period, __BeginningEmployees, we use the COUNTROWS function to count the rows in our fact table, R01_Table, that have a Hire Date greater than or equal to the start of the chosen time period and a Leave Date greater than the end of the chosen time period. This assumes that each row in the employee table represents a unique employment instance.

The calculation for the number of employees at the end of our defined time, __EndingEmployees, is similar to the calculation for __BeginningEmployees. This time, however, our FILTER clause specifies employees that have a Hire Date less than or equal to the end of our chosen time period as well as either a Leave Date greater than the end of our chosen time period or have a value for Leave Date that equals our special value for employees still employed with the organization. In our case, we have a special value for Leave Date that is always greater than the time period within context, but this would not be the case for a special value such as 1/1/1900.

Calculating the number of lost employees, __LostEmployees, is again similar to the calculations for __BeginningEmployees and __EndingEmployees. This time our FILTER clause specifies employees that have a Leave Date within the period of time defined by our __StartPeriod and __EndPeriod variables.

Now that we have the components of our calculation, we can return the annual ETR by dividing the number of lost employees within the time period, __LostEmployees, by the average number of employees within the time period. The average number of employees within the time period is simply the sum of the number of employees at the beginning and end of the time period divided by two.

There's more...

While this recipe computes an annual ETR for the sake of simplicity, the formula can be easily modified to account for any range of time. To do this, remove the row where the __Year variable is set to 2019. Then, set the __StartPeriod variable to the minimum date within the current context using the MIN or MINX functions. Similarly, set the __EndPeriod variable to the maximum date within the current context using the MAX or MAXX functions. To see an example of how this is done, please see the next recipe, *Computing absenteeism*.

See also

For more details of the functions in this recipe, refer to the following links:

- DATE: https://docs.microsoft.com/en-us/dax/date-function-dax
- COUNTROWS: https://docs.microsoft.com/en-us/dax/countrows-function-dax
- DIVIDE: https://docs.microsoft.com/en-us/dax/divide-function-dax
- FILTER: https://docs.microsoft.com/en-us/dax/filter-function-dax

Computing absenteeism

Absenteeism is a measure of how much time employees are unavailable for work. Most often, this means that the amount of time employees are unavailable for work that is unexpected, in other words, employees calling off work for being sick or simply not showing up for work as opposed to absences that are planned such as vacations, holidays, family leave or long-term disability. Employees with chronic absenteeism can be a drain on business productivity and thus, in certain organizations, absenteeism is an important measure to track and analyze.

The basic formula for calculating an absenteeism rate is extremely simple—divide the number of days or hours of absence within a given time period by the total number of available days or hours within the same given time period. While this sounds extremely simple, it becomes harder when computing absenteeism across a business unit or the entire organization since new employees may be hired, existing employees may leave, and absences may span multiple separate time periods.

This recipe presents a single measure that can compute absenteeism at an individual level as well as a group level. In addition, this measure will compute absenteeism for any time range within context.

Getting ready

To prepare for this recipe, do the following:

1. Open Power BI Desktop.
2. Use an **Enter Data** query to create a table called `R02_Table` with the following data:

Employee	Hire Date	Leave Date
Greg	3/1/2015	1/1/9999
Julie	12/1/2016	1/1/9999
Scott	6/1/2017	1/1/9999
Bob	8/1/2017	1/1/9999
Jimmy	9/1/2017	2/1/2019
John	1/1/2018	1/1/9999
Terry	3/1/2018	1/1/9999
Billy	1/1/2018	12/1/2018
Sam	3/1/2019	1/1/9999

Harry	8/1/2018	1/1/9999
Jerry	9/1/2019	1/1/9999
Rob	9/1/2019	1/1/9999
Sajith	9/1/2019	1/1/9999
Pam	9/1/2019	1/1/9999
Mike	9/1/2019	1/1/9999
Aaron	9/1/2019	1/1/9999

3. Use an **Enter Data** query to create a table called `R02_Absent` with the following data:

Employee	AbsentStartDate	AbsentReturnDate
Jimmy	1/15/2019	1/17/2019
Jerry	6/1/2019	6/2/2019
Jerry	7/1/2019	7/3/2019
Aaron	3/3/2019	3/6/2019
Aaron	4/3/2019	4/6/2019
Aaron	5/3/2019	5/6/2019
Aaron	6/3/2019	6/6/2019
Aaron	7/3/2019	7/6/2019
Aaron	12/28/2019	1/4/2020

4. Relate tables `R02_Table` and `R02_Absent` on the `Employee` columns and ensure that no other relationships exist for the `R02_Table` and `R02_Absent` tables. The relationship should be one-to-many, with the one side being `R02_Table` and the many side being `R02_Absent`.

5. Create a table called `R02_Calendar` using the following formula:

```
R02_Calendar = CALENDAR(DATE(2019,1,1), DATE(2019,12,31))
```

6. Ensure that the `R02_Calendar` table is not related to any other table.

`R02_Table` represents a typical employee table that contains dates for when the employee was hired by the organization and when the employee left the organization. Many such systems track leave dates by using a nonsensical date such as 1/1/1900 or 1/1/9999 as the `Leave Date` for employees that are still with the company. Other systems use a blank or null value. The recipe presented here can be easily adjusted to account for these differences between systems.

How to do it...

Computing absenteeism can be done in the following steps:

1. Create the following measure:

```
Absenteeism =
    VAR __StartPeriod = MIN('R02_Calendar'[Date])
    VAR __EndPeriod = MAX('R02_Calendar'[Date])
    VAR __Employees =
        ADDCOLUMNS(
            ADDCOLUMNS(
                FILTER(
                    'R02_Table',
                    [Hire Date] <= __EndPeriod &&
                    ([Leave Date] >= __StartPeriod ||
                        [Leave Date] = DATE(9999,1,1)
                    )
                ),
                "__MinDate",
                    IF([Hire Date] > __StartPeriod,
                        [Hire Date],
                        __StartPeriod
                    ),
                "__MaxDAte",
                    IF([Leave Date] < __EndPeriod,
                        [Leave Date],
                        __EndPeriod
                    )
            ),
            "__DaysInPeriod",([__MaxDate] - [__MinDate]) * 1 + 1
        )
    VAR __TotalDaysInPeriod = SUMX(__Employees,[__DaysInPeriod])
    VAR __AbsentTable =
        ADDCOLUMNS(
            ADDCOLUMNS(
                FILTER(
                    'R02_Absent',
                    ([AbsentStartDate] >= __StartPeriod &&
                        [AbsentReturnDate] <= __EndPeriod
                    ) ||
                        ([AbsentStartDate] < __StartPeriod &&
                            [AbsentReturnDate] > __StartPeriod &&
                                [AbsentReturnDate] <= __EndPeriod
                        ) ||
                            ([AbsentStartDate] >= __StartPeriod &&
                                [AbsentStartDate] <= __EndPeriod &&
                                    [AbsentReturnDate] >
```

```
        __EndPeriod
                                )
                    ),
                    "__AbsentStartDateInPeriod",
                        IF([AbsentStartDate]<__StartPeriod,
                            __StartPeriod,
                            [AbsentStartDate]
                        ),
                    "__AbsentEndDateInPeriod",
                        IF([AbsentReturnDate]>__EndPeriod,
                            __EndPeriod,
                            [AbsentReturnDate]
                        )
                ),
                "__DaysAbsent",
                    ([__AbsentEndDateInPeriod]-
    [__AbsentStartDateInPeriod])*1+1
            )
        VAR __TotalDaysAbsent = SUMX(__AbsentTable,[__DaysAbsent])
        VAR __AbsenteeismRatio =
            DIVIDE(__TotalDaysAbsent, __TotalDaysInPeriod, 0)
    RETURN
        IF(ISBLANK(__AbsenteeismRatio),0,__AbsenteeismRatio)
```

2. Format the `Absenteeism` measure as a percentage.

3. On a report page, create a Card visualization and place the `Absenteeism` measure in the **Fields** area of the visualization.

4. On the same report page, create a Matrix visualization and place the `Employee` column from the `R02_Table` table in the **Rows** area, `Absenteeism` in the **Values** area, and `Date` from the `R02_Calendar` table in the **Columns** area. Edit the `Date` column in the **Columns** area of the visualization to display the `Date Hierarchy,` but only the `Year` from that hierarchy.

5. On the same report page, create a Line chart visualization and place `Absenteeism` in the **Values** area and `Date` from the `R02_Calendar` table in the **Axis** area. Edit the `Date` column in the **Axis** area of the visualization to display the `Date Hierarchy,` but only the `Month` from that hierarchy.

How it works...

First, it should be noted that this recipe assumes a seven-day work week. If this is not the case for your organization, see the *Replacing Excel's NETWORKDAYS function* recipe in `Chapter 2`, *Dealing with Dates and Calendars.*

We start by setting the start and end of our time period for analysis. This is done by setting the __StartPeriod variable to the minimum Date in the R02_Calendar table currently within the context, as well as setting the __EndPeriod variable to the maximum Date in the R02_Calendar table currently within the context. By setting these variables dynamically based upon the context, this allows the measure to work within any time interval chosen.

We know from our basic formula for absenteeism that we need the number of available days or hours. While this seems straightforward, we must take into account that employees may be hired or leave the organization during the time period under analysis. Thus, we must compute a table, __Employees, that accounts for employees coming into and leaving the organization during the time period in question. We do this by first using FILTER to get the employees that have a Hire Date before the end of our period, __EndPeriod, and have a Leave Date of after the start of our time period, __StartPeriod, or have a special Leave Date value that denotes that they are still employed by the organization, in this case, 1/1/9999.

We use ADDCOLUMNS to compute each employee's relevant starting and ending dates, __MinDate and __MaxDate, within the period in question. For __MinDate, we check if the employee's Hire Date is after the start of our period, __StartPeriod, and, if so, their Hire Date is used. Otherwise, the start of the period, __StartPeriod is used. Similarly, for __MaxDate, we check if the employee's Leave Date is before the end of our period, __EndPeriod, and, if so, their Leave Date is used. Otherwise, the end of the period, __EndPeriod is used. We then use ADDCOLUMNS again to create the __DaysInPeriod column, which is the number of days between __MaxDate and __MinDate. The __Employees variable now contains a table with only the employees relevant to the time period under analysis, as well as the number of relevant days within that period.

We can now calculate the total number of available days within the time period across all employees that worked during that time period, __TotalDaysInPeriod. We do this by simply using SUMX to sum the values in the __DaysInPeriod column within the __Employees table variable. Note that this method works whether one employee is within context or multiple employees are within context. If only one employee is within context, then the __Employees table variable will contain, at most, one employee.

Now that we have the denominator for our basic absenteeism calculation, __TotalDaysInPeriod, we can move on to calculating the numerator, the number of days of absence. To do this, we must determine the number of absent days within the time period in question. We must be concerned with three types of absence periods:

- Absences that begin and end within the time period in question
- Absences that begin prior to the start of the time period in question but end during the time period in question
- Absences that begin prior to the end of the time period in question but end after the time period in question

For the last two types of absences, we do not wish to count absent days that fall outside of the time period in question. To accomplish this, we start by using FILTER to filter our R02_Absent table. The first filter clause handles the first type of absence, those absences that begin and end within the time period in question. The second filter clause handles including those absences that start prior to the time period in question, __StartPeriod, but also have an AbsentReturnDate that is both after the __StartPeriod and before or equal to the __EndPeriod. The third clause handles our third type of absence, those absences with an AbsentStartDate that is both after or equal to the start of our period, __StartPeriod, and before or equal to the end of our period, __EndPeriod. In addition, these types of absences must have an AbsentReturnDate that is after the end of our period, __EndPeriod.

We use ADDCOLUMNS to compute each absence's relevant starting and ending dates, __AbsentStartDateInPeriod and __AbsentEndDateInPeriod, within the period in question. For __AbsentStartDateInPeriod, we check if the AbsentStartDate is before the start of our period, __StartPeriod, and, if so, __StartPeriod is used. Otherwise, the start of the absence, AbsentStartDate, is used. Similarly, for __AbsentEndDateInPeriod, we check if AbsentReturnDate is after the end of our period, __EndPeriod, and, if so, __EndPeriod is used. Otherwise, the end of the absence, AbsentReturnDate, is used. We then use ADDCOLUMNS again to create the __DaysAbsent column, which is the number of days between __AbsentEndDateInPeriod and __AbsentStartDateInPeriod. The __AbsentTable variable now contains a table with only the absences relevant to the time period under analysis as well as the number of relevant days of absence within that period.

We can now calculate the total number of absence days within the time period across all absences relevant during that time period, __TotalDaysAbsent. We do this by simply using SUMX to sum the values in the __DaysAbsent column within the __AbsentTable table variable.

We now have both the numerator and the denominator for our simple base absenteeism formula. Thus, we now simply divide __TotalDaysAbsent by __TotalDaysInPeriod to arrive at our absenteeism ratio, __AbsenteeismRatio. Since we wish to return zeros and not blanks, we make a quick check using ISBLANK and return 0 if true or __AbsenteeismRatio if false.

There's more...

Another common metric used in absenteeism is the Bradford Factor. The underlying assumption with the Bradford Factor is that frequent short unplanned absences are more disruptive than infrequent longer unplanned absences. The Bradford Factor is given by the following equation:

$$\text{Bradford Factor} = \text{Instances}^2 \times \text{Days Absent}$$

The Bradford Factor is intended to be computed annually and only at the individual employee level. To calculate the Bradford Factor, create the following measure:

```
Bradford Factor =
    VAR __StartPeriod = MIN('R02_Calendar'[Date])
    VAR __EndPeriod = MAX('R02_Calendar'[Date])
    VAR __AbsentTable =
        ADDCOLUMNS(
            ADDCOLUMNS(
                FILTER(
                    'R02_Absent',
                    ([AbsentStartDate] >= __StartPeriod &&
                        [AbsentReturnDate] <= __EndPeriod
                    ) ||
                        ([AbsentStartDate] < __StartPeriod &&
                            [AbsentReturnDate] > __StartPeriod &&
                                [AbsentReturnDate] <= __EndPeriod
                        ) ||
                        ([AbsentStartDate] >= __StartPeriod &&
                            [AbsentStartDate] <= __EndPeriod &&
                                [AbsentReturnDate] > __EndPeriod
                        )
                ),
                "__AbsentStartDateInPeriod",
                    IF([AbsentStartDate]<__StartPeriod,
                        __StartPeriod,
                        [AbsentStartDate]
                    ),
                "__AbsentEndDateInPeriod",
```

```
                    IF([AbsentReturnDate]>__EndPeriod,
                        __EndPeriod,
                        [AbsentReturnDate]
                    )
                ),
                "__DaysAbsent",
                ([__AbsentEndDateInPeriod]-[__AbsentStartDateInPeriod])*1+1
            )
        VAR __TotalDaysAbsent = SUMX(__AbsentTable,[__DaysAbsent])
        VAR __Instances = COUNTROWS(__AbsentTable)
        VAR __BradfordFactor = POWER(__Instances,2) * __TotalDaysAbsent
    RETURN
        IF(ISBLANK(__BradfordFactor),0,__BradfordFactor)
```

See also

For more details of the functions in this recipe, refer to the following links:

- MIN: https://docs.microsoft.com/en-us/dax/min-function-dax
- MAX: https://docs.microsoft.com/en-us/dax/max-function-dax
- ADDCOLUMNS: https://docs.microsoft.com/en-us/dax/addcolumns-function-dax
- IF: https://docs.microsoft.com/en-us/dax/if-function-dax
- SUMX: https://docs.microsoft.com/en-us/dax/sumx-function-dax
- ISBLANK: https://docs.microsoft.com/en-us/dax/isblank-function-dax
- COUNTROWS: https://docs.microsoft.com/en-us/dax/countrows-function-dax
- DIVIDE: https://docs.microsoft.com/en-us/dax/divide-function-dax
- FILTER: https://docs.microsoft.com/en-us/dax/filter-function-dax
- POWER: https://docs.microsoft.com/en-us/dax/power-function-dax
- **Bradford Factor:** https://en.wikipedia.org/wiki/Bradford_Factor

Evaluating employee engagement

Employee engagement or satisfaction at work is an important human resource metric for organizations to measure and analyze on a regular basis. In short, happier employees are more productive employees that are most likely not considering quitting their jobs. Employee engagement has been shown to correlate with employee productivity as well as employee turnover rates.

Despite its importance, there is actually no single method of evaluating and calculating employee engagement or satisfaction. For example, there is the **Utrecht Work Engagement Scale (UWES)** and the **Gallup Workplace Audit (GWA)** as well as perhaps less rigorously defined methods such as **Employee Satisfaction (ESAT)** and the **Employee Engagement Index (EEI)**. However, all of these methods have similarities. With all of these methods, employees are asked to respond to a survey of questions and rank their answers to those questions on a scale. The number of questions on the survey as well as the scale can vary wildly between methods. For example, UWES uses 17, 9 or 3 questions while GWA uses 12. Scales also vary from UWES's 0 to 6 scale to Gallup's 1 to 6 scale to other scales that rank answers from 1 to 5.

This recipe will demonstrate how to create calculations regarding employee engagement using a generic format for questions and scale. In this way, the recipe can be easily adapted to any particular employee engagement methodology. In our recipe, we will use 3 questions numbered 1 to 3 and a ranking scale from 1 to 5 with 5 being the best, most positive response and 1 being the worst, least positive response. We will not list specific questions or specific scale categorizations due to the copyrights held by various legal entities that have developed proprietary methodologies for employee engagement and satisfaction.

Getting ready

To prepare for this recipe, do the following:

1. Open Power BI Desktop.
2. Use an **Enter Data** query to create a table called R03_Table with the following data:

Employee	Question	Answer
1	1	5
1	2	5
1	3	5
2	1	4
2	2	4
2	3	4
3	1	3
3	2	3
3	3	3

4	1	2
4	2	2
4	3	2
5	1	1
5	2	1
5	3	1
6	1	4
6	2	3
6	3	2
7	1	2
7	2	3
7	3	4
8	1	3
8	2	2
8	3	2
9	1	4
9	2	3
10	2	3
10	3	4

The data in this table represents ten separate responses to the three survey questions, although not all questions were answered by all survey responders.

How to do it...

Evaluating employee engagement can be done in the following steps:

1. Create the following measures:

```
Count = COUNT(R03_Table[Answer])
Average = AVERAGE('R03_Table'[Answer])
Standard Deviation = STDEV.P('R03_Table'[Answer])
Variance = VAR.P('R03_Table'[Answer])
Median = MEDIAN('R03_Table'[Answer])

Employee Engagement =
    VAR __BestScore = 5
    VAR __TotalCount = COUNTROWS('R03_Table')
    VAR __Table =
```

```
ADDCOLUMNS (
    SUMMARIZE (
        'R03_Table',
        [Answer],
        "__Count", COUNT([Answer])
    ),
    "__Score", [__Count] * [Answer]
)
VAR __MaxScore = __TotalCount * __BestScore
VAR __TotalScore = SUMX(__Table, [__Score])
RETURN
    DIVIDE(__TotalScore, __MaxScore, 0)
```

2. Format `Employee Engagement` as a percentage.

3. Set the default summarization for the `Question` column to `Don't summarize`.

4. On a report page, create a Table visualization and place the `Question` column from the `R03_Table` table as well as the `Average`, `Standard Deviation`, `Variance`, `Median` and `Employee Engagement` measures into the **Values** area of the visualization.

5. On the same report page, create a Matrix visualization and place the `Question` column from the `R03_Table` table into the **Rows** area, the `Answer` column from the `R03_Table` table into the **Columns** area and the `Count` measure into the **Values** area.

How it works...

The `Average`, `Standard Deviation`, `Variance`, and `Median` measures simply provide the DAX equivalent formulas for the default aggregations used within the Power BI Desktop. It is perhaps worth noting that the default aggregations for standard deviation and variance use the `STDEV.P` and `VAR.P` functions as opposed to the `STDEV.S` and `VAR.S` functions. Another base metric that would perhaps be valuable here is the mode of the answer for each question and the survey as a whole. The mode is the frequently occurring value. If this is of interest, see the *Calculating mode for single and multiple columns* recipe in `Chapter 4`, *Transforming Text and Numbers*.

The `Employee Engagement` measure presents one method of calculating an employee engagement score or metric at both the question level as well as the overall survey. The methodology is straightforward. Calculate the maximum total score based upon the number of responses and the maximum scoring value on the answer scale. Also calculate the survey or question score based upon the number of responses and the value of those responses on the measuring scale. Then simply divide the question or survey score by the maximum potential score.

To implement this methodology, we start by first setting the maximum (best) answer value for our survey. In our case, this is the number 5, and thus we set the __BestScore variable to 5. Next, we count the number of responses by using COUNTROWS to count the number of rows in the R03_Table table that are within the current context and store this number in the __TotalCount variable. This enables the `Employee Engagement` measure to work when individual questions are within the context or all questions are within the context.

We now need to determine the count of responses that we have for each scoring value in our scale. We do this by creating the table variable, __Table. The table held by the __Table variable is computed by first using SUMMARIZE to group the responses within the current context by the value of the Answer column and at the same time creating the __Count column within this table that stores the count of responses with each particular value in the Answer column. We then use ADDCOLUMNS to add the __Score column to __Table, which is simply the __Count column multiplied by the value in the Answer column.

We can now compute our numerator and denominator for calculating `Employee Engagement`. The maximum score for the question or survey is simply the count of the number of responses within context, __TotalCount, multiplied by the best possible score for a question, __BestScore. This value is stored in the __MaxScore variable. The total score for the question or survey, __TotalScore, is computed by simply summing the __Score column in the __Table variable using SUMX.

The value to return for `Employee Engagement` is now simply the total score for the question or survey, __TotalScore divided by the maximum possible score, __MaxScore.

There's more...

As mentioned previously, there are multiple methods of calculating employee engagement. Another popular method is to evaluate the minimum scores of employee responses across all questions within the survey. To implement this metric, do the following:

1. Create the following measure:

```
Employee Engagement 2 =
    VAR __Score = MAX('R03_Table'[Answer])
    VAR __TotalEmployees =
        COUNTROWS(
            DISTINCT(
                ALL('R03_Table'[Employee])
            )
        )
    VAR __Table =
        SUMMARIZE(
            ALL('R03_Table'),
            [Employee],
            "__MinimumScore",MIN([Answer])
        )
    VAR __Employees =
        COUNTROWS(
            DISTINCT(
                SELECTCOLUMNS(
                    FILTER(__Table,[__MinimumScore] = __Score),
                    "__Employee",[Employee]
                )
            )
        )
RETURN
    DIVIDE(__Employees,__TotalEmployees,0)
```

2. Format `Employee Engagement 2` as a percentage.
3. On a report page, create a Table visualization and place the `Answer` column from the `R03_Table` table as well as the `Employee Engagement 2` measure into the **Values** area of the visualization.

Here, we can see that 50% of the employees surveyed rated at least one answer to a question either with a 1 or a 2.

See also

For more details of the functions in this recipe, refer to the following links:

- COUNT: https://docs.microsoft.com/en-us/dax/count-function-dax
- AVERAGE: https://docs.microsoft.com/en-us/dax/average-function-dax
- STDEV.P: https://docs.microsoft.com/en-us/dax/stdev-p-function-dax
- VAR.P: https://docs.microsoft.com/en-us/dax/var-p-function-dax
- MEDIAN: https://docs.microsoft.com/en-us/dax/median-function-dax
- COUNTROWS: https://docs.microsoft.com/en-us/dax/countrows-function-dax
- SUMMARIZE: https://docs.microsoft.com/en-us/dax/summarize-function-dax
- ADDCOLUMNS: https://docs.microsoft.com/en-us/dax/addcolumns-function-dax
- SUMX: https://docs.microsoft.com/en-us/dax/sumx-function-dax
- DIVIDE: https://docs.microsoft.com/en-us/dax/divide-function-dax
- FILTER: https://docs.microsoft.com/en-us/dax/filter-function-dax
- MAX: https://docs.microsoft.com/en-us/dax/max-function-dax
- MIN: https://docs.microsoft.com/en-us/dax/min-function-dax
- DISTINCT: https://docs.microsoft.com/en-us/dax/distinct-function-dax
- ALL: https://docs.microsoft.com/en-us/dax/all-function-dax
- SELECTCOLUMNS: https://docs.microsoft.com/en-us/dax/selectcolumns-function-dax

Determining human capital value added

Human capital value added, or **HCVA**, is a measure that quantifies the profit that the average employee contributes to an organization within a specified period of time. HCVA is quite distinct from the **Revenue Per Employee (RPE)** metric, which is simply the amount of revenue for the organization divided by the number of **full-time equivalent employees (FTEs)**. In contrast, HCVA measures the average profitability an employee contributes to the organization versus the average revenue. The formula for HCVA is given by the following:

$$HCVA = (Revenue - (Total\ Costs - Employment\ Costs)) \div FTE$$

This recipe demonstrates how to calculate HCVA on a quarterly basis, which is the recommended frequency for calculating HCVA.

Getting ready

To prepare for this recipe, do the following:

1. Open Power BI Desktop.
2. Use an **Enter Data** query to create a table called `R02_Table` with the following data:

Employee	Hire Date	Leave Date	Annual Salary
Greg	3/1/2015	1/1/9999	100000
Julie	12/1/2016	1/1/9999	150000
Scott	6/1/2017	1/1/9999	120000
Bob	8/1/2017	1/1/9999	75000
Jimmy	9/1/2017	2/1/2019	45000
John	1/1/2018	1/1/9999	110000
Terry	3/1/2018	1/1/9999	90000
Billy	1/1/2018	12/1/2018	80000
Sam	3/1/2019	1/1/9999	70000
Harry	8/1/2018	1/1/9999	60000
Jerry	9/1/2019	1/1/9999	100000
Rob	9/1/2019	1/1/9999	150000
Sajith	9/1/2019	1/1/9999	90000
Pam	9/1/2019	1/1/9999	100000
Mike	9/1/2019	1/1/9999	110000
Aaron	9/1/2019	1/1/9999	80000

3. Create a table called `R04_Calendar` using the following formula:

```
R04_Calendar = CALENDAR(DATE(2019,1,1), DATE(2019,12,31))
```

4. Ensure that both the `R04_Table` table and the `R04_Calendar` table do not have any relationships with any other tables, including each other.

This data represents a typical employee table that contains dates for when the employee was hired by the organization and when the employee left the organization. Many such systems track leave dates by using a nonsensical date such as 1/1/1900 or 1/1/9999 as the `Leave Date` for employees that are still with the company. Other systems use a blank or null value. The recipe presented here can be easily adjusted to account for these differences between systems.

How to do it...

Determining HCVA can be done in the following steps:

1. Create the following measures:

```
Total Annual Revenue = 4000000
Total Annual Costs = 3900000
Employee Overhead Cost Factor = 1.4

Revenue =
    VAR __StartPeriod = MIN('R04_Calendar'[Date])
    VAR __EndPeriod = MAX('R04_Calendar'[Date])
    VAR __DaysInPeriod = DATEDIFF(__StartPeriod, __EndPeriod,DAY) +
1
    VAR __Year = YEAR(__StartPeriod)
    VAR __DaysInYear = DATEDIFF(DATE(__Year,1,1),
DATE(__Year,12,31),DAY)+1
RETURN
    [Total Annual Revenue] / __DaysInYear * __DaysInPeriod

Total Costs =
    VAR __StartPeriod = MIN('R04_Calendar'[Date])
    VAR __EndPeriod = MAX('R04_Calendar'[Date])
    VAR __DaysInPeriod = DATEDIFF(__StartPeriod, __EndPeriod,DAY) +
1
    VAR __Year = YEAR(__StartPeriod)
    VAR __DaysInYear = DATEDIFF(DATE(__Year,1,1),
DATE(__Year,12,31),DAY)+1
RETURN
    [Total Annual Costs] / __DaysInYear * __DaysInPeriod
```

2. Create the FTE measure using the code found in the R04_FTE.txt file located in the GitHub repository.

3. Create the Employment Costs measure using the code found in the R04_EmploymentCosts.txt file located in the GitHub repository.

4. Create the following measure:

```
HCVA = ([Revenue] - ([Total Costs] - [Employment Costs])) / [FTE]
```

5. Format `FTE` to have two decimal places.

6. On a report page, create a Table visualization and place the `Date` column from the `R04_Table` table as well as the `FTE`, `Employment Costs`, `Total Costs`, `Revenue`, and `HCVA` measures into the **Values** area of the visualization. Edit the `Date` column in the **Values** area of the visualization to display the `Date Hierarchy` but only the `Quarter` from that hierarchy.

How it works...

For this recipe, we assume that the organization's `Total Annual Revenue`, `Total Annual Cost`, and `Employee Overhead Cost Factor` are all known values. The `Total Annual Revenue` measure represents the total amount of revenue earned during the year under analysis. Similarly, the `Total Annual Cost` measure represents the total of all costs to the organization, including employee costs. The `Employee Overhead Cost Factor` measure represents the multiplier by which employee annual salaries are adjusted to account for employee benefits such as health care.

The next data point we need is the amount of revenue earned by the organization during the time period under analysis. This is the purpose of the `Revenue` measure. While the actual revenue earned per quarter may be known to the organization, we can approximate this revenue from the `Total Annual Revenue` measure. To accomplish this, we make the assumption that the amount of revenue earned per day is evenly distributed across each day of the year. Therefore, we start by getting the starting and ending dates of the period under review, `__StartPeriod` and `__EndPeriod`. We use this information to determine the number of days within the period in question, `__DaysInPeriod`, by using `DATEDIFF` to calculate the number of days between `__StartPeriod` and `__EndPeriod`. We then determine the year of our analysis, `__Year`, and use this to determine the total number of days within the year, `__DaysInYear`. We can then calculate the amount of revenue earned in the period by dividing the total annual revenue, `Total Annual Revenue`, by the number of days in the year, `__DaysInYear`, and then multiplying by the number of days in the period, `__DaysInPeriod`.

We also need the total costs incurred by the organization during the period in question, the `Total Costs` measure. This calculation is made by making the same assumption as was made with `Total Annual Revenue` and the equation is identical to our `Revenue` calculation, except that we use `Total Annual Cost` instead of `Total Annual Revenue`.

We now need to determine how many FTEs worked during the time period under analysis. This is the `FTE` measure. To do this, we start by getting the starting and ending dates of the period under review, `__StartPeriod` and `__EndPeriod`. We use this information to determine the number of days within the period in question, `__TotalDaysInPeriod`, by using `DATEDIFF` to calculate the number of days between `__StartPeriod` and `__EndPeriod`. We then compute a table, `__Employees`, that accounts for employees coming into and leaving the organization during the time period in question. We do this by first using `FILTER` to get the employees that have a `Hire Date` before the end of our period, `__EndPeriod`, and have a `Leave Date` of after the start of our time period, `__StartPeriod`, or have a special `Leave Date` value that denotes that they are still employed by the organization, in this case, 1/1/9999.

We use `ADDCOLUMNS` to compute each employee's relevant starting and ending dates, `__MinDate` and `__MaxDate`, within the period in question. For `__MinDate`, we check if the employee's `Hire Date` is after the start of our period, `__StartPeriod`, and, if so, their `Hire Date` is used. Otherwise, the start of the period, `__StartPeriod` is used. Similarly, for `__MaxDate`, we check if the employee's `Leave Date` is before the end of our period, `__EndPeriod`, and, if so, their `Leave Date` is used. Otherwise, the end of the period, `__EndPeriod` is used. We then use `ADDCOLUMNS` again to create the `__DaysInPeriod` column, which is the number of days between `__MaxDate` and `__MinDate`. The `__Employees` variable now contains a table with only the employees relevant to the time period under analysis and the number of relevant days within that period.

We determine how many full-time employees are included in the `__Employees` table variable; this is our `__FullTimeEmployees` variable. To compute `__FullTimeEmployees`, we use `FILTER` to restrict the rows to only those employees whose `__DaysInPeriod` column equal the `__TotalDaysInPeriod` variable. We then count the number of rows using `COUNTROWS`. This number is stored in the `__FullTimeEmployees` variable.

Determining the FTEs for all employees that worked for a portion of the time period in question, `__PartTimeEmployees`, is similar to `__FullTimeEmployees`. We use `FILTER` to restrict the rows to those employees whose `__DaysInPeriod` column is less than the `__TotalDaysInPeriod` variable. We sum the values of the `__DaysInPeriod` column using `SUMX` and then divide this value by the number of days in the period, the `__TotalDaysInPeriod` variable. The final value for the FTE measure is simply the sum of the full-time employees, `__FullTimeEmployees`, and the part-time employees, `__PartTimeEmployees`.

The final component for calculating HVCA is to determine the cost of employees during the time period in question, the `Employment Costs` measure. The formula for `Employment Costs` starts out identically to the formula for `FTE`. However, we add an additional `ADDCOLUMS` function to the calculation of our `__Employees` table variable that adds the `__TotalCostInPeriod` column. This column spreads the annual cost of the employee, the `Annual Salary` column, over each day of the year, `__DaysInYear`, and then multiplies that value by the employee's `__DaysInPeriod` column. We can determine the final value for `Employment Cost`, `__TotalCostInPeriod`, by using `SUMX` to sum the `__TotalCostInPeriod` column within our `__Employees` table variable and then multiplying this sum by the `Employee Overhead Cost Factor`.

Finally, the `HVCA` measure can be calculated through the implementation of the HCVA formula using the `Revenue`, `Total Costs`, `Employment Costs`, and `FTE` measures.

See also

For more details of the functions in this recipe, refer to the following links:

- MIN: https://docs.microsoft.com/en-us/dax/min-function-dax
- MAX: https://docs.microsoft.com/en-us/dax/max-function-dax
- DATEDIFF: https://docs.microsoft.com/en-us/dax/datediff-function-dax
- YEAR: https://docs.microsoft.com/en-us/dax/year-function-dax
- ADDCOLUMNS: https://docs.microsoft.com/en-us/dax/addcolumns-function-dax
- FILTER: https://docs.microsoft.com/en-us/dax/filter-function-dax
- COUNTROWS: https://docs.microsoft.com/en-us/dax/countrows-function-dax
- SUMX: https://docs.microsoft.com/en-us/dax/sumx-function-dax

Finding the full-time equivalent

The **full-time equivalent**, or **FTE**, is the number of hours worked by a full-time employee. When businesses employ numerous part-time employees, it is often beneficial to understand how the hours worked by these part-time employees translate into the equivalent number of full-time employees. The FTE metric is used in numerous other metrics and calculations and is useful for budget analysis, project scheduling, industry analysis, and when comparing the number of FTEs to such things as office square footage, revenues, and profits.

Generally, an FTE is considered to have a theoretical maximum of 2,080 hours. This number is found by multiplying 8 working hours per day by 5 working days per week by 52 weeks per year. 8 * 5 * 52 = 2,080. However, some organizations use a lower figure to account for vacation days, sick days, and holidays.

This recipe is designed to calculate the number of FTE employees based upon hours worked by part-time employees and operate at any date hierarchy level, such as year, quarter, month, or day.

Getting ready

To prepare for this recipe, do the following:

1. Open Power BI Desktop.
2. Create a table called `R05_Table` using the following formula:

```
R05_Table =
    VAR __Calendar =
        EXCEPT(
            FILTER(
                SELECTCOLUMNS(
GENERATESERIES(DATE(2019,1,1),DATE(2019,12,31),1),
                    "Date",[Value]
                ),
                WEEKDAY([Date],2) < 6
            ),
            SELECTCOLUMNS(
                { DATE(2019,12,25), DATE(2019,4,1), DATE(2019,2,2)
},
                "Date",[Value]
            )
        )
    VAR __FT = { "Greg", "Julie", "Scott", "Bob", "John" }
    VAR __PT1 = { "Jimmy", "Terry", "Billy", "Sam", "Harry" }
    VAR __PT2 = { "Jerry", "Rob", "Sajith", "Pam", "Mike", "Aaron"
}
    VAR __FTHours =
        ADDCOLUMNS(
            GENERATE(__Calendar,__FT),
            "Type","FT",
            "Hours",RANDBETWEEN(6,8)
        )
    VAR __PT1Hours =
        ADDCOLUMNS(
            GENERATE(__Calendar,__PT1),
```

```
                    "Type","PT",
                    "Hours",RANDBETWEEN(3,5)
            )
        VAR __PT2Hours =
            ADDCOLUMNS(
                GENERATE(__Calendar,__PT2),
                "Type","PT",
                "Hours",RANDBETWEEN(2,4)
            )
    RETURN
        ADDCOLUMNS(
            UNION(__FTHours,__PT1Hours,__PT2Hours),
            "Work Hours",8
        )
```

3. Rename the `Value` column in the `R05_Table` table to `Employee`.

This data represents timesheet information reported by 16 different employees. Five of these employees are full-time employees, denoted by the value `FT` in the `Type` column. The other 11 employees are part-time employees, denoted by the value `PT` in the `Type` column. Five of these part-time employees work between 3 to 5 hours in a day, while the other 6 part-time employees work between 2 to 4 hours per day. The hours reported are for all working days in the calendar year 2019, meaning Monday through Friday of each week and excluding the holidays Christmas (December 25th), April Fool's Day (April 1st), and Groundhog Day (February 2nd). Each row in this table has a `Work Hours` column that contains the value `8`, which is the maximum number of work hours per day.

 Note that, since this is a purely calculated table that uses random dates (`RANDBETWEEN`), the data in this table will change if a data refresh or reload event is triggered.

How to do it...

Finding full-time equivalent can be done in the following steps:

1. Create the following measure:

```
FTEs =
    VAR __FT =
        COUNTROWS(
            SUMMARIZE(
                FILTER('R05_Table', [Type] = "FT"),
                [Employee]
```

```
            )
        )
    VAR __PT =
        SUMMARIZE(
            FILTER('R05_Table', [Type] = "PT"),
            [Employee],
            "__Hours",SUM([Hours])
        )
    VAR __WorkHours =
        SUMMARIZE(
            'R05_Table',
            [Date],
            "__WorkHours",AVERAGE([Work Hours])
        )
    VAR __TotalPartTimeHours = SUMX(__PT,[__Hours])
    VAR __TotalWorkHours = SUMX(__WorkHours,[__WorkHours])
    RETURN
        __FT + DIVIDE(__TotalPartTimeHours, __TotalWorkHours, 0)
```

2. Format FTEs to have two decimal places.
3. On a report page create a clustered column chart visualization and place the Date column from the R05_Table table into the **Axis** area of the visualization; also place the FTEs measure into the **Value** area of the visualization.
4. Use the forked arrow icon, **Expand all down one level in the hierarchy**, as well as the up arrow, **Drill up**, to drill down and up within the Date hierarchy and observe the varying values for the FTEs measure.

How it works...

The FTEs measure is designed to work at all levels of a date hierarchy, accounting for the fact that there are different numbers of working hours in different months and quarters of the year.

We start by counting the number of full-time employees, __FT. Employees designated as full time are always considered FTEs. We do this by using FILTER to restrict the R05_Table table to just those rows that have the value FT in the Type column. We then use SUMMARIZE to group the rows in that table by the Employee column. This effectively returns a table with distinct values for the Employee column. We can then simply use COUNTROWS to count the number of full-time employees.

Next, we calculate a table variable that contains information on part-time employees, __PT. This table uses FILTER to restrict the R05_Table table to just those rows that have the value PT in the Type column. We then use SUMMARIZE to group the rows in that table by the Employee column. Within this SUMMARIZE function, we add a column called __Hours that contains the SUM of the hours worked by each part-time employee.

We now need to determine the number of working hours within the period in question, __WorkHours. Because the R05_Table table contains multiple rows of the same date, we again use SUMMARIZE to group the rows in the R05_Table table by the Date column. Within this SUMMARIZE function, we add a column called __WorkHours that contains the AVERAGE of the Work Hours column.

We can use the __PT table variable to determine the total amount of part-time employee hours reported in the period, __TotalPartTimeHours, by using the SUMX function to sum the __Hours column in the __PT table variable. Similarly, we can calculate the total amount of work hours available in the period, __TotalWorkHours, by using the SUMX function to sum the __WorkHours column in the __WorkHours table variable.

Finally, we can return the value for the FTEs measure by dividing __TotalPartTimeHours by __TotalWorkHours. This quotient represents the number of full-time employees that is equivalent to the hours worked by part-time employees. We add this number to the number of full-time employees, __FT, to return the total number of full-time equivalent employees.

See also

For more details of the functions in this recipe, refer to the following links:

- EXCEPT: https://docs.microsoft.com/en-us/dax/min-function-dax
- SELECTCOLUMNS: https://docs.microsoft.com/en-us/dax/max-function-dax
- WEEKDAY: https://docs.microsoft.com/en-us/dax/weekday-function-dax
- DATE: https://docs.microsoft.com/en-us/dax/date-function-dax
- GENERATE: https://docs.microsoft.com/en-us/dax/generate-function-dax
- UNION: https://docs.microsoft.com/en-us/dax/union-function-dax

- DIVIDE: https://docs.microsoft.com/en-us/dax/divide-function-dax
- SUMMARIZE: https://docs.microsoft.com/en-us/dax/summarize-function-dax
- ADDCOLUMNS: https://docs.microsoft.com/en-us/dax/addcolumns-function-dax
- FILTER: https://docs.microsoft.com/en-us/dax/filter-function-dax
- COUNTROWS: https://docs.microsoft.com/en-us/dax/countrows-function-dax
- SUMX: https://docs.microsoft.com/en-us/dax/sumx-function-dax
- RANDBETWEEN: https://docs.microsoft.com/en-us/dax/randbetween-function-dax

Using Kaplan-Meier survival curves

The Kaplan-Meier estimator, also known as the **product-limit estimator**, is a statistical measure used to estimate the percentage chance of survival of a population over a given length of time. The formula for the Kaplan-Meier estimator is given as follows:

$$Survival(t) = \prod_{i:t_i <= t} (1 - \frac{d_i}{n_i})$$

In plain English, this formula means that the survivability at any time (t) is the product of 1 minus the number of end events (d), the non-surviving population, divided by the number of the population that have not reached an end event (n), the surviving population, for all increments of time (t) that are less than or equal to the current time (t).

Think of this as essentially a running product over time. This means that values for the function are calculated for each increment of time (t) less than or equal to the present time and then multiplied together to get a new value. Obviously, this is similar in concept to a running sum except that multiplication is being used instead of addition.

Perhaps most associated with use in the clinical sciences, the Kaplan-Meier estimator morbidly allows the estimation of the percentage chance of survival over time once a patient has been diagnosed with a disease or received treatment for a disease. This is accomplished by using historical data that contains information on when patients have died after being diagnosed with the same disease or received similar treatment.

However, all that is really required to use the Kaplan-Meier estimator is a defined population and a duration of time between the start and end of an event. This means that there are numerous applications for the Kaplan-Meier estimator. For instance, the Kaplan-Meier estimator can be used to analyze the historical record of machine failures in order to determine the length of time when an additional failure is likely. In this case, the start time is when the machine started operation and the end event time is a failure or repair of the machine. Similarly, the Kaplan-Meier estimator can be used to determine the length of time someone might remain jobless. In this instance, the starting event is the loss of one's job and the end event is finding a new job.

This recipe uses the Kaplan-Meier estimator to determine the expected tenure of employees within an organization using simple human resources data that should be available to nearly all businesses. In this case, the start time is the date of hire for an employee and the end event time is the date of that employee leaving the organization. This recipe demonstrates how to compare the survival rates between two segments of the population. In this recipe, we use two different departments. However, any segmentation could be used, such as employees voluntarily leaving or involuntarily leaving.

Getting ready

To prepare for this recipe, do the following:

1. Open Power BI Desktop.
2. Create a table called `R06_Table` using the following formula:

```
R06_Table =
    VAR __Initialize =
        SELECTCOLUMNS (
            {
                ( 0 , DATE(2012,1,1), DATE(2012,1,1), "DeptA" ),
                ( 0 , DATE(2012,1,1), DATE(2012,1,1), "DeptB" )
            },
            "Value",[Value1],
            "Hire Date",[Value2],
            "End Date",[Value3],
            "Department",[Value4]
        )
    VAR __Table =
        ADDCOLUMNS (
            ADDCOLUMNS (
                GENERATESERIES(1,250,1),
                "Hire
Date",RANDBETWEEN(DATE(2012,1,1),DATE(2012,6,30)) +
```

```
DATE(1899,12,30)
            ),
        "End Date",
            IF([Value] < 80,
                IF(MOD([Value],3) = 0,
                    BLANK(),
                    RANDBETWEEN([Hire
Date]+180,DATE(2019,10,15)) + DATE(1899,12,30)
                ),
                IF(MOD([Value],11) = 0,
                    BLANK(),
                    RANDBETWEEN([Hire Date],DATE(2019,10,15)) +
DATE(1899,12,30)
                )
            ),
        "Department",IF([Value] < 80,"DeptA","DeptB")
    )
RETURN
    UNION(__Initialize, __Table)
```

3. Rename the `Value` column in the `R06_Table` table to `Employee`.

This data represents data on 250 unique employees and contains the date those employees were hired into the organization, `Hire Date`, left the organization, `End Date`, and their department, `Department`. This data has been specifically engineered to produce greater survivability in `DeptA` rather than `DeptB`.

 It should be noted that, since this is a purely calculated table that uses random dates (RANDBETWEEN), the data in this table will change if a data refresh or reload event is triggered.

How to do it...

To implement this recipe, do the following:

1. In the `R06_Table` table, create the following columns:

```
Count = 1
Event = IF(ISBLANK([End Date]),0,1)

Count = 1

Event = IF(ISBLANK([End Date]),0,1)
```

```
Days =
    IF (
        [Event],
        DATEDIFF ('R06_Table'[Hire Date],'R06_Table'[End Date],DAY),
        DATEDIFF ('R06_Table'[Hire Date],TODAY(),DAY)
    )

DeptDayKey =
    CONCATENATE (
        'R06_Table'[Department],
        FORMAT (
        'R06_Table'[Days],
            "0000"
        )
    )
```

2. Create a table called R06_KM using the following formula:

```
R06_KM =
    VAR __DeptA =
        ADDCOLUMNS (
            GENERATESERIES(0,MAX('R06_Table'[Days]),1),
            "Department","DeptA",
"DeptDayKey",CONCATENATE("DeptA",FORMAT([Value],"0000"))
        )
    VAR __DeptB =
        ADDCOLUMNS (
            GENERATESERIES(0,MAX('R06_Table'[Days]),1),
            "Department","DeptB",
"DeptDayKey",CONCATENATE("DeptB",FORMAT([Value],"0000"))
        )
RETURN
    UNION(__DeptA,__DeptB)
```

3. Rename the Value column in the R06_KM table to Days.

4. Relate the R06_KM table to the R06_Table table using the DeptDateKey columns in both tables. The relationship should be one-to-many with the R06_KM table on the one side of the relationship and the R06_Table table on the many side of the relationship.

5. In the R06_KM table, create the following columns:

```
Count =
    VAR __Count =
SUMX(RELATEDTABLE('R06_Table'),'R06_Table'[Count])
RETURN
    IF(ISBLANK(__Count),0,__Count)
```

```
Running Count =
    SUMX(
        FILTER(
            ALL('R06_KM'),
            [Department]=EARLIER([Department]) &&
            [DeptDayKey]<=EARLIER([DeptDayKey])
        ),
        [Count]
    )


d(i) =
    VAR __Events =
SUMX(RELATEDTABLE('R06_Table'),'R06_Table'[Event])
RETURN
    IF(ISBLANK(__Events),0,__Events)


n(i) =
    [Count] +
    SUMX(
        FILTER(
            ALL('R06_KM'),
            [Department]=EARLIER([Department])
        ),
        [Count]
    ) -
    [Running Count]
```

6. Create the following measure:

```
Survivability =
    CALCULATE(
        PRODUCT('R06_KM'[1-d(i)/n(i)]),
        FILTER(
            ALLSELECTED('R06_KM'[Days]),
            ISONORAFTER('R06_KM'[Days], MAX('R06_KM'[Days]), DESC)
        )
    )
```

7. Format the `Survivability` measure as a percentage.

8. On a report page, create a line chart visualization and place the `Days` column from the `R06_KM` table in the **Axis** area, the `Department` column from the `R06_KM` table into the **Legend** area, and the `Survivability` measure into the **Values** area.

Note that, overall, `DeptA` has higher survivability than `DeptB`, particularly towards the end of the curves where the `Days` number is the highest.

How it works...

We start by adding four columns to our main fact table, R06_Table. The first column, Count, is set to a static value of 1 for all rows in the table. This may seem superfluous, but it will make certain later calculations a bit easier and more consistent. The second column, Event, is set to 1 if the employee has reached an end event (termination) and set to 0 if they have not. The Event column is our indicator of whether or not the employee is still employed by the organization. The third column is the number of days of tenure with the organization, Days. In the event that an employee has reached an end event, the Days column is calculated to be the difference between the End Date for the employee and the Hire Date for the employee. Otherwise, the Days column is the difference between the current date as returned by the TODAY function and the Hire Date for the employee. The fourth column, DeptDateKey, provides a key column that will later be used to relate the R06_KM table. The DeptDateKey column is created by using the CONCATENATE function to join the Department column with the Days column, with the latter column being formatted, using the FORMAT function, to always have four digits with leading zeros if necessary.

With operations on our base table, R06_Table, completed, our next step is to construct a new table that will become the basis for our Kaplan-Meier estimator calculations. This is necessary in order to create the running product that the Kaplan-Meier estimator function requires. Because we desire to compare estimations for two distinct segments of our population, we create two similar table variables, __DeptA and __DeptB, and use the UNION function to combine these two table variables into a single table. For both the __DeptA and __DeptB variables, we start by using GENERATESERIES to create a table that contains all the possible days of tenure for an employee from 0 to the maximum number of tenure days listed in the Days column in the R06_Table table. To this table of values returned by the GENERATESERIES function, we add a column, Department, that specifies the appropriate segment of our population as well as a similar DeptDateKey formula as used previously to create a unique key per row of the table. Importantly, because of the use of our population segmentation column, Department, within DeptDateKey, this key remains unique within the R06_KM table, even after a union of the two table variables, __DeptA and __DeptB.

We now have the base table required for our Kaplan-Meier estimator calculations. These Kaplan-Meier calculations consist of five columns. The first column, `Count`, simply records the number of the segment of the population that has reached the particular tenure milestone, `Days`. This is accomplished by essentially counting the related records for the segment of the population in our base table, `R06_Table`, only we use the `Count` column created previously in the `R06_Table` table, which is always 1, and use `SUMX` to sum the values in the column. The next column, `Running Count`, keeps a running total of the `Count` column in the `R06_KM` table. This is essentially a running total of all employees that have a tenure that is less than or equal to the current tenure as represented in the `Days` column for each row. This is achieved by using the `EARLIER` function to `FILTER` the `R06_KM` table to only the rows that have a tenure, `Days`, that is less than or equal to the current row's value for the `Days` column and have the same segmentation, `Department`, as the current row.

The third column, `d(i)`, stores the number of employees that have exited the segmented population at the tenure denoted by the `Days` column and is the numerator in our Kaplan-Meier estimator equation. The `d(i)` column is calculated by using `SUMX` to sum the `Event` column of related records in the base table, `R06_Table`. Recall that the `Event` column in the `R06_Table` table contains a 1 if an end event has occurred and 0 if not. Thus, the `d(i)` column becomes the number of non-surviving members of the population segment for each tenure denoted by the `Days` column. Our fourth column, `n(i)`, stores the number of employees still surviving within the segmented population at the tenure denoted by the `Days` column and is the denominator in our Kaplan-Meier estimator equation. The `n(i)` column is calculated by adding our `Count` column to the total original population and then subtracting our `Running Count` column. We can now finally calculate the value of our Kaplan-Meier function at each tenure of `Days` by creating our fifth column, `1-d(i)/n(i)`, which simply implements the Kaplan-Meier estimation function using our previous created columns.

Now that we have the Kaplan-Meier estimation function calculated for every possible time (*t*), our final step is to implement the running product. This is the purpose of the `Survivability` measure. The `Survivability` measure is calculated similarly to the `Running Total` quick measure in Power BI's DAX Quick Measures gallery. Using the `CALCULATE` function, we return the `PRODUCT` of the `1-d(i)/n(i)` column multiplied across all rows in the `R06_KM` table that have a value for the `Days` column that is less than or equal to the current maximum value for the `Days` column within the current context.

See also

For more details of the functions in this recipe, refer to the following links:

- **Kaplan-Meier Estimator:** `https://en.wikipedia.org/wiki/Kaplan-Meier_estimator`
- **Table Constructor:** `https://docs.microsoft.com/en-us/dax/table-constructor`
- SELECTCOLUMNS: `https://docs.microsoft.com/en-us/dax/max-function-dax`
- ADDCOLUMNS: `https://docs.microsoft.com/en-us/dax/addcolumns-function-dax`
- GENERATESERIES: `https://docs.microsoft.com/en-us/dax/generateseries-function-dax`
- UNION: `https://docs.microsoft.com/en-us/dax/union-function-dax`
- IF: `https://docs.microsoft.com/en-us/dax/if-function-dax`
- DATE: `https://docs.microsoft.com/en-us/dax/date-function-dax`
- MOD: `https://docs.microsoft.com/en-us/dax/mod-function-dax`
- BLANK: `https://docs.microsoft.com/en-us/dax/blank-function-dax`
- RANDBETWEEN: `https://docs.microsoft.com/en-us/dax/randbetween-function-dax`
- DATEDIFF: `https://docs.microsoft.com/en-us/dax/datediff-function-dax`
- CONCATENATE: `https://docs.microsoft.com/en-us/dax/concatenate-function-dax`
- FORMAT: `https://docs.microsoft.com/en-us/dax/format-function-dax`
- SUMX: `https://docs.microsoft.com/en-us/dax/sumx-function-dax`
- RELATEDTABLE: `https://docs.microsoft.com/en-us/dax/relatedtable-function-dax`
- ISBLANK: `https://docs.microsoft.com/en-us/dax/isblank-function-dax`
- EARLIER: `https://docs.microsoft.com/en-us/dax/earlier-function-dax`
- ALL: `https://docs.microsoft.com/en-us/dax/all-function-dax`
- CALCULATE: `https://docs.microsoft.com/en-us/dax/calculate-function-dax`
- PRODUCT: `https://docs.microsoft.com/en-us/dax/product-function-dax`
- ALLSELECTED: `https://docs.microsoft.com/en-us/dax/allselected-function-dax`
- ISONORAFTER: `https://docs.microsoft.com/en-us/dax/isonorafter-function-dax`

8
Processing Project Performance

Projects are carefully planned endeavors that involve one or more individuals engaging in tasks that are designed to accomplish particular aims or goals. Most organizations engage in projects in one form or another. For example, an organization may wish to redesign its website. Often, this becomes a project with specific tasks designed to ensure that the website is redesigned and deployed on time and within a specific budget. Being carefully planned, projects have an array of metrics and KPIs that project managers find critical to their role: keeping project expenses within specified budgets and reaching the goals of the project within specified timelines. This chapter is all about how to calculate many of these key metrics and KPIs. By calculating and tracking these project metrics and KPIs, project managers can identify projects at risk of exceeding specified budgets and timelines; they can also measure overall project performance.

The following is a list of recipes in this chapter:

- Calculating utilization
- Projecting planned value
- Estimating earned value
- Achieving actual cost
- Creating project schedule variance
- Computing project cost variance
- Constructing burndown charts

Technical requirements

The following are required to complete all of the recipes in this chapter:

- Power BI Desktop
- This book's GitHub repository at `https://github.com/PacktPublishing/DAX-Cookbook/tree/master/Chapter08`

Calculating utilization

Utilization is the concept of comparing productive time to unproductive time. Utilization is generally expressed as a percentage and is calculated as the ratio between productive time and all productive and unproductive time. Utilization is often used in project management to determine where resources are being expended and can be helpful in finding project resources that are underutilized.

This recipe demonstrates how to calculate utilization, with productive time being categorized as billable time and unproductive time being categorized as non-billable time.

Getting ready

To prepare for this recipe, do the following:

1. Open Power BI Desktop.
2. Import the data from the `Ch08R01Data.xlsx` Excel file located in this book's GitHub repository. Ensure that the table that's created is called `R01_Table`.
3. Create a table called `R01_Calendar` using the following formula:

   ```
   R01_Calendar = CALENDAR(DATE(2019,1,1),DATE(2019,3,31))
   ```

4. Create the following column in the `R01_Calendar` table:

   ```
   Work Hours = IF(WEEKDAY('R01_Calendar'[Date],2) < 6,8,0)
   ```

5. Create a relationship between the `Date` columns in the `R01_Table` and `R01_Calendar` tables and ensure that `Cross filter direction` is set to `Both`.

Each row in the R01_Table table represents daily hours reported by employees against various projects and tasks within those projects. Each project has a unique JobID that identifies the project and each task has a TaskID that identifies the task within the project. In addition, each employee has a PayType that identifies the employee as either an internal resource (ADMINISTRATION) or as some form of billable employee (SALARY, HOURLY, SUB-CONTRACTOR). Finally, each combination of project and task code is given a Category of either Billable or a non-billable category such as Bench, Int Admin, or PTO.

The Work Hours column in the R01_Calendar table simply determines if the Date in each row is a weekday or a weekend. If the Date is a weekday, a value of **8** hours is assigned; otherwise, a value of 0 hours is assigned. Thus, the Work Hours column represents the total number of potential billable hours available for each day.

How to do it...

To implement this recipe, do the following:

1. Create the following measures:

```
Total Billable Hours =
    VAR __Category = MAX('R01_Table'[PayType])
RETURN
    IF(
        __Category = "ADMINISTRATION",
        0,
        SUMX(
            FILTER(
                'R01_Table',
                'R01_Table'[Category] = "Billable"
            ),
            'R01_Table'[Hours]
        )
    )

Total Hours =
    SWITCH(
        MAX('R01_Table'[PayType]),
        "HOURLY",[Total Billable Hours],
        "SUB-CONTRACTOR",[Total Billable Hours],
        "SALARY",SUM('R01_Calendar'[Work Hours]),
        BLANK()
    )
```

```
% Utilization =
    VAR __Table = SUMMARIZE('R01_Table','R01_Table'[EmployeeID])
    VAR __TotalBillableHours = SUMX(__Table,[Total Billable Hours])
    VAR __TotalHours = SUMX(__Table,[Total Hours])
    VAR __Utilization = DIVIDE(__TotalBillableHours,__TotalHours,0)
RETURN
    IF(ISBLANK(__Utilization),0,__Utilization)
```

2. On a **Report** page, create a matrix visualization and place the `JobID` and `EmployeeID` columns from the `R01_Table` table into the `Rows` area, with the `JobID` column being at the top and the `EmployeeID` column at the bottom.
3. In the same matrix visualization, place the `% Utilization` measure into the **Value** area.

How it works...

The first measure, `Total Billable Hours`, calculates the total amount of billable or productive time. This is done by checking whether the `PayType` of the employee is equal to `ADMINISTRATION`. If so, then `0` is returned as the employee is not expected to be billable. Otherwise, the amount of billable time is computed by using `FILTER` to return only the rows in `R01_Table` that have a `Category` of `Billable` and then using `SUMX` to sum the `Hours` column.

The next measure, `Total Hours`, calculates the total amount of billable (productive) and non-billable time (unproductive). However, the `PayType` of each billable employee affects how `Total Hours` is calculated. We do this by using a `SWITCH` statement based upon the `PayType` column. Since we must use an aggregating function such as `MAX` when referencing columns within a measure, it is important to realize that this measure is only valid when it's used within the context of a single `EmployeeID` and that the employee must not have changed `PayType`.

For `HOURLY` and `SUB-CONTRACTOR` employees, since these employees are only paid for billable hours, we simply return the value from our `Total Billable Hours` measure for these employees. This means that `HOURLY` and `SUB-CONTRACTOR` employees are always considered to have 100% utilization. However, if the employee has a `PayType` of `SALARY`, then the sum of all potential work hours is returned from the `R01_Calendar` table.

Now that we have measures for productive time (Total Billable Hours) and all productive and unproductive time (Total Hours), we can calculate utilization in our % Utilization measure. This is fairly straightforward: we create a base table variable called __Table that uses SUMMARIZE to return a unique list of EmployeeID values that are currently in context. We can then use SUMX to sum our Total Billable Hours measure and store this value in the __TotalBillableHours variable. We can perform the same process to calculate __TotalHours. Then, we simply need to divide __TotalBillableHours by __TotalHours to get our utilization (__Utilization). In our RETURN statement, we simply check if __Utilization is blank (ISBLANK) and, if so, return 0. Otherwise, we return __Utilization.

See also

For more details about this recipe, please refer to the following links:

- FILTER: https://docs.microsoft.com/en-us/dax/filter-function-dax
- SWITCH: https://docs.microsoft.com/en-us/dax/switch-function-dax
- SUM: https://docs.microsoft.com/en-us/dax/sum-function-dax
- DIVIDE: https://docs.microsoft.com/en-us/dax/divide-function-dax
- COUNTROWS: https://docs.microsoft.com/en-us/dax/countrows-function-dax
- HASONEVALUE: https://docs.microsoft.com/en-us/dax/hasonevalue-function-dax
- IF: https://docs.microsoft.com/en-us/dax/if-function-dax
- BLANK: https://docs.microsoft.com/en-us/dax/blank-function-dax
- ISBLANK: https://docs.microsoft.com/en-us/dax/isblank-function-dax
- SUMX: https://docs.microsoft.com/en-us/dax/sumx-function-dax
- MAX: https://docs.microsoft.com/en-us/dax/max-function-dax
- FILTER: https://docs.microsoft.com/en-us/dax/filter-function-dax
- SUMMARIZE: https://docs.microsoft.com/en-us/dax/summarize-function-dax

Projecting planned value

Within project management circles, planned value is a crucial metric that's required to calculate numerous project-related **key performance indicators**, or **KPIs**. Simply stated, **planned value**, or **PV**, is the expected baseline cost of a project. In practical terms, this then becomes the budget for the project. Thus, planned value plays a key role in determining whether a project was completed under budget or over budget. Tracking actual costs against a planned value can help project managers identify projects that are at risk of going over budget. Planned value is also known as the **Budgeted Cost of Work Scheduled**, or **BCWS**.

While project costs can consist of both the cost for people performing the project work (salaries or hourly costs for consultants) and the costs of materials or physical assets, this recipe provides a calculation for the planned value that focuses on the costs of people performing project work.

Getting ready

To prepare for this recipe, do the following:

1. Open Power BI Desktop.
2. Use an **Enter Data** query to create a table called R02_Project that contains the following data:

ID	Project	Phase	Name	Scheduled_Work	Start_Date	Finish_Date
3	The Project	Phase 1	Task 1	24	1/13/2020	1/13/2020
4	The Project	Phase 1	Task 2	160	1/14/2020	1/27/2020
5	The Project	Phase 1	Task 3	40	1/28/2020	2/3/2020
7	The Project	Phase 2	Task 4	240	2/4/2020	2/24/2020
8	The Project	Phase 2	Task 5	200	2/25/2020	3/30/2020
9	The Project	Phase 2	Task 6	160	3/31/2020	4/27/2020
11	The Project	Phase 3	Task 7	120	4/28/2020	5/4/2020
12	The Project	Phase 3	Task 8	240	5/5/2020	5/25/2020
13	The Project	Phase 3	Task 9	80	5/26/2020	6/8/2020

3. Use another **Enter Data** query to create a table called `R02_Assignments` that contains the following data:

ID	Scheduled_Work	Resource_Name
3	8	Greg
3	8	Julie
3	8	Pam
4	80	Greg
4	80	Julie
5	40	Julie
7	120	Greg
7	120	Julie
8	200	Greg
9	160	Julie
11	40	Greg
11	40	Pam
11	40	Mike
12	120	Pam
12	120	Mike
13	80	Pam

4. Use another **Enter Data** query to create a table called `R02_Resources` that contains the following data:

Cost_Per_Hour	Resource_Name
95	Greg
85	Julie
75	Pam
75	Mike

5. Create a table called `R02_Calendar` using the following formula:

```
R02_Calendar = CALENDAR(DATE(2020,1,1),DATE(2020,6,30))
```

6. Create a relationship between the `ID` column in the `R02_Project` table and the `ID` column in the `R02_Assignments` table.

7. Create a relationship between the `Resource_Name` column in the `R02_Assignments` table and the `Resource_Name` column in the `R02_Resources` table. Ensure that this relationship has a `Cross filter direction` of `Both`.

8. Ensure that no other relationships exist in the data model for the tables that we created.

The `R02_Project` table represents the project plan. This project plan has three phases and nine tasks. The `Scheduled_Work` column in the `R02_Project` table provides the number of hours each task is expected to take to complete. The `R02_Assignments` table represents the resources assigned to each task and the number of hours (`Scheduled_Work`) these resources are expected to work on each task. Finally, the `R02_Resources` table provides the hourly per-resource cost for working on the project.

How to do it...

To implement this recipe, do the following:

1. Create a column in the `R02_Project` table using the following formula:

```
Planned Value =
    VAR __Table =
        ADDCOLUMNS (
            ADDCOLUMNS (
                RELATEDTABLE ('R02_Assignments'),
                "__Cost_Per_Hour",
                RELATED ('R02_Resources'[Cost_Per_Hour])
            ),
            "__PV",
            [Scheduled_Work] * [__Cost_Per_Hour]
        )
    RETURN
        SUMX (__Table, [__PV])
```

2. On a **Report** page, create a matrix visualization and place the `Project`, `Phase`, and `Name` columns from the `R02_Project` table into the `Rows` area with the `Project` column being at the top, then the `Phase` column, and then the `Name` column at the bottom.

3. In the same matrix visualization, place the `Planned Value` column from the `R02_Project` table into the **Value** area.

How it works...

We start by creating a table variable, __Table, that contains all of the related records from the R02_Assignments table and their respective costs. We do this by using the RELATEDTABLE function to return all the rows from the R02_Assignments table that are related to the current row in the R02_Projects table. To this table, we add a column called __Cost_Per_Hour using the ADDCOLUMNS function. This cost per hour comes from the R02_Resources table, so we use the RELATED function to return the related Cost_Per_Hour for each row of the R02_Assignments table. Then, we add an additional column called __PV, which is simply the product of the Scheduled_Work column from the R02_Assignments table, and our new __Cost_Per_Hour column. Finally, we need to return the sum of the __PV column using SUMX. By using a column, we are assured that our Planned Value provides the correct value at each level of the ad hoc hierarchy we created in our matrix visualization.

There's more...

Project managers often like to see the cumulative planned value of a project displayed over the course of time. To implement this, do the following:

1. Create a measure using the following formula:

```
PV =
    VAR __MaxDate = MAX('R02_Project'[Finish_Date])
    VAR __Date = MAX('R02_Calendar'[Date])
    VAR __Table =
        ADDCOLUMNS(
            ADDCOLUMNS(
                FILTER('R02_Project','R02_Project'[Start_Date] <
__Date),
                "__TaskDaysDuration",
DATEDIFF('R02_Project'[Start_Date],'R02_Project'[Finish_Date],DAY)
+ 1,
                "__Days",
                DATEDIFF('R02_Project'[Start_Date],__Date,DAY) + 1
            ),
            "__PV",
            IF(
                __Date > __MaxDate,
                BLANK(),
                IF(
```

```
                [__Days] >= [__TaskDaysDuration],
                'R02_Project'[Planned Value],
    [__Days]/[__TaskDaysDuration]*'R02_Project'[Planned Value]
                )
            )
        )
    RETURN
        SUMX(__Table,[__PV])
```

2. On a **Report** page, create a line chart visualization and place the `Date` column from the `R02_Calendar` table into the **Axis** area. Ensure that this field is set to `Date` and not `Date Hierarchy`.

3. In the same line chart visualization, place the `PV` measure into the **Value** area.

To explain how this measure operates, we start by simply getting the maximum `Finish_Date` within the `R02_Project` table, `__MaxDate`, and the maximum date within the current context of our line chart visualization, `__Date`.

Next, since we wish to display the cumulative sum of the planned value for each date, we construct a table variable, `__Table`, by using `FILTER` to return only those rows within the `R02_Project` table that have a `Start_Date` that is less than our current date, `__Date`. We add two columns to this base table using `ADDCOLUMNS`. The first column, `__TaskDaysDuration`, uses `DATEDIFF` to calculate the total duration in days of each task (row) within the filtered `R02_Project` table. This duration is the number of days between the `Start_Date` and `Finish_Date` of each task. The second column, `__Days`, again uses `DATEDIFF` but this time calculates the total duration in days between the `Start_Date` of each task (row) within the filtered `R02_Project` table and the current date, `__Date`.

Now, we use `ADDCOLUMNS` once more to add the `__PV` column. The calculation for `__PV` consists of two nested `IF` statements. The first `IF` statement checks if the current date, `__Date`, is greater than the maximum date within our project plan, `__MaxDate`. If so, then `BLANK` is returned. This prevents extraneous values from being displayed in the event that the dates in our calendar table exceed the end of the project. If the current date, `__Date`, is not greater than the maximum date within our project plan, `__MaxDate`, then our second `IF` statement executes. This `IF` statement checks to see if the number of days between the `Start_Date` of a task and the current date, `__Days`, is greater than or equal to the total duration in days for the task, `__TaskDaysDuration`. If so, then the full `Planned Value` amount for the task is returned. However, if the number of days between the `Start_Date` of a task and the current date, `__Days`, is not greater than or equal to the total duration in days for the task, `__TaskDaysDuration`, then we apportion the `Planned Value` of the task based upon a ratio of how many days of the task duration have been accrued.

Finally, we simply need to return the sum of our calculated planned values in the __PV column using SUMX in order to return the cumulative planned value of the project at any particular date.

See also

For more details about this recipe, please refer to the following links:

- ADDCOLUMNS: https://docs.microsoft.com/en-us/dax/addcolumns-function-dax
- RELATEDTABLE: https://docs.microsoft.com/en-us/dax/relatedtable-function-dax
- RELATED: https://docs.microsoft.com/en-us/dax/related-function-dax
- SUMX: https://docs.microsoft.com/en-us/dax/sumx-function-dax
- MAX: https://docs.microsoft.com/en-us/dax/max-function-dax
- FILTER: https://docs.microsoft.com/en-us/dax/filter-function-dax
- DATEDIFF: https://docs.microsoft.com/en-us/dax/datediff-function-dax
- IF: https://docs.microsoft.com/en-us/dax/if-function-dax
- BLANK: https://docs.microsoft.com/en-us/dax/blank-function-dax

Estimating earned value

Earned value, or **EV**, is a common metric that's used within the discipline of project management. The concept of earned value is relatively straightforward. Earned value is simply calculated by multiplying the completion percentage of a task by that task's planned value. Thus, the planned value of tasks is a necessary input in order to calculate the earned value. To learn how to calculate **Planned Value**, please refer to the *Projecting planned value* recipe in Chapter 8, *Processing Project Performance*. The earned value metric is often used as an early warning indicator that a project may be in danger of running over budget or past its expected end date.

This recipe demonstrates how to calculate the earned value for individual tasks as well as how to display the cumulative earned value of a project over time.

Getting ready

To prepare for this recipe, do the following:

1. Open Power BI Desktop.
2. Use an **Enter Data** query to create a table called `R03_Project` that contains the following data:

ID	Project	Phase	Name	Scheduled_Work	Start_Date	Finish_Date	% Complete	Planned Value
3	The Project	Phase 1	Task 1	24	1/13/2020	1/13/2020	1	2,040
4	The Project	Phase 1	Task 2	160	1/14/2020	1/27/2020	1	14,400
5	The Project	Phase 1	Task 3	40	1/28/2020	2/3/2020	1	3,400
7	The Project	Phase 2	Task 4	240	2/4/2020	2/24/2020	.75	21,600
8	The Project	Phase 2	Task 5	200	2/25/2020	3/30/2020	.5	19,000
9	The Project	Phase 2	Task 6	160	3/31/2020	4/27/2020	.25	13,600
11	The Project	Phase 3	Task 7	120	4/28/2020	5/4/2020	0	9,800
12	The Project	Phase 3	Task 8	240	5/5/2020	5/25/2020	0	18,000
13	The Project	Phase 3	Task 9	80	5/26/2020	6/8/2020	0	6,000

3. Create a table called `R03_Calendar` using the following formula:

```
R03_Calendar = CALENDAR(DATE(2020,1,1),DATE(2020,6,30))
```

The `R03_Project` table represents the project plan. This project plan has three phases and nine tasks. The `Scheduled_Work` column in the `R03_Project` table provides the number of hours each task is expected to take in order to complete the task. The `% Complete` column indicates how complete each task is. The `% Complete` figure is generally assigned by the project manager based on a decision with regard to how complete the task is. `% Complete` does not necessarily correspond to how much work has been reported against each task as tasks may take more or fewer hours to complete than scheduled. The `Planned Value` column is a necessary input for calculating `Earned Value`. The `Planned Value`, or PV, is the expected cost of each task according to the baseline project schedule.

How to do it...

To implement this recipe, do the following:

1. Create a column in the `R03_Project` table using the following formula:

```
Earned Value = 'R03_Project'[Planned Value] * 'R03_Project'[%
Complete]
```

2. Create the following measure:

```
EV =
    VAR __ReportingDate = DATE(2020,4,1)
    VAR __MaxDate = MAX('R03_Project'[Finish_Date])
    VAR __Date = MAX('R03_Calendar'[Date])
    VAR __Table =
        ADDCOLUMNS(
            ADDCOLUMNS(
                FILTER('R03_Project','R03_Project'[Start_Date] <
__Date),
                "__TaskDaysDuration",
DATEDIFF('R03_Project'[Start_Date],'R03_Project'[Finish_Date],DAY)
+ 1,
                "__Days",
                DATEDIFF('R03_Project'[Start_Date],__Date,DAY)
            ),
            "__EV",
            IF(
                __Date > __MaxDate,
                BLANK(),
                IF(
                    [__Days] >= [__TaskDaysDuration],
```

```
                          [Earned Value],
                          [__Days]/[__TaskDaysDuration] * [Earned Value]
                      )
                  )
              )
      RETURN
          IF(__Date > __ReportingDate, BLANK(), SUMX(__Table,[__EV]))
```

3. On a **Report** page, create a matrix visualization and place the `Project`, `Phase`, and `Name` columns from the `R03_Project` table into the **Rows** area with the `Project` column being at the top, then the `Phase` column and the `Name` column at the bottom.

4. In the same matrix visualization, place the `Earned Value` column from the `R03_Project` table into the **Value** area.

5. On the same **Report** page, create a line chart visualization and place the `Date` column from the `R03_Calendar` table into the **Axis** area. Ensure that this field is set to `Date` and not `Date Hierarchy`.

6. In the same line chart visualization, place the `EV` measure into the **Value** area.

How it works...

The basic formula for the `Earned Value` column is very straightforward. `Earned Value` is simply the `% Complete` of a task multiplied by the `Planned Value` of the same task.

Project managers often like to see the cumulative earned value of a project displayed over the course of time. This is the purpose of the `EV` measure. To explain how this measure operates, we start by specifying the current reporting date, `__ReportingDate`. We then get the maximum `Finish_Date` within the `R03_Project` table, `__MaxDate`, and the maximum date within the current context of our line chart visualization, `__Date`.

Next, since we wish to display the cumulative sum of the earned value for each date, we construct a table variable, `__Table`, by first using `FILTER` to return only those rows within the `R03_Project` table that have a `Start_Date` that is less than our current date, `__Date`. We add two columns to this base table using `ADDCOLUMNS`. The first column, `__TaskDaysDuration`, uses `DATEDIFF` to calculate the total duration in days of each task (row) within the filtered `R03_Project` table. This duration is the number of days between the `Start_Date` and `Finish_Date` of each task. The second column, `__Days`, again uses `DATEDIFF` but this time calculates the total duration in days between the `Start_Date` of each task (row) within the filtered `R03_Project` table and the current date, `__Date`.

Now, we use ADDCOLUMNS once more to add the __EV column. The calculation for __EV consists of two nested IF statements. The first IF statement checks if the current date, __Date, is greater than the maximum date within our project plan, __MaxDate. If so, then BLANK is returned. This prevents extraneous values from being displayed in the event that the dates in our calendar table exceed the end of the project. If the current date, __Date, is not greater than the maximum date within our project plan, __MaxDate, then our second IF statement executes. This IF statement checks to see if the number of days between the Start_Date of a task and the current date, __Days, is greater than or equal to the total duration in days for the task, __TaskDaysDuration. If so, then the full Earned Value amount for the task is returned.

However, if the number of days between the Start_Date of a task and the current date, __Days, is not greater than or equal to the total duration in days for the task, __TaskDaysDuration, then we apportion the Earned Value of the task-based upon a ratio of how many days of the task duration have been accrued.

Finally, we simply need to return the sum of our calculated earned values in the __EV column using SUMX in order to return the cumulative earned value of the project at any particular date. However, we first check if __Date exceeds our __ReportingDate and, if so, we return BLANK since we do not wish to display __EV values for dates exceeding our current __ReportingDate.

There's more...

In practice, project managers have varying methods of assigning earned value. One method is to assign a percentage of the planned value for the task once the task is started and then assign the full planned value once the task is completed. A common practice today is to assign 20% of the planned value when a task is started and the remaining 80% only when the task is completed. To implement this version of earned value, do the following:

1. Create a column in the R03_Project table using the following formula:

```
Earned Value 1 =
    IF(
        [% Complete] = 1,
        'R03_Project'[Planned Value],
        IF('R03_Project'[% Complete] > 0,
            'R03_Project'[Planned Value] * .2,
            0
```

```
            )
        )
```

2. Create the following measure:

```
EV1 =
    VAR __ReportingDate = DATE(2020,4,1)
    VAR __MaxDate = MAX('R03_Project'[Finish_Date])
    VAR __Date = MAX('R03_Calendar'[Date])
    VAR __Table =
        ADDCOLUMNS(
            ADDCOLUMNS(
                FILTER('R03_Project','R03_Project'[Start_Date] <
__Date),
                "__TaskDaysDuration",
DATEDIFF('R03_Project'[Start_Date],'R03_Project'[Finish_Date],DAY)
+ 1,
                "__Days",
                DATEDIFF('R03_Project'[Start_Date],__Date,DAY)
            ),
            "__EV",
            IF(
                __Date > __MaxDate,
                BLANK(),
                IF(
                    [__Days] >= [__TaskDaysDuration],
                    [Earned Value 1],
                    [__Days]/[__TaskDaysDuration] * [Earned Value
1]
                )
            )
        )
    RETURN
        IF(__Date > __ReportingDate, BLANK(), SUMX(__Table,[__EV]))
```

3. In the same line chart visualization we created previously, place the `EV1` measure into the **Value** area of the visualization.

From the line chart visualization, we can see how the different methods of assigning earned value affect its cumulative value over time.

In this version of earned value, the `Earned Value 1` column is simply two nested `IF` statements. The first `IF` statement checks to see if the task is complete (`% Complete` equals 1). If the task is complete, the full value of the `Planned Value` column is assigned. Otherwise, if the task is started and has a `% Complete` value greater than 0, then 20% of the `Planned Value` column is assigned. If the task is not started, `% Complete` equals 0, so the earned value is also 0.

The `EV1` measure is identical to the `EV` measure except that all references to the `Earned Value` column have been replaced with references to the `Earned Value 1` column.

See also

For more details about this recipe, please refer to the following links:

- MAX: https://docs.microsoft.com/en-us/dax/max-function-dax
- FILTER: https://docs.microsoft.com/en-us/dax/filter-function-dax
- DATEDIFF: https://docs.microsoft.com/en-us/dax/datediff-function-dax
- IF: https://docs.microsoft.com/en-us/dax/if-function-dax
- BLANK: https://docs.microsoft.com/en-us/dax/blank-function-dax
- SUMX: https://docs.microsoft.com/en-us/dax/sumx-function-dax

Achieving actual cost

Actual cost, or **AC**, of a project is, as its name implies, the costs of delivering a project based upon the material goods that have been purchased and the costs associated with project resources. The cost of project resources is generally calculated by multiplying the hours each resource worked on a project by the hourly rate or cost of each resource. This recipe demonstrates how to calculate the actual costs of a project and its tasks using the hours each resource reported as project work and the hourly cost of those resources.

Getting Ready

To prepare for this recipe, do the following:

1. Open Power BI Desktop.
2. Use an **Enter Data** query to create a table called `R04_Project` that contains the following data:

ID	Project	Phase	Name	Scheduled_Work	Start_Date	Finish_Date
3	The Project	Phase 1	Task 1	24	1/13/2020	1/13/2020
4	The Project	Phase 1	Task 2	160	1/14/2020	1/27/2020
5	The Project	Phase 1	Task 3	40	1/28/2020	2/3/2020
7	The Project	Phase 2	Task 4	240	2/4/2020	2/24/2020
8	The Project	Phase 2	Task 5	200	2/25/2020	3/30/2020
9	The Project	Phase 2	Task 6	160	3/31/2020	4/27/2020
11	The Project	Phase 3	Task 7	120	4/28/2020	5/4/2020
12	The Project	Phase 3	Task 8	240	5/5/2020	5/25/2020
13	The Project	Phase 3	Task 9	80	5/26/2020	6/8/2020

3. Use another **Enter Data** query to create a table called `R04_Resources` that contains the following data:

Cost_Per_Hour	Resource_Name
95	Greg
85	Julie
75	Pam
75	Mike

4. Create a table called `R04_Calendar` using the following formula:

```
R04_Calendar = CALENDAR(DATE(2020,1,1),DATE(2020,6,30))
```

5. Create another table called `R04_Hours` using the following formula:

```
R04_Hours =
    VAR __Greg = SELECTCOLUMNS({ ("Greg", 8) },"Resource
Name",[Value1],"Hours",[Value2])
    VAR __Julie = SELECTCOLUMNS({ ("Julie", 8) },"Resource
Name",[Value1],"Hours",[Value2])
    VAR __Pam = SELECTCOLUMNS({ ("Pam", 8) },"Resource
```

```
Name",[Value1],"Hours",[Value2])
    VAR __TaskID3 = SELECTCOLUMNS({ (3, DATE(2020,1,13))
},"ID",[Value1],"Date",[Value2])
    VAR __TaskID4 =
        SELECTCOLUMNS(
            ADDCOLUMNS(
                GENERATESERIES(DATE(2020,1,14),DATE(2020,1,27),1),
                "ID",4
            ),
            "ID",[ID],"Date",[Value]
        )
    VAR __TaskID5 =
        SELECTCOLUMNS(
            ADDCOLUMNS(
                GENERATESERIES(DATE(2020,1,28),DATE(2020,1,31),1),
                "ID",5
            ),
            "ID",[ID],"Date",[Value]
        )
    VAR __TaskID7 =
        SELECTCOLUMNS(
            ADDCOLUMNS(
                GENERATESERIES(DATE(2020,2,4),DATE(2020,2,12),1),
                "ID",7
            ),
            "ID",[ID],"Date",[Value]
        )
    VAR __TaskID8 =
        SELECTCOLUMNS(
            ADDCOLUMNS(
                GENERATESERIES(DATE(2020,2,25),DATE(2020,3,12),1),
                "ID",8
            ),
            "ID",[ID],"Date",[Value]
        )
    VAR __TaskID9 =
        SELECTCOLUMNS(
            ADDCOLUMNS(
                GENERATESERIES(DATE(2020,3,31),DATE(2020,4,1),1),
                "ID",9
            ),
            "ID",[ID],"Date",[Value]
        )
    VAR __Table1 =
        UNION(
            GENERATE(__Greg, __TaskID3),
            GENERATE(__Julie,__TaskID3),
            GENERATE(__Pam, __TaskID3)
```

```
            )
        VAR __Table2 = UNION(GENERATE(__Greg, __TaskID4),
    GENERATE(__Julie,__TaskID4))
        VAR __Table3 = GENERATE(__Julie,__TaskID5)
        VAR __Table4 = UNION(GENERATE(__Greg, __TaskID7),
    GENERATE(__Julie,__TaskID7))
        VAR __Table5 = GENERATE(__Greg,__TaskID8)
        VAR __Table6 = GENERATE(__Julie,__TaskID9)
    RETURN
        UNION(__Table1, __Table2, __Table3, __Table4, __Table5,
    __Table6)
```

6. Create a relationship between the `ID` column in the `R04_Project` table and the `ID` column in the `R04_Hours` table.

7. Create a relationship between the `Resource_Name` column in the `R04_Hours` table and the `Resource_Name` column in the `R04_Resources` table. Ensure that this relationship has a `Cross filter direction` of `Both`.

8. Ensure that no other relationships exist in the data model for the tables that were created.

The `R04_Project` table represents the project plan. This project plan has three phases and nine tasks. The `Scheduled_Work` column in the `R04_Project` table shows the number of hours each task is expected to complete. The `R04_Hours` table represents the hours of work that project resources assigned to each task have reported as expended against each task. The `Date` column within this table is the date upon which the reported hours were worked. Finally, the `R04_Resources` table provides the hourly cost for each resource when working on the project.

How to do it...

To implement this recipe, do the following:

1. Create a column in the `R04_Project` table using the following formula:

```
Actual Cost =
    VAR __Table =
        ADDCOLUMNS(
            ADDCOLUMNS(
                RELATEDTABLE('R04_Hours'),
                "__Cost_Per_Hour",
                RELATED('R04_Resources'[Cost_Per_Hour])
```

```
        ),
        "__Actual Cost",
        [Hours] * [__Cost_Per_Hour]
    )
RETURN
    SUMX(__Table,[__Actual Cost])
```

2. Create the following measure:

```
AC =
    VAR __Date = MAX('R04_Calendar'[Date])
    VAR __Table =
        ADDCOLUMNS(
            ADDCOLUMNS(
                FILTER('R04_Hours', 'R04_Hours'[Date] <= __Date),
                "__Cost_Per_Hour",
                RELATED('R04_Resources'[Cost_Per_Hour])
            ),
            "__AC",
            [Hours] * [__Cost_Per_Hour]
        )
RETURN
    SUMX(__Table,[__AC])
```

3. On a **Report** page, create a matrix visualization and place the `Project`, `Phase`, and `Name` columns from the `R04_Project` table into the **Rows** area with the `Project` column being at the top, then the `Phase` column, and the `Name` column at the bottom.

4. In the same matrix visualization, place the `Actual Cost` column from the `R04_Project` table into the **Value** area.

5. On the same **Report** page, create a line chart visualization and place the `Date` column from the `R04_Calendar` table into the **Axis** area. Ensure that this field is set to `Date` and not `Date Hierarchy`.

6. In the same line chart visualization, place the `AC` measure into the **Value** area.

How it works...

For the `Actual Cost` column, we start by creating a table variable, `__Table`, that contains all of the related records from the `R04_Hours` table and their respective costs. We do this by using the `RELATEDTABLE` function to return all the rows from the `R04_Hours` table that are related to the current row in the `R04_Projects` table. We add a column called `__Cost_Per_Hour` to this table using the `ADDCOLUMNS` function. This cost per hour comes from the `R04_Resources` table, so we use the `RELATED` function to return the related `Cost_Per_Hour` for each row of the `R04_Hours` table. Then, we add an additional column called `__AC`, which is simply the product of the `Hours` column from the `R04_Hours` table, and our new `__Cost_Per_Hour` column. Finally, we simply need to return the sum of the `__AC` column using `SUMX`. By using a column, we are assured that our `Actual Cost` provides the correct value at each level of the ad hoc hierarchy we created in our matrix visualization.

To display the cumulative actual costs over time, we use the `AC` measure. The calculation of this `AC` measure is nearly identical to our `Actual Cost` column. There are only two differences. The first difference is that we start by getting the maximum date within the current context of our line chart visualization, `__Date`. The second difference is that, instead of starting with a table that has been built using the `RELATEDTABLE` function, we use the `FILTER` function to filter rows within the `R04_Hours` table that have a Date column that is less than or equal to `__Date`.

See also

For more details about this recipe, please refer to the following links:

- MAX: https://docs.microsoft.com/en-us/dax/max-function-dax
- RELATEDTABLE: https://docs.microsoft.com/en-us/dax/relatedtable-function-dax
- RELATED: https://docs.microsoft.com/en-us/dax/related-function-dax
- FILTER: https://docs.microsoft.com/en-us/dax/filter-function-dax
- SUMX: https://docs.microsoft.com/en-us/dax/sumx-function-dax

Creating project schedule variance

The project schedule variance metric is the difference between the planned value of a project and the earned value of a project. Planned value, or PV, is the expected baseline cost of a project. Earned value, or EV, is calculated by multiplying the percent that's been completed by a task with the task's planned value. A project's schedule variance can be expressed in terms of both cost and time. A project's schedule variance in terms of cost is calculated as the difference between the planned value of a project and the earned value of a project at the same point in time. A project's schedule variance in terms of time is calculated by determining the difference in time between the date for a particular earned value and the date when the planned value equaled that earned value.

This recipe demonstrates how to calculate a project's schedule variance in terms of cost as well as time.

Getting ready

To prepare for this recipe, do the following:

1. Open Power BI Desktop.
2. Use an **Enter Data** query to create a table called `R05_Project` that contains the following data:

ID	Project	Phase	Name	Scheduled_Work	Start_Date	Finish_Date	% Complete	Planned Value	Earned Value
3	The Project	Phase 1	Task 1	24	1/13/2020	1/13/2020	1	2,040	2,040
4	The Project	Phase 1	Task 2	160	1/14/2020	1/27/2020	1	14,400	14,400
5	The Project	Phase 1	Task 3	40	1/28/2020	2/3/2020	1	3,400	3,400
7	The Project	Phase 2	Task 4	240	2/4/2020	2/24/2020	.75	21,600	16,200
8	The Project	Phase 2	Task 5	200	2/25/2020	3/30/2020	.5	19,000	9,500
9	The Project	Phase 2	Task 6	160	3/31/2020	4/27/2020	.25	13,600	3,400

11	The Project	Phase 3	Task 7	120	4/28/2020	5/4/2020	0	9,800	0
12	The Project	Phase 3	Task 8	240	5/5/2020	5/25/2020	0	18,000	0
13	The Project	Phase 3	Task 9	80	5/26/2020	6/8/2020	0	6,000	0

3. Create a table called `R05_Calendar` using the following formula:

```
R05_Calendar = CALENDAR(DATE(2020,1,1),DATE(2020,6,30))
```

The `R05_Project` table represents the project plan. This project plan has three phases and nine tasks. The `Scheduled_Work` column in the `R05_Project` table provides the number of hours each task is expected to take to complete. The `Planned Value` and `Earned Value` columns are necessary inputs to create a schedule variance. To learn how to calculate `Planned Value` and `Earned Value`, please refer to the *Projecting planned value* and *Estimating earned value* recipes in `Chapter 8`, *Processing Project Performance*.

How to do it...

To implement this recipe, do the following:

1. Create the following measures:

```
SV_PV =
    VAR __MaxDate = MAX('R05_Project'[Finish_Date])
    VAR __Date = MAX('R05_Calendar'[Date])
    VAR __Table =
        ADDCOLUMNS (
            ADDCOLUMNS (
                FILTER('R05_Project','R05_Project'[Start_Date] <
__Date),
                "__TaskDaysDuration",
DATEDIFF('R05_Project'[Start_Date],'R05_Project'[Finish_Date],DAY)
+ 1,
                "__Days",
                DATEDIFF('R05_Project'[Start_Date],__Date,DAY) + 1
            ),
            "__PV",
            IF(
                __Date > __MaxDate,
                BLANK(),
```

```
                                IF(
                                    [__Days] >= [__TaskDaysDuration],
                                    [Planned Value],
                                    [__Days]/[__TaskDaysDuration] * [Planned Value]
                                )
                            )
                        )
            RETURN
                SUMX(__Table,[__PV])


            SV_EV =
                VAR __ReportingDate = DATE(2020,4,1)
                VAR __MaxDate = MAX('R05_Project'[Finish_Date])
                VAR __Date = MAX('R05_Calendar'[Date])
                VAR __Table =
                        ADDCOLUMNS(
                            ADDCOLUMNS(
                                FILTER('R05_Project','R05_Project'[Start_Date]
            < __Date),
                                "__TaskDaysDuration",
            DATEDIFF('R05_Project'[Start_Date],'R05_Project'[Finish_Date],DAY)
            + 1,
                                "__Days",
                                DATEDIFF('R05_Project'[Start_Date],__Date,DAY)
                            ),
                            "__EV",
                            IF(
                                __Date > __MaxDate,
                                BLANK(),
                                IF(
                                    [__Days] >= [__TaskDaysDuration],
                                    [Earned Value],
                                    [__Days]/[__TaskDaysDuration] * [Earned
            Value]
                                )
                            )
                        )
            RETURN
                IF(__Date > __ReportingDate, BLANK(), SUMX(__Table,[__EV]))
```

2. Create the following additional measures:

```
            SV$ =
            IF(ISBLANK([SV_EV]),
                BLANK(),
                [SV_PV] - [SV_EV]
            )
```

```
Current SV$ =
    VAR __Table =
        ADDCOLUMNS(
            'R05_Calendar',
            "__SV$",
            [SV$]
        )
    VAR __CurrentDate =
MAXX(FILTER(__Table,NOT(ISBLANK([__SV$]))),[Date])
RETURN
    MAXX(FILTER(__Table,[Date] = __CurrentDate),[__SV$])

SVDays =
    VAR __Table =
        ADDCOLUMNS(
            'R05_Calendar',
            "__PV",
            [SV_PV],
            "__EV",
            [SV_EV]
        )
    VAR __EVDate =
MAXX(FILTER(__Table,NOT(ISBLANK([__EV]))),[Date])
    VAR __CurrentEV = MAXX(__Table,[__EV])
    VAR __Table1 =
        ADDCOLUMNS(
            FILTER(__Table,NOT(ISBLANK([SV_EV]))),
            "__Diff",
            ABS([__PV] - __CurrentEV)
        )
    VAR __MinDiff = MINX(__Table1,[__Diff])
    VAR __PVDate = MAXX(FILTER(__Table1,[__Diff] =
__MinDiff),[Date])
RETURN
    DATEDIFF(__PVDate, __EVDate,DAY) + 1
```

3. On a **Report** page, create a line chart visualization and place the `Date` column from the `R05_Calendar` table into the **Axis** area. Ensure that this field is set to `Date` and not `Date Hierarchy`.

4. In the same line chart visualization, place the `SV_PV`, `SV_EV`, and `SV$` measures into the **Value** area.

5. On the same **Report** page, create a card visualization and place the `Current SV$` measure into the **Fields** area.

6. On the same **Report** page, create another card visualization and place the `SVDays` measure into the **Fields** area.

How it works...

The SV_PV measure represents the cumulative planned value of the project over time. For the SV_PV measure, we start by simply getting the maximum Finish_Date within the R05_Project table, __MaxDate, and the maximum date within the current context of our line chart visualization, __Date.

Next, since we wish to display the cumulative sum of the planned value for each date we construct a table variable, __Table, by using FILTER to return only those rows within the R05_Project table that have a Start_Date that is less than our current date, __Date. We add two columns to this base table using ADDCOLUMNS. The first column, __TaskDaysDuration, uses DATEDIFF to calculate the total duration in days of each task (row) within the filtered R05_Project table. This duration is the number of days between the Start_Date and Finish_Date of each task. The second column, __Days, again uses DATEDIFF but this time calculates the total duration in days between the Start_Date of each task (row) within the filtered R05_Project table and the current date, __Date.

Now, we use ADDCOLUMNS once more to add the __PV column. The calculation for __PV consists of two nested IF statements. The first IF statement checks if the current date, __Date, is greater than the maximum date within our project plan, __MaxDate. If so, then BLANK is returned. This prevents extraneous values from being displayed in the event that the dates in our calendar table exceed the end of the project. If the current date, __Date, is not greater than the maximum date within our project plan, __MaxDate, then our second IF statement executes. This IF statement checks to see if the number of days between the Start_Date of a task and the current date, __Days, is greater than or equal to the total number of days the task lasted, __TaskDaysDuration. If so, then the full Planned Value amount for the task is returned. However, if the number of days between the Start_Date of a task and the current date, __Days, is not greater than or equal to the total duration in days for the task, __TaskDaysDuration, then we apportion the Planned Value of the task based upon a ratio bases on how many days of the task duration have been accrued.

Finally, we simply need to return the sum of our calculated planned values in the __PV column using SUMX in order to return the cumulative planned value of the project at any particular date.

The SV_EV measure represents the cumulative earned value of the project over time. The SV_EV measure is nearly identical to the SV_PV measure. The exception is that, at the start of the formula, we specify a reporting date, __ReportingDate. Then, in the RETURN statement, we check to see if __Date is greater than __ReportingDate and, if so, we return BLANK since we do not want to report SV_EV values that are past our __ReportingDate.

The SV$ measure is the scheduled variable of the project measured in terms of cost. The calculation for SV$ is simply subtracting the SV_EV measure from the SV_PV measure. However, first, we check to see if SV_EV is BLANK and, if so, return BLANK.

To get the current value of the schedule variance in terms of cost, Current SV$, we start by creating a table variable, __Table, that contains all of the dates from our R05_Calendar table and use ADDCOLUMNS to add a column called __SV$. The value for the __SV$ column is simply the SV$ measure. Then, we find the maximum date where __SV$ is not blank using MAXX and FILTER. This is the most current date for SV$. Thus, we can simply FILTER our __Table to this specific date and return the value in the __SV$ column.

The SVDays measure provides the schedule variance between the baseline project schedule and the current state of the project in terms of the number of days the project is ahead or behind the baseline project schedule. This is done by creating a table variable, __Table, that contains all of the dates from our R05_Calendar table and then adding two columns, __PV and __EV. We use the ADDCOLUMNS function to add both the __PV and __EV columns. The values for these columns are simply our SV_PV and SV_EV measures, respectively. Then, we use __Table to find the maximum value of the Date column where the __EV column is not BLANK; that is, __EVDate. In addition, we use __Table to find the maximum value of the __EV column, that is, __CurrentEV. Since our SV_EV measure is cumulative, we are assured that this value corresponds to the __EVDate value calculated on the previous line.

Now, we want to find the corresponding date for SV_PV where the value for SV_PV is the same as, or as close as possible to, the current earned value, __CurrentEV. To accomplish this, we add an additional column to __Table called __Diff using ADDCOLUMNS. This new version of the table is called __Table1. The value for the __Diff column is the absolute value of each row's __PV column, minus the __CurrentEV variable. Now, we can determine the minimum value of the __Diff column, __MinDiff, by using MINX with __Table1 as the first parameter.

Once we have a value for __MinDiff, we can use this value to look up the date in the table that corresponds with this value. This is the date where the __PV column closely matches __CurrentEV. Then, we simply need to return the number of days between these two dates using DATEDIFF.

See also

For more details about this recipe, please refer to the following links:

- ADDCOLUMNS: https://docs.microsoft.com/en-us/dax/addcolumns-function-dax
- SUMX: https://docs.microsoft.com/en-us/dax/sumx-function-dax
- MAX: https://docs.microsoft.com/en-us/dax/max-function-dax
- FILTER: https://docs.microsoft.com/en-us/dax/filter-function-dax
- DATEDIFF: https://docs.microsoft.com/en-us/dax/datediff-function-dax
- IF: https://docs.microsoft.com/en-us/dax/if-function-dax
- BLANK: https://docs.microsoft.com/en-us/dax/blank-function-dax
- ISBLANK: https://docs.microsoft.com/en-us/dax/isblank-function-dax
- MAXX: https://docs.microsoft.com/en-us/dax/maxx-function-dax
- MINX: https://docs.microsoft.com/en-us/dax/minx-function-dax
- ABS: https://docs.microsoft.com/en-us/dax/abs-function-dax

Computing project cost variance

The project cost variance is the difference between the earned value of a project and the actual cost of a project. The EV is calculated by multiplying the percentage of a task that's been completed by that task's planned value. The AC of a project is the cost of delivering a project based upon the material goods that have been purchased and the costs associated with project resources. A project's cost variance is calculated as the difference between the earned value of a project and the actual cost of a project at the same point in time.

This recipe demonstrates how to calculate a project's cost variance.

Getting Ready

To prepare for this recipe, do the following:

1. Open Power BI Desktop.
2. Use an **Enter Data** query to create a table called R03_Project that contains the following data:

ID	Project	Phase	Name	Scheduled_Work	Start_Date	Finish_Date	% Complete	Earned Value	Actual Cost
3	The Project	Phase 1	Task 1	24	1/13/2020	1/13/2020	1	2,040	2,040
4	The Project	Phase 1	Task 2	160	1/14/2020	1/27/2020	1	14,400	20,160
5	The Project	Phase 1	Task 3	40	1/28/2020	2/3/2020	1	3,400	2,720
7	The Project	Phase 2	Task 4	240	2/4/2020	2/24/2020	.75	16,200	12,960
8	The Project	Phase 2	Task 5	200	2/25/2020	3/30/2020	.5	9,500	12,920
9	The Project	Phase 2	Task 6	160	3/31/2020	4/27/2020	.25	3,400	1,360
11	The Project	Phase 3	Task 7	120	4/28/2020	5/4/2020	0	0	0
12	The Project	Phase 3	Task 8	240	5/5/2020	5/25/2020	0	0	0
13	The Project	Phase 3	Task 9	80	5/26/2020	6/8/2020	0	0	0

3. Create a table called R06_Calendar using the following formula:

```
R06_Calendar = CALENDAR(DATE(2020,1,1),DATE(2020,6,30))
```

The R06_Project table represents the project plan. This project plan has three phases and nine tasks. The Scheduled_Work column in the R06_Project table provides the number of hours each task is expected to take to complete. The Earned Value and Actual Cost columns are necessary inputs to create a schedule variance. To learn how to calculate Earned Value and Actual Cost, refer to the *Estimating earned value* and *Achieving actual cost* recipes in Chapter 8, *Processing Project Performance*.

How to do it...

To implement this recipe, do the following:

1. Create the following measures:

```
CV_EV =
    VAR __ReportingDate = DATE(2020,4,1)
    VAR __MaxDate = MAX('R06_Project'[Finish_Date])
    VAR __Date = MAX('R06_Calendar'[Date])
    VAR __Table =
            ADDCOLUMNS(
                ADDCOLUMNS(
                    FILTER('R06_Project','R06_Project'[Start_Date]
< __Date),
                    "__TaskDaysDuration",
DATEDIFF('R06_Project'[Start_Date],'R06_Project'[Finish_Date],DAY)
+ 1,
                    "__Days",
                    DATEDIFF('R06_Project'[Start_Date],__Date,DAY)
                ),
                "__EV",
                IF(
                    __Date > __MaxDate,
                    BLANK(),
                    IF(
                        [__Days] >= [__TaskDaysDuration],
                        [Earned Value],
                        [__Days]/[__TaskDaysDuration]*[Earned
Value]
                    )
                )
            )
    RETURN
        IF(__Date > __ReportingDate, BLANK(), SUMX(__Table,[__EV]))

CV_AC =
    VAR __ReportingDate = DATE(2020,4,1)
    VAR __MaxDate = MAX('R06_Project'[Finish_Date])
    VAR __Date = MAX('R06_Calendar'[Date])
    VAR __Table =
            ADDCOLUMNS(
                ADDCOLUMNS(
                    FILTER('R06_Project','R06_Project'[Start_Date]
< __Date),
                    "__TaskDaysDuration",
```

```
DATEDIFF('R06_Project'[Start_Date],'R06_Project'[Finish_Date],DAY)
+ 1,
                "__Days",
                DATEDIFF('R06_Project'[Start_Date],__Date,DAY)
            ),
            "__AC",
            IF(
                __Date > __MaxDate,
                BLANK(),
                IF(
                    [__Days] >= [__TaskDaysDuration],
                    [Actual Cost],
                    [__Days]/[__TaskDaysDuration]*[Actual Cost]
                )
            )
        )
RETURN
    IF(__Date > __ReportingDate, BLANK(), SUMX(__Table,[__AC]))

CV = [CV_AC] - [CV_EV]

Current CV =
    VAR __Table =
        ADDCOLUMNS(
            'R06_Calendar',
            "__CV",
            [CV]
        )
    VAR __CurrentDate =
MAXX(FILTER(__Table,NOT(ISBLANK([CV]))),[Date])
RETURN
    MAXX(FILTER(__Table,[Date] = __CurrentDate),[__CV])
```

2. On a **Report** page, create a line chart visualization and place the `Date` column from the `R06_Calendar` table into the **Axis** area. Ensure that this field is set to `Date` and not `Date Hierarchy`.

3. In the same line chart visualization, place the `CV_EV`, `CV_AC`, and `CV` measures into the **Value** area.

4. On the same **Report** page, create a card visualization and place the `Current CV` measures into the **Fields** area.

How it works...

The `CV_EV` measure represents the cumulative earned value of the project over time. To calculate the `CV_EV` measure, we start by specifying the current reporting date, `__ReportingDate`. Then, we get the maximum `Finish_Date` within the `R03_Project`, table `__MaxDate`, and the maximum date within the current context of our line chart visualization, `__Date`.

Next, since we wish to display the cumulative sum of the earned value for each date, we construct a table variable, `__Table`. We use `FILTER` to return only those rows within the `R06_Project` table that have a `Start_Date` that is less than our current date, `__Date`. We add two columns to this base table using `ADDCOLUMNS`. The first column, `__TaskDaysDuration`, uses `DATEDIFF` to calculate the total duration in days of each task (row) within the filtered `R06_Project` table. This duration is the number of days between the `Start_Date` and `Finish_Date` of each task. The second column, `__Days`, again uses `DATEDIFF` but this time calculates the total duration in days between the `Start_Date` of each task (row) within the filtered `R06_Project` table and the current date, `__Date`.

Now, we use `ADDCOLUMNS` once more to add the `__EV` column. The calculation for `__EV` consists of two nested `IF` statements. The first `IF` statement checks if the current date, `__Date`, is greater than the maximum date within our project plan, `__MaxDate`. If so, then `BLANK` is returned. This prevents extraneous values from being displayed in the event that the dates in our calendar table exceed the end of the project. If the current date, `__Date`, is not greater than the maximum date within our project plan, `__MaxDate`, then our second `IF` statement executes. This `IF` statement checks to see if the number of days between the `Start_Date` of a task and the current date, `__Days`, is greater than or equal to the total duration in days for the task, `__TaskDaysDuration`. If so, then the full `Earned Value` amount for the task is returned. However, if the number of days between the `Start_Date` of a task and the current date, `__Days`, is not greater than or equal to the total duration in days for the task, `__TaskDaysDuration` then we apportion the `Earned Value` of the task based upon a ratio of how many days of the task duration have been accrued.

Finally, we simply need to return the sum of our calculated earned values in the `__EV` column using `SUMX` in order to return the cumulative earned value of the project at any particular date. However, first we check if `__Date` exceeds our `__ReportingDate` and if so, we return `BLANK` since we do not wish to display `__EV` values for dates exceeding our current `__ReportingDate`.

The CV_AC measure represents the cumulative actual cost of the project over time. The CV_AC measure is nearly identical to the CV_EV measure. The only difference is that we refer to the Actual Cost column in the R06_Project table instead of the Earned Value column.

The CV measure is the cost variance of the project and is simply the difference between our CV_EV measure and our CV_AC measure.

To get the current value of the cost variance, Current CV, we start by creating a table variable, __Table, that contains all of the dates from our R06_Calendar table and use ADDCOLUMNS to add a column called __CV. The value for the __CV column is simply the CV measure. Then, we find the maximum date where __CV is not blank using MAXX and FILTER. This is the most current date for CV. Thus, we can simply FILTER our __Table to this specific date and return the value in the __CV column.

See also

For more details about this recipe, please refer to the following links:

- ADDCOLUMNS: https://docs.microsoft.com/en-us/dax/addcolumns-function-dax
- SUMX: https://docs.microsoft.com/en-us/dax/sumx-function-dax
- MAX: https://docs.microsoft.com/en-us/dax/max-function-dax
- FILTER: https://docs.microsoft.com/en-us/dax/filter-function-dax
- DATEDIFF: https://docs.microsoft.com/en-us/dax/datediff-function-dax
- IF: https://docs.microsoft.com/en-us/dax/if-function-dax
- BLANK: https://docs.microsoft.com/en-us/dax/blank-function-dax
- ISBLANK: https://docs.microsoft.com/en-us/dax/isblank-function-dax
- MAXX: https://docs.microsoft.com/en-us/dax/maxx-function-dax

Creating burndown charts

A burndown chart graphs the amount of work that's been performed against a project over time and subtracts this value from the total amount of work for the entire project. This allows project managers to gather a general sense of whether enough work is being performed on the project to meet expected deadlines, and of the overall amount of work that's left to do on the project.

This recipe demonstrates how to create a burndown chart in Power BI.

Getting Ready

To prepare for this recipe, do the following:

1. Open Power BI Desktop.
2. Use an **Enter Data** query to create a table called `R07_Project` that contains the following data:

ID	Project	Phase	Name	Scheduled_Work	Start_Date	Finish_Date
3	The Project	Phase 1	Task 1	24	1/13/2020	1/13/2020
4	The Project	Phase 1	Task 2	160	1/14/2020	1/27/2020
5	The Project	Phase 1	Task 3	40	1/28/2020	2/3/2020
7	The Project	Phase 2	Task 4	240	2/4/2020	2/24/2020
8	The Project	Phase 2	Task 5	200	2/25/2020	3/30/2020
9	The Project	Phase 2	Task 6	160	3/31/2020	4/27/2020
11	The Project	Phase 3	Task 7	120	4/28/2020	5/4/2020
12	The Project	Phase 3	Task 8	240	5/5/2020	5/25/2020
13	The Project	Phase 3	Task 9	80	5/26/2020	6/8/2020

3. Create a table called `R07_Calendar` using the following formula:

```
R07_Calendar = CALENDAR(DATE(2020,1,1),DATE(2020,6,30))
```

4. Create another table called `R07_Hours` using the following formula:

```
R07_Hours =
    VAR __Greg = SELECTCOLUMNS({ ("Greg", 8) },"Resource
Name",[Value1],"Hours",[Value2])
    VAR __Julie = SELECTCOLUMNS({ ("Julie", 8) },"Resource
Name",[Value1],"Hours",[Value2])
    VAR __Pam = SELECTCOLUMNS({ ("Pam", 8) },"Resource
Name",[Value1],"Hours",[Value2])
    VAR __TaskID3 = SELECTCOLUMNS({ (3, DATE(2020,1,13))
},"ID",[Value1],"Date",[Value2])
    VAR __TaskID4 =
        SELECTCOLUMNS (
            ADDCOLUMNS (
                GENERATESERIES(DATE(2020,1,14),DATE(2020,1,27),1),
                "ID",4
            ),
            "ID",[ID],"Date",[Value]
        )
    VAR __TaskID5 =
        SELECTCOLUMNS (
            ADDCOLUMNS (
                GENERATESERIES(DATE(2020,1,28),DATE(2020,1,31),1),
                "ID",5
            ),
            "ID",[ID],"Date",[Value]
        )
    VAR __TaskID7 =
        SELECTCOLUMNS (
            ADDCOLUMNS (
                GENERATESERIES(DATE(2020,2,4),DATE(2020,2,12),1),
                "ID",7
            ),
            "ID",[ID],"Date",[Value]
        )
    VAR __TaskID8 =
        SELECTCOLUMNS (
            ADDCOLUMNS (
                GENERATESERIES(DATE(2020,2,25),DATE(2020,3,12),1),
                "ID",8
            ),
            "ID",[ID],"Date",[Value]
        )
    VAR __TaskID9 =
        SELECTCOLUMNS (
            ADDCOLUMNS (
                GENERATESERIES(DATE(2020,3,31),DATE(2020,4,1),1),
                "ID",9
```

```
        ),
        "ID",[ID],"Date",[Value]
    )
VAR __Table1 =
    UNION(
        GENERATE(__Greg, __TaskID3),
        GENERATE(__Julie,__TaskID3),
        GENERATE(__Pam, __TaskID3)
    )
VAR __Table2 = UNION(GENERATE(__Greg, __TaskID4),
GENERATE(__Julie,__TaskID4))
VAR __Table3 = GENERATE(__Julie,__TaskID5)
VAR __Table4 = UNION(GENERATE(__Greg, __TaskID7),
GENERATE(__Julie,__TaskID7))
VAR __Table5 = GENERATE(__Greg, __TaskID8)
VAR __Table6 = GENERATE(__Julie,__TaskID9)
RETURN
    UNION(__Table1, __Table2, __Table3, __Table4, __Table5,
__Table6)
```

5. Create a relationship between the `ID` column in the `R07_Project` table and the `ID` column in the `R07_Hours` table.

6. Ensure that no other relationships exist in the data model for the tables we created.

The `R07_Project` table represents the project plan. This project plan has three phases and nine tasks. The `Scheduled_Work` column in the `R07_Project` table provides the number of hours each task is expected to take in order to complete the task. The `R07_Hours` table represents the hours of work that the project resources assigned to each task have been reported as expending against each task. The `Date` column within this table is the date that the reported hours were worked on.

How to do it...

To implement this recipe, do the following:

1. Create the following measures:

```
Burndown =
    VAR __ReportingDate = DATE(2020,4,1)
    VAR __Date = MAX('R07_Calendar'[Date])
    VAR __StartDate = MINX('R07_Project','R07_Project'[Start_Date])
```

```
        VAR __FinishDate =
MAXX('R07_Project','R07_Project'[Finish_Date])
        VAR __TotalProjectHours =
SUMX(ALL('R07_Project'),'R07_Project'[Scheduled_Work])
        VAR __TotalConsumedHours =
            SUMX(
                FILTER(
                    ALL('R07_Hours'),
                    'R07_Hours'[Date] <= __Date
                ),
                'R07_Hours'[Hours])
    RETURN
        IF(
            __Date < __StartDate - 1 || __Date > __ReportingDate,
            BLANK(),
            __TotalProjectHours - __TotalConsumedHours
        )


Idealized Burndown =
    VAR __ReportingDate = DATE(2020,4,1)
    VAR __Date = MAX('R07_Calendar'[Date])
    VAR __StartDate = MINX('R07_Project','R07_Project'[Start_Date])
    VAR __FinishDate =
MAXX('R07_Project','R07_Project'[Finish_Date])
    VAR __TotalProjectHours =
SUMX(ALL('R07_Project'),'R07_Project'[Scheduled_Work])
    VAR __IdealHoursPerDay =
        DIVIDE(
            __TotalProjectHours,
            DATEDIFF(__StartDate,__FinishDate,DAY) + 1,
            0
        )
    VAR __IdealConsumedHours =
            __IdealHoursPerDay * (DATEDIFF(__StartDate,__Date,DAY)
+ 1)
    RETURN
        IF(
            __Date < __StartDate - 1 || __Date > __FinishDate,
            BLANK(),
            __TotalProjectHours - __IdealConsumedHours
        )
```

2. On a **Report** page, create a line chart visualization and place the Date column from the R05_Calendar table into the **Axis** area. Ensure that this field is set to Date and not Date Hierarchy.

3. In the same line chart visualization, place the SV_PV, SV_EV, and SV$ measures into the **Value** area.

4. On the same **Report** page, create a card visualization and place the `Current SV$` measure into the **Fields** area.

5. On the same **Report** page, create another card visualization and place the `SVDays` measure into the **Fields** area.

How it works...

The `Burndown` measure represents the cumulative number of hours reported as work against the project over time. To calculate this measure, we start by setting the current reporting date, `__ReportingDate`. Then, we get the maximum date within the current context of our line chart visualization, `__Date`. Next, we get the starting and finishing dates, `__StartDate` and `__FinishDate`, by using `MINX` and `MAXX` to retrieve the minimum value in the `Start_Date` column and the maximum date in the `Finish_Date` column, respectively. The next variable, `__TotalProjectHours`, stores the total amount of planned hours of work within the project plan in the `R07_Table` table. To calculate `__TotalProjectHours`, we simply use `SUMX` to sum all of the values in the `Scheduled_Work` column. We also need `__TotalConsumedHours`, which is the cumulative total of hours reported as work that are less than or equal to `__Date`.

The return value for the `Burndown` measure is simply the `__TotalProjectHours` minus the `__TotalConsumedHours`. However, first, we check to see if `__Date` is less than the start date of the project, `__StartDate`, or greater than the reporting date, `__ReportingDate` and, if so, return `BLANK`.

The `Idealized Burndown` measure represents an even distribution of consumed hours for the project over time. This means that the same number of hours is consumed every day over the course of the entire project. The calculations for the `__ReportingDate`, `__StartDate`, `__FinishDate`, and `__TotalProjectHours` variables are identical to the same variables in our `Burndown` measure. However, we then calculate `__IdealHoursPerDay`, which is an even distribution of the total project hours over the entire length of the project. To calculate `__IdealHoursPerDay`, we divide the total project hours, `__TotalProjectHours`, by the number of days between the start of the project, `__StartDate`, and the end of the project, `__EndDate`. By doing this, we can find the ideal hours consumed at any point in our project timeline, `__IdealConsumedHours`, by multiplying `__IdealHoursPerDay` by the difference in days between the start of the project, `__StartDate`, and the current date, `__Date`.

The return value for the `Idealized Burndown` measure is simply the `__TotalProjectHours` minus the `__IdealConsumedHours`. However, first, we check to see if `__Date` is less than the start date of the project, `__StartDate`, or greater than the end of the project, `__FinishDate`, and if so, return `BLANK`.

See also

For more details about this recipe, please refer to the following links:

- ADDCOLUMNS: https://docs.microsoft.com/en-us/dax/addcolumns-function-dax
- SUMX: https://docs.microsoft.com/en-us/dax/sumx-function-dax
- MAX: https://docs.microsoft.com/en-us/dax/max-function-dax
- FILTER: https://docs.microsoft.com/en-us/dax/filter-function-dax
- DATEDIFF: https://docs.microsoft.com/en-us/dax/datediff-function-dax
- IF: https://docs.microsoft.com/en-us/dax/if-function-dax
- BLANK: https://docs.microsoft.com/en-us/dax/blank-function-dax
- MAXX: https://docs.microsoft.com/en-us/dax/maxx-function-dax
- MINX: https://docs.microsoft.com/en-us/dax/minx-function-dax
- ALL: https://docs.microsoft.com/en-us/dax/all-function-dax

9
Calculating Common Industry Metrics

Across various industries, there are hundreds, if not thousands, of KPIs that businesses use to measure themselves. The previous chapters of this book have focused on metrics that are common to most businesses, such as metrics dealing with dates and times, finances, customers, employees, and projects. This chapter focuses on measures of business processes that are more particular to specific industries, such as manufacturing, health care, and supply chains.

We will cover the following recipes in this chapter:

- Calculating Days of Supply
- Computing the mean time between failures
- Constructing a patient cohort (AND slicer)
- Determining overall equipment effectiveness
- Optimizing On Time in Full
- Analyzing Order Cycle Time

Technical requirements

The following are required to complete all of the recipes in this chapter:

- Power BI Desktop
- This book's GitHub repository at `https://github.com/PacktPublishing/DAX-Cookbook/tree/master/Chapter09`

Calculating Days of Supply

Days of Supply, or **DoS**, is also known as **Days In Inventory** (**DII**). This metric is used in various ways but is often used as an efficiency metric to measure the average number of days organizations stock their inventory before selling that inventory. DoS is a useful measure for any organization that stocks inventory and can be a key metric when analyzing your supply chain. The calculation for DoS is given by the following formula:

$$DoS = AverageInventory/AverageSoldPerDay$$

Here, the numerator, *AverageInventory*, is the average inventory levels during an accounting period. The denominator, *AverageSoldPerDay*, is simply the average amount of inventory taken out of stock per day. *AverageSoldPerDay* can be calculated across any timeline, although often, 365 days or a year is used when calculating the average number or value of goods sold.

This recipe demonstrates how to calculate DoS when considering weekly sales and inventory levels. Two versions of DoS are provided, the calculation described here, as well as a special form of DoS that's used by supply chain managers when considering forecasted sales and inventory levels.

Getting ready

To prepare for this recipe, do the following:

1. Open Power BI Desktop.
2. Use an **Enter Data** query to create a table called `R01_Table` that contains the following data:

Week	Demand	Ending Inventory
2/3/2020	0	49,813
2/10/2020	11,360	36,961
2/17/2020	7,952	37,859
2/24/2020	7,485	32,876
3/2/2020	7,131	24,875
3/9/2020	6,785	76,385
3/16/2020	6,854	73,152
3/23/2020	7,132	80,563

3/30/2020	5,820	76,131
4/6/2020	7,272	68,177
4/13/2020	7,344	58,538
4/20/2020	7,200	54,853
4/27/2020	3,994	52,142
5/4/2020	2,577	44,728
5/11/2020	2,629	44,950
5/18/2020	2,706	42,347
5/25/2020	4,279	37,142
6/1/2020	8,158	28,262
6/8/2020	8,319	31,203
6/15/2020	7,835	22,365

The R01_Table table represents the weekly inventory and sales levels. The Demand column represents inventory that is sold or taken out of stock during the week, while the Ending Inventory column represents the stock level of inventory at the end of the week. It should be noted that you cannot simply subtract the next week's demand from the current week's Ending Inventory to arrive at the figure for next week's Ending Inventory as additional inventory may be added during any given week.

How to do it...

To implement this recipe, do the following:

1. Create a column in the R01_Table table using the following formula:

```
DoS =
    VAR __EndingInventory = 'R01_Table'[Ending Inventory]
    VAR __BeginningInventoryTemp =
        MAXX(
            FILTER(
                ALL('R01_Table'),
                'R01_Table'[Week] = EARLIER('R01_Table'[Week]) - 7
            ),
            'R01_Table'[Ending Inventory]
        )
    VAR __BeginningInventory =
        IF(
            ISBLANK(__BeginningInventoryTemp),
            __EndingInventory + [Demand],
```

```
        __BeginningInventoryTemp)
    VAR __AverageInventory = (__BeginningInventory +
__EndingInventory) / 2
    VAR __AverageDemand =
AVERAGEX(ALL('R01_Table'[Demand]),'R01_Table'[Demand])
RETURN
    __AverageInventory / __AverageDemand * 7
```

2. On a **Report** page, create a line chart visualization and place the `Week` column from the `R01_Table` table into the **Axis** area. Ensure that this field is set to `Week` and not `Date Hierarchy`.

3. In the same matrix visualization, place the `DoS` column from the `R01_Table` table into the **Values** area.

How it works...

To calculate the numerator, we want to calculate the average value or units of inventory at the beginning and end of our period (week) and divide this by **2**. Since our data specifies the ending inventory for each week in the `Ending Inventory` column, we simply store the value of this column for the current row in the `__EndingInventory` variable. To find our beginning inventory, `__BeginningInventory`, we store the value of the `Ending Inventory` column for the previous week in the `__BeginningInventoryTemp` variable. This is done by using `ALL` to break out of row context and then by using `FILTER` to return the previous row. Since our data is weekly, we know that the previous row has a `Week` column value that is our current `Week` column value (`EARLIER`) minus 7 days. Once we have filtered down to a single row, we can use `MAXX` or really any other similar function to return the value of the `Ending Inventory` column. Then, we can do a quick check to account for the beginning of the table where we have no previous week's inventory data. This is done by using an `IF` statement and checking if `__BeginningInventoryTemp` is blank (`ISBLANK`). If `__BeginningInventoryTemp` is blank, we know that we are at the beginning of our table and thus we can estimate the beginning inventory for the week by adding the `Demand` column to our `__EndingInventory`. Otherwise, we simply assign the value of `__BeginningInventoryTemp`.

Now, we can calculate the __AverageInventory variable by adding __EndingInventory and __BeginningInventory and then dividing by 2. We can also calculate the average amount of product sold or otherwise taken out of stock per week, __AverageDemand, by simply getting the average of the Demand column for ALL of our rows using the AVERAGEX function. Finally, we can RETURN a value for DoS by simply dividing __AverageInventory by __AverageDemand and multiplying by 7, since there are seven days in a week.

There's more...

In our recipe thus far, we have treated our data table, R01_Table, in terms of a historical record showing ending inventory levels and demand levels per week. However, supply chain managers often use forecasting tables for inventory and demand. These forecasting tables are generated from **Advanced Shipping Notices (ASNs)** that are received from suppliers indicating when stock will be received as well as sales forecasts or other information regarding when stock will be depleted. In these cases, supply chain managers are attempting to forecast and optimize Days of Supply so that they keep the minimum possible amount of stock in hand, without the risk of running out of that stock.

We can implement this version of calculating Days of Supply by considering our data table as a forecast of future weeks versus a historical record. To implement this version of Days of Supply, do the following:

1. In Power BI Desktop, create the following measure:

```
Days of Supply =
    VAR __Week = MAX('R01_Table'[Week])
    VAR __Inventory = MAX('R01_Table'[Ending Inventory])
    VAR __Table =
        ADDCOLUMNS (
            FILTER(ALL('R01_Table'),'R01_Table'[Week] > __Week),
            "__Start",__Inventory
        )
    VAR __Table2 =
        ADDCOLUMNS (
            ADDCOLUMNS (
                __Table,
                "__Demand",SUMX(FILTER(__Table,[Week] <=
EARLIER([Week])),[Demand])
            ),
            "__Left",[__Start] - [__Demand]
        )
    VAR __Table3 = FILTER(__Table2, [__Left] >= 0)
```

```
        VAR __BaseDays = COUNTROWS(__Table3) * 7
        VAR __Min = MINX(__Table3,[__Left])
        VAR __Max = MAXX(FILTER(__Table2,[__left] < 0),[__left])
        VAR __ExtraDays = IF(ISBLANK(__Max),7,__Min / ABS(__Max) * 7)
    RETURN
        __BaseDays + __ExtraDays
```

2. In the same line chart visualization we created previously, place the Days of Supply measure into the **Values** area.

In this version of days of supply, we start by getting our current week within context, __Week, as well as our current Ending Inventory, __Inventory. Next, we create a table variable, __Table, that contains all the future weeks and add a column using ADDCOLUMNS called __Start that simply contains the value of our current inventory, __Inventory. What we are doing is creating a table of future weeks and essentially projecting our current inventory level onto each of those weeks.

Now, we create a second table variable, __Table2, based upon our first table variable, __Table. We add two columns. The first column, __Demand, is a cumulative sum of the Demand column for all the weeks that are prior to the current row. This is done by using FILTER to filter our original table, __Table, for all the rows where the Week column is less than or equal to our current row's Week column (EARLIER) and then using SUMX to sum the Demand column for these rows. The second column, __Left, simply subtracts this cumulative demand, __Demand, from our projected starting inventory, __Start.

Let's take a moment to consider the methodology being implemented here. The goal is to determine how many future weeks or days we have given forecast inventory levels and demand for, before our current inventory is fully depleted. In most programming languages, this would be accomplished by using a for or while loop. However, DAX lacks any looping constructs. Thus, we are using the combination of __Table and __Table2 to emulate a looping construct using DAX. By projecting our starting inventory, __Start, to all future weeks, we can use the cumulative sum of Demand and subtract that value from __Start, thereby essentially forecasting the depletion of our current stock over future weeks. The goal here is to find the last week where the cumulative Demand in future weeks has not exceeded our original starting inventory, __Start. This threshold is reached when our calculation for __Last reaches zero or goes negative.

Now, we can determine the base number of days of supply. We do this by creating a third table variable, __Table3, that uses FILTER to return only the rows from __Table2 that have a positive value or zero for the __Left column. Then, we can determine our base days of supply, __BaseDays, by simply using COUNTROWS to count the number of rows in __Table3, which gives us the number of weeks of supply, and then multiplying by 7 to get days.

Now, we have a number for our base days of supply, __BaseDays. However, since our data is provided in weeks and we are attempting to determine Days of Supply, there may be a portion of the week where __Left goes negative that we need to include as additional Days of Supply. To calculate these additional days, we start by getting the minimum amount of our __Left column from __Table3, which only includes values for __Left that are greater than or equal to zero. This value, __Min, is the value for __Left in the week just prior to our supply running out the following week. Then, we calculate __Max by using FILTER to return all the rows from Table2 that are less than zero and return the maximum value for __Left. This is the value for __Left in the week just after our supply runs out. By doing this, we can calculate the additional Days of Supply, __ExtraDays, during the week where our supply runs out by creating a ratio of our __Min and __Max values and multiplying by 7. The ratio between __Min and __Max provides the fraction of the week where we still have inventory remaining, assuming an even distribution for the depletion of stock during the week. However, since our forecast future weeks may never fully deplete our starting inventory, we must check if __Max is blank (ISBLANK) and, if so, simply assign a full week's worth of days to __ExtraDays.

Now, we can simply add __BaseDays and __ExtraDays together to return a value for our Days of Supply measure.

See also

For more details about the functions in this recipe, please refer to the following links:

- MAXX: https://docs.microsoft.com/en-us/dax/maxx-function-dax
- FILTER: https://docs.microsoft.com/en-us/dax/filter-function-dax
- ALL: https://docs.microsoft.com/en-us/dax/all-function-dax
- EARLIER: https://docs.microsoft.com/en-us/dax/earlier-function-dax
- IF: https://docs.microsoft.com/en-us/dax/if-function-dax
- ISBLANK: https://docs.microsoft.com/en-us/dax/isblank-function-dax
- AVERAGEX: https://docs.microsoft.com/en-us/dax/averagex-function-dax

- ADDCOLUMNS: https://docs.microsoft.com/en-us/dax/addcolumns-function-dax
- SUMX: https://docs.microsoft.com/en-us/dax/sumx-function-dax
- COUNTROWS: https://docs.microsoft.com/en-us/dax/countrows-function-dax
- MINX: https://docs.microsoft.com/en-us/dax/minx-function-dax
- ABS: https://docs.microsoft.com/en-us/dax/abs-function-dax

Computing the mean time between failures

While there are a variety of applications for the concept of **mean time between failures (MBTF)**, this metric is perhaps most often used in the manufacturing industry. MTBF measures the average amount of uptime a mechanical or electrical system has before some kind of failure interrupts normal operation. This concept is perhaps best conveyed in the following diagram:

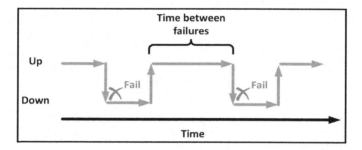

Starting from the left of the preceding diagram, the machine or system is operational up until the point of failure. At this point, the machine or system must be repaired. After repairs have been completed, the system is operational once again, up until the point of a second failure. The time between the system becoming operational after the first failure and the time of the second failure is the time between failures. MTBF averages this amount of time between failures over the life of the system or many similar systems. This can be a key metric when considering things such as productivity and system reliability. In addition, MTBF can help organizations weigh the cost-benefit of more frequent or less frequent preventative maintenance schedules and can even be used to assist in predicting future failures.

This recipe demonstrates how to calculate MTBF given the repair log of a set of machines. In addition to MTBF, an associated metric, **mean down time (MDT)**, is also presented, along with a demonstration of the potential predictive value of MTBF.

Getting ready

To prepare for this recipe, do the following:

1. Open Power BI Desktop.
2. Import the data from the `Ch09R02Data.xlsx` Excel file located in this book's GitHub repository. Ensure that the created table is called `R02_Table`.

This data represents a repair log. Each row in the `R02_Table` table represents a repair or preventative maintenance operation being performed on a machine. Included in the data is the type of repair, `RepairType`. Preventative maintenance tasks are denoted as having a value of `PM` within the `RepairType` column. Also included are the start time of the procedure, `RepairStarted`, and the end time of the procedure, `RepairCompleted`. Finally, the cause of the procedure is also included in the `Cause` columns. Any time that isn't logged in this table is considered uptime.

How to do it...

To implement this recipe, do the following:

1. Create the following measure:

```
MTBF (Hours) =
    VAR __Table = 'R02_Table'
    VAR __Table1 =
        ADDCOLUMNS (
            ADDCOLUMNS (
                __Table,
                "__Next",
                MINX (
                    FILTER(__Table,
                            [MachineName] = EARLIER([MachineName])
&&
                            [RepairStarted] >
EARLIER([RepairStarted]) &&
                            [RepairType] <> "PM"
                    ),
                    [RepairStarted]
                )
            ),
            "__Uptime",
            IF([RepairType] = "PM",
                0,
                IF(ISBLANK([__Next]),
```

```
                              DATEDIFF([RepairCompleted],NOW(),SECOND),
                              DATEDIFF([RepairCompleted],[__Next],SECOND)
                    )
                )
            )
    VAR __TotalUptime = SUMX(__Table1,[__Uptime])
        VAR __Repairs = COUNTROWS(FILTER(__Table,[RepairType] <> "PM"))
    RETURN
            DIVIDE(__TotalUptime,__Repairs,BLANK())/3600
```

2. On a **Report** page, create a card visualization and place the MTBF (Hours) measure into the **Fields** area of the visualization.

3. On the same **Report** page, create a table visualization and place the MachineName column as well as the MTBF (Hours) measure into the **Values** area of the visualization.

4. On the same **Report** page, create a second table visualization and place the Cause column as well as the MTBF (Hours) measure into the **Values** area of the visualization.

The card visual provides a value for MTBF across all machines (MachineName) and all causes (Cause). The first table visualization demonstrates how MTBF can be analyzed to determine which machines are more reliable than others. Finally, the second table demonstrates that some causes of failure are more frequent than others.

How it works...

We start by getting all the rows from the R02_Table table that are currently in context and storing these rows in the __Table table variable. Now, we add two columns to this table, __Next and __Uptime, in order to create the new table variable called __Table1.

To calculate the uptime of machines between failures, we must know the time of the next failure. This is the purpose of the __Next column. For each failure event (row), __Next computes the time of the next failure after the current row. To accomplish this, we use FILTER to return only the rows from __Table where the MachineName is equal to the current row's MachineName (EARLIER) and RepairStarted is greater than the current row's RepairStarted (EARLIER) and where RepairType is not preventative maintenance (PM). Then, we can simply take the minimum RepairStarted time from this filtered set using MINX in order to arrive at the start time of the next subsequent failure.

Now we can add our second column, __Uptime. For the __Uptime calculation, we check to see if the row is a preventative maintenance row by checking to see if RepairType is PM. If this is a preventative maintenance row, __Uptime is set to zero since preventative maintenance time is still non-operational downtime. If the row is not a preventative maintenance row, we check to see if the value for __Next is blank (ISBLANK). If __Next is blank, then we are at the end of our data since there is no subsequent failure in the data. Thus, we set __Uptime to the difference in seconds between when the current row's completed failure (RepairCompleted) and the current time provided by the NOW function. Otherwise, if this is not a preventative maintenance row and __Next is not blank, we compute __Uptime by taking the difference in seconds between the current row's RepairCompleted column and the computed subsequent failure event for the row, __Next.

Now we can compute the total uptime for all rows within context, __TotalUptime. To do this, we simply need to use SUMX to sum our __Uptime column across all of the rows in the table variable, __Table1.

Now that we have the total uptime for all machines, we need to determine how many repairs occurred over the same set of rows, __Repairs. To this, we simply need to count the number of rows in __Table using COUNTROWS but filter out preventative maintenance rows.

Now we can return the final value for MTBF (hours) by dividing our total uptime, __TotalUptime, by the number of repairs, __Repairs, and then divide this by 3600. Dividing by 3600 is necessary since we want our MTBF in hours. We computed our __Uptime in seconds and there are 3600 seconds in an hour (60 seconds/minute * 60 minutes/hour).

There's more...

A metric that is often computed along with MTBF is MDT. MDT is the average amount of downtime (repair time) that is required in order to fix a failed machine or system. To compute MDT, do the following:

1. In Power BI Desktop, create the following measure:

```
MDT (Hours) =
    VAR __Table =
        ADDCOLUMNS (
            'R02_Table',
            "__Hours",
```

```
                    DATEDIFF(
                        'R02_Table'[RepairStarted],
                        'R02_Table'[RepairCompleted],
                        SECOND
                    )/3600
                )
        RETURN
            DIVIDE(SUMX(__Table, [__Hours]), COUNTROWS(__Table), 0)
```

2. On the same **Report** page we created earlier, create a card visualization and place the MDT (Hours) measure into the **Fields** area of the visualization.

3. On the same **Report** page, place the MDT (Hours) measure into the **Values** area of both table visualizations.

Now we can see that certain machines and causes of failure take longer to repair than others.

Finally, to demonstrate the predictive value of MTBF, do the following:

1. In Power BI Desktop, create the following measure:

```
Next Expected Repair =
    VAR __LastRepair = MAX('R02_Table'[RepairCompleted])
RETURN
    __LastRepair + [MTBF (Hours)]/24
```

2. On the same **Report** page we created earlier, add Next Expected Repair to the **Values** area of the table visualization that includes the MachineName column.

Now, we can see by MachineName when the next expected failure event is likely to occur.

See also

For more details about the functions in this recipe, please refer to the following links:

- DATEDIFF: https://docs.microsoft.com/en-us/dax/datediff-function-dax
- FILTER: https://docs.microsoft.com/en-us/dax/filter-function-dax
- NOW: https://docs.microsoft.com/en-us/dax/now-function-dax
- EARLIER: https://docs.microsoft.com/en-us/dax/earlier-function-dax

- IF: https://docs.microsoft.com/en-us/dax/if-function-dax

- ISBLANK: https://docs.microsoft.com/en-us/dax/isblank-function-dax

- DIVIDE: https://docs.microsoft.com/en-us/dax/divide-function-dax

- ADDCOLUMNS: https://docs.microsoft.com/en-us/dax/addcolumns-function-dax

- SUMX: https://docs.microsoft.com/en-us/dax/sumx-function-dax

- COUNTROWS: https://docs.microsoft.com/en-us/dax/countrows-function-dax

- MINX: https://docs.microsoft.com/en-us/dax/minx-function-dax

Constructing a patient cohort (AND slicer)

In the healthcare industry, researchers often desire to create what are called patient cohorts. Patient cohorts are groups of patients that all share the same diagnoses, treatments, or other characteristics. These patient cohorts are used for research and study purposes. It is important to stress here that these cohorts generally contain multiple criteria and that every patient included in the cohort must meet all of the criteria. In other words, the inclusion requirements generally represent a logical AND of conditions, not a logical OR.

This recipe demonstrates how to construct a patient cohort from a set of patient diagnoses. To accomplish this, this recipe effectively changes the normal operation of a Power BI Slicer visualization from a logical OR to a logical AND. Thus, it has many other potential applications outside of just building patient cohorts.

Getting ready

To prepare for this recipe, do the following:

1. Open Power BI Desktop.
2. Import the data from the Ch09R03Data.xlsx Excel file located in this book's GitHub repository. Ensure that the created table is called R03_Table.

Each row in the R03_Table table represents a diagnosis on a patient. The patient's de-identified ID is contained in the Patient column, while the diagnosis code is contained in the Diagnosis column.

How to do it...

To implement this recipe, do the following:

1. Create the following measure:

```
Cohort =
    VAR __Table =
        GENERATE (
            DISTINCT ('R03_Table' [Patient]),
            EXCEPT (
                DISTINCT ('R03_Table' [Diagnosis]),
                CALCULATETABLE (DISTINCT ('R03_Table' [Diagnosis]))
            )
        )
    VAR __Table2 = SUMMARIZE (__Table, [Patient])
    VAR __Table3 = EXCEPT (DISTINCT ('R03_Table' [Patient]), __Table2)
RETURN
    CONCATENATEX (__Table3, [Patient], ",")
```

2. On a **Report** page, create a slicer visualization and place the `Diagnosis` column into the **Field** area of the visualization.
3. On the same **Report** page, create a card visualization and place the `Cohort` measure into the **Fields** area of the visualization.
4. Choose two or more diagnosis codes in the slicer by using the *Ctrl* key to select multiple items and note how the card values in the card visualization change.

The card visualization is displaying only those patient IDs that have been diagnosed with all of the diagnosis codes that were chosen in the slicer. For example, if you choose diagnosis codes **F91** and **K78**, you will note that only a single patient is displayed, **168947287**. If you additionally select **K85**, the card visualization displays **(Blank)**, indicating that no patient has been diagnosed with code **F91** and **F78** and **K85**.

How it works...

For such a small amount of DAX code, the `Cohort` measure hides perhaps one of the trickiest DAX computations ever devised, a computation that would likely give even DAX masters a moment's pause to understand how the calculation works. This calculation is only possible because of the peculiar interaction between particular, individual features of three DAX functions: `GENERATE`, `DISTINCT`, and `CALCULATETABLE`. Exactly how this calculation operates and why it does will be explained shortly, but first, let's go over the overall measure calculation.

The first table variable we created, ___Table, contains a list of patients and diagnosis codes for patients that do NOT have all of the diagnoses selected in the slicer. This table contains both the patient identifier, Patient, and diagnosis code, Diagnosis. The next table variable, ___Table2, simply uses SUMMARIZE to group ___Table by Patient, resulting in a single column table that only includes the Patient column. The third table variable, ___Table3 uses EXCEPT to remove any patients listed in ___Table2 from a list of distinct patients in the base table, R03_Table. The ___Table3 variable now contains a list of only the patients that do have all of the diagnoses selected in the slicer. Then, we use the CONCATENATEX function to return a comma-delimited list of the patients contained in ___Table3.

Thus, the key to this measure is in the calculation of the ___Table variable. But how does this calculation work? At a glance, it would appear that the ___Table variable should always be blank, since the two tables specified in the EXCEPT function appear to be identical, except the second table is wrapped with the CALCULATETABLE function. Using EXCEPT on two identical tables should result in an empty set. However, the two tables specified in the EXCEPT function are not identical. To understand why, you must truly understand exactly how GENERATE, DISTINCT, and CALCULATETABLE perform their calculations and how those three functions interoperate.

It is sometimes mistakenly believed that the GENERATE function creates the Cartesian product of the two tables specified. While this is true for unrelated tables, it is not true for related tables. In actuality, the GENERATE function creates the Cartesian product between each row in the first table and the table that results from the evaluation of the second table in the context of the current row from the first table. This is an important distinction and means that the current row context from the first table is passed along when evaluating the second table. To generate the Cartesian product of all the rows from all the specified tables, you would use CROSSJOIN. Thus, since the first table argument to our GENERATE function is the distinct list of patient IDs from the R03_Table table, the second table specified will be evaluated within the row context of each row of this table.

The second table specified in our GENERATE function is actually the resulting table from an EXCEPT function. The first table specified in the EXCEPT function is simply a distinct list of diagnosis codes provided by using the DISTINCT function. We must understand that the DISTINCT function ignores row context. You can prove this to yourself by creating a column in the R03_Table table using the following formula:

```
Column = COUNTROWS(DISTINCT('R03_Table'[Diagnosis]))
```

You will note that the value for each row in the table is 21, which is the total number of diagnosis codes in the R03_Table table. This is done despite the fact that not every patient has been diagnosed with every diagnosis code. However, DISTINCT does respect the filter context provided by our slicer visualization. Thus, the table that's returned by the first table argument in our EXCEPT clause is simply a list of diagnosis codes that were chosen in our slicer.

Now, we come to the second table specified in our EXCEPT function, which is simply the same distinct list of diagnosis codes wrapped in a CALCULATETABLE function with no additional filters specified. Here, we must understand that CALCULATETABLE operates exactly like the CALCULATE function, except that CALCULATETABLE returns a table while CALCULATE returns a scalar value. The CALCULATE function, and thus the CALCULATETABLE function, has a particular order of operations in which it performs its calculation. The first step in this order of operations for CALCULATETABLE is to evaluate the specified table in the original row and filter context. Thus, by wrapping our DISTINCT function with CALCULATETABLE, we force row context back into the evaluation. What row context? The row context provided by the first table parameter of our GENERATE function! Thus, the second table specified in our EXCEPT function returns only the diagnosis codes for each patient, which is not necessarily all of the diagnosis codes specified in our slicer. In fact, the only time that the tables in our EXCEPT function where all of the diagnosis codes specified in our slicer have matches in the second table, is for patients that have all of the diagnosis codes specified in the slicer. In this case, the EXCEPT function returns an empty set. This is the reason why __Table does not include patients that meet all of the criteria specified in the slicer.

And that is how you turn the normal operation of a slicer (OR logic) into AND logic!

See also

For more details about the functions in this recipe, please refer to the following links:

- GENERATE: https://docs.microsoft.com/en-us/dax/generate-function-dax
- DISTINCT: https://docs.microsoft.com/en-us/dax/distinct-function-dax
- EXCEPT: https://docs.microsoft.com/en-us/dax/except-function-dax
- CALCULATETABLE: https://docs.microsoft.com/en-us/dax/calculatetable-function-dax
- CALCULATE: https://docs.microsoft.com/en-us/dax/calculate-function-dax
- SUMMARIZE: https://docs.microsoft.com/en-us/dax/summarize-function-dax

- CONCATENATEX: `https://docs.microsoft.com/en-us/dax/concatenatex-function-dax`

Determining overall equipment effectiveness

Overall equipment effectiveness, or **OEE**, is a metric that's used in manufacturing to measure how efficiently production resources are being utilized versus their maximum potential. OEE is actually a combination of three other metrics: availability, performance, and quality. Availability is a measure of uptime. 100% availability means that resources are available for all of their scheduled operational time. In other words, there's no unscheduled downtime. Performance is a measure of production speed or capacity. 100% performance means that production is occurring at maximum speed or capacity. Quality is a measure of the production of good parts versus bad parts. 100% quality means that only good parts are being produced. Availability, performance, and quality are measured as percentages, and OEE is simply the product of multiplying availability, performance, and quality.

This measure demonstrates how to calculate availability, performance, quality, and ultimately, OEE.

Getting ready

To prepare for this recipe, do the following:

1. Open Power BI Desktop.
2. Use an **Enter Data** query to create a table called `R04_Machines` that contains the following data:

MachineName
Machine1
Machine2
Machine3
Machine4
Machine5
Machine6
Machine7
Machine8
Machine9
Machine10
Machine11

3. Import the data from the `Ch09R04Data.xlsx` Excel file located in this book's GitHub repository. Ensure that the created table is called `R04_Availability`.

4. Create a new table called `R04_Production` using the following formula:

```
R04_Production =
    VAR __Machines =
        { ( "Machine1", 1000 ),
          ( "Machine2", 800 ),
          ( "Machine3", 1200 ),
          ( "Machine4", 500 ),
          ( "Machine5", 1000 ),
          ( "Machine6", 800 ),
          ( "Machine7", 750 ),
          ( "Machine8", 1000 ),
          ( "Machine9", 120 ),
          ( "Machine10", 500 ),
          ( "Machine11", 750 ) }
    VAR __Calendar = CALENDAR(DATE(2010,1,7),DATE(2013,12,26))
    VAR __Table =
        ADDCOLUMNS(
            ADDCOLUMNS(
                SELECTCOLUMNS(
                    GENERATE(__Machines,__Calendar),
                    "MachineName",[Value1],
                    "Capacity",[Value2],
                    "Date",[Date]
                ),
                "Actual",
                RANDBETWEEN([Capacity]*.8,[Capacity])
            ),
            "Good",
            RANDBETWEEN([Actual]*.9,[Actual])
        )
    RETURN
        __Table
```

5. Create a relationship between the `MachineName` column in the `R04_Machines` table and the `MachineName` column in `R04_Availability`.

6. Create a relationship between the `MachineName` column in the `R04_Machines` table and the `MachineName` column in `R04_Production`.

7. Ensure that no other relationships exist for `R04_Machines`, `R04_Availability`, and `R04_Production`.

The `R04_Machines` table simply lists the names of the machines being analyzed.

The `R04_Availability` table represents a repair log. Each row in the `R04_Availability` table represents a repair or a preventative maintenance operation being performed on a machine. Included in the data is the type of repair, `RepairType`. Preventative maintenance tasks are denoted as having a value of `PM` within the `RepairType` column. Also included are the start time of the procedure, `RepairStarted`, and the end time of the procedure, `RepairCompleted`. Finally, the cause of the procedure is also included in the `Cause` columns. Any times that are not logged in this table are considered uptime.

The `R04_Production` table represents a production log. Each row in the `R04_Production` table represents production data for each `MachineName` for every `Date`. Included in the rows are the maximum daily production capacity of the machine, `Capacity`, how many parts per were actually produced, `Actual`, and how many of the parts produced did not have defects, `Good`.

How to do it...

To implement this recipe, do the following:

1. Create the following measures:

```
Availability =
    VAR __Table = 'R04_Availability'
    VAR __Table1 =
        ADDCOLUMNS (
            ADDCOLUMNS (
                __Table,
                "__Next",
                MINX (
                    FILTER (
                        __Table,
                        [MachineName] = EARLIER ([MachineName]) &&
                        [RepairStarted] > EARLIER ([RepairStarted])
                    ),
                    [RepairStarted]
                )
            )
```

```
            ),
            "__Uptime",
            IF(ISBLANK([__Next]),
DATEDIFF([RepairCompleted],DATE(2013,12,31),SECOND),
                DATEDIFF([RepairCompleted],[__Next],SECOND)
            )
        )
    VAR __TotalUptime = SUMX(__Table1,[__Uptime])
    VAR __Days =
        DATEDIFF(
            DATE(2010,1,1),
            DATE(2013,12,31),
            DAY) + 1
    VAR __MaxAvailable = 24 * 60 * 60 * __Days
RETURN
    DIVIDE(__TotalUptime, __MaxAvailable)

Performance =
    DIVIDE(
        SUMX('R04_Production','R04_Production'[Actual]),
        SUMX('R04_Production','R04_Production'[Capacity]),
        0
    )

Quality =
    DIVIDE(
        SUMX('R04_Production','R04_Production'[Good]),
        SUMX('R04_Production','R04_Production'[Actual]),
        0
    )

OEE = [Availability] * [Performance] * [Quality]
```

2. On a **Report** page, create a table visualization and place the `MachineName` column from the `R04_Machines` table into the **Values** area along with the `Availability`, `Performance`, `Quality`, and `OEE`. measures.

How it works...

The first measure is `Availability`. To calculate `Availability`, we start by getting all the rows from the `R04_Availability` table that are currently in context and store these rows in the `__Table` table variable. Now, we add two columns to this table, `__Next` and `__Uptime`, in order to create the new table variable, `__Table1`.

To calculate the uptime of machines between failures, we must know the time of the next failure. This is the purpose of the __Next column. For each failure event (row), __Next computes the time of the next failure after the current row. To accomplish this, we use FILTER to return only the rows from __Table where MachineName is equal to the current row's MachineName (EARLIER) and RepairStarted is greater than the current row's RepairStarted (EARLIER). Then, we can simply take the minimum RepairStarted time from this filtered set in order using MINX, in order to arrive at the start time of the next subsequent failure.

Now we can add our second column, __Uptime. For the __Uptime calculation, we check to see if the value for __Next is blank (ISBLANK). If __Next is blank, then we are at the end of our data since there is no subsequent failure in the data. Thus, we set __Uptime to the difference in seconds between when the current row's failure completed (RepairCompleted) and the end of our data, which we have set to December 31, 2013. Otherwise, if __Next is not blank, we compute __Uptime by taking the difference in seconds between the current row's RepairCompleted column and the computed subsequent failure event for the row, __Next.

Now we can compute the total uptime for all rows within the context of __TotalUptime. To do this, we simply need to use SUMX to sum our __Uptime column across all of the rows in the table variable, __Table1.

Now that we have the total uptime for all machines, we need to determine the maximum available time for the machines to operate. For our recipe, we have set our data start and end dates to January 1, 2010 and December 31, 2013, respectively. We also assume a 24/7 operation with no breaks. Thus, to get the maximum availability, __MaxAvailable, we compute the number of days in our dataset, __Days. Then, we can simply multiply __Days by 24 * 60 * 60, the number of seconds in a day. If we did include time for breaks or shift changes, we would deduct the amount of time for those breaks and shift changes from our __MaxAvailable value since the machines are not expected to be in operation during those times.

Now we can return the final value for Availability by dividing our total uptime, __TotalUptime, by the maximum availability, __MaxAvailability.

The Performance measure deals with data in the R04_Production table and is much simpler to calculate than Availability. For the Performance measure, we simply need to divide the sum of the actual parts produced, Actual, and the sum of the maximum production capacity, Capacity.

The `Quality` measure is nearly identical to the `Performance` measure, except that we are dividing the sum of the good (non-defective) parts produced, `Good`, and the sum of the actual parts produced, `Actual`.

Finally, for the `OEE` measure, we simply need to multiply our three measures together, that is, `Availability`, `Performance`, and `Quality`.

See also

For more details about the functions in this recipe, please refer to the following links:

- ADDCOLUMNS: https://docs.microsoft.com/en-us/dax/addcolumns-function-dax
- FILTER: https://docs.microsoft.com/en-us/dax/filter-function-dax
- MINX: https://docs.microsoft.com/en-us/dax/minx-function-dax
- EARLIER: https://docs.microsoft.com/en-us/dax/earlier-function-dax
- IF: https://docs.microsoft.com/en-us/dax/if-function-dax
- ISBLANK: https://docs.microsoft.com/en-us/dax/isblank-function-dax
- DATEDIFF: https://docs.microsoft.com/en-us/dax/datediff-function-dax
- SUMX: https://docs.microsoft.com/en-us/dax/sumx-function-dax
- DATE: https://docs.microsoft.com/en-us/dax/date-function-dax
- DIVIDE: https://docs.microsoft.com/en-us/dax/divide-function-dax

Optimizing On Time In Full

On Time In Full, or **OTIF**, is a measure of supply chain logistics. OTIF is of interest to any organization that ships products as OTIF measures whether the expected product was delivered in the quantity ordered, at the expected time, and to the desired location. In short, OTIF measures whether customers get what they want when they want it. The calculation for OTIF can be measured in a variety of ways, including the following:

- Number of deliveries
- Number of orders
- Number of order lines
- Percentage of the ordered quantity being delivered on time

This measure presents the methods for calculating OTIF at both the order line and order levels.

Getting ready

To prepare for this recipe, do the following:

1. Open Power BI Desktop.
2. Import the data from the Ch09R05Data.xlsx Excel file located in this book's GitHub repository. Ensure that the created table is called R05_Table.

The R05_Table table contains a list of customer orders. Customer orders may have multiple line items and require multiple shipments to fulfill. The rows in the R05_Table table are at the line item level. Each line item includes the ordered amount (Ordered), shipped amount (Shipped), customer (Customer), and product segment (Segment), as well as when the customer expects the product (CustomerDueDate) and when the line item was actually delivered (DeliveredDate).

How to do it...

To implement this recipe, do the following:

1. Create the following column:

```
OTIF =
    IF (
        'R05_Table'[Ordered] = 'R05_Table'[Shipped] &&
            'R05_Table'[DeliveredDate] <=
'R05_Table'[CustomerDueDate],
            1,
            0
    )
```

2. On a **Report** page, create a line chart visualization and place the DeliveredDate column from the R05_Table table into the **Axis** area and ensure that this is set to DeliveredDate and not Date Hierarchy.

3. In the same line chart visualization, place the `OTIF` column from the `R05_Table` table into the **Values** area and change the aggregation for the `OTIF` field to `Average`.

4. Create a table visualization and place the `Plant` and `OTIF` columns from the `R05_Table` table into the **Values** area, ensuring that the aggregation for `OTIF` is set to `Average`.

5. Create a second table visualization and place the `Segment` and `OTIF` columns from the `R05_Table` table into the **Values** area, ensuring that the aggregation for `OTIF` is set to `Average`.

How it works...

The `OTIF` column calculates on time in full at the line item level of orders. This calculation is quite trivial. For each line, we simply check if the `Shipped` column equals the `Ordered` column and whether the `DeliveredDate` is less than or equal to the `CustomerDueDate`. If both conditions are true, we assign a value of 1 (100%). If not, we assign a value of 0 (0%).

Since `OTIF` is a column, we can safely aggregate across multiple different dimensions such as time (`DeliveredDate`), product group (`Segment`), or source (`Plant`). However, it is important that we use an aggregation of `Average` to return a meaningful result.

There's more...

Calculating OTIF at a line level can be useful but can also obfuscate serious deficiencies. Customers likely do not care about individual lines of orders but rather about whether their complete orders are being fulfilled on time and in full. To calculate OTIF at the order level, do the following:

1. Create the following measure:

```
On Time In Full =
    VAR __Ordered =
        SUMMARIZE(
            'R05_Table',
            'R05_Table'[Order],
            "__Ordered",
            SUM('R05_Table'[Ordered]))
        )
    VAR __OTIF =
        SUMMARIZE(
```

```
                    FILTER(
                        'R05_Table',
                        'R05_Table'[Ordered] = 'R05_Table'[Shipped] &&
                            'R05_Table'[DeliveredDate] <=
'R05_Table'[CustomerDueDate]
                    ),
                    [Order],
                    "__OTIF",
                    SUM('R05_Table'[Shipped])
                )
        VAR __Table =
            ADDCOLUMNS(
                NATURALLEFTOUTERJOIN(__Ordered,__OTIF),
                "__Percent",
                IF(ISBLANK([__OTIF]),0,[__OTIF] / [__Ordered])
            )
    RETURN
        DIVIDE(
            COUNTROWS(FILTER(__Table,[__OTIF] = 1)),
            COUNTROWS(__Table),
            0
        )
```

2. Add the `On Time In Full` measure to the **Values** area of the line chart and table charts we created previously.

Here, the calculation for the `On Time In Full` measure is more complex. We start by creating a table variable, `__Orders`, that uses SUMMARIZE to group the `R05_Table` table by the `Order` column. We use ADDCOLUMNS to add the `__Ordered` column. The `__Ordered` column sums the `Ordered` column. Thus, the `__Orders` table now contains a row for each order with the total amount of products requested for the entire order.

Now, we create the table variable, `__OTIF`. For this table, we filter the `R05_Table` table to only those lines that meet the `OTIF` criteria. Specifically, we return only the rows in the `R05_Table` table that have an `Ordered` value that equals the `Shipped` value and have a `DeliveredDate` that is less than or equal to the `CustomerDueDate`. Again, we use SUMMARIZE to group this filtered table by the `Order` column. We use ADDCOLUMNS to add the `__Shipped` column. The `__Shipped` column sums the `Shipped` column. Thus, the `__OTIF` table now contains a row for each order with the total amount of products shipped on time for the entire order.

Next, we create a third table variable called __Table. We use the NATURALLEFTOUTERJOIN function as the basis for our table. NATURALLEFTOUTERJOIN uses natural left outer join semantics to merge the __Orders and __OTIF tables. This means that all of the rows from the left table (__Orders) are included and match the rows from the right table (__OTIF). Then, we use ADDCOLUMNS to add the __Percent column, which is simply a division of the __OTIF and __Ordered columns in our new table. However, since there may be no matching records in the right table, __OTIF may be blank. Thus, we check for this and, if __OTIF is blank (ISBLANK), we assign a value of zero.

Now, we can return a value for On Time In Full by simply dividing the rows in __Table where the __Percent column is 1 by the total number of rows in __Table.

> Note that, if we wish to calculate On Time In Full by the percentage of ordered products being delivered on time, we would simply need to replace the entire RETURN section with the AVERAGEX(__Table,__Percent) formula.

See also

For more details about the functions in this recipe, please refer to the following links:

- ADDCOLUMNS: https://docs.microsoft.com/en-us/dax/addcolumns-function-dax
- FILTER: https://docs.microsoft.com/en-us/dax/filter-function-dax
- SUM: https://docs.microsoft.com/en-us/dax/sum-function-dax
- SUMMARIZE: https://docs.microsoft.com/en-us/dax/summarize-function-dax
- NATURALLEFTOUTERJOIN: https://docs.microsoft.com/en-us/dax/naturalleftouterjoin-function-dax
- ISBLANK: https://docs.microsoft.com/en-us/dax/isblank-function-dax
- COUNTROWS: https://docs.microsoft.com/en-us/dax/countrows-function-dax
- DIVIDE: https://docs.microsoft.com/en-us/dax/divide-function-dax
- IF: https://docs.microsoft.com/en-us/dax/if-function-dax

Analyzing order cycle time

There are many types of cycle times when it comes to businesses, especially when it comes to analyzing manufacturing and supply chain processes. In general, all of these various cycle times are simply the time between two events. For example, **order cycle time**, or **OCT**, is the time between orders being placed. In other words, OCT compares the time of the first order with the time of the second order and calculates the duration between the two events.

This recipe demonstrates how to calculate OCT as well as a closely associated metric, **order lead time (OLT)**.

Getting ready

To prepare for this recipe, do the following:

1. Open Power BI Desktop.
2. Import the data from the Ch09R06Data.xlsx Excel file located in this book's GitHub repository. Ensure that the created table is called R06_Table.

The R06_Table table contains a list of customer orders. Customer orders may have multiple line items and require multiple shipments to fulfill. The rows in the R06_Table table are at the line item level. Each line item includes the ordered amount (Ordered), shipped amount (Shipped), customer (Customer), and product segment (Segment), as well as when the order was received (ReceiveDate) and when the line item was actually delivered (DeliveredDate).

How to do it...

To implement this recipe, do the following:

1. Create the following measure:

```
OCT (Hours) =
    VAR __Table =
        GROUPBY(
            'R06_Table',
            'R06_Table'[Order],
"__ReceiveDate",MINX(CURRENTGROUP(),'R06_Table'[ReceiveDate])
            )
        VAR __Max = MAXX(__Table,[__ReceiveDate])
```

```
VAR __Min = MINX(__Table,[__ReceiveDate])
VAR __Count = COUNTROWS(__Table)
VAR __OCT =
    DIVIDE(
        DATEDIFF(__Min,__Max,HOUR),
        __Count,
        0
    )
RETURN
    __OCT
```

2. On a **Report** page, create a card visualization and place the OCT measure in the **Fields** area.

3. Create a table visualization and place the Plant column from the R06_Table table, as well as the OCT measure, into the **Values** area.

4. Create a second table visualization and place the Segment column from the R06_Table table, as well as the OCT measure, into the **Values** area.

How it works...

Since our data is at the line level, we start by using GROUPBY to summarize our data by Order and storing this table within the __Table variable. Within our GROUPBY function, we calculate the minimum value of the ReceiveDate column per Order. Next, we calculate the maximum and minimum ReceiveDate within __Table by using MAXX and MINX, respectively. The maximum ReceiveDate is stored in the __Max variable, while the minimum ReceiveDate is stored in the __Min variable. We also calculate the number of rows within __Table using COUNTROWS and store this number in the __Count variable.

Now, we can calculate the frequency of orders by using DATEDIFF to find the difference between __Min and __Max in hours (HOUR) and then dividing by the number of orders with __Count. We store this value in the __OCT variable and simply return the value of __OCT as the value of the OCT (Hours) measure.

There's more...

A closely related measure to OCT is OLT. OLT is a measure of how long it takes to fulfill an order, once it's been received. To calculate OLT, follow these steps:

1. Create the following measure:

```
OLT (Days) =
    VAR __Table =
        ADDCOLUMNS (
            GROUPBY (
                'R06_Table',
                'R06_Table'[Order],
"__Delivered",MAXX(CURRENTGROUP(),'R06_Table'[DeliveredDate]),
"__Ordered",MINX(CURRENTGROUP(),'R06_Table'[ReceiveDate])
            ),
            "__Days",
            DATEDIFF([__Ordered],[__Delivered],DAY)
        )
RETURN
    AVERAGEX(__Table,[__Days])
```

2. Add the OLT measure to the **Values** area of the table charts we created previously.

To calculate the OLT (Days) measure, we start by using GROUPBY to summarize our base data table, R06_Table, by Order. For each Order, we calculate the ordered date, __Ordered, and the delivered date, __Delivered. Then, we use ADDCOLUMNS to calculate the number of days, __Days, between __Ordered and __Delivered. The calculation for __Days uses DATEDIFF with the DAY parameter. Finally, we can simply return the average value for the __Days column within __Table using the AVERAGEX function.

See also

For more details about the functions in this recipe, please refer to the following links:

- ADDCOLUMNS: https://docs.microsoft.com/en-us/dax/addcolumns-function-dax
- FILTER: https://docs.microsoft.com/en-us/dax/filter-function-dax
- MINX: https://docs.microsoft.com/en-us/dax/minx-function-dax

- MAXX: https://docs.microsoft.com/en-us/dax/maxx-function-dax
- GROUPBY: https://docs.microsoft.com/en-us/dax/groupby-function-dax
- COUNTROWS: https://docs.microsoft.com/en-us/dax/countrows-function-dax
- DIVIDE: https://docs.microsoft.com/en-us/dax/divide-function-dax
- DATEDIFF: https://docs.microsoft.com/en-us/dax/datediff-function-dax
- AVERAGEX: https://docs.microsoft.com/en-us/dax/averagex-function-dax

Using Uncommon DAX Patterns

10

Previous chapters have largely focused on the calculation of specific metrics and KPIs that are common to most businesses. This chapter instead focuses on DAX patterns and techniques that can be applied in a variety of different circumstances. While these patterns and techniques are perhaps more uncommon, the recipes provided in this chapter can be critical and instrumental in achieving the desired calculations within DAX.

We will cover the following recipes in this chapter:

- Aggregating multiple columns
- Finding not-in-common/in-common things
- Crafting linear interpolation
- Creating an inverse aggregator
- Finding childless nodes
- Calculating transitive closure
- Computing advanced measure totals
- Using measures where you are not allowed to
- Evaluating permutations and combinations
- Creating a dynamic temporal scale
- Emulating loops
- Simulating recursion

Technical requirements

The following are required to complete all of the recipes in this chapter:

- Power BI Desktop
- The GitHub repository: `https://github.com/PacktPublishing/DAX-Cookbook/tree/master/Chapter10`

Aggregating multiple columns

As DAX is built around dealing with tables, aggregating single columns of table data is incredibly easy. All standard aggregation functions, such as SUM, AVERAGE, MAX, and MIN, take a column as input as well as their corresponding iterative aggregation functions, such as SUMX, AVERAGEX, MAXX, and MINX. However, sometimes performing aggregations against a single column is not enough. Sometimes we need to aggregate against multiple columns at the same time.

This recipe demonstrates how to perform aggregations across multiple columns simultaneously.

Getting ready

To prepare for this recipe, do the following:

1. Open Power BI Desktop.
2. Use an **Enter Data** query to create a table called `R01_Table` with the following data:

ID	Value1	Value2	Value3	Value4
1	1	2	3	4
2	10	20	30	40
3	100	200	300	400
4	1000	2000	3000	4000
5	10	10	10	10
6	10	10	0	0
7	5	10	15	20
8	50	100	150	200

9	10	100	1000	10000
10	1	200	30	4000

How to do it...

To complete this recipe, do the following:

1. Create the following measure:

```
MC Sum =
    VAR __Column1 =
SELECTCOLUMNS('R01_Table',"__Column",'R01_Table'[Value1])
    VAR __Column2 =
SELECTCOLUMNS('R01_Table',"__Column",'R01_Table'[Value2])
    VAR __Column3 =
SELECTCOLUMNS('R01_Table',"__Column",'R01_Table'[Value3])
    VAR __Column4 =
SELECTCOLUMNS('R01_Table',"__Column",'R01_Table'[Value4])
    VAR __Table = UNION(__Column1,__Column2,__Column3,__Column4)
RETURN
    SUMX(__Table,[__Column])
```

2. On a **Report** page, create a **Card** visualization and place the MC Sum measure into the **Fields** area.

How it works...

For each column we wish to aggregate, we create a table variable, __Column1, __Column2, __Column3, and __Column4. Each of these table variables follows the same pattern. SELECTCOLUMNS is used to select all rows in the R01_Table table currently in context for a particular column. The columns chosen are Value1, Value2, Value3, and Value4. Critically, each of these selected columns is essentially renamed to the same column name, __Column, within our SELECTCOLUMNS statements. We then use the UNION function to create another table variable, __Table, which connects each of our other table variables, __Column1, __Column2, __Column3, and __Column4, together. The end result is that the __Table variable now contains a single-column table with all of the values from all of our selected columns. This single column is called __Column. Thus we can now use any of our iterative aggregation functions, such as SUMX, to return an aggregation against our __Table variable for the __Column column.

There's more...

This technique will work with any of DAX's iterative aggregation functions, X functions, including AVERAGEX, COUNTAX, COUNTX, GEOMEANX, MAXX, MEDIANX, MINX, PRODUCTX, STDEVX.P, STDEVX.S, SUMX, VARX.P, and VARX.S.

 It is also important to note that, when aggregating multiple columns, they do not have to come from the same table but can come from different tables. Also, because this recipe does not override any row or filter contexts, this recipe will perform aggregations under any filtering conditions, such as the use of slicers and cross filtering.

See also

For more details about the functions used in this recipe, refer to the following links:

- SELECTCOLUMNS: https://docs.microsoft.com/en-us/dax/selectcolumns-function-dax
- UNION: https://docs.microsoft.com/en-us/dax/union-function-dax
- SUMX: https://docs.microsoft.com/en-us/dax/sumx-function-dax
- AVERAGEX: https://docs.microsoft.com/en-us/dax/averagex-function-dax
- COUNTAX: https://docs.microsoft.com/en-us/dax/countax-function-dax
- COUNTX: https://docs.microsoft.com/en-us/dax/countx-function-dax
- GEOMEANX: https://docs.microsoft.com/en-us/dax/goemeanx-function-dax
- MAXX: https://docs.microsoft.com/en-us/dax/maxx-function-dax
- MEDIANX: https://docs.microsoft.com/en-us/dax/medianx-function-dax
- MINX: https://docs.microsoft.com/en-us/dax/minx-function-dax
- PRODUCTX: https://docs.microsoft.com/en-us/dax/productx-function-dax
- STDEVX.P: https://docs.microsoft.com/en-us/dax/stdevx-p-function-dax
- STDEVX.S: https://docs.microsoft.com/en-us/dax/stdevx-s-function-dax
- VARX.P: https://docs.microsoft.com/en-us/dax/varx-p-function-dax
- VARX.S: https://docs.microsoft.com/en-us/dax/varx-s-function-dax

Finding in-common and not-in-common things

When performing data analysis, sometimes it is important to understand which data shares common groups or attributes and, conversely, which data does not share common groups and attributes. This recipe provides techniques you can use to identify data that shares common groups and attributes (**in-common**) as well as data that does not share common groups and attributes (**not-in-common**).

Getting ready

To prepare for this recipe, do the following:

1. Open Power BI Desktop.
2. Use an **Enter Data** query to create a table called `R02_Students` with the following data:

Teacher	Student
Teacher A	Student 1
Teacher A	Student 2
Teacher A	Student 3
Teacher A	Student 4
Teacher B	Student 1
Teacher B	Student 5
Teacher B	Student 7
Teacher B	Student 8
Teacher C	Student 3
Teacher C	Student 4

Teacher C	Student 7
Teacher C	Student 8
Teacher D	Student 5
Teacher D	Student 9
Teacher D	Student 10

3. Create the following tables:

```
R02_Teachers1 = DISTINCT('R02_Students'[Teacher])

R02_Teachers2 = DISTINCT('R02_Students'[Teacher])
```

4. Ensure that a one-to-many relationship exists between the R02_Teachers1 and R02_Students tables.

5. Ensure that a one-to-many relationship exists between the R02_Teachers2 and R02_Students tables.

6. Ensure that no other relationships between the R02_Students, R02_Teachers1, and R02_Teachers2 tables exist.

The data in the R02_Students table contains a list of teachers and their students. We wish to identify the number of students that teachers have in common. In addition, we also wish to identify the students that teachers do not share.

How to do it...

To complete this recipe, do the following:

1. Create the following measure:

```
InCommon =
    VAR __Students1 =
        SELECTCOLUMNS(
            FILTER('R02_Students'),
                'R02_Students'[Teacher] =
MAX('R02_Teachers1'[Teacher])
            ),
                "__Student",'R02_Students'[Student]
```

```
            )
    VAR __Students2 =
        SELECTCOLUMNS(
            FILTER(
                ALL('R02_Students'),
                'R02_Students'[Teacher] =
MAX('R02_Teachers2'[Teacher])
            ),
            "__Student",'R02_Students'[Student]
        )
    VAR __InCommon = COUNTROWS(INTERSECT(__Students1,__Students2))
RETURN
    IF(ISBLANK(__InCommon),0,__InCommon)
```

2. On a **Report** page, create a **Matrix** visualization and place the `Teacher` column from the `R02_Teachers1` table into the **Rows** area.

3. In the same **Matrix** visualization, place the `Teacher` column from the `R02_Teachers2` table into the **Columns** area.

4. In the same **Matrix** visualization, place the `InCommon` measure into the **Values** area.

How it works...

We started by creating a table variable, `__Students1`, to store values from the `Students` column in the `R02_Students` table that have the current context value of the `Teacher` column from the `R02_Teachers1` table. We did this by first using the `FILTER` function coupled with the `ALL` function. The `ALL` function gets all of the rows for the `R02_Students` column regardless of the filter context. We then filtered this table down to only those students that have a `Teacher` that equals the `MAX` of the `Teacher` column from the `R02_Teachers1` table. Since we are using this measure in a matrix visualization where row values are not repeated, using the `MAX` function in this manner simply returns the current `Teacher` within the current matrix row filter context. We then used `SELECTCOLUMNS` to select only the `Student` column and named our new column `__Student`. The `__Students1` table now contains a single-column table with a column called `__Student`.

Then, we created a second table variable, __Students2, to store values from the Students column in the R02_Students table that have the current context value of the Teacher column from the R02_Teachers2 table. We did this in the same manner as our __Students1 table variable except that we replaced references to the R02_Teachers1 table with the R02_Teachers2 table. Critically, our SELECTCOLUMNS statement uses the same name for the column, __Student.

We then calculate how many students that different pairs of teachers have in common and store this value in the __InCommon variable. Because both of our table variables, __Students1 and __Students2, have the same column name, __Students, we can use the INTERSECT function to determine matching rows within the two table variables. We then use COUNTX to count the number of rows, and thus shared students.

In our RETURN statement, we can now simply check whether our __InCommon variable is blank (no matching students) and if so, return 0. Otherwise, we simply return the value of __InCommon.

There's more...

Suppose we now wish to find the students that various teachers do not have in common. To do this, follow these steps:

1. Create the following measure:

```
NotInCommon =
    VAR __Students1 =
        CALCULATETABLE (
            DISTINCT('R02_Students'[Student]),
            ALLEXCEPT('R02_Students','R02_Teachers1'[Teacher])
        )
    VAR __Students2 =
        CALCULATETABLE (
            DISTINCT('R02_Students'[Student]),
            ALLEXCEPT('R02_Students','R02_Teachers2'[Teacher])
        )
    VAR __Table =
        UNION (
            EXCEPT(__Studens1,__Students2),
            EXCEPT(__Students2,__Students1)
        )
    RETURN
        CONCATENATEX(__Table,[Student],",")
```

2. On a **Report** page, create a **Slicer** visualization and place the `Teacher` column from the `R02_Teachers1` table into the **Fields** area.

3. On the same **Report** page, create a second **Slicer** visualization and place the `Teacher` column from the `R02_Teachers2` table into the **Fields** area.

4. On the same **Report** page, create a **Card** visualization and place the `NotInCommon` measure into the **Fields** area.

Select different combinations of teachers in the slicers to see what students are not shared between them.

`NotInCommon` follows a similar pattern to `InCommon`; however, we use entirely different DAX functions to essentially achieve similar results. This has been done purposefully to demonstrate different DAX techniques for achieving the same or similar results.

Here, again, we start by creating a table variable, `__Students1`, to store values from the `Students` column in the `R02_Students` table that have the current context value of the `Teacher` column from the `R02_Teachers1` table. This time, we do it by using the `CACULATETABLE` function to override our current filter context. Instead of using `ALL` and then filtering down to the `MAX` value of the `Teacher` column from the `R02_Teachers1` table, we use a filter clause that utilizes the `ALLEXCEPT` function. The `ALLEXCEPT` function removes all filter contexts except those explicitly referenced within the `ALLEXCEPT` function, in this case the `Teacher` column from the `R02_Teachers1` table. The filter context for the `Teacher` column from the `R02_Teachers1` table comes from our first **Slicer** visualization. Instead of using `SELECTCOLUMNS` to select only the `Student` column, we use `DISTINCT` to return only the unique values in the `Student` column. The end result of this calculation is essentially the same as in our `InCommon` calculation for the `__Students1` variable. The `__Students1` table now contains a single-column table with a column called `Student`.

We now create a second table variable, `__Students2`, to store values from the `Students` column in the `R02_Students` table that have the current context value of the `Teacher` column from the `R02_Teachers2` table. We do this in the same manner as our `__Students1` table variable except that we replace references to the `R02_Teachers1` table with `R02_Teachers2`. The filter context for the `Teacher` column from the `R02_Teachers2` table comes from our second **Slicer** visualization. Critically, our `DISTINCT` statement references the same name for the column, `Student`.

We can now calculate the students that teachers do not have in common and store this value in the __NotInCommon variable. Because both of our table variables, __Students1 and __Students2, have the same column name, Students, we can use the EXCEPT function to determine non-matching rows within the two table variables. We use UNION coupled with two EXCEPT functions with our table variables referenced in different orders so that we can determine students that our first teacher does not have in common with our second teacher, as well as students that our second teacher does not have in common with our first teacher.

We can now use CONCATENATEX to return a concatenated string of students that the teachers do not have in common.

If we were only interested in students that our first teacher has and that our second teacher does not have, we would replace the entire UNION statement with just EXCEPT(__Students1,__Students2).

See also

For more details about the functions used in this recipe, refer to the following links:

- DISTINCT: https://docs.microsoft.com/en-us/dax/distinct-function-dax
- SELECTCOLUMNS: https://docs.microsoft.com/en-us/dax/selectcolumns-function-dax
- FILTER: https://docs.microsoft.com/en-us/dax/filter-function-dax
- CONCATENATEX: https://docs.microsoft.com/en-us/dax/concatenatex-function-dax
- ALL: https://docs.microsoft.com/en-us/dax/all-function-dax
- UNION: https://docs.microsoft.com/en-us/dax/union-function-dax
- INTERSECT: https://docs.microsoft.com/en-us/dax/intersect-function-dax
- COUNTROWS: https://docs.microsoft.com/en-us/dax/countrows-function-dax
- MAX: https://docs.microsoft.com/en-us/dax/max-function-dax
- IF: https://docs.microsoft.com/en-us/dax/if-function-dax
- ISBLANK: https://docs.microsoft.com/en-us/dax/isblank-function-dax
- CALCULATETABLE: https://docs.microsoft.com/en-us/dax/calculatetable-function-dax
- ALLEXCEPT: https://docs.microsoft.com/en-us/dax/allexcept-function-dax

Crafting linear interpolation

Linear interpolation is a mathematical curve fitting technique. The goal of linear interpolation is to take known data points and create new data points as estimations based upon known values. For example, suppose we know that a car starts at a velocity of 0 miles per hour (mph). After 1,000 feet, we use a laser to clock the speed of the car at 60 mph. If we assume a constant rate of acceleration (linear), then we could use linear interpolation to estimate the speed of the car after 10 feet, 20 feet, 30 feet, and so on. Even though we only know the speed of the car at 0 feet and 1,000 feet, we can estimate the speed at any distance traveled between 0 and 1,000 feet using linear interpolation.

The formula for linear interpolation solved for an unknown variable y (think of this as the speed of the car in the example) can be given as follows:

$$y = y0 + (x + x0) * (y1 - y0)/(x1 - x0)$$

Continuing our example, the variables in the formula are defined as follows:

- y = the unknown speed of the car
- $y0$ = the initial speed of the car (0 mph)
- $y1$ = the ending speed of the car (60 mph)
- x = the distance at which we wish to calculate the speed of the car
- $x0$ = the initial distance traveled by the car (0 feet)
- $x1$ = the ending distance traveled by the car (1,000 feet)

This recipe provides a method for performing linear interpolation in DAX.

Getting ready

To prepare for this recipe, do the following:

1. Open Power BI Desktop.
2. Import the data from the `Ch10R03Data.xlsx` Excel file located in the GitHub repository. Ensure that the table you create is called `R03_Table`.

The data in `R03_Table` represents a thermodynamics chart for water listing the pressure, volume, energy, enthalpy, and entropy for water in 5° Celsius increments of temperature. Do not be too concerned about the subject matter of thermodynamics; this is just an example of data where values for such things as the pressure, volume, energy, enthalpy, and entropy of water are considered to be linear between incremental measured values of temperature.

How to do it...

To complete this recipe, do the following:

1. Create the following table:

```
R03_Interpolation =
    SELECTCOLUMNS (
        GENERATESERIES(1,373,1),
        "Temp (C)",
        [Value]
    )
```

2. Create the following measure in the `R03_Interpolation` table:

```
Pressure (MPa) =
    VAR __x = MAX('R03_Interpolation'[Temp (C)])
    VAR __match =
    LOOKUPVALUE (
        'R03_Table'[Pressure (MPa)],
        'R03_Table'[Temp (C)],__x,
        BLANK()
    )
RETURN
    IF (
        ISBLANK(__match),
            VAR __x0 =
                MAXX(
                    FILTER('R03_Table','R03_Table'[Temp (C)]<__x),
                    'R03_Table'[Temp (C)]
                )
            VAR __x1 =
                MINX(
                    FILTER('R03_Table','R03_Table'[Temp (C)]>__x),
                    'R03_Table'[Temp (C)]
                )
            VAR __y0 =
                LOOKUPVALUE (
```

```
                        'R03_Table'[Pressure (MPa)],
                        'R03_Table'[Temp (C)],__x0,
                        BLANK()
                    )
            VAR __y1 =
                LOOKUPVALUE(
                    'R03_Table'[Pressure (MPa)],
                    'R03_Table'[Temp (C)],__x1,
                    BLANK()
                )
            RETURN __y0 + (__x - __x0) * (__y1 - __y0)/(__x1 - __x0),
            __match
    )
```

3. On a **Report** page, create a **Scatter chart** visualization and place the Temp (C) column from the R03_Table table into the **X Axis** field. Set Temp (C) to Don't summarize.

4. In the same visual, place the Pressure (MPa) column from the R03_Table table into the **Y Axis** field.

5. On the same **Report** page, create a second **Scatter chart** visualization and place the Temp (C) column from the R03_Interpolation table into the **X Axis** field. Set Temp (C) to Don't summarize.

6. In this second visual, place the Pressure (MPa) measure from the R03_Table table into the **Y Axis** field.

The first visualization demonstrates the holes in the data. The R03_Table table only contains data about certain values of Temp (C). The second visualization demonstrates the smooth curve created by the linear interpolation of values between known data points.

How it works...

We start by getting the current value for the Temp (C) in the R03_Interpolation table within the current context. This is stored in the __x variable and represents the point on the x axis at which we are attempting to perform interpolation. Next, we create the __match variable. The __match variable attempts to find a matching record for the current temperature, __x, within the R03_Table table. If a match is found, __match is assigned the value of the Pressure (MPA) column for the corresponding row in the R03_Table table. Otherwise, if no match is found, __match is assigned the BLANK value.

We now start our first RETURN statement. We first check whether __match is blank (ISBLANK). If __match is blank, then we will need to interpolate. If __match is not blank, then there is no reason to interpolate and we simply return the value of __match. If interpolation is required, we start by calculating the __x0 variable. The __x0 variable represents the temperature value, Temp (C), within the R03_Table table that is the highest temperature that is less than our current temperature value, __x. We can find this by using FILTER to filter the R03_Table table for all rows with a Temp (C) that is less than the current temperature, __x, and then using MAXX to find the maximum value of Temp (C) within this filtered set of rows.

The calculation of the __x1 variable is very similar to the calculation for __x0. The __x1 variable represents the temperature value, Temp (C), within the R03_Table table that is the lowest temperature that is greater than our current temperature value, __x. We can find this by using FILTER to filter the R03_Table table for all rows with a Temp (C) that is greater than the current temperature, __x, and then using MINX to find the minimum value of Temp (C) within this filtered set of rows.

We can now use our values for __x0 and __x1 when calculating the __y0 and __y1 variables. Both __y0 and __y1 are calculated nearly identically to our calculation for __match except that we are now looking up the temperature values for __x0 and __x1, respectively. Our second RETURN statement then simply implements the linear interpolation formula to return the estimated value.

See also

For more details about the functions used in this recipe, refer to the following links:

- MAXX: https://docs.microsoft.com/en-us/dax/maxx-function-dax
- FILTER: https://docs.microsoft.com/en-us/dax/filter-function-dax
- MAX: https://docs.microsoft.com/en-us/dax/max-function-dax
- LOOKUPVALUE: https://docs.microsoft.com/en-us/dax/lookupvalue-function-dax
- BLANK: https://docs.microsoft.com/en-us/dax/blank-function-dax
- ISBLANK: https://docs.microsoft.com/en-us/dax/isblank-function-dax

Creating an inverse aggregator

We are all familiar with normal aggregations, such as sum, average, maximum, minimum, and count. Usually, this is exactly what we want when analyzing data: displaying aggregated data based upon filtering that we specify. However, sometimes the desired behavior lies in seeing the aggregation of values for the items that we do not filter. In other words, we wish to instead specify the items that we do not want included in an aggregation as opposed to the items we do want included in an aggregation.

This recipe demonstrates how to implement a measure that performs an inverse sum; in other words, it sums the items that we have not selected. While this recipe performs a sum aggregation, this same technique can be used for any type of aggregation.

Getting ready

To prepare for this recipe, do the following:

1. Open Power BI Desktop.
2. Use an **Enter Data** query to create a table called R04_Table with the following data:

Category	Value
A	10
B	20
C	100
D	200
E	300

How to do it...

To complete this recipe, do the following:

1. Create the following measures:

```
AllSum = SUMX(ALL('R04_Table'),'R04_Table'[Value])

NormalSum = SUM('R04_Table'[Value])

InverseSum =
    IF(
        ISFILTERED('R04_Table'[Category]),
```

```
CALCULATE (
    SUM ('R04_Table'[Value]),
    EXCEPT (
        ALL ('R04_Table'[Category]),
        VALUES ('R04_Table'[Category])
    )
),
SUM ('R04_Table'[Value])
)
```

2. On a **Report** page, create a **Slicer** visualization and place the `Category` column from the `R04_Table` table into the **Fields** area.

3. On the same **Report** page, create a **Table** visualization and place the `Category` and `Value` columns from the `R04_Table` table into the **Values** area.

4. On the same **Report** page, create a **Card** visualization and place the `AllSum` measure into the **Fields** area.

5. On the same **Report** page, create a second **Card** visualization and place the `NormalSum` measure into the **Fields** area.

6. On the same **Report** page, create a third **Card** visualization and place the `InverseSum` measure into the **Fields** area.

The `AllSum` measure always displays the total amount of the `Value` column for all items in the table. The `NormalSum` measure displays the sum of the `Value` column for all items selected in the **Slicer** visualization. The `InverseSum` measure displays the sum of the `Value` column for all items not selected in the **Slicer** visualization. The sum of `NormalSum` and `InverseSum` always equals the value of `AllSum`.

How it works...

For the `AllSum` measure, we use `SUMX` coupled with an `ALL` filter to sum the `Value` column for all rows in the `R04_Table` table, regardless of any filters. The `NormalSum` measure simply implements the `SUM` function for the `Value` column in the `R04_Table` table.

For the `InverseSum` measure, we start by checking whether the `Category` column in the `R04_Table` table is filtered using the `ISFILTERED` function. If the `Category` column is not filtered, we simply use the same DAX we used in the `NormalSum` measure. If the `Category` column in the `R04_Table` table is filtered, then we need to calculate the sum of the `Value` column for the rows that are not selected in the slicer. To do this, we use `CALCULATE` to `SUM` the `Value` column with a filter that returns non-matching rows from the `R04_Table` table.

To return non-matching rows, we use the EXCEPT function. For the first parameter of the EXCEPT function, we use the ALL function to return all values from the Category column in the R04_Table table. For the second parameter of the EXCEPT function, we use VALUES to return distinct, filtered values from the Category column (the items chosen in the slicer). Thus, the end result of the EXCEPT function is a table that contains only non-matching rows from the R04_Table table. CALCULATE applies this filter to the calculation of our SUM of the Value column.

See also

For more details about the functions used in this recipe, refer to the following links:

- SUMX: https://docs.microsoft.com/en-us/dax/sumx-function-dax
- ALL: https://docs.microsoft.com/en-us/dax/all-function-dax
- SUM: https://docs.microsoft.com/en-us/dax/sum-function-dax
- ISFILTERED: https://docs.microsoft.com/en-us/dax/isfiltered-function-dax
- IF: https://docs.microsoft.com/en-us/dax/if-function-dax
- CALCULATE: https://docs.microsoft.com/en-us/dax/calculate-function-dax
- EXCEPT: https://docs.microsoft.com/en-us/dax/except-function-dax
- VALUES: https://docs.microsoft.com/en-us/dax/values-function-dax

Finding childless nodes

DAX has a number of parent-child functions, including PATH, PATHCONTAINS, PATHITEM, PATHITEMREVERSE, and PATHLENGTH. These functions help us analyze data presented in the format of a parent-child hierarchy. While the parent-child functions help us determine such things as the entire lineage of rows of parent-child hierarchy data, the number of levels within a hierarchy, and who is the nth level down in the hierarchy, there is some useful functionality that is not included. For example, it can be useful to know the top and bottom levels of the hierarchy or, essentially, where hierarchies begin and end. Determining the top level of a hierarchy is very easy: we simply need to filter for the row or rows that have no parent. However, finding the bottom of the hierarchy, nodes that have no children, is somewhat more difficult since these may occur at any level within the hierarchy.

This recipe provides two different methods for finding childless nodes within a hierarchy.

Getting ready

To prepare for this recipe, do the following:

1. Open Power BI Desktop.
2. Use an **Enter Data** query to create a table called R05_Table with the following data:

EmployeeKey	ParentKey
112	
14	112
3	14
11	3
13	3
162	3
117	162
221	162
81	162

This data is the same as the data provided in the Microsoft documentation on parent-child functions, which can be found here: https://docs.microsoft.com/en-us/dax/understanding-functions-for-parent-child-hierarchies-in-dax.

Our purpose is to demonstrate the usefulness of this recipe with the same data used to explain DAX's built-in parent-child functions.

How to do it...

To complete this recipe, do the following:

1. Create the following measure:

```
Childless =
    VAR __Table =
        ADDCOLUMNS(
            'R05_Table',
            "__Count",
            COUNTX(
                FILTER(
                    'R05_Table',
'R05_Table'[ParentEmployeeKey]=EARLIER('R05_Table'[EmployeeKey])
```

```
            )
                ,'R05_Table'[EmployeeKey]
            )
        )
    RETURN
        CONCATENATEX(FILTER(__Table,[__Count]<1),[EmployeeKey],",")
```

2. On a **Report** page, create a **Card** visualization and place the `Childless` measure into the **Fields** area of the visualization.

How it works...

We start by creating a table variable, `__Table`, based on our data table, `R05_Table`. In this base table we use the `ADDCOLUMNS` function to add the `__Count` column. The formula for the `__Count` column counts the number of times the `ParentEmployeeKey` column matches the current row's `EmployeeKey` column. We do this by using the `FILTER` function to filter the base data table, `R05_Table`, to those rows where the `ParentEmployeeKey` matches our current row's `EmployeeKey` (`EARLIER`), and then by counting the number of `EmployeeKey` values (rows) using `COUNTX`. Employees that have no children will have a `__Count` of zero. Thus, we can simply use `CONCATENATEX` to concatenate all `EmployeeKey` values in `__Table` where the `__Count` column is less than 1.

There's more...

The preceding solution to the problem of finding childless nodes was developed prior to the introduction of the `EXCEPT` function. The `EXCEPT` function perhaps makes the calculation somewhat more elegant and easier to understand. To implement the `Childless` measure using the `EXCEPT` function, do the following:

1. Create the following measure:

```
Childless 2 =
    CONCATENATEX(
        EXCEPT(
            VALUES('R05_Table'[EmployeeKey]),
            VALUES(R05_Table[ParentEmployeeKey])
        ),
        'R05_Table'[EmployeeKey],
        ","
    )
```

2. On the same **Report** page, create a second **Card** visualization and place the `Childless 2` measure into the **Fields** area of the visualization.

In this version, we simply use the `EXCEPT` function and for the first table provide distinct values for the `EmployeeKey` column. For the second table, we provide distinct values from the `ParentEmployeeKey` column. Since childless nodes will not be parents, the table returned by the `EXCEPT` function is a table of childless nodes, which we can then concatenate using `CONCATENATEX`.

See also

For more details about the functions used in this recipe, refer to the following links:

- Understanding functions for parent-child hierarchies in DAX: `https://docs.microsoft.com/en-us/dax/understanding-functions-for-parent-child-hierarchies-in-dax`
- ADDCOLUMNS: `https://docs.microsoft.com/en-us/dax/addcolumns-function-dax`
- COUNTX: `https://docs.microsoft.com/en-us/dax/countx-function-dax`
- FILTER: `https://docs.microsoft.com/en-us/dax/filter-function-dax`
- CONCATENATEX: `https://docs.microsoft.com/en-us/dax/concatenatex-function-dax`
- EARLIER: `https://docs.microsoft.com/en-us/dax/earlier-function-dax`
- EXCEPT: `https://docs.microsoft.com/en-us/dax/except-function-dax`
- VALUES: `https://docs.microsoft.com/en-us/dax/values-function-dax`

Calculating transitive closure

The concept of transitive closure can be a formidable topic to discuss, often devolving into purely mathematical discussions of binary relationships, graph theory, relationships, set theory, and so on. In plain English, transitive closure basically involves a set of origins, a set of destinations, and the paths between these origins and destinations. Given such a dataset, transitive closure provides a list of destinations that are reachable from any given origin.

You could think of this in terms of plane trips. There may not be a direct flight from Columbus, OH to Dubai in the United Arab Emirates, but if there is a flight from Columbus, OH to Toronto, Canada, a flight from Toronto, Canada to Frankfurt, Germany, and a flight from Frankfurt, Germany to Dubai, then there is transitive closure between Columbus, OH and Dubai since the trip can be made from the origin (Columbus, OH) to the destination (Dubai) in one or more flights.

This recipe presents a DAX implementation of transitive closure.

Getting ready

To prepare for this recipe, do the following:

1. Open Power BI Desktop.
2. Use an **Enter Data** query to create a table called `R06_Table` with the following data:

Origin	Destination
1	2
1	3
2	4
3	8
5	6
6	7
6	8

The `R06_Table` table represents origins and destinations for direct plane flights. For example, there is a direct flight from origin 1 to destinations 2 and 3 and a direct flight from origin 2 to destination 4.

How to do it...

To complete this recipe, do the following:

1. Create the following measure:

```
Destinations =
    VAR __Table1 = 'R06_Table'
    VAR __Table1a =
```

```
            DISTINCT(
                SELECTCOLUMNS(
                    __Table1,
                    "__Destination",[Destination]
                )
            )
        VAR __Table2 =
            FILTER(
                ALL('R06_Table'),
                'R06_Table'[Origin] IN __Table1a
            )
        VAR __Table2a =
            DISTINCT(
                SELECTCOLUMNS(
                    __Table2,
                    "__Destination",[Destination])
                )
    RETURN
        CONCATENATEX(
            DISTINCT(
                UNION(__Table1a,__Table2a)
            ),
            [__Destination],
            ","
        )
```

2. On a **Report** page, create a **Table** visualization and place the `Origin` column into the **Fields** area of the visualization. Ensure that `Origin` is set to `Don't summarize`.

3. In the same **Table** visualization, place the `Destinations` measure into the **Fields** area.

The `Destinations` measure lists all values from the `Destination` column to which travel is possible from the `Origin`.

How it works...

Let's first discuss what will not work. You may be tempted to try to use the `PATH` function here in order to derive the paths between origins and destinations. Unfortunately, the `PATH` function will return an error because the data in the `R06_Table` table is not a true parent-child hierarchy, which is what the `PATH` function expects.

Since we cannot use the PATH function, we instead start by defining a table variable called __Table1. __Table1 is set to equal all of the rows from the R06_Table table that are currently within context. Next, we create a second table variable, __Table1a, that is based on __Table1. From __Table1, we select the Destination column and return distinct values from this column using DISTINCT. We now have a list of all values in the Destination column that can be directly traveled to from the current row value for Origin.

We now create a third table variable, __Table2. For __Table2, we use ALL to break out of the row context and return all rows in our base data table, R06_Table. We use FILTER to return only values in the Origin column that match rows in __Table1a using the DAX IN operator. __Table2 now contains all values for the Origin column that match the destinations directly reachable from our original Origin. We then repeat the pattern of __Table1a to calculate __Table2a but replace the reference to __Table1 with a reference to __Table2. Thus, __Table2a now has a list of all values in the Destination column that can be indirectly traveled to after an intermediate flight from the current row value for Origin.

We can now use UNION to concatenate __Table1a and __Table2a, use DISTINCT to return only unique values, and finally use CONCATENATEX to return all in the distinct values of the __Destination column.

Note that the dataset in R06_Table only requires a maximum of two flights to reach any destination from any origin. Thus, the pattern implemented here is only required twice. If three flights were required between origins and possible destinations, the pattern would need to be implemented three times. If four flights were required, the pattern would need to be implemented four times, and so on. For example, if three flights were required, you would create __Table3 and __Table3a variables based upon the same DAX calculations as __Table2 and __Table2a. In the __Table3 calculation, you would replace the reference to __Table1a with __Table2a and in the __Table3a calculation you would replace the reference to __Table2 with __Table3. Your UNION statement would now need to include __Table1a, __Table2a, and __Table3a. This pattern can be repeated up to the limits of DAX. Thus, if you are unsure of how many intermediate steps there may be between origins and destinations you can use a reasonable maximum approach since returning blank tables will not affect the calculation.

There's more...

Transitive closure is a useful concept and technique outside plane flights or even outside the general concept of origins and destinations. For example, take something such as a referral program where customers receive a bonus for referring their friends and family to your business. For every direct referral, the customer receives a gift card of $100. For every indirect referral, the customer receives a $50 gift card. For every referral from an indirect referral (more than twice removed), the customer receives a $5 gift card.

To see how transitive closure can be used in this case, do the following:

1. Use an **Enter Data** query to create a table called R06_Referrals with the following data:

Client	Referral
John	
Tom	John
Dick	Tom
Harry	
David	Harry
Eric	David
Dre	Dick
Lex	Dick

2. Create the following column:

```
Path =
    VAR __Table1 =
        FILTER('R06_Referrals','R06_Referrals'[Client] =
EARLIER('R06_Referrals'[Client]))
    VAR __Table1a =
        DISTINCT(SELECTCOLUMNS(__Table1,"__Referral",[Referral]))
    VAR __Table2 =
        FILTER(ALL('R06_Referrals'),[Client] IN __Table1a)
    VAR __Table2a =
        DISTINCT(SELECTCOLUMNS(__Table2,"__Referral",[Referral]))
    VAR __Table3 =
        FILTER(ALL('R06_Referrals'),[Client] IN __Table2a)
    VAR __Table3a =
        DISTINCT(SELECTCOLUMNS(__Table3,"__Referral",[Referral]))
    VAR __Table4 =
        FILTER(ALL('R06_Referrals'),[Client] IN __Table3a)
    VAR __Table4a =
```

```
                   DISTINCT(SELECTCOLUMNS(__Table4,"__Referral",[Referral]))
     RETURN
         CONCATENATEX(
             DISTINCT(
                 UNION(__Table1a,__Table2a,__Table3a,__Table4a)
             ),
             [__Referral],
             "|"
         )
```

3. Create this additional column:

```
Gift Card =
    VAR __Table =
        ADDCOLUMNS(
            ADDCOLUMNS(
                ADDCOLUMNS(
                    'R06_Referrals',
    "__Include",PATHCONTAINS('R06_Referrals'[Path],EARLIER('R06_Referra
ls'[Client]))
                ),
                "__Level",
                IF(
                    ISBLANK([Path]),
                    0,
                    VAR __Pos = FIND(EARLIER([Client]),[Path],,-1)
                    RETURN
                        IF(
                            __Pos = -1,
                            0,
                            LEN(
                                LEFT(
                                    [Path],
                                    __Pos
                                )
                            ) -
                                LEN(
                                    SUBSTITUTE(
                                        LEFT([Path],__Pos),
                                        "|",
                                        ""
                                    )
                                ) + 1
                        )
                )
            ),
            "__Value",
            SWITCH(
```

```
            [__Level],
            1, 100,
            2, 50,
            5
        )
    )
RETURN
    SUMX(FILTER(__Table, [__Include]), [__Value])
```

Here, the `Path` column implements our transitive closure pattern to a reasonable maximum of four repetitions of the pattern, even though our dataset only includes a maximum of three levels of referrals. We use our transitive closure pattern to return pipe characters (|) so that we can now use parent-child hierarchy functions such as PATHCONTAINS in our subsequent column, `Gift Card`. The `Gift Card` column uses PATHCONTAINS to determine if the current `Client` is part of the referral path for each row (__Include). We then use arduous text parsing to determine the level of the referral in the hierarchy (__Level). Next, we set the value of each referral (__Value) based upon the __Level. Finally, we simply need to FILTER our table variable, __Table, to only those rows where __Include is TRUE and sum the __Value column.

See also

For more details about the functions used in this recipe, refer to the following links:

- DISTINCT: https://docs.microsoft.com/en-us/dax/distinct-function-dax
- SELECTCOLUMNS: https://docs.microsoft.com/en-us/dax/selectcolumns-function-dax
- FILTER: https://docs.microsoft.com/en-us/dax/filter-function-dax
- CONCATENATEX: https://docs.microsoft.com/en-us/dax/concatenatex-function-dax
- ALL: https://docs.microsoft.com/en-us/dax/all-function-dax
- UNION: https://docs.microsoft.com/en-us/dax/union-function-dax
- ADDCOLUMNS: https://docs.microsoft.com/en-us/dax/addcolumns-function-dax
- PATHCONTAINS: https://docs.microsoft.com/en-us/dax/pathcontains-function-dax
- EARLIER: https://docs.microsoft.com/en-us/dax/earlier-function-dax
- IF: https://docs.microsoft.com/en-us/dax/if-function-dax
- ISBLANK: https://docs.microsoft.com/en-us/dax/isblank-function-dax

- FIND: https://docs.microsoft.com/en-us/dax/find-function-dax
- LEN: https://docs.microsoft.com/en-us/dax/len-function-dax
- LEFT: https://docs.microsoft.com/en-us/dax/left-function-dax
- SUBSTITUTE: https://docs.microsoft.com/en-us/dax/substitute-function-dax
- SWITCH: https://docs.microsoft.com/en-us/dax/switch-function-dax
- SUMX: https://docs.microsoft.com/en-us/dax/sumx-function-dax

Computing advanced measure totals

Measure totals have been a problem since the dawn of placing DAX measures into table and matrix visualizations. This issue strikes at the core of the DAX language itself, context. The problem arises because the context in a subtotal or total line for a table or matrix is effectively all rows within context. However, evaluating a DAX calculation in the context of all current rows can often produce very different and expected results. Most users want the total of the numbers displayed in the rows of the table. However, DAX does not even consider the actual numbers displayed in the rows of a table or matrix visualization when calculating the total line for a table or matrix visualization. The *Totaling measures* recipe in Chapter 4, *Transforming Text and Numbers*, demonstrates how to solve this problem. However, there are times when we actually want different types of aggregation performed at the subtotal and total levels when displaying a hierarchy.

This recipe demonstrates an advanced scenario with measure totals where different types of aggregations are performed at different levels in a hierarchy.

Getting ready

To prepare for this recipe, do the following:

1. Open Power BI Desktop.
2. Use an **Enter Data** query to create a table called R07_Table with the following data:

Country	Hotel	Date	% Occupancy
UK	Hotel 1	1/1/2019	.8
UK	Hotel 2	1/1/2019	.75
UK	Hotel 3	1/1/2019	.9

USA	Hotel 4	1/1/2019	.9
USA	Hotel 5	1/1/2019	.75
USA	Hotel 6	1/1/2019	.9
UK	Hotel 1	1/2/2019	.9
UK	Hotel 2	1/2/2019	.8
UK	Hotel 3	1/2/2019	.95
USA	Hotel 4	1/2/2019	.95
USA	Hotel 5	1/2/2019	.8
USA	Hotel 6	1/2/2019	.95

The R07_Table table represents hotel occupancy data. The business rules for reporting on this data specify that it should be presented in the following hierarchy: Country first, then Hotel, and finally Date. Furthermore, business rules dictate that, at the Hotel or Date level, the minimum % Occupancy should be reported. However, at the subtotal level for Country, the average of the minimum % Occupancy for all hotels in that Country should also be reported. Finally, at the grand total level, the maximum value of the averages of the minimum % Occupancy for all hotels should be reported.

How to do it...

To complete this recipe, do the following:

1. Create the following measure:

```
Occupancy % =
    VAR __Table =
        SUMMARIZE(
            'R07_Table',
            'R07_Table'[Country],
            'R07_Table'[Hotel],
            "Aggregation",MIN('R07_Table'[% Occupancy])
        )
RETURN
    SWITCH(TRUE(),
        ISINSCOPE('R07_Table'[Date]) ||
            ISINSCOPE('R07_Table'[Hotel]),MIN('R07_Table'[%
Occupancy]),
    ISINSCOPE('R07_Table'[Country]),AVERAGEX(__Table,[Aggregation]),
        MAXX(
            GROUPBY(
                __Table,
```

```
                    [Country],
                    "GTAggregation",
                    AVERAGEX (CURRENTGROUP (), [Aggregation])
                ),
                [GTAggregation]
            )
        )
```

2. On a **Report** page, create a **Matrix** visualization and place the `Country` and `Hotel` columns from the `R07_Table` table into the **Rows** area of the visualization with `Country` at the top and `Hotel` at the bottom.

3. In the same **Matrix** visualization, place the `Occupancy %` measure into the `Values` area of the visualization.

4. Right-click the **UK** cell and choose **Expand** and then **All**.

How it works...

We start by creating a table variable, `__Table`. The calculation for `__Table` uses the SUMMARIZE function to summarize the rows in the `R07_Table` table as we expect our data to be summarized within visualizations. Specifically, we group our rows by `Country` and `Hotel`. We also add the `Aggregation` column and use MIN to compute the minimum value for the `% Occupancy` column.

In our RETURN statement, we use the alternative version of the SWITCH statement since we have multiple conditions to test and do not want nested IF statements. The first condition that we test is using ISINSCOPE to identify whether we are at the `Date` or `Hotel` level of our hierarchy. If so, we simply return the minimum value of the `% Occupancy` column using the MIN function. Next, we use ISINSCOPE again to determine whether we are at the `Country` level of our hierarchy. If so, we return the average of the `Aggregation` column in `__Table` using AVERAGEX. This is the subtotal level for `Country`. Finally, if none of the `Date`, `Hotel`, or `Country` columns are in scope, we need to return the maximum value for the averages at the `Country` subtotal level. To accomplish this, we use GROUPBY to group the rows in `__Table` by `Country`. We add the `GTAggregation` column, which uses AVERAGEXX to calculate the average of our `Aggregation` column. We then use MAXX to return the maximum value for the `GTAggregation` column.

This recipe can be modified for any number of aggregation levels within a hierarchy by simply extending our SWITCH statement and using ISINSCOPE to determine where we are within a hierarchy.

See also

For more details about the functions used in this recipe, refer to the following links:

- SUMMARIZE: https://docs.microsoft.com/en-us/dax/summarize-function-dax
- MIN: https://docs.microsoft.com/en-us/dax/min-function-dax
- SWITCH: https://docs.microsoft.com/en-us/dax/switch-function-dax
- ISINSCOPE: https://docs.microsoft.com/en-us/dax/isinscope-function-dax
- AVERAGEX: https://docs.microsoft.com/en-us/dax/averagex-function-dax
- MAXX: https://docs.microsoft.com/en-us/dax/maxx-function-dax
- GROUPBY: https://docs.microsoft.com/en-us/dax/groupby-function-dax

Using measures where you are not allowed to

DAX measures are incredibly powerful, allowing a single DAX calculation to be used in seemingly endless circumstances. Given the right dataset, a single DAX calculation for something such as year-over-year revenue could be used in the context of customers, products, product groups, locations, business divisions, and so on. Perhaps even more amazingly, you could even evaluate that same single measure within all of those contexts simultaneously! However, measures are not without their limitations. Specifically, measures cannot be used in Power BI for things such as slicers and chart axes and legends.

This recipe demonstrates how to do the impossible: to essentially use measures where you are really not allowed to use measures. This is, of course, a trick, and it is specifically known as the **Disconnected Table Trick**.

Getting ready

To prepare for this recipe, do the following:

1. Open Power BI Desktop.
2. Import the data from the Ch10R08Data.xlsx Excel file located in the GitHub repository. Ensure that the tables you create are called R08_Hours and R08_Training.

3. Use an **Enter Data** query to create a table called R08_Employees with the following data:

Employee
Greg
Bill
Joe
David
Jimbo

4. Ensure that there is a relationship between the R08_Employees and R08_Hours tables using the Employee column in both tables and that this relationship's Cross filter direction is set to Both.

5. Ensure that there is a relationship between the R08_Employees and R08_Training tables using the Employee column in both tables and that this relationship's Cross filter direction is set to Single.

The data in the R08_Employees, R08_Training, and R08_Hours tables represents safety data that you might find at a typical construction firm. For any week that an employee works, that employee is required to attend the weekly safety briefing. We wish to analyze this data such that we can identify employees that are attending the weekly safety briefings and those that are not. The R08_Training table contains data regarding which employees attended which weekly training. The R08_Hours table contains the log of employee hours on the weeks those employees worked. Finally, the R08_Employees table simply contains a list of employees.

How to do it...

To complete this recipe, do the following:

1. Use an **Enter Data** query to create a table called R08_Attendance with the following data:

Attendance
Attended
Not Attended

2. Create the following measure:

```
Attendance =
    VAR __Training =
        CALCULATE(
            MAX('R08_Training'[Training]),
            ALLEXCEPT('R08_Training','R08_Training'[Training])
        )
    VAR __TrainingDate =
        MAXX(
            FILTER(
                ALL('R08_Training'),
                'R08_Training'[Training] = __Training
            ),
            [Date]
        )
    RETURN
        IF(
            COUNTROWS(
                FILTER('R08_Hours','R08_Hours'[Week] = __TrainingDate)
            ) >= 1,
            IF(
                ISBLANK(MAX('R08_Training'[Date])),
                "Not Attended",
                "Attended"
            ),
            BLANK()
        )
```

3. Create the following additional measure:

```
Worked =
    VAR __Training =
        CALCULATE(
            MAX('R08_Training'[Training]),
            ALLEXCEPT('R08_Training','R08_Training'[Training])
        )
    VAR __TrainingDate =
        MAXX(
            FILTER(
                ALL('R08_Training'),
                'R08_Training'[Training] = __Training
            ),
            'R08_Training'[Date]
        )
    RETURN
        IF(
            COUNTROWS(
```

```
            FILTER('R08_Hours','R08_Hours'[Week] = __TrainingDate)
        ) >= 1,
        TRUE(),
        FALSE()
    )
```

4. Create the following additional measures:

```
Attended =
    IF([Worked],
        IF(
            ISBLANK(MAX('R08_Training'[Date])),
            BLANK(),
            "Attended"
        ),
        BLANK()
    )

NotAttended =
    IF([Worked],
        IF(
            ISBLANK(MAX('R08_Training'[Date])),
            "Not Attended",
            BLANK()
        ),
        BLANK()
    )

Attendance Measure to Show =
    IF(HASONEVALUE('R08_Attendance'[Attendance]),
        SWITCH(
            MAX('R08_Attendance'[Attendance]),
            "Attended",[Attended],
            "Not Attended",[NotAttended]
        ),
        MAX('R08_Training'[Date])
    )
```

5. On a **Report** page, create a **Matrix** visualization and place the Employee column from the R08_Employees table into the **Rows** area of the visualization.

6. In the same **Matrix** visualization, place the Training column from the R08_Training table into the **Columns** area of the visualization.

7. In the same **Matrix** visualization, place the Attendance measure into the **Values** area.

8. On the same **Report** page, create a **Slicer** visualization and place the `Attendance` column from the `R08_Attendance` table into the **Fields** area.

9. On the same **Report** page, create a second **Matrix** visualization and place the `Employee` column from the `R08_Employees` table into the **Rows** area of the visualization.

10. In this second **Matrix** visualization, place the `Training` column from the `R08_Training` table into the **Columns** area of the visualization.

11. In this second **Matrix** visualization, place the `Attendance Measures to Show` measure into the **Values** area.

How it works...

Our first matrix visualization uses the `Attendance` measure. This measure displays `Attended` if the employee attended the training session in a week the employee worked and displays `Not Attended` if the employee did not attend the training session in a week the employee worked. To accomplish this, we start by getting the current training session, `__Training`, within the current context regardless of `Employee`. This is done by using `CALCULATE` coupled with `ALLEXCEPT` to override the filter context in order to remove all filters, including `Employee` from the `R08_Employees` table, but excluding the filter for the `Training` column in the `R08_Training` table.

We can now determine the date for the training, `__TrainingDate`. This is done by using `ALL` to strip away all filters from the `R08_Training` table, using `FILTER` to filter down to rows where the `Training` column equals `__Training`, and finally simply returning the maximum value for filtered rows using `MAXX`.

In our `RETURN` statement, we now first check to see whether the employee worked during the week in question, `__TrainingDate`. We do this by using `FILTER` to select only rows from the `R08_Hours` table where the `Week` column equals `__TrainingDate`, by counting the number of rows using `COUNTROWS`, and then by checking to ensure the value returned is greater than or equal to 1. If the value is not greater than or equal to 1, we simply return `BLANK`, as the employee did not work during that week. If the value is greater than or equal to 1, then the employee worked during that week. We then check to see whether the employee attended training by using `MAX` to return the `Date` column from the `R08_Training` table. If the value returned by this `MAX` statement is blank (`ISBLANK`), then the employee did not attend training and we return a value of `Not Attended`. Conversely, if the value returned by this `MAX` statement is not blank, then the employee attended training and we return a value of `Attended`.

When this Attendance measure is used within our matrix, we can see where employees attended and did not attend training, as well as blank values where employees did not work during the training week. However, you can imagine a grid of hundreds of training sessions and hundreds of employees where it would become quite cumbersome to visually review which employees did or did not attend training. What we would really like to do is use our Attendance measure in a slicer visualization to display Attended and Not Attended within the slicer, so that we could easily filter down to those employees that did not attend training. Unfortunately, we cannot use measures within slicers.

Enter the *Disconnected Table Trick*. As the name implies, to implement the Disconnected Table Trick, we need a disconnected table. In other words, we need a table that is not related to any other table in our model. This is the purpose of the R08_Attendance table. This table contains only two rows, Attended and Not Attended, which are the same as the values returned by our Attendance measure. We can now use the R08_Attendance table in our slicer. However, we need a method by which to relate the values in the R08_Attendance table back to our measure for attendance.

To relate the values in the R08_Attendance table back to our measure for attendance, we start by splitting our Attendance measure into multiple measures. While we only need two measures, one for attendance and one for non-attendance, here we use three measures, Worked, Attended, and Not Attended, because there is a significant portion of shared code.

Our Worked measure implements the first portion of our Attendance measure where we determine if an employee worked or did not work during the week of training. The code for the Worked measure is the same as the code for the Attendance measure except that we remove the portions of the code where we determine attendance and instead simply return TRUE or FALSE depending on whether the employee worked during the week of training or not.

We now break the portion of the Attendance measure that determines attendance into two separate measures, Attended and Not Attended. These measures first look at the return value from the Worked measure and, if the employee did not work during the training week, we simply return BLANK. If the employee did work during the training week, we use the same code as we did in the Attendance measure to determine whether the employee attended training. The Attended measure returns BLANK if the employee did not attend training and returns Attended if the employee did attend training. The Not Attended measure returns BLANK if the employee attended training and Not Attended if the employee did not attend training.

We now come to the measure that ties everything together, `Attendance Measure to Show`. The `Attendance Measure to Show` measure forms the bridge or relationship between our disconnected table, `Attendance`, and our `Attended` and `Not Attended` measures. We start by first checking to see if we have a single value for the `Attendance` column in the `R08_Attendance` table. We do this using the `HASONEVALUE` value function. If we do not have a single value for the `Attendance` column, we simply return the maximum value for the `Date` column in the `R08_Training` table. If we do have a single value for the `Attendance` column, we then implement a `SWITCH` statement based upon the value of the `Attendance` column. If the value in the `Attendance` column is `Attended`, we return the value from our `Attended` measure. If the value in the `Attendance` column is `Not Attended`, we return the value from our `Not Attended` measure. We have thus created the illusion of using our measure within a slicer.

There's more...

The Disconnected Table Trick can be used essentially anywhere that measures are not typically allowed to be used. For example, the Disconnected Table Trick can be used with chart axes as well as chart legends. To demonstrate this, do the following:

1. Create the following measure:

```
Attendance Count =
    VAR __Table =
        ADDCOLUMNS (
            'R08_Employees',
            "__Attendance",
            [Attendance]
        )
RETURN
    SWITCH (
        MAX ('R08_Attendance'[Attendance]),
        "Attended",
        COUNTX (
            FILTER (__Table, [__Attendance]="Attended"),
            [Employee]
        ),
        "Not Attended",
        COUNTX (
            FILTER (__Table, [__Attendance]="Not Attended"),
            [Employee]
        ),
        BLANK ()
    )
```

2. Clear any selections in the **Slicer** visualization.

3. Create a **Clustered column chart** visualization and place the `Training` column from the `R08_Training` table into the **Axis** area, the `Attendance` column from the `R08_Attendance` table into the **Legend** area, and the `Attendance Count` measure into the **Values** area.

4. Create a second **Clustered column chart** visualization and place the `Training` column from the `R08_Training` table into the **Legend** area, the `Attendance` column from the `R08_Attendance` table into the **Axis** area, and the `Attendance Count` measure into the **Values** area.

See also

For more details about the functions used in this recipe, refer to the following links:

- CALCULATE: https://docs.microsoft.com/en-us/dax/calculate-function-dax
- MAX: https://docs.microsoft.com/en-us/dax/max-function-dax
- MAXX: https://docs.microsoft.com/en-us/dax/maxx-function-dax
- FILTER: https://docs.microsoft.com/en-us/dax/filter-function-dax
- ALL : https://docs.microsoft.com/en-us/dax/all-function-dax
- ALLEXCEPT: https://docs.microsoft.com/en-us/dax/allexcept-function-dax
- COUNTROWS: https://docs.microsoft.com/en-us/dax/countrows-function-dax
- IF: https://docs.microsoft.com/en-us/dax/if-function-dax
- ISBLANK: https://docs.microsoft.com/en-us/dax/isblank-function-dax
- BLANK: https://docs.microsoft.com/en-us/dax/blank-function-dax
- SWITCH: https://docs.microsoft.com/en-us/dax/switch-function-dax
- HASONEVALUE: https://docs.microsoft.com/en-us/dax/hasonevalue-function-dax
- COUNTX: https://docs.microsoft.com/en-us/dax/countx-function-dax
- ADDCOLUMNS: https://docs.microsoft.com/en-us/dax/addcolumns-function-dax

Evaluating permutations and combinations

When we are performing data analysis, there are times when we wish to determine whether items are alike or not alike and how many of these like items or unalike items we have in our data. When considering such circumstances, we often have data for things that have multiple attributes expressed in multiple columns. Sometimes it is important which values are in which attributes (columns) and sometimes this is not the case.

One can think of this in terms of combinations versus permutations. With combinations, order does not matter. With permutations, order does matter.

This recipe demonstrates how to determine how many distinct things we have in our data, based upon values in multiple attribute columns. This recipe provides calculations where the order (the values in specific columns) matters (permutation) and where it does not matter (combination).

Getting ready

To prepare for this recipe, do the following:

1. Open Power BI Desktop.
2. Use an **Enter Data** query to create a table called R09_Table with the following data:

ID	DimKey1	DimKey2	DimKey3	DimKey4
1	blue	red	green	green
2	blue	blue	red	blue
3	blue	red	blue	blue
4	green	green	red	green
5	green	green	blue	green
6	red	red	red	red
7	blue	blue	blue	blue
8	green	green	green	green
9	blue	green	red	green
10	blue	red	green	green

The `R09_Table` table represents a list of items (`ID`) with various attributes (`DimKey1`, `DimKey2`, `DimKey3`, `DimKey4`). In this recipe, we only care about distinct combinations of `DimKey1`, `DimKey2`, and `DimKey3`.

How to do it...

To complete this recipe, do the following:

1. Create the following measures:

```
Row Count = COUNTROWS('R09_Table')

Permutations =
    VAR __Table =
        SELECTCOLUMNS (
            'R09_Table',
            "__Key1",'R09_Table'[DimKey1],
            "__Key2",'R09_Table'[DimKey2],
            "__Key3",'R09_Table'[DimKey3]
        )
RETURN
    COUNTROWS(DISTINCT(__Table))
```

2. On a **Report** page, create a **Card** visualization and place the `Row Count` measure into the **Fields** area of the visualization.
3. On the same **Report** page, create a second **Card** visualization and place the `Permutations` measure into the **Fields** area.

We can see that the `Permutations` measure has correctly identified that ID 1 and ID 10 are the same.

How it works...

This recipe is quite simple because the `DISTINCT` function does all of the hard work for us. We simply need to create a table variable, `__Table`, that uses `SELECTCOLUMNSX` to return only columns that we care about from the `R06_Table` table. These columns are `DimKey1`, `DimKey2`, and `DimKey3`. We rename these columns `__Key1`, `__Key2`, and `__Key3` respectively.

While the `DISTINCT` function is perhaps most often used for returning a distinct list of values from a column, it has an alternate form that can accept a table reference or table expression. We can thus use this form of the `DISTINCT` function to return only unique rows from our `__Table` variable and then simply use `COUNTROWS` to count the number of distinct rows. It is important to keep in mind here that this form of the `DISTINCT` function respects the order of values in columns. In other words, while IDs 1, 9, and 10 each have values of red, green, and blue; only ID 1 and ID 10 are identical because the values red, green, and blue occur in the same columns.

There's more...

While it may be interesting to know about the alternative form of the `DISTINCT` function, this recipe is perhaps a bit too easy. Never fear, this was really just preparatory to the more complex problem of finding distinct column combinations where the order does not matter. In other words, for instances such as ID 1, 9, and 10 where each row contains red, green, and blue, if we do not care about the order then all three of these rows should only be counted as 1 combination.

To implement this version of the recipe, do the following:

1. Create the following measure:

```
Combinations =
    VAR __Table =
        ADDCOLUMNS (
            SELECTCOLUMNS (
                'R09_Table',
                "__Key1", 'R09_Table'[DimKey1],
                "__Key2", 'R09_Table'[DimKey2],
                "__Key3", 'R09_Table'[DimKey3]
            ),
            "__Max",
            MAX (
                MAX ([__Key1], [__Key2]),
                [__Key3]
            ),
            "__Min",
            MIN (
                MIN ([__Key1], [__Key2]),
                [__Key3])
        )
    VAR __Table2 =
        SELECTCOLUMNS (
            ADDCOLUMNS (
```

```
        __Table,
        "__Mid",
        SUBSTITUTE(
            SUBSTITUTE(
                [__Key1] & [__Key2] & [__Key3],
                [__Max],"",1
            ),
            [__Min],"",1
        )
    ),
    "__Max",[__Max],
    "__Min",[__Min],
    "__Mid",[__Mid]
)
RETURN COUNTROWS(DISTINCT(__Table2))
```

2. On the same **Report** page as before, create a third **Card** visualization and place the `Combinations` measure into the **Fields** area of the visualization.

Here, we start out similarly to our `Permutations` measure by creating a table variable, `__Table`, that uses SELECTCOLUMNS to return only columns that we care about from the `R06_Table` table. These columns are `DimKey1`, `DimKey2`, and `DimKey3`, and we rename these columns `__Key1`, `__Key2`, and `__Key3` respectively. However, this time when calculating `__Table` we also use ADDCOLUMNS to add two columns, `__Max` and `__Min`. For the `__Max` column, we use an alternative version of the MAX function that accepts two DAX expressions as input as opposed to the normal single column reference. Since we desire the MAX of our three columns, `__Key1`, `__Key2`, and `__Key3`, we first find the MAX of `__Key1` and `__Key2` and then use this as the input to a second MAX function that evaluates the output of this expression along with `__Key3`. The calculation for our `__Min` column is identical to our `__Max` column except that we use the alternative form of the MIN function instead of the MAX function.

We now use our `__Table` variable as the basis for creating a second table variable, `__Table2`. Here, we use ADDCOLUMNS to add the `__Mid` column to our `__Table` variable. The calculation of our `__Mid` column uses two nested SUBSTITUTE functions. The first SUBSTITUTE function concatenates our `__Key1`, `__Key2`, and `__Key3` columns and then substitutes the first occurrence of the value in our `__Max` column with nothing (""). We then use the output of this SUBSTITUTE function to feed our second SUBSTITUTE function, where we replace the first occurrence of the value in our `__Min` column with nothing (""). The value left from these two SUBSTITUTE statements is thus the third value from our `__Key1`, `__Key2`, and `__Key3` columns. We now use SELECTCOLUMNS to select our three added columns, `__Max`, `__Min`, and `__Mid`.

Because of the calculations we have performed, we have effectively reordered rows with the same values in different columns into the same values in the same columns. Thus, we can now use `DISTINCT` coupled with `COUNTROWS` to return the count of the distinct rows within `__Table2`.

See also

For more details about the functions used in this recipe, refer to the following links:

- `DISTINCT (Table)`: https://docs.microsoft.com/en-us/dax/distinct-table-function-dax
- `SELECTCOLUMNS`: https://docs.microsoft.com/en-us/dax/selectcolumns-function-dax
- `COUNTROWS`: https://docs.microsoft.com/en-us/dax/countrows-function-dax
- `ADDCOLUMNS`: https://docs.microsoft.com/en-us/dax/addcolumns-function-dax
- `MAX`: https://docs.microsoft.com/en-us/dax/max-function-dax
- `MIN`: https://docs.microsoft.com/en-us/dax/min-function-dax
- `SUBSTITUTE`: https://docs.microsoft.com/en-us/dax/substitute-function-dax

Creating a dynamic temporal scale

Recently, I came across a visualization that aggregated data based upon a varying time scale. For those dates that were in the current quarter, weekly summaries were displayed, while for those dates that were not in the current quarter, quarterly summaries were displayed. Replicating this visualization within Power BI originally took the form of two visuals squished together with transparent backgrounds. The result was less than ideal and took a significant amount of formatting and alignment.

This recipe presents a method of creating a dynamic temporal scale that can be used within Power BI visualizations, such that a single visual can display different time scales simultaneously.

Getting ready

To prepare for this recipe, do the following:

1. Open Power BI Desktop.
2. Create a table called `R10_Table` using the following formula:

```
R10_Table =
    ADDCOLUMNS(
        GENERATESERIES(DATE(2016,1,1),TODAY()),
        "Inventory",RANDBETWEEN(10000,30000)
    )
```

This table represents inventory amounts per day. With this data, we wish to display average inventory levels summarized by week in the current quarter and by year, and by quarter for dates that are not in the current quarter.

How to do it...

To complete this recipe, do the following:

1. Create the following columns in the `R10_Table` table:

```
IsCurrentQuarter =
    VAR __Today = TODAY()
    VAR __CurrentYear = YEAR(__Today)
    VAR __CurrentQuarter = QUARTER(__Today)
    VAR __Year = YEAR('R10_Table'[Value])
    VAR __Quarter = QUARTER('R10_Table'[Value])
RETURN
    IF(
        __Year = __CurrentYear &&
            __Quarter = __CurrentQuarter,
        TRUE,
        FALSE
    )

DTS =
    IF(
        'R10_Table'[IsCurrentQuarter],
        "W" & WEEKNUM('R10_Table'[Value]) & " - " &
YEAR('R10_Table'[Value]),
        "Q" & QUARTER('R10_Table'[Value]) & " - " &
YEAR('R10_Table'[Value])
    )
```

```
DTS Sort By =
    IF(
        'R10_Table'[IsCurrentQuarter],
        YEAR('R10_Table'[Value]) & QUARTER('R10_Table'[Value]) &
    WEEKNUM('R10_Table'[Value]),
        YEAR('R10_Table'[Value]) & QUARTER('R10_Table'[Value])
    )
```

2. Set the `Sort by column` for the `DTS` column in the `R10_Table` table to the `DTS Sort By` column in the `R10_Table` table.

3. On a **Report** page, create a **Clustered column chart** visualization and place the `DTS` column from the `R10_Table` table into the **Axis** area.

4. For the same **Clustered column chart**, place the `IsCurrentQuarter` column from the `R10_Table` table into the **Legend** area.

5. For the same **Clustered column chart**, place the `Inventory` column from the `R10_Table` table into the **Values** area and change the aggregation to `Average`.

How it works...

We start by creating the `IsCurrentQuarter` column. The `IsCurrentQuarter` column evaluates the current row's `Value` column, which contains dates. The `IsCurrentQuarter` column values are `True` if the date falls within the current quarter and `False` if the date does not fall within the current quarter. We do this by first getting the current date using the `TODAY` function and storing the value in the `__Today` variable. We then create the `__CurrentYear` and `__CurrentQuarter` variables, which store the `YEAR` and `QUARTER` for `__Today`. Next, we get the `YEAR` and `QUARTER` for the current row's `Value` column and store these in the `__Year` and `__Quarter` variables, respectively. We now simply need to compare our `__Year` and `__CurrentYear` variables as well as our `__Quarter` and `__CurrentQuarter` variables. If `__Year` and `__CurrentYear` are equal to one another and `__Quarter` and `__CurrentQuarter` are equal to one another, then we return `TRUE`. Otherwise, if either `__Year` is not equal to `__CurrentYear` or `__Quarter` is not equal to `__CurrentQuarter`, then we return `FALSE`.

We can now use our `IsCurrentQuarter` column in the calculation of both of our `DTS` and `DTS Sort By` columns. The `DTS` column calculates a display value depending upon whether `IsCurrentQuarter` is `True` or `False`. If `IsCurrentQuarter` is `True`, `DTS` takes on the format *W# - yyyy*, where # is the week number of the year and *yyyy* is the four-digit year. If `IsCurrentQuarter` is `False`, `DTS` takes on the format *Q# - yyyy*, where # is the quarter number of the year and *yyyy* is the four-digit year.

Since we cannot be certain that our display value for our dynamic temporal scale, DTS, will sort correctly, we create DTS Sort By. The calculation for DTS Sort By is similar to DTS except that we return the concatenation of either YEAR, QUARTER, and WEEKNUM or YEAR and QUARTER.

See also

For more details about the functions used in this recipe, refer to the following links:

- DAX syntax: https://docs.microsoft.com/en-us/dax/dax-syntax-reference
- IF: https://docs.microsoft.com/en-us/dax/if-function-dax

Emulating loops

Unlike the vast majority of coding language, DAX has no code constructs to perform true looping. This can be somewhat challenging, and perhaps a bit disconcerting, for individuals new to DAX who come from a coding background in a more traditional programming language. Most developers have come to rely heavily upon control flow statements such as the for and while loops. The for and while loops have a similar structure. Each has a header portion that specifies the boundary conditions or limits for iteration. Each also has a body, which is a group of coding statements that are executed once per iteration.

This recipe provides methods for emulating for and while loops in DAX using table constructs.

Getting ready

To prepare for this recipe, do the following:

1. Open Power BI Desktop.
2. Create a new table called R11_Table using the following code:

```
R11_Table = { "Value" }
```

The `R11_Table` table is just here to serve as a place to create our measures. Let's also get ready for this recipe by quickly reviewing loops. We start by reviewing the `while` loop. A `while` loop in most programming languages looks similar to the following:

```
int i=10;
int j=0
while(i>1) {
    j=j+10
    i=i-1;
}
```

In this pseudo-code, we declare a variable, `i`, and set the starting value for `i` to `10`. We also declare a variable called `j` and set the starting value for `j` to `0`. We then have the declaration of our `while` loop header, where we specify that we want to continue iterating only while the `i` variable is greater than 1. The body of the `while` loop is encapsulated by brackets: `{` and `}`. In this body, we add `10` to the value of `j` each time we go through the loop and we decrement `i` by 1. Thus, we would expect this loop to iterate nine times and for the value of `j` to be `90` once the loop finishes execution.

How to do it...

To complete this recipe, do the following:

1. Create the following measure:

```
While Loop =
    VAR __i = 10
    VAR __j = 0
    VAR __loopTable =
        ADDCOLUMNS (
            GENERATESERIES(1,__i),
            "__j",10,
            "__i",[Value] - 1
        )
RETURN
    SUMX (
        FILTER(__loopTable,[__i]>=1),
        [__j]
    )
```

2. On a **Report** page, create a **Card** visualization and place the `While Loop` measure into the **Fields** area

How it works...

To emulate a while loop in DAX, we essentially use the rows of a table as the iterations of the loop. We start by specifying starting values for the __i and __j variables as 10 and 0 respectively. We then create a table variable, __loopTable. The basis for __loopTable is the GENERATESERIES function, which creates a single-column table with the numbers from 1 to the value of __i (10). We use ADDCOLUMNS to add the __j column and the __i column to this table. For the __j column, we specify the value of 10. For the __i column, we subtract 1 from the current row's value for the Value column.

Thus, each row in our table emulates an iteration through a loop with the __i column keeping track of the loop iteration and the __j column tracking how much we wish to add to our final number for each iteration through the loop. In our RETURN statement we can then filter our __loopTable to the last iteration and use the iterative summing function, SUMX, to sum the __j column.

While all of this may seem a bit theoretical, a variation of this technique is actually used in the *Calculating days of supply* recipe in Chapter 9, *Calculating Common Industry Metrics*. For the *Days of supply* recipe, we essentially emulate a while loop in order to find when our days of supply go negative.

There's more...

We can also emulate for loops. A for loop in most programming languages looks similar to the following:

```
int sum = 0;
for(int i = 1; i = 5) {
    sum = sum + i
    i = i + 1
}
```

In this pseudo-code, we declare a variable, sum, and set the starting value for sum to 0. We then have the declaration of our for loop header, where we specify that we want to start iterating with the i variable equaling 1 and stop iterating when i equals 5. The body of the for loop is encapsulated by brackets: { and }. In this body, we add i to the value of sum each time we go through the loop, and we increment i by 1. Thus, we would expect this loop to iterate 5 times and for the value of sum to be 15 once the loop finishes executing: (0+1) -> (1+2) -> (3+3) -> (6+4) -> (10+5) = 15.

To emulate this `for` loop, do the following:

1. Create the following measure:

```
For Loop =
    VAR __n = 5
    VAR __sum = 0
    VAR __loopTable = GENERATESERIES(1,__n)
    VAR __loopTable1 =
        ADDCOLUMNS(
            __loopTable,
            "__Sum",
            __sum + SUMX(
                        FILTER(
                            __loopTable,
                            [Value]<=EARLIER([Value])
                        ),
                        [Value])
            )
    RETURN
        MAXX(
            FILTER(__loopTable1,[Value]=__n),
            [__sum]
        )
```

2. On a **Report** page, create a **Card** visualization and place the `While Loop` measure into the **Fields** area

The `For Loop` measure follows a very similar pattern to the `While Loop` measure, using table rows in the table variable, `__loopTable`, as the iterations of the loop.

See also

For more details about the functions used in this recipe, refer to the following links:

- GENERATESERIES: https://docs.microsoft.com/en-us/dax/generateseries-function-dax
- ADDCOLUMNS: https://docs.microsoft.com/en-us/dax/addcolumns-function-dax
- FILTER: https://docs.microsoft.com/en-us/dax/filter-function-dax
- SUMX: https://docs.microsoft.com/en-us/dax/sumx-function-dax
- EARLIER: https://docs.microsoft.com/en-us/dax/earlier-function-dax
- MAXX: https://docs.microsoft.com/en-us/dax/maxx-function-dax

Simulating recursion

Recursion is a common coding pattern that involves a calculation being defined in terms of itself. While this may seem bizarre to non-coders, recursion is an extremely powerful coding pattern. Perhaps the most commonly known recursive example is the Fibonacci sequence. The Fibonacci sequence is defined like so: after the two starting numbers, 0 and 1, each number is the sum of the two preceding numbers. Mathematically, Fibonacci numbers are denoted as F_n and are defined formally as follows:

$$
F_0 = 0 \\
F_1 = 1 \\
F_n = F_{n-1} + F_{n12}
$$

Regrettably, It is impossible to perform true recursion in DAX. In fact, DAX has logic that specifically prevents any type of recursive behavior. However, there are calculations that require recursive behavior, and thus this recipe provides a method for simulating recursion in DAX. Specifically, this recipe calculates the first six Fibonacci numbers.

Getting ready

To prepare for this recipe, do the following:

1. Open Power BI Desktop.
2. Create a new table called `R12_Table` using the following code:

```
R12_Table = GENERATESERIES(0,6,1)
```

How to do it...

To complete this recipe, do the following:

1. Create the following measure:

```
Fibonacci =
    VAR __Value = MAX('R12_Table'[Value])
    VAR __Table0 =
        ADDCOLUMNS(
            { 0 },
            "Fib",0
        )
    VAR __Table1 =
```

```
            ADDCOLUMNS (
                { 1 },
                "Fib",1
            )
    VAR __Table2 =
        ADDCOLUMNS (
            { 2 },
            "Fib",SUMX(UNION(__Table0,__Table1),[Fib])
        )
    VAR __Table3 =
        ADDCOLUMNS (
            { 3 },
            "Fib",SUMX(UNION(__Table1,__Table2),[Fib])
        )
    VAR __Table4 =
        ADDCOLUMNS (
            { 4 },
            "Fib",SUMX(UNION(__Table2,__Table3),[Fib])
        )
    VAR __Table5 =
        ADDCOLUMNS (
            { 5 },
            "Fib",SUMX(UNION(__Table3,__Table4),[Fib])
        )
    VAR __Table6 =
        ADDCOLUMNS (
            { 6 },
            "Fib",SUMX(UNION(__Table4,__Table5),[Fib])
        )
    VAR __Table =
        UNION (
__Table0,__Table1,__Table2,__Table3,__Table4,__Table5,__Table6
        )
RETURN
    SUMX(FILTER(__Table,[Value]=__Value),[Fib])
```

2. On a **Report** page, create a **Table** visualization and place the `Value` column from the `R12_Table` table into the **Values** area of the visualization. Set the aggregation for `Value` to `Don't summarize`.

3. In the same **Table** visualization, place the `Fibonacci` measure into the **Values** area of the visualization.

How it works...

Because DAX does not have any true recursive capabilities or the ability to recall previous values of a calculation, we must essentially build up each recursive step within its own table and store calculated values within variables.

We start by simply noting the current Fibonacci number being calculated and storing this value in the __Value variable. Next, we calculate the first two values of the Fibonacci sequence in the table variables, __Table0 and __Table1. The calculations for __Table0 and __Table1 are essentially the same. For each, we add the Fib column and simply specify the values as 0 and 1 respectively.

The rest of the table variables, __Table2, __Table3, __Table4, __Table5, and __Table6, all follow the same pattern. For each of these variables, the Fib column uses SUMX to sum the Fib column across the UNION of the two previous steps.

See also

For more details about the functions used in this recipe, refer to the following links:

- SELECTCOLUMNS: https://docs.microsoft.com/en-us/dax/selectcolumns-function-dax
- ADDCOLUMNS: https://docs.microsoft.com/en-us/dax/addcolumns-function-dax
- FILTER: https://docs.microsoft.com/en-us/dax/filter-function-dax
- SUMX: https://docs.microsoft.com/en-us/dax/sumx-function-dax
- ALL: https://docs.microsoft.com/en-us/dax/all-function-dax
- MAX: https://docs.microsoft.com/en-us/dax/max-function-dax
- UNION: https://docs.microsoft.com/en-us/dax/union-function-dax

11
Solving Statistical and Mathematical Formulas

Properly analyzing data can often turn into a statistical and mathematical exercise. There is a wid On a Report page, create a Card visualization and place the alpha measure into e array of statistical and mathematical tools available to businesses today that can assist organizations in analyzing operational efficiencies, hiring practices, customer profiles, and more. In addition, while DAX has a fair number of statistics and math functions, many of the more complex mathematical and statistical formulas and methods are missing. Furthermore, many of these more complex mathematical and statistical methods require the use of interesting and uncommon DAX functions and techniques. This chapter, then, focuses on adding a number of useful statistical and mathematical formulas and techniques to the repertoire of DAX.

The following is the list of recipes that we will cover in this chapter:

- Calculating Shannon entropy
- Approximating the area under a curve
- Using Runge-Kutta
- Measuring covariance
- Utilizing the Mann-Kendall test
- Finding Kendall's Tau
- Analyzing kurtosis
- Utilizing the Jarque-Bera test

- Determining Pearson's coefficient of skewness
- Applying the hypergeometric distribution formula
- Determining the required sample size

Technical requirements

The following are required to complete all of the recipes in this chapter:

- Power BI Desktop
- The GitHub repository for this chapter, available at `https://github.com/PacktPublishing/DAX-Cookbook/tree/master/Chapter11`

Calculating Shannon entropy

Shannon entropy, or more generally information entropy, is an important concept in information theory, the field of study that concerns the quantification of information used in communication. In thermodynamics and other fields, entropy generally refers to the disorder or uncertainty within a system. Claude Shannon introduced the concept of information entropy in the late 1940s, and its definition is effectively equivalent to the definition used in the field of thermodynamics.

Today, the concept of information entropy has a wide range of uses spanning security, encryption, and even such things as machine learning and artificial intelligence. The mathematical definition for information entropy is as follows:

$$H(X) = -\sum_{i=1}^{n} P(x_i) \log_b P(x_i)$$

Here, X is a random variable that has x_i possible outcomes. P is the probability. The b in this formula can be one of several values, but is most often 2. H is the designation for information entropy.

This recipe demonstrates how to calculate the Shannon entropy of a column of values using DAX.

Getting ready

To prepare for this recipe, do the following:

1. Open Power BI Desktop.
2. Create a table called R01_Table using the following formula:

```
R01_Table =
    SELECTCOLUMNS (
        ADDCOLUMNS (
            GENERATESERIES(1,20,1),
            "Number",
            RANDBETWEEN(1,5)
        ),
        "Value",[Number]
    )
```

How to do it...

To complete this recipe, do the following:

1. Create the following measure:

```
ShannonEntropy =
    SUMX (
        ADDCOLUMNS (
            SUMMARIZE (
                'R01_Table',
                'R01_Table'[Value],
                "Probability",
                DIVIDE (
                    COUNTROWS('R01_Table'),
                    COUNTROWS(ALL('R01_Table'))
                )
            ),
            "H(X)",
            -1 * [Probability] * LOG([Probability],2)
        ),
        [H(X)]
    )
```

2. On a **Report** page, create a **Card** visualization and place the ShannonEntropy measure into the **Fields** area.

How it works...

We start by using `SUMMARIZE` to group our base data table, `R01_Table`, by the values in the `Value` column. To this table we add the `Probability` column, which simply divides the count of the grouped values by the count of all rows within the table. We then use `ADDCOLUMNS` to add an additional column to this table called `H(X)`, which simply implements the equation for Shannon entropy. We then use `SUMX` to sum the `H(X)` column for all of the rows within the summarized table and return the result.

> Because this recipe computes probabilities and thus uses `COUNTROWS`, the data within the base data table can be either numeric or text.

There's more...

The recipe provided thus far computes the overall entropy of the values in the column. To see the individual entropy of each distinct value, follow these steps:

1. Create the following measure:

```
IndividualShannonEntropy =
    VAR __Probability =
        DIVIDE(
            COUNTROWS('R01_Table'),
            COUNTROWS(ALL('R01_Table'))
        )
    VAR __HX = -1 * __Probability * LOG(__Probability,2)
RETURN __HX
```

2. On a **Report** page, create a **Table** visualization and place the `Value` column into the **Values** area of the visualization. Set the aggregation for the `Value` column to `Don't summarize`.

3. In the same **Table** visualization, place the `IndividualShannonEntropy` measure into the **Values** area.

See also

For more details about functions used in this recipe, refer to the following links:

- **Entropy (information theory):** `https://en.wikipedia.org/wiki/Entropy_(information_theory)`
- ADDCOLUMNS: `https://docs.microsoft.com/en-us/dax/addcolumns-function-dax`
- SUMX: `https://docs.microsoft.com/en-us/dax/sumx-function-dax`
- SUMMARIZE: `https://docs.microsoft.com/en-us/dax/summarize-function-dax`
- DIVIDE: `https://docs.microsoft.com/en-us/dax/divide-function-dax`
- COUNTROWS: `https://docs.microsoft.com/en-us/dax/countrows-function-dax`
- LOG: `https://docs.microsoft.com/en-us/dax/log-function-dax`

Approximating the area under a curve

Using polygons to approximate the area of curved shapes is a technique that has been known since ancient times. The concept is simple: draw polygons such as triangles or rectangles within the confines of a curved shape, calculate the area of those triangles and polygons, and you have approximated the area of a curved shape or under a curved line. Today, the technique is called a Riemann sum and is named after Bernhard Riemann, a German mathematician from the nineteenth century.

This recipe provides a method of approximating the area under a curve based upon the Riemann sum technique.

Getting ready

To prepare for this recipe, do the following:

1. Open Power BI Desktop.
2. Create a table called `R02_Table` using the following formula:

```
R02_Table =
    SELECTCOLUMNS(
        GENERATESERIES(-50, 50, 1),
        "X",[Value]
    )
```

How to do it...

To complete this recipe, do the following:

1. Create the following columns in the R02_Table table:

```
Y = SQRT(POWER(50,2) - POWER('R02_Table'[X],2))

A =
    VAR __Table = ALL('R02_Table')
    VAR __Max = MAXX(__Table,[X])
    VAR __Min = MINX(__Table,[X])
    VAR __Increment =
        DIVIDE(
            __Max - __Min + 1,
            COUNTROWS(__Table)
        )
RETURN
    [Y]*__Increment
```

2. Create the following measures:

```
AreaSemiCircle = PI()*POWER(50,2)/2

AreaApproximation =
    VAR __Table = ALL('R02_Table')
    VAR __Max = MAXX(__Table,[X])
    VAR __Min = MINX(__Table,[X])
    VAR __Increment =
        DIVIDE(
            __Max - __Min + 1,
            COUNTROWS(__Table)
        )
RETURN
    ABS(
        SUMX(
            ADDCOLUMNS(
                __Table,
                "__Area",[Y]*__Increment
            ),
            ABS([__Area])
        )
    )

% Error =
    DIVIDE(
```

```
            [AreaApproximation] - [AreaSemiCircle],
            [AreaSemiCircle]
        )
```

3. On a **Report** page, create a **Line and clustered column chart** visualization and place the X column from the R02_Table table into the **Shared axis** area.

4. In the same **Line and clustered column chart** visualization, place the A column from the R02_Table table into the **Column values** area and the Y column from the R02_Table table into the **Line values** area.

5. On the same **Report** page, create a **Card** visualization and place the AreaApproximation measure into the **Fields** area for the visual.

6. On the same **Report** page, create a second **Card** visualization and place the AreaSemiCircle measure into the **Fields** area for the visual.

7. On the same **Report** page, create a third **Card** visualization and place the % Error measure into the **Fields** area for the visual.

How it works...

The Y column simply provides a list of *y*-axis values to draw our semicircle line. The equation for a semicircle is as follows:

$$ y = y_0 - \sqrt{r^{-2} - (x - x_0)^2} $$

Here, *r* is the radius of the semicircle. Since we have defined our X column to be from -50 to 50, our radius is 50. y_0 and x_0 are the midpoint of our semicircle. Since our semicircle is centered on point *x=0* and *y=0*, we just drop those from the DAX equation. Used together, the values in the X and Y columns provide a nice semicircle line when plotted on a line graph that spans from X equal to -50 to X equal to 50.

The A column is used to provide a visual representation of the rectangles that we will build in our measure to approximate the area under the semicircle. We start by creating a table variable, __Table, that contains all (ALL) of the rows in our data table, R02_Table. We then use MAXX and MINX to return the maximum and minimum values of the X column and store these values in the __Max and __Min variables, respectively.

We next calculate the __Increment variable. The calculation for __Increment tells us how many rows we have in our table between our __Max and __Min values. This essentially becomes the *x* component of the rectangle that we *draw* and find the area of when performing our Riemann sum. To find the value of __Increment, we subtract our __Min from our __Max and add one. We then divide by the number of rows (COUNTROWS) in the R02_Table table using the DIVIDE function. Now, this makes some assumptions such as the fact that there are no repeated values for X, and it only really works well visually if your __Increment calculates to 1. We can now return the area of the rectangle that we have drawn by multiplying our Y column by __Increment.

The first measure that we calculate is called AreaSemiCircle. AreaSemiCircle simply implements the equation for finding the area of a semicircle, which is as follows:

$$A = \frac{\pi r^2}{2}$$

We use the PI function for π and 50 for the radius of our circle. The POWER function is used to square our radius.

The next measure is AreaApproximation. AreaApproximation calculates an estimate of the area of our semicircle using the Riemann sum method. The code above our RETURN statement is identical to the code above the RETURN statement in our A column. Remember that this calculates the __Increment variable, which is used to calculate the area of our individual rectangles. Thus, to get the sum of all of our individual rectangles, we first use ADDCOLUMNS to add a column called __Area. The __Area column holds the value of the area for each rectangle for each value of X within our R02_Table table. To get the sum of all of these rectangles, we then use SUMX to sum the __Area column.

Our last measure, % Error, calculates how close our approximate value, AreaApproximation, is to the actual area of the semicircle, AreaSemiCircle. We express this as a percentage by subtracting AreaSemiCircle from AreaApproximation and then dividing the result by AreaSemiCircle. A positive value indicates that we overestimated, while a negative value indicates that we underestimated.

There's more...

The recipe presented works for the common shape of a semicircle. However, any line can use the same technique, including lines that form triangles, lines with exponential equations, and even sine waves. To prove this is the case, do the following:

1. Create the following columns in the `R02_Table` table:

```
Y1 = RANDBETWEEN(15,50)

A1 =
    VAR __Table = ALL('R02_Table')
    VAR __Max = MAXX(__Table,[X])
    VAR __Min = MINX(__Table,[X])
    VAR __Increment =
        DIVIDE(
            __Max - __Min + 1,
            COUNTROWS(__Table)
        )
RETURN
    [Y1]*__Increment
```

2. Create the following measure:

```
AreaApproximation1 =
    VAR __Table = ALL('R02_Table')
    VAR __Max = MAXX(__Table,[X])
    VAR __Min = MINX(__Table,[X])
    VAR __Increment =
        DIVIDE(
            __Max - __Min + 1,
            COUNTROWS(__Table)
        )
RETURN
    SUMX(
        ADDCOLUMNS(
            __Table,
            "__Area",[Y1]*__Increment
        ),
        ABS([__Area])
    )
```

3. On a **Report** page, create a **Line and clustered column chart** visualization and place the X column from the R02_Table table into the **Shared axis** area.

4. In the same **Line and clustered column chart** visualization, place the A1 column from the R02_Table table into the **Column values** area, and the Y1 column from the R02_Table table into the **Line values** area.

5. On the same **Report** page, create a **Card** visualization and place the AreaApproximation1 measure into the **Fields** area for the visual.

The formulas for the A1 column and the AreaApprimation1 measure are identical to the formulas for the A column and the AreaApproximation measure except that both refer to the Y1 column instead of the Y column.

See also

For more details about the functions used in this recipe, refer to the following links:

- Archimedes and the area of a parabolic segment: https://www.intmath.com/blog/mathematics/archimedes-and-the-area-of-a-parabolic-segment-1652
- Riemann sum: https://en.wikipedia.org/wiki/Riemann_sum
- SQRT: https://docs.microsoft.com/en-us/dax/sqrt-function-dax
- POWER: https://docs.microsoft.com/en-us/dax/power-function-dax
- MAXX: https://docs.microsoft.com/en-us/dax/maxx-function-dax
- MINX: https://docs.microsoft.com/en-us/dax/minx-function-dax
- DIVIDE: https://docs.microsoft.com/en-us/dax/divide-function-dax
- COUNTROWS: https://docs.microsoft.com/en-us/dax/countrows-function-dax
- ALL: https://docs.microsoft.com/en-us/dax/all-function-dax
- PI: https://docs.microsoft.com/en-us/dax/pi-function-dax
- SIGN: https://docs.microsoft.com/en-us/dax/sign-function-dax

Using Runge-Kutta

Runge-Kutta is a set of numerical methods for approximating the solutions of differential equations. A differential equation is an equation that consists of the derivative of a variable (think the rate of change) defined in terms of another, independent variable (think physical property). For example, consider a virus. As a virus spreads, its rate of infection becomes faster and faster. The same is true for population growth in most species. Most often used in such fields as biology, engineering, physics, and economics, differential equations are extremely handy for expressing complex systems. Unfortunately, only the most trivial of differential equations can be explicitly solved. For the rest, we use numerical methods such as Runge-Kutta, which was developed by mathematicians Carl Runge and Wilhelm Kutta.

While Runge-Kutta is technically a set of numerical methods, the fourth-order Runge-Kutta method is the most widely used and is often abbreviated **RK4**. Runge-Kutta essentially attempts to find the next point on a line. The next point on the line is expressed in terms of a function of two variables, such as the independent variable time and some other dependent value.

Formally, the Runge-Kutta is expressed in terms of the initial conditions:

$$(t_0) = y_0$$
$$\frac{dy}{dt} = f(t, y)$$

The variable y is an unknown function of time. However, we know that the rate at which y changes is a function of time (t) and y itself. The rate of change is the first derivative. The Runge-Kutta methods specify that we choose a *step size* for time, defined as the variable h. All this means is that we have chosen how far in the future we wish to calculate the next value of the variable y. We can now define the following two equations as the values for our next value of time and our next value of y:

$$t_{n+1} = t_n + h$$
$$y_{n+1} = y_n + \frac{1}{6}(k_1 + 2k_2 + 2k_3 + k_4)$$

The values for k_1, k_2, k_3, and k_4 are defined as follows:

$$k_1 = hf(t_n, y_n)$$
$$k_2 = hf(t_n + \frac{h}{2}, y + \frac{k_1}{2})$$
$$k_2 = hf(t_n + \frac{h}{2}, y + \frac{k_1}{2})$$
$$k_4 = hf(t_n + h, y_n + k_3)$$

That's a lot of math. What's more, we can pick a step size, h, that is smaller than the actual next point in time that we are interested in. When we do this, we can compute the preceding formulas iteratively until we arrive at the point in time of interest. In other words, if we begin at time (t) = 0 and are interested in t = 2 seconds, we could define h as .5 seconds. We would then compute the calculations for Runge-Kutta four times, with the value for k_4 from each iterative step feeding into the next computation of k_1 as y_n.

If this all makes your brain hurt, never fear; this recipe demonstrates an implementation for multiple iterations of RK4 in DAX. Runge-Kutta was specifically chosen because of its iterative (recursive) behavior. Thus, this recipe demonstrates a method of simulating recursion within DAX. For an alternative method of simulating recursion, see the *Simulating recursion* recipe in Chapter 10, *Using Uncommon DAX Patterns*.

Getting ready

To prepare for this recipe, do the following:

1. Open Power BI Desktop.
2. Use an **Enter Data** query to create a table called R03_Table with the following data:

t
0
.5
1
1.5
2

The initial conditions that we specify for our problem to solve include the following:

$$\frac{dy}{dt} = y - t^2 + 1$$
$$y_0 = 0.5$$

y_0 defines the value of y at time equal to 0. We wish to find the value for $t = 2$. We choose a step size (h) of 0.5. This means that we will need to perform four iterations of the RK4 method.

How to do it...

To complete this recipe, do the following:

1. Create the RK4 measure using the code in the R03_RK4.txt file located in the GitHub repository.
2. On a **Report** page, create a **Table** visualization and place the t column from the R03_Table table as well as the RK4 measure into the **Fields** area of the visualization.
3. On the same **Report** page, create a **Line chart** visualization and place the t column from the R03_Table table into the **Axis** area and the RK4 measure into the **Values** area of the visualization.

How it works...

First, it is important to understand that the RK4 measure is intended to be used within a table or other visualization that provides the values of time (t) that correspond with the chosen step sizes (h) for the time period of interest. Second, because subsequent steps of the implementation of the Runge-Kutta formulas require the values from the previous calculations of the Runge-Kutta formulas, the implementation of the Runge-Kutta method is essentially a recursive process. Because there is no true recursion in DAX, this recipe simulates recursion by using nested variables.

We start by capturing the current value of our t column from the R03_Table table within the current context and store this value in the tCurrent variable. Next, we define the initial parameters of our Runge-Kutta implementation. The initial value for t is set to 0. The initial value of our line at time 0, w, is set to .5. Finally, our step size, h, is set to our chosen value of .5.

We now define the `step1` variable. `step1` is intended to calculate the first step of our Runge-Kutta calculation. However, we may be at time equal to 0 and thus not need to run through our Runge-Kutta calculations. Thus, we first check to see if `tCurrent` is equal to 0. If so, we simply return the current value of our variable, `w`. Otherwise, we implement our Runge-Kutta calculations. To do this, we first set our `k1t` variable to `t`. Next, we increment our `t` variable by `h`. We can reuse variable names here because we are working within nested variables. The *scope* of this new value for `t` is only used for calculations further down within the nested variables. In other words, the value of `t` outside of the `step1` variable is still the original value of `t` (0). We also set our `k1w` variable equal to `w`. We can now calculate our values for `k1`, `k2`, `k3`, and `k4` using `k1t`, `k1w`, and `h` and plugging these values into our Runge-Kutta formulas. Finally, we compute the next point on our line, `w`.

The next variable, `step2`, is a essentially a repeat of `step1`. Here, we first check if `tCurrent` is equal to our step size of `h`. If so, we set `step2` equal to the current value of `w`. Critically, the value of `w` is the value computed during `step1`, which is the next point on our line. Otherwise, we repeat the process, setting `k1t` equal to `t` (which is the value of `t` computed in `step1`). We also increment `t` (the value of `t` computed in `step1`) by `h`. Additionally, we set `k1w` to the value of `w` (which is the value of `w` computed in `step1`).

We repeat this pattern for `step3` and `step4`. Thus, at the first increment of `h`, `step1`, we are actually returning the `w` value computed in `step1` as the value of `step2`, which then becomes the value of `step1` and thus the value of `RK4`. At the second increment of `h`, `step2`, we are actually returning the `w` value computed in `step2` as the value of `step3`, which becomes the value of `step2`, which becomes the value of `step1`, which becomes the value of `RK4`, and so on.

It is OK if your brain hurts.

See also

For more details about functions used in this recipe, refer to the following links:

- Runge-Kutta method: https://math.okstate.edu/people/yqwang/teaching/math4513_fall11/Notes/rungekutta.pdf
- DAX operators: https://docs.microsoft.com/en-us/dax/dax-operator-reference
- MAX: https://docs.microsoft.com/en-us/dax/max-function-dax

Measuring covariance

Covariance is a measure of how two variables are related to one another and has a wide array of applications, from feature extraction (machine learning) to meteorology, molecular biology, financial economics, and more. Covariance can either be positive or negative. Positive covariance means that the two variables are directly related. In other words, the large values in the first variable generally correspond with large values in the second variable and the small values in the first variable generally correspond with the small values in the second variable. Negative covariance means that the two variables are inversely related. This means that the large values in the first variable generally correspond with the smaller values in the second variable and that the smaller values in the first variable generally correspond with the larger values in the second variable. It must be stressed here that covariance does not generally measure the strength of the relationship, just whether the relationship is directly or inversely related.

The formula for covariance is as follows:

$$cov(X, Y) = \sum_{i}^{N} \frac{(x_i - \bar{x})(y_i - \bar{y})}{N}$$

If you do not speak math, what we are doing is that for every value of the variables x and y, we are subtracting the value of x from the average (mean) of x, subtracting the value of y from the average (mean) of y, multiplying these two numbers together and dividing by the total number (count) of our variable pairs. We sum all of these numbers, and this becomes our value of covariance.

This recipe demonstrates how to calculate covariance using DAX.

Getting ready

To prepare for this recipe, do the following:

1. Open Power BI Desktop.
2. Use an **Enter Data** query to create a table called R04_Table with the following data:

A	B
1	11
2	12

3	13
4	14
5	15
6	16
7	17
8	18
9	19
10	20

This table represents two variables, A and B. Each row has a value for both variables. We wish to determine how the variables are related to one another.

How to do it...

To complete this recipe, do the following:

1. Create the following measure:

```
Covariance =
    VAR __Table = 'R04_Table'
    VAR __Count = COUNTROWS(__Table)
    VAR __AvgA = AVERAGEX(__Table,[A])
    VAR __AvgB = AVERAGEX(__Table,[B])
    VAR __Table1 =
        ADDCOLUMNS(
            __Table,
            "__Covariance",
            DIVIDE(
                ([A] - __AvgA) * ([B]) - __AvgB),
                __Count
            )
        )
RETURN
    SUMX(__Table1,[__Covariance])
```

2. On a **Report** page, create a **Table** visualization and place the t column from the R03_Table table as well as the RK4 measure into the **Fields** area of the visualization.

3. On the same **Report** page, create a **Line chart** visualization and place the `t` column from the `R03_Table` table into the **Axis** area and the `RK4` measure into the **Values** area of the visualization.

How it works...

The covariance measure is relatively straightforward. We first create a table variable, `__Table`, that simply references our base data table, `R04_Table`. Next, we use `COUNTROWS` to count the number of rows in `__Table` and store this in the variable called `Count`. This is the *N* from our formula for covariance. We then use `AVERAGEX` to calculate the mean (average) of both the `A` and `B` columns and store these values in the `__AvgA` and `__AvgB` variables respectively.

We now create a second table variable, `__Table1`. We use `__Table` as the initial table and then use `ADDCOLUMNS` to add a column called `__Covariance`. For the formula for the `__Covariance` column, we implement our covariance formula. We subtract `__AvgA` from the `A` column, subtract `__AvgB` from the `B` column, multiply the two numbers together, and divide by the count of the rows in the table, `__Count`.

Finally, we implement the last part of the covariance formula and use `SUMX` to sum all of the values in our `__Covariance` column.

See also

For more details about functions used in this recipe, refer to the following links:

- Covariance: https://en.wikipedia.org/wiki/Covariance
- Covariance: http://mathworld.wolfram.com/Covariance.html
- Covariance: https://www.investopedia.com/terms/c/covariance.asp
- SUMMARIZE: https://docs.microsoft.com/en-us/dax/summarize-function-dax
- COUNTROWS: https://docs.microsoft.com/en-us/dax/countrows-function-dax
- AVERAGEX: https://docs.microsoft.com/en-us/dax/averagex-function-dax
- SUMX: https://docs.microsoft.com/en-us/dax/sumx-function-dax
- DIVIDE: https://docs.microsoft.com/en-us/dax/divide-function-dax
- MAX: https://docs.microsoft.com/en-us/dax/max-function-dax

Utilizing the Mann-Kendall test

The Mann-Kendall test is a method of identifying whether or not there is a trend in a set of data points. The nice thing about the Mann-Kendall test is that the test can identify trends even if there is a seasonal component to the data (but not if the data is collected seasonally!). Also, the Mann-Kendall test is a non-parametric test. This means that the Mann-Kendall test works for data that does not fit a normal distribution (bell curve). The Mann-Kendall test is a useful computation that is perhaps most often used within the environmental, health, and social sciences but can be used in any situation where trends are important.

This recipe provides an implementation of the Mann-Kendall test in DAX.

Getting ready

To prepare for this recipe, do the following:

1. Open Power BI Desktop.
2. Use an **Enter Data** query to create a table called R05_Table with the following data:

ID	Value
1	6.8
2	5.9
3	5.7
4	5.5
5	5.5
6	4.5
7	4
8	5.1
9	4.5
10	4.5
11	3.3
12	4.8

The data in the R05_Table table represents measurement data taken over time. We wish to identify if there is a trend in the data.

How to do it...

To complete this recipe, do the following:

1. Create the following measures:

```
alpha = .05

n = COUNTROWS('R05_Table')

S =
    VAR __Table =
        ADDCOLUMNS(
            'R05_Table',
            "__S",
                VAR __Value = 'R05_Table'[Value]
                VAR __Table =
                    FILTER(
                        'R05_Table',
                        'R05_Table'[ID] < EARLIER('R05_Table'[ID])
                    )
                VAR __Pos =
                    COUNTX(
                        FILTER(__table,[Value]<__Value),
                        [ID]
                    )
                VAR __Neg =
                    COUNTX(
                        FILTER(__table,[Value]>__Value),
                        [ID]
                    )
                RETURN
                    __Pos - __Neg
        )
    RETURN
        SUMX(__Table,[__S])

freq =
    VAR __Table =
        ADDCOLUMNS(
            ADDCOLUMNS(
                GROUPBY(
                    'R05_Table',
                    'R05_Table'[Value],
                    "__Count",COUNTX(CURRENTGROUP(),[ID])
                ),
                "__Ties",[__Count] - 1
            ),
```

```
            "__Freq",
            IF([__ties]=0,
                0,
                [__ties] * ([__ties]+1) * (2*[__ties]+7)
            )
        )
    VAR __Sum = SUMX(__Table,[__Freq])
RETURN
    IF(ISBLANK(__Sum),0,__Sum)

se =
    SQRT(
        DIVIDE(
            ([n] * ([n]-1) * (2*[n]+5) - [freq] ),
            18
        )
    )

z-stat =
    SWITCH(TRUE(),
        [S]>0,([S] - 1)/[se],
        [S]<0,([S] + 1)/[se],
        0
    )

p-value = 2 * NORM.S.DIST(-ABS([z-stat]),TRUE)

trend = IF([p-value] < [alpha],"Yes","No")
```

2. On a **Report** page, create a **Card** visualization and place the `alpha` measure into the **Fields** area of the visualization.

3. On the same **Report** page, create another **Card** visualization and place the `n` measure into the **Fields** area of the visualization.

4. On the same **Report** page, create another **Card** visualization and place the `S` measure into the **Fields** area of the visualization.

5. On the same **Report** page, create another **Card** visualization and place the `freq` measure into the **Fields** area of the visualization.

6. On the same **Report** page, create another **Card** visualization and place the `se` measure into the **Fields** area of the visualization.

7. On the same **Report** page, create another **Card** visualization and place the z-stat measure into the **Fields** area of the visualization.

8. On the same **Report** page, create another **Card** visualization and place the p-value measure into the **Fields** area of the visualization.

9. On the same **Report** page, create another **Card** visualization and place the trend measure into the **Fields** area of the visualization.

10. On the same **Report** page, create a **Line chart** visualization and place the ID column from the R05_Table table into the **Axis** area and the Value column from the R05_Table table into the **Values** area of the visualization.

How it works...

The Mann-Kendall test requires a number of elements to be calculated or set, including alpha, n, S, freq, se, z-stat, and p-value. Each of these elements is a measure within our recipe, and each is explained in turn here.

The first measure, alpha, is the significance level. In statistics, this generally defaults to 0.05, so we simply set our alpha variable to .05.

The second measure, n, is simply the count of the number of observations, or rows in our data table, R05_Table. We simply use COUNTROWS to compute this value.

The next element, measure S, is much more tricky to calculate. The formula for S is as follows:

$$S = \sum_{i}^{n-1} \sum_{j=k+1}^{n} sign(x_j - x_i)$$

To implement this formula in DAX, we first have to understand what the formula for S is trying to accomplish. Essentially, what is going on here is that every value in the series is compared with every preceding value and we record a -1 if the preceding value is larger and a 1 if the preceding value is smaller. Ties are 0. The idea is that if there is a trend present, the sign values will tend to either be constantly negative or constantly positive. A negative value of S indicates that values tend to be lower, and a positive value for S indicates that values tend to be higher.

The implementation of this in DAX starts by creating the table variable, __Table. __Table begins with our base table, R05_Table, and then adding the __S column using ADDCOLUMNS. The calculation of the __S column uses nested variables. We start by simply recording the current value of the row, __Value. We then construct the nested table variable, __Table. We can reuse the variable name __Table here because we are nesting variables. The nested variable, __Table, uses FILTER to select only the rows where the ID column is less than the current ID column (EARLIER). We can now use COUNTX to count how many previous rows have a Value column that is less than our current row's Value column, __Value. This count is stored in the __Pos variable. We then compute the __Neg variable in the same manner as the __Pos variable except that we count how many previous values are greater than our current value. Finally, we simply RETURN the difference between __Pos and __Neg. The final step for computing S is to simply sum our __S column in __Table using SUMX.

From the sign of S, we now know whether our values tend to be larger or smaller over time. Our next task is to determine if this tendency is significant. The first step in this process is to account for ties. This is the purpose of the freq measure. To compute the freq measure, we start by creating the table variable, __Table, using GROUPBY to group our data by the Value column and add the __Count column. The __Count column uses COUNTX to count the number if ID values in the CURRENTGROUP. We then use ADDCOLUMNS to add the __Ties column, which is simply our __Count minus 1. Next, we use ADDCOLUMNS again to add the __Freq column. If the __Ties column is 0, then the value of our __Freq column is also set to 0. Otherwise, our __Freq column is set to __Ties multiplied by __Ties plus 1, multiplied by 2 times __Ties plus 7. We can now create the __Sum variable by simply using SUMX to sum our __Freq column within __Table. Finally, we make certain that __Sum is not blank (ISBLANK) and either return 0 if __Sum is blank or __Sum if it's not blank.

The next step is to compute se. se is the square root of our variance, and our variance is given by the following formula:

$$var = \frac{1}{18}[n(n-1)(2n+5) - \sum_t f_t(f_t-1)(2f_t+5)]$$

As we have seen, n is simply the number of observations or values in our data. The summation part of the formula is simply our frequency summed over time t. We have already computed our frequency as the freq measure. Thus, our calculation for se is relatively straightforward, and we simply implement the formula for the variance, substituting our freq measure for the summation portion of the formula and calculate the square root using the SQRT function.

The `z-stat` measure is next. `z-stat` is based on the following formula:

$$z - stat = \begin{cases} (S-1)/se, & S > 0 \\ 0, & S = 0 \\ (S+1)/se, & S < 0 \end{cases}$$

We can easily implement this logic using a `SWITCH` statement, with its first parameter being the `TRUE` function.

We can now calculate our `p-value` measure by finding the normal distribution of the negative absolute value of our `z-stat` measure using the `NORM.S.DIST` function.

Finally, we can compare our `p-value` measure to our `alpha` measure to determine if the trend is significant. This is the `trend` measure. If our `p-value` measure is less than our `alpha` measure, then the `trend` is significant and we return `Yes`. Otherwise, we return `No`.

See also

For more details about functions used in this recipe, refer to the following links:

- **Mann-Kendall test:** `https://www.real-statistics.com/time-series-analysis/time-series-miscellaneous/mann-kendall-test/`
- **Mann-Kendall Analysis:** `https://www.statisticshowto.datasciencecentral.com/wp-content/uploads/2016/08/Mann-Kendall-Analysis-1.pdf`
- **What is the Mann-Kendall trend test?:** `https://www.statisticshowto.datasciencecentral.com/mann-kendall-trend-test/`
- `SUMMARIZE:` `https://docs.microsoft.com/en-us/dax/summarize-function-dax`
- `COUNTROWS:` `https://docs.microsoft.com/en-us/dax/countrows-function-dax`
- `ADDCOLUMNS:` `https://docs.microsoft.com/en-us/dax/addcolumns-function-dax`
- `SUMX:` `https://docs.microsoft.com/en-us/dax/sumx-function-dax`
- `DIVIDE:` `https://docs.microsoft.com/en-us/dax/divide-function-dax`
- `COUNTX:` `https://docs.microsoft.com/en-us/dax/countx-function-dax`
- `FILTER:` `https://docs.microsoft.com/en-us/dax/filter-function-dax`
- `ALLSELECTED:` `https://docs.microsoft.com/en-us/dax/allselected-function-dax`
- `EARLIER:` `https://docs.microsoft.com/en-us/dax/earlier-function-dax`
- `GROUPBY:` `https://docs.microsoft.com/en-us/dax/groupby-function-dax`

- ISBLANK: https://docs.microsoft.com/en-us/dax/isblank-function-dax
- SQRT: https://docs.microsoft.com/en-us/dax/sqrt-function-dax
- SWITCH: https://docs.microsoft.com/en-us/dax/switch-function-dax
- NORM.S.DIST: https://docs.microsoft.com/en-us/dax/norm-s-dist-function-dax
- IF: https://docs.microsoft.com/en-us/dax/if-function-dax

Finding Kendall's Tau

Kendall's Tau is a measure of the strength of the relationship between two variables. The calculation for Kendall's Tau returns a value between zero and one. A value of zero means that there is no relationship between the two variables. A value of one means that there is a perfect relationship between the two variables.

Several versions of Kendall's Tau exist, including Tau-A, Tau-B, and Tau-C. This recipe implements Tau-B in DAX, comparing two columns of values.

Getting ready

To prepare for this recipe, do the following:

1. Open Power BI Desktop.
2. Use an **Enter Data** query to create a table called R06_Table with the following data:

Candidate	Interviewer1	Interviewer2
A	1	1
B	2	2
C	3	3
D	4	3
E	5	6
F	6	5
G	7	8
H	8	7
I	9	10
J	10	9

| K | 11 | 12 |
| L | 12 | 11 |

The data in the `R06_Table` table represents two interviewers' rankings of candidates for a job. The `Candidate` column is simply for reference and is not critical to the recipe.

> It is critical to the functioning of this recipe that the first interviewer's rankings are sorted in order from lowest to highest.

How to do it...

To complete this recipe, do the following:

1. Create the following columns in the `R06_Table` table:

```
Concordant =
    VAR __Count =
        COUNTROWS (
            FILTER (
                ALL('R06_Table'),
                'R06_Table'[Interviewer1] >
EARLIER('R06_Table'[Interviewer1])
                    && 'R06_Table'[Interviewer2] >
EARLIER('R06_Table'[Interviewer2])
            )
        )
    RETURN
        IF(ISBLANK(__count),0,__count)

Discordant =
    VAR __Count =
        COUNTROWS (
            FILTER (
                ALL('R06_Table'),
                'R06_Table'[Interviewer1] >
EARLIER('R06_Table'[Interviewer1])
                    && 'R06_Table'[Interviewer2] <
EARLIER('R06_Table'[Interviewer2])
            )
        )
    RETURN
        IF(ISBLANK(__Count),0,__Count)
```

2. Create the following measure:

```
Kendall's Tau =
    VAR __Data = 'R06_Table'
    VAR __Table =
        ADDCOLUMNS (
            __Data,
            "__Concordant",
            COUNTROWS (
                FILTER (
                    __Data,
                    [Interviewer1] > EARLIER([Interviewer1]) &&
                        [Interviewer2] > EARLIER([Interviewer2])
                )
            ),
            "__Discordant",
            COUNTROWS (
                FILTER (
                    __Data,
                    [Interviewer1] > EARLIER([Interviewer1]) &&
                        [Interviewer2] < EARLIER([Interviewer2])
                )
            )
        )
    VAR __C = SUMX(__Table,[__Concordant])
    VAR __D = SUMX(__Table,[__Discordant])
    RETURN
        ABS(DIVIDE(__C - __D , __C + __D,0))
```

3. On a **Report** page, create a **Card** visualization, place the `Concordant` column from the `R06_Table` table into the **Fields** area of the visualization and set the aggregation to `Sum`.

4. On the same **Report** page, create a second **Card** visualization, place the `Discordant` column from the `R06_Table` table into the **Fields** area of the visualization and set the aggregation to `Sum`.

5. On the same **Report** page, create a third **Card** visualization and place the `Kendall's Tau` measure into the **Fields** area of the visualization.

How it works...

The `Concordant` and `Discordant` columns are simply for visualization purposes, but their calculations are nearly identical to equivalent calculations in our `Kendall's Tau` measure, so we will start by explaining the calculation of the `Concordant` and `Discordant` columns.

The purpose of the `Concordant` column is to find the number of rows in the data table, `R06_Table`, where both interviewers have larger values than the current row value for `Interviewer1` and `Interviewer2`. Because `Concordant` is a column, we use the `ALL` function to break out of the row context. We then use the `FILTER` function to select only the rows where the `Interviewer1` column is larger than the current value of the `Interviewer1` column (`EARLIER`) and the `Interviewer2` column is larger than the current value for the `Interviewer2` column (`EARLIER`). We then use `COUNTROWS` to count the number of rows returned from the `FILTER` function.

The calculation of the `Discordant` column is almost identical to the `Concordant` column. The only difference is that we count the number of rows where the `Interviewer1` column is larger than the current value for the `Interviewer1` column (`EARLIER`) and the `Interviewer2` column is *smaller* than the current value for the `Interviewer2` column (`EARLIER`).

For our `Kendall's Tau` measure, we start by creating the table variable, `__Data`, and setting the value for `__Data` equal to our base table, `R06_Table`. This is done for ease of reference. Next, we create the table variable, `__Table`. For our `__Table` variable, we start with our table variable, `__Data`. To this table, we add the `__Concordant` and `__Discordant` columns. The `__Concordant` and `__Discordant` columns are simply implementations of our `Concordant` and `Discordant` columns described previously.

We now sum our `__Concordant` and `__Discordant` columns and store these values in the `__C` and `__D` variables respectively. Finally, we `RETURN` the absolute value of `__C` minus `__D` divided by the sum of `__C` and `__D`.

See also

For more details about functions used in this recipe, refer to the following links:

- Kendall rank correlation coefficient: `https://en.wikipedia.org/wiki/Kendall_rank_correlation_coefficient`
- Kendall's Tau (Kendall Rank Correlation Coefficient): `https://www.statisticshowto.datasciencecentral.com/kendalls-tau/`

- Kendall's Tau: `https://stanfordphd.com/KendallsTau.html`
- COUNTROWS: `https://docs.microsoft.com/en-us/dax/countrows-function-dax`
- FILTER: `https://docs.microsoft.com/en-us/dax/filter-function-dax`
- ALL: `https://docs.microsoft.com/en-us/dax/all-function-dax`
- EARLIER: `https://docs.microsoft.com/en-us/dax/earlier-function-dax`
- IF: `https://docs.microsoft.com/en-us/dax/if-function-dax`
- ISBLANK: `https://docs.microsoft.com/en-us/dax/isblank-function-dax`
- ADDCOLUMNS: `https://docs.microsoft.com/en-us/dax/addcolumns-function-dax`
- SUMX: `https://docs.microsoft.com/en-us/dax/sumx-function-dax`
- ABS: `https://docs.microsoft.com/en-us/dax/abs-function-dax`
- DIVIDE: `https://docs.microsoft.com/en-us/dax/divide-function-dax`

Analyzing kurtosis

Kurtosis is a measure of how the distribution of a set of data compares with a normal distribution. Specifically, kurtosis measures the *tailedness* of a distribution with respect to a normal bell curve. We should think of this in terms of the distribution of probability. A normal bell curve is said to be **mesokurtic**. Distributions that have more kurtosis than a normal bell curve are called **leptokurtic**. Leptokurtic distributions have wide tails, meaning that they have a wide range of outliers, with some of those outliers being extreme. Distributions with less kurtosis than a normal bell curve are called **platykurtic**. Platykurtic distributions are stable with a paucity of extreme outliers. Kurtosis is a useful computation for decision-making in that kurtosis directly speaks to risk. For example, investors who invest in stocks with a leptokurtic distribution are engaging in more risk than investors who invest in stocks with a platykurtic distribution. The reason is the extreme outliers that exist in a leptokurtic distribution and the greater probability of events involving outliers.

Often of interest when computing kurtosis is the concept of skewness. Skewness measures the asymmetry of the probability distribution compared with the normal distribution. While we must be careful when interpreting skewness, in plain English this means that a positive skew generally indicates that the tail is on the right while negative skew generally indicates that the tail is on the left. This is compared to a normal distribution with two equal tails.

This recipe demonstrates how to calculate the skewness and kurtosis of a set of values.

Getting ready

To prepare for this recipe, do the following:

1. Open Power BI Desktop.
2. Use an **Enter Data** query to create a table called `R07_Table` with the following data:

Index	Values
1	12
2	13
3	54
4	56
5	25

How to do it...

To complete this recipe, do the following:

1. Create the following measures:

```
Kn = COUNTROWS(ALL('R07_Table'))

Kmean = AVERAGEX(ALL('R07_Table'),'R07_Table'[Values])

KStdDev = STDEVX.S(ALL('R07_Table'),'R07_Table'[Values])

Skewness =
    VAR __Mean = [Kmean]
    VAR __StdDev = [KStdDev]
    VAR __n = [Kn]
    VAR __Table =
        ADDCOLUMNS(
            'R07_Table',
            "__Skew",POWER(('R07_Table'[Values]-__Mean),3)
        )
RETURN
    DIVIDE(
        SUMX(__Table,[__Skew]),
        POWER(__StdDev,3),
        0
    ) * DIVIDE(1,__n,0)

Kurtosis =
```

```
VAR __Mean = [Kmean]
VAR __StdDev = [KStdDev]
VAR __n = [Kn]
VAR __Table =
    ADDCOLUMNS(
        'R07_Table',
        "__Skew",POWER(('R07_Table'[Values]-__Mean),4)
    )
RETURN
    DIVIDE(
        SUMX(__Table,[__Skew]),
        POWER(__StdDev,4),
        0
    ) * DIVIDE(1,__n,0)

Excess Kurtosis = [Kurtosis] - 3

Kurtosis Type =
    SWITCH(TRUE(),
        [Excess Kurtosis]>0,"Leptokurtic",
        [Excess Kurtosis]<0,"Platykurtic",
        "Mesokurtic"
    )
```

2. On the same **Report** page, create a **Card** visualization and place the Kn measure into the **Fields** area of the visualization.

3. On the same **Report** page, create another **Card** visualization and place the Kmean measure into the **Fields** area of the visualization.

4. On the same **Report** page, create another **Card** visualization and place the KStdDev measure into the **Fields** area of the visualization.

5. On the same **Report** page, create another **Card** visualization and place the Skewness measure into the **Fields** area of the visualization.

6. On the same **Report** page, create another **Card** visualization and place the Kurtosis measure into the **Fields** area of the visualization.

7. On the same **Report** page, create another **Card** visualization and place the Excess Kurtosis measure into the **Fields** area of the visualization.

8. On the same **Report** page, create another **Card** visualization and place the Kurtosis Type measure into the **Fields** area of the visualization.

9. On the same **Report** page, create a **Line chart** visualization and place the Index column from the R07_Table table into the **Axis** area and the Values column from the R07_Table table into the **Values** area of the visualization.

How it works...

The formulas for skewness and kurtosis are as follows:

$$\text{Skewness} = \frac{1}{n} \frac{\sum_{i=1}^{n} (X_i - \overline{X})^3}{S^3}$$

$$\text{Kurtosis} = \frac{1}{n} \frac{\sum_{i=1}^{n} (X_i - \overline{X})^4}{S^4}$$

As we can see, the formulas are nearly identical. Each requires n, the number of data points. In addition, each requires the average or mean of those data points (the X with the bar over it). Finally, each requires the standard deviation of the data points, S.

To implement these formulas, we start with the Kn measure. Kn is the count of the number of data points in our data table, R07_Table. This is n in our formulas for skewness and kurtosis.

Next, we calculate the Kmean measure. To calculate Kmean, we simply use AVERAGEX to return the average of the Values column in the R07_Table table.

We also need the sample standard deviation of our data points, KStdDev. To calculate KStdDev, we simply use the STDEVX.S function to calculate the standard deviation of the Values column in the R07_Table table.

Now that we have the base measures for our formulas, we can now calculate our Skewness and Kurtosis measures. We start our Skewness measure by simply setting the __Mean, __StdDev, and __n variables equal to the Kmean, KStdDev, and Kn measures, respectively. Since we must calculate the sum of the cube of the differences between each row's Value column and the mean of the Value column, we create the table variable, __Table, and use our base data table, R07_Table, as a starting point. We use ADDCOLUMNS to add the __Skew column to our table and simply implement the summation portion of the formula for skewness. We can now implement the rest of the formula for skewness by dividing the sum of our __Skew column by the __StdDev to the third power (cubed). We then divide this quotient by 4.

The calculation for the Kurtosis measure is identical to the calculation for the Skewness measure, except that powers of 4 are used instead of powers of 3.

We can now find our Excess Kurtosis by subtracting 3 from our Kurtosis measure. Finally, we can return the Kurtosis Type by using a SWITCH statement.

See also

For more details about functions used in this recipe, refer to the following links:

- **Kurtosis and Skewness:** `https://analystprep.com/cfa-level-1-exam/quantitative-methods/kurtosis-and-skewness-types-of-distributions/`

- **Kurtosis Formula:** `https://www.macroption.com/kurtosis-formula/`

- **Symmetry, Skewness, and Kurtosis:** `http://www.real-statistics.com/descriptive-statistics/symmetry-skewness-kurtosis/`

- **Kurtosis: Definition, Leptokurtic, Platykurtic:** `https://www.statisticshowto.datasciencecentral.com/probability-and-statistics/statistics-definitions/kurtosis-leptokurtic-platykurtic/`

- **BREAKING DOWN Kurtosis:** `https://www.investopedia.com/terms/k/kurtosis.asp`

- **Kurtosis:** `https://en.wikipedia.org/wiki/Kurtosis`

- **Skewness:** `https://en.wikipedia.org/wiki/Skewness`

- COUNTROWS: `https://docs.microsoft.com/en-us/dax/countrows-function-dax`

- ALL: `https://docs.microsoft.com/en-us/dax/all-function-dax`

- AVERAGEX: `https://docs.microsoft.com/en-us/dax/averagex-function-dax`

- STDEVX.S: `https://docs.microsoft.com/en-us/dax/stdevx-s-function-dax`

- ADDCOLUMNS: `https://docs.microsoft.com/en-us/dax/addcolumns-function-dax`

- POWER: `https://docs.microsoft.com/en-us/dax/power-function-dax`

- DIVIDE: `https://docs.microsoft.com/en-us/dax/divide-function-dax`

- SUMX: `https://docs.microsoft.com/en-us/dax/sumx-function-dax`

- SWITCH: `https://docs.microsoft.com/en-us/dax/switch-function-dax`

Utilizing the Jarque-Bera test

The Jarque-Bera test is named after Carlos Jarque and Anil K. Bera. It measures whether a set of data points is normally distributed or not. The formula for the Jarque-Bera test is as follows:

$$JB = \frac{n}{6}\left(S^2 + \frac{1}{4}(K - 3)^2\right)$$

In this formula, *n* is the number of data points, *S* is the sample skewness, and *K* is the sample kurtosis. For an explanation of skewness and kurtosis, see the previous *Analyzing kurtosis* recipe in this chapter. The Jarque-Bera test is an important test in statistics because many statistical methods rely on having a normal distribution. Thus, if your data is not normally distributed, the application of certain statistical methods would be invalid.

This recipe demonstrates how to utilize the Jarque-Bera test on a set of data.

Getting ready

To prepare for this recipe, do the following:

1. Open Power BI Desktop.
2. Use an **Enter Data** query to create a table called R08_Table with the following data:

Index	Values
1	12
2	13
3	54
4	56
5	25

How to do it...

To complete this recipe, do the following:

1. Create the following measures:

```
Jarque-Bera =
    VAR __Table = 'R08_Table'
    VAR __Mean = AVERAGEX(__Table,[Values])
    VAR __StdDev = STDEVX.S(__Table,[Values])
    VAR __n = COUNTROWS(__Table)
    VAR __TableSkew =
        ADDCOLUMNS(
            __Table,
            "__Skew",POWER(([Values]-__Mean),3)
        )
    VAR __Skewness =
        DIVIDE(
            SUMX(__TableSkew,[__SKew]),
```

```
                        POWER(__StdDev,3),0
                    ) * DIVIDE(1,__n,0)
            VAR __TableKurtosis =
                ADDCOLUMNS(
                    __Table,
                    "__Kurtosis",POWER(([Values]-__Mean),4)
                )
            VAR __Kurtosis =
                DIVIDE(
                    SUMX(__TableKurtosis,[__Kurtosis]),
                    POWER(__StdDev,4),0
                ) * DIVIDE(1,__n,0)
            VAR __FirstPart = DIVIDE(__n,6,0)
            VAR __SecondPart =
                POWER(__Skewness,2) +
                    1/4*(POWER(__Kurtosis - 3,2))
        RETURN
            __FirstPart * __SecondPart

        JB Type =
            SWITCH(TRUE(),
                [Jarque-Bera]>0,"Not Normally Distributed",
                "Normally Distributed"
            )
```

2. On a **Report** page, create a **Card** visualization and place the `Jarque-Bera` measure into the **Fields** area of the visualization.

3. On the same **Report** page, create another **Card** visualization and place the `JB Type` measure into the **Fields** area of the visualization.

4. On the same **Report** page, create a **Line chart** visualization and place the `Index` column from the `R08_Table` table into the **Axis** area and the `Values` column from the `R08_Table` table into the **Values** area of the visualization.

How it works...

For the `Jarque-Bera` measure, we start by creating the table variable, `__Table`, and setting this as equal to our base data table, `R08_Table`. This is done for ease of reference. Next, we calculate the mean (`__Mean`), standard deviation (`__StdDev`), and count (n) of the data points in our `Values` column. This is done by using `AVERAGEX`, `STDEVX.S`, and `COUNTROWS` respectively.

Next, we need to calculate the skewness of our data. The formula for skewness is as follows:

$$Skewness = \frac{1}{n} \frac{\sum_{i=1}^{n}(X_i - \overline{X})^3}{S^3}$$

This formula requires n, the number of data points, the average or mean of those data points (the X with the bar over it) and the standard deviation of the data points, S. Since we must calculate the sum of the cube of the differences between each row's `Value` column and the mean of the `Value` column, we create the table variable, `__TableSkew`, and use our base data table, `__Table`, as a starting point. We use `ADDCOLUMNS` to add the `__Skew` column to our table and simply implement the summation portion of the formula for skewness. We can now implement the rest of the formula for skewness in our `__Skewness` variable by dividing the sum of our `__Skew` column by the `__StdDev` to the third power (cubed). We then divide this quotient by 4.

The calculation for the `__TableKurtosis` and `__Kurtosis` variables are identical to the calculation for the `__TableSkew` and `__Skewness` variable except that powers of 4 are used instead of powers of 3.

Now that we have calculated all of the required parts of the Jarque-Bera test formula, we can calculate our final value for the `Jarque-Bera` measure. The `__FirstPart` variable simply calculates the quotient of `__n` divided by 6. The `__SecondPart` variable calculates the rest of the formula for the Jarque-Bera test. We then simply need to return the multiplication of the `__FirstPart` variable and the `__SecondPart` variable.

For the `JB Type` measure, we simply need to check if the value of our `Jarque-Bera` measure is greater than zero. If our `Jarque-Bera` measure is greater than zero then the data is not normally distributed. Otherwise, the data is normally distributed.

See also

For more details about functions used in this recipe, refer to the following links:

- Jarque-Bera Test: `https://www.statisticshowto.datasciencecentral.com/jarque-bera-test/`
- Jarque-Bera test: `https://en.wikipedia.org/wiki/Jarque–Bera_test`
- COUNTROWS: `https://docs.microsoft.com/en-us/dax/countrows-function-dax`
- ALL: `https://docs.microsoft.com/en-us/dax/all-function-dax`

- AVERAGEX: https://docs.microsoft.com/en-us/dax/averagex-function-dax
- STDEVX.S: https://docs.microsoft.com/en-us/dax/stdevx-s-function-dax
- ADDCOLUMNS: https://docs.microsoft.com/en-us/dax/addcolumns-function-dax
- POWER: https://docs.microsoft.com/en-us/dax/power-function-dax
- DIVIDE: https://docs.microsoft.com/en-us/dax/divide-function-dax
- SUMX: https://docs.microsoft.com/en-us/dax/sumx-function-dax
- SWITCH: https://docs.microsoft.com/en-us/dax/switch-function-dax

Determining Pearson's coefficient of skewness

Skewness measures the asymmetry of the probability distribution compared with the normal distribution. In other words, compared to a normal distribution (bell curve), is the data skewed to one side or the other in terms of having a longer tail to the right or left? While we must be careful when interpreting skewness, a positive skew generally means that the tail is on the right, while negative skew indicates that the tail is on the left. This is compared to a normal distribution with two equal tails.

This recipe demonstrates how to calculate Karl Pearson's coefficient of skewness (the second method), which is given by the following formula:

$$Skewness = \frac{3(\overline{x} - \tilde{x})}{s}$$

In plain English, to find the skewness you subtract the median (the middle value) from the mean (average), multiply by three, and then divide by the standard deviation.

Getting ready

To prepare for this recipe, do the following:

1. Open Power BI Desktop.
2. Import the data from the Ch11R09Data.xlsx Excel file located in the GitHub repository. Ensure that the created table is called R09_Table.

How to do it...

To complete this recipe, do the following:

1. Create the following measures:

```
09_Skewness =
    VAR __Table =
SELECTCOLUMNS('R09_Table',"__Value",'R09_Table'[Column1])
RETURN
    DIVIDE(
        3 * (AVERAGEX(__Table,[__Value]) -
MEDIANX(__Table,[__Value])),
        STDEVX.P(__Table,[__Value]),
        0
    )
```

2. On a **Report** page, create a **Card** visualization and place the `09_Skewness` measure into the **Fields** area of the visualization.
3. On the same **Report** page, create a **Line chart** visualization and place the `Index` column from the `R09_Table` table into the **Axis** area and the `Column1` column from the `R09_Table` table into the **Value** area of the visualization.

How it works...

The implementation of this recipe is fairly straightforward. Our `09_Skewness` measure first uses `SELECTCOLUMNS` to select `Column1` from our base table, `R09_Table`. The `SELECTCOLUMNS` function returns a one-column table with the column named `__Value`. Our `RETURN` statement simply implements the skewness formula using the `AVERAGEX` function to calculate the mean of the `__Value` column, the `MEDIANX` function to calculate the median of the `__Value` column, and the `STDEVX.P` function to calculate the standard deviation of the `__Value` column.

There's more...

To observe how different lines can give different values for skewness, do the following:

1. Create the following measures:

```
09_Skewness2 =
    VAR __Table =
SELECTCOLUMNS('R09_Table',"__Value",'R09_Table'[Column2])
```

```
RETURN
    DIVIDE(
        3 * (AVERAGEX(__Table,[__Value]) -
MEDIANX(__Table,[__Value])),
        STDEVX.P(__Table,[__Value]),
        0
    )

09_Skewness3 =
    VAR __Table =
SELECTCOLUMNS('R09_Table',"__Value",'R09_Table'[Column3])
RETURN
    DIVIDE(
        3 * (AVERAGEX(__Table,[__Value]) -
MEDIANX(__Table,[__Value])),
        STDEVX.P(__Table,[__Value]),
        0
    )
```

2. On the same **Report** page as before, create another **Card** visualization and place the `09_Skewness2` measure into the **Fields** area of the visualization.

3. On the same **Report** page, create another **Card** visualization and place the `09_Skewness3` measure into the **Fields** area of the visualization.

4. On the same **Report** page, create another **Line chart** visualization and place the `Index` column from the `R09_Table` table into the **Axis** area and the `Column2` column from the `R09_Table` table into the **Values** area of the visualization.

5. On the same **Report** page, create another **Line chart** visualization and place the `Index` column from the `R09_Table` table into the **Axis** area and the `Column3` column from the `R09_Table` table into the **Values** area of the visualization.

See also

For more details about functions used in this recipe, refer to the following links:

- Skewness: https://en.wikipedia.org/wiki/Skewness
- How to Find Pearson's Coefficient of Skewness in Excel: https://www.statisticshowto.datasciencecentral.com/find-pearsons-coefficient-skewness-excel/
- DIVIDE: https://docs.microsoft.com/en-us/dax/divide-function-dax
- AVERAGEX: https://docs.microsoft.com/en-us/dax/averagex-function-dax
- STDEVX.P: https://docs.microsoft.com/en-us/dax/stdevx-p-function-dax

- MEDIANX: https://docs.microsoft.com/en-us/dax/medianx-function-dax
- SELECTCOLUMNS: https://docs.microsoft.com/en-us/dax/selectcolumns-function-dax

Applying the hypergeometric distribution formula

The hypergeometric distribution is a probability distribution that defines the probability of having a specified amount of success (k) within a specified number of attempts (n) for a given population of N with K items with the desired feature. So, if we consider a deck of cards, what is the probability of drawing 2 (k) jacks within 10 (n) draws from a deck of 52 (N) cards in which there are 4 (K) jacks? The formula for the hypergeometric distribution formula is as follows:

$$P(X = k) = \frac{\binom{K}{k}\binom{N-K}{n-k}}{\binom{N}{n}}$$

Those odd-looking things in parenthesis are binomial distributions (combinations).

Not only constrained to gambling, the hypergeometric distribution has a wide range of uses and can be used to determine the statistical significance of specific events (successes). Thus, we can use the hypergeometric distribution to determine under- or over-representation of a sub-population within a given population sample. In other words, businesses could use the hypergeometric distribution formula to determine the characteristics of their customer base.

This recipe demonstrates how to implement the formula for hypergeometric distribution in DAX.

Getting ready

To prepare for this recipe, do the following:

1. Open Power BI Desktop.
2. Create the following tables:

```
R10_K =
    SELECTCOLUMNS (
        GENERATESERIES(1, 25, 1),
        "K",
```

```
              [Value]
          )

R10__k =
      SELECTCOLUMNS(
          GENERATESERIES(1, 25, 1),
          "k",
          [Value]
      )

R10_N =
      SELECTCOLUMNS(
          GENERATESERIES(1, 25, 1),
          "N",
          [Value]
      )

R10__n =
      SELECTCOLUMNS(
          GENERATESERIES(1, 25, 1),
          "n",
          [Value]
      )
```

These four tables represent the inputs to our geometric distribution formula.

How to do it...

To complete this recipe, do the following:

1. Create the following measures:

```
K Value = SELECTEDVALUE('R10_K'[K], 6)

k Value 2 = SELECTEDVALUE('R10__k'[k], 1)

N Value = SELECTEDVALUE('R10_N'[N], 1)

n Value 2 = SELECTEDVALUE('R10__n'[n], 1)

Probability =
    VAR __Error =
        IF(ISBLANK([K Value]) ||
            ISBLANK([k Value 2]) ||
                ISBLANK([N Value]) ||
                    ISBLANK([n Value 2]) ||
```

```
                                        [n Value 2]<[k Value 2] ||
                                          [K Value]<[k Value 2] ||
                                            [N Value]<[n Value 2] ||
                                              [N Value]<[K Value],
                    TRUE(),
                    FALSE()
                )
        VAR __Numerator =
            IF(
                ISERROR(
                    COMBIN([K Value],[k Value 2]) *
                        COMBIN([N Value]-[K Value],[n Value 2]-[k Value
    2])
                ),
                -1,
                COMBIN([K Value],[k Value 2]) *
                    COMBIN([N Value]-[K Value],[n Value 2]-[k Value 2])
            )
        VAR __Denominator =
            IF(
                ISERROR(COMBIN([N Value],[n Value 2])),
                -1,
                COMBIN([N Value],[n Value 2])
            )
    RETURN
        IF(
            __Error || __Denominator = -1 || __Numerator = -1,
            "Bad Parameters",
            DIVIDE(__Numerator,__Denominator,0)
        )
```

2. On a **Report** page, create a **Slicer** visualization, place the K column from the `R10_K` table into the **Field** area of the visualization, and format the slicer as a `List`.

3. On the same **Report** page, create a second **Slicer** visualization, place the k column from the `R10__k` table into the **Field** area of the visualization, and format the slicer as a `List`.

4. On the same **Report** page, create a third **Slicer** visualization, place the N column from the `R10_N` table into the **Field** area of the visualization, and format the slicer as a `List`.

5. On the same **Report** page, create a fourth **Slicer** visualization, place the n column from the R10__n table into the **Field** area of the visualization, and format the slicer as a List.

6. On the same **Report** page, create a **Card** visualization and place the Probability measure into the **Field** area of the visualization.

How it works...

The first four measures, K Value, k Value 2, N Value, and n Value 2 simply capture the current value selections from our tables, R10_K, R10__k, R10_N, and R10__n respectively. This is done by using the SELECTCOLUMNS function. As part of the SELECTCOLUMNS function, we provide default values for each of these measures.

To compute our Probability using the geometric distribution formula, we start by creating the __Error variable. The purpose of __Error is to determine whether the user has selected impossible values in the slicers. The entire __Error variable calculation is a series of logical OR statements that test various conditions. The first four conditions tested are whether or not the values of the four inputs to the geometric distribution formula are blank (ISBLANK). The second four conditions tested are for impossible conditions, such as the population size (N) being less than the desired number of successes (K).

We now calculate the numerator of our geometric distribution formula, __Numerator. This is accomplished by using the COMBIN function. The COMBIN function does all of the hard work of computing the binomial distributions (combinations). We wrap the calculation in an ISERROR statement to catch any other possible errors not accounted for by our __Error variable. If there is an error, our __Numerator is set to an impossible value, -1. Otherwise, we repeat our calculation. The calculation of our __Denominator variable is done in the same manner as our __Numerator variable.

Finally, in our RETURN statement we check if there has been an error by using a logical OR construct to see if __Error is FALSE or if __Numerator or __Denominator is -1. If there has been an error, we return Bad Parameters. Otherwise, we simply divide our __Numerator by our __Denominator.

See also

For more details about functions used in this recipe, refer to the following links:

- Hypergeometric Distribution: Examples and Formula: `https://www.statisticshowto.datasciencecentral.com/hypergeometric-distribution-examples/`
- Hypergeometric distribution: `https://en.wikipedia.org/wiki/Hypergeometric_distribution`
- `SELECTEDVALUE`: `https://docs.microsoft.com/en-us/dax/selectedvalue-function-dax`
- `DIVIDE`: `https://docs.microsoft.com/en-us/dax/divide-function-dax`
- `IF`: `https://docs.microsoft.com/en-us/dax/if-function-dax`
- `TRUE`: `https://docs.microsoft.com/en-us/dax/true-function-dax`
- `FALSE`: `https://docs.microsoft.com/en-us/dax/false-function-dax`
- `ISERROR`: `https://docs.microsoft.com/en-us/dax/iserror-function-dax`
- `COMBIN`: `https://docs.microsoft.com/en-us/dax/combin-function-dax`

Determining the required sample size

Sample size is an important concept in statistics. In order to make reliable inferences of a population based upon a sample of that population, it is necessary to have a statistically significant sample size. One method of calculating the required sample size is Cochran's formula, named after the statistician William Gemmell Cochran.

Cochran's formula is as follows:

$$n = \frac{Z^2 p(1-p)}{e^2}$$

Here, p is the expected percent of the population with the desired attribute. e is the desired precision or margin of error. Z is something called the z-score, which is found in a z-score table (it's a statistics thing). In order to find the z-score, we must choose a desired confidence value (how confident are we in the results).

This recipe implements Cochran's formula for determining sample size in DAX based upon the chosen confidence levels, the proportion of the population with the desired attribute, and the desired precision.

Getting ready

To prepare for this recipe, do the following:

1. Open Power BI Desktop.
2. Import the data from the `Ch11R11Data.xlsx` Excel file located in the GitHub repository. Ensure that the created table is called `R11_2TailZScores`.
3. Create the following tables:

```
R11_Precision =
    SELECTCOLUMNS(
        GENERATESERIES(.01,.1,.01),
        "Precision",
        [Value]
    )

R11_Proportion =
    SELECTCOLUMNS(
        GENERATESERIES(.1,.9,.1),
        "Proportion",
        [Value]
    )
```

These three tables represent inputs into our sample size formula. The `R11_2TailZScores` table is also a lookup table for the z-score corresponding to a desired confidence level.

How to do it...

To complete this recipe, do the following:

1. Create the following measures:

```
Confidence Value =
SELECTEDVALUE('R11_2TailZScores'[Confidence],.95)

Precision Value = SELECTEDVALUE('R11_Precision'[Precision],.05)

Proportion Value = SELECTEDVALUE('R11_Proportion'[Proportion],.5)

Sample Size =
    VAR __ZScore =
        LOOKUPVALUE(
            'R11_2TailZScores'[Z-Score],
            'R11_2TailZScores'[Confidence],
            [Confidence Value]
```

```
        )
RETURN
    DIVIDE(
        __ZScore^2 * [Proportion Value] * (1 - [Proportion Value]),
        [Precision Value]^2,
        0
    )
```

2. On a **Report** page, create a **Slicer** visualization, place the `Confidence` column from the `R11_2TailZScores` table into the **Field** area of the visualization, and format the slicer as a `Dropdown`.

3. On the same **Report** page, create a second **Slicer** visualization, place the `Precision` column from the `R11_Precision` table into the **Field** area of the visualization, and format the slicer as a `Dropdown`.

4. On the same **Report** page, create a third **Slicer** visualization, place the `Proportion` column from the `R11_Proportion` table into the **Field** area of the visualization, and format the slicer as a `Dropdown`.

5. On the same **Report** page, create a **Card** visualization and place the `Sample Size` measure into the **Field** area of the visualization.

How it works...

The first three measures, `Confidence Value`, `Precision Value`, and `Proportion Value`, simply capture the current value selections from our tables, `R11_2TailZScores`, `R11_Precision`, and `R11_Proportion` respectively. This is done by using the `SELECTCOLUMNS` function. As part of the `SELECTCOLUMNS` function, we provide default values for each of these measures.

To calculate our `Sample Size` measure, we first must determine the corresponding `Z-Score` for our selected `Confidence Value`. This is done using the `LOOKUPVALUE` function. Once we have our `Z-Score`, we simply need to plug our measures into the formula for computing the sample size to arrive at the required sample size for the input values we have selected.

See also

For more details about functions used in this recipe, refer to the following links:

- **Sample Size in Statistics (How to Find It): Excel, Cochran's Formula, General Tips:** https://www.statisticshowto.datasciencecentral.com/probability-and-statistics/find-sample-size/
- SELECTEDVALUE: https://docs.microsoft.com/en-us/dax/selectedvalue-function-dax
- LOOKUPVALUE: https://docs.microsoft.com/en-us/dax/lookupvalue-function-dax
- DIVIDE: https://docs.microsoft.com/en-us/dax/divide-function-dax

12
Applying Advanced DAX Patterns

This chapter contains some of the more mind-bogglingly hard problems to solve in DAX that I have encountered over the years, as well as a few DAX oddities such as creating **Scalable Vector Graphics (SVG)** graphics and animations. This is not to say that the previous chapters do not have some very hard DAX recipes. This chapter, however, has an abundance of truly complex DAX code that solves some of the more vexing problems you might encounter. Either through brute force or DAX code wizardry, this chapter should put to rest any notion that DAX cannot solve just about any calculation you might throw at it!

The following is the list of recipes that we will cover in this chapter:

- Using dynamic ABC classification
- Creating an inverse slicer
- Unpivoting columns in DAX
- Transposing tables
- Repeating counter with criteria
- Using across then down
- Using matrix multiplication
- Forecasting with a de-seasonalized correlation coefficient
- Creating an SVG graphic
- Creating an SVG animation
- Making things anonymous

Technical requirements

The following are the technical requirements in order to complete all of the recipes in this chapter:

- Power BI Desktop
- This book's GitHub repository: `https://github.com/PacktPublishing/DAX-Cookbook/tree/master/Chapter12`

Using dynamic ABC classification

In general, ABC classification is an implementation of the 80/20 rule. Succinctly stated, the 80/20 rule says that about 80% of what you care about comes from about 20% of what you have. In other words, if you are a manufacturer of goods, 80% of your sales comes from about 20% of your products. This concept is applicable to sales, inventories, purchasing, and many other areas of business. The most important items are tagged with the A label, which generally represents about 80% of the total dollars spent by a company or received as revenue by a company. B items are not as important as A items and generally represent an additional 10% to 15% of the dollars that are spent or received by a company. Making up the remainder are C items, which are the least important.

I was first introduced to ABC classification when I went to `https://www.daxpatterns.com/`, which is maintained by two giants in the Microsoft business intelligence world: Marco Russo and Alberto Ferrari. This pattern, as implemented back then, used columns to implement ABC classification. This meant that the ABC classifications that were created were static and did not change dynamically based upon filtering within a report. I took this as an opportunity to implement ABC classification as a measure in order to make the calculation of the ABC classifications dynamic.

While Marco Russo and Alberto Ferrari now have their own take on dynamic ABC classification within DAX, this recipe implements my original dynamic ABC classification based upon their original, static implementation of ABC classification.

Getting ready

To prepare for this recipe, do the following:

1. Open Power BI Desktop.
2. Import the data from the `Ch12R01Data.xlsx` Excel file located in this book's GitHub repository. Ensure that you import all the sheets and that the tables that you create are called `R01_Categories`, `R01_Products`, `R01_Sales`, and `R01_SubCategories`.
3. Create a relationship between the `ProductCategoryID` column in the `R01_Categories` table and the `ProductCategoryID` column in the `R01_SubCategories` table. Ensure that `Cross filter direction` is set to `Single`.
4. Create a relationship between the `ProductSubCategoryID` column in the `R01_SubCategories` table and the `ProductSubCategoryID` column in the `R01_Products` table. Ensure that `Cross filter direction` is set to `Single`.
5. Create a relationship between the `ProductID` column in the `R01_Sales` table and the `ProductID` column in the `R01_Products` table. Ensure that `Cross filter direction` is set to `Single`.
6. Ensure that no other relationships exist between the `R01_Categories`, `R01_Products`, `R01_Sales`, and `R01_SubCategoreis` tables and any other tables.

The data for this recipe is a subset of Microsoft's AdventureWorks 2014 database and includes products and sales information, as well as categories and subcategories for products.

How to do it...

To implement this recipe, do the following:

1. Create the following measure:

```
ABC =
    VAR __ProductID = MAX('R01_Products'[ProductID])
    VAR __Table =
        GROUPBY(
            ALLSELECTED('R01_Sales'),
            'R01_Sales'[ProductID],
            "__Sales", SUMX(CURRENTGROUP(), 'R01_Sales'[SaleTotal])
```

```
            )
        VAR __TotalSales = SUMX(__Table,[__Sales])
        VAR __Table1 =
            ADDCOLUMNS(
                ADDCOLUMNS(
                    __Table,
                    "__RunningSales%",
                        VAR __Percent = 1 -
                                        SUMX(
                                            FILTER(__Table,
[__Sales]<=EARLIER([__Sales])
                                        ),
                                        [__Sales] / __TotalSales)
                        RETURN
                        IF(__Percent < 0,0,__Percent)
                ),
                "__ABC Class",
                SWITCH(
                    TRUE(),
                    [__RunningSales%] <.8,"A",
                    [__RunningSales%]<.95,"B",
                    "C"
                )
            )
    RETURN
        MAXX(
            FILTER(
                __Table1,
                [ProductID] = __ProductID
            ),
            [__ABC Class]
        )
```

2. On the same **Report** page, create a **Table** visualization and place
   the Name column from the R01_Products table into the **Values** area of the
   visualization. Also, place the ABC measure into the **Values** area of the
   visualization.

3. On a **Report** page, create a **Slicer** visualization and place the Name column from
   the R01_Categories table into the **Field** area of the visualization.

4. On the same **Report** page, create a second **Slicer** visualization and place
   the Name column from the R01_SubCategories table into the **Field** area of the
   visualization.

How it works...

We start by simply getting the current `ProductID` within the current context from the `R01_Products` table and storing this in the `__ProductID` variable. Next, we create the table variable, `__Table`. `__Table` is based upon our `R01_Sales` table and uses GROUPBY to summarize the `R01_Sales` table by the `ProductID` column and adds the `__Sales` column, which simply sums the `SaleTotal` column. Now, we sum the `__Sales` column in `__Table` to get the total sum of sales for all the products within the current context, `__TotalSales`.

Now, we create the table variable, `__Table1`. We start with our `__Table` variable and add two columns using ADDCOLUMNS. The first column, `__RunningSales%`, sums the quotient of the `__Sales` column in `__Table` divided by `__TotalSales` for all the rows where the number of `__Sales` is less than or equal to the current row's value for the `__Sales` column (EARLIER). This value is subtracted from 1 to create a nested variable called `__Percent`. `__Percent` is checked to see if it is less than zero and, if so, `0` is returned; otherwise, we just return `__Percent` as the value for `__RunningSales%`. Thus, what is happening here is that we are keeping a running total of the percentage of sales each product makes up of the total sales for all the products within the current context. Importantly, this running total is in rank order of the highest to the lowest product sales. Thus, the lowest sales item will have a value of 1 for `__RunningSales%`, since 100% of `__TotalSales` comes from itself and other products. Conversely, the highest sales item will have its value for `__RunningSales%` simply be the percentage of `__TotalSales` that comes from itself.

The next column in `__Table1` is our ABC classification, `__ABC Class`. We use a SWITCH statement here to, in essence, implement a while loop in a more traditional programming language. For each product, we check if the `__RunningSales%` column is less than our A threshold of `.8` (80%). If so, we assign a value of A. In a more traditional programming language, you might loop through the products and while `__RunningSales%` is less than `.8`, you would assign a value of A. Similarly, next, we check if `__RunningSales%` is less than our B threshold of `.95` (our A threshold of `.8`, plus an additional `.15`) and, if so, we assign a value of B. Otherwise, if `__RunningSales%` is greater than `.95`, we assign the value C.

Now, we can return a value for the ABC classification of a product by using FILTER to return only the row where the `ProductID` column in `__Table` equals our `__ProductID`, and then use MAXX to return the value of the `__ABC Class` column.

See also

For more details regarding the functions that were used in this recipe, please refer to the following links:

- **ABC classification:** https://www.daxpatterns.com/abc-classification/
- **ABC classification – dynamic:** https://www.daxpatterns.com/abc-classification-dynamic/
- MAX: https://docs.microsoft.com/en-us/dax/max-function-dax
- ALLSELECTED: https://docs.microsoft.com/en-us/dax/allselected-function-dax
- FILTER: https://docs.microsoft.com/en-us/dax/filter-function-dax
- GROUPBY: https://docs.microsoft.com/en-us/dax/groupby-function-dax
- SUMX: https://docs.microsoft.com/en-us/dax/sumx-function-dax
- IF: https://docs.microsoft.com/en-us/dax/if-function-dax
- ADDCOLUMNS: https://docs.microsoft.com/en-us/dax/addcolumns-function-dax
- EARLIER: https://docs.microsoft.com/en-us/dax/earlier-function-dax
- SWITCH: https://docs.microsoft.com/en-us/dax/switch-function-dax
- TRUE: https://docs.microsoft.com/en-us/dax/true-function-dax
- MAXX: https://docs.microsoft.com/en-us/dax/maxx-function-dax

Creating an inverse slicer

In Power BI, slicer visualizations are used as a handy method to filter data to only those items that have been selected within the slicer. However, there are times when you would rather use a slicer visualization to exclude items (filter items out). Effectively, you want the inverse of the normal slicer operation. Unfortunately, Power BI has no native functionality to make slicers operate in an exclude fashion.

This recipe turns slicer visualizations into exclude filters rather than the normal (include) slicer operation.

Getting ready

To prepare for this recipe, do the following:

1. Open Power BI Desktop.
2. Use an **Enter Data** query to create a table called `R02_Table` that contains the following data:

Department	Category	ProductID
Sports	AA	1
Education	BB	2
Health	AB	3
Sports	AA	4
Health	BB	5

3. Create the following table called `R02_Categories`:

```
R02_Categories = DISTINCT('R02_Table'[Category])
```

4. Create a relationship between the `Category` column in the `R02_Categories` table and the `Category` column in the `R02_Table` table. Ensure that `Cross filter direction` is set to `Single`.

How to do it...

To implement this recipe, do the following:

1. Create the following measure:

```
Inverse Selector =
    VAR __Category = MAX('R02_Table'[Category])
    VAR __Categories = VALUES('R02_Categories'[Category])
    VAR __Table =
        SELECTCOLUMNS(
            FILTER(
                ALL('R02_Table'),
                'R02_Table'[Category] IN __Categories
            ),
            "__Category",'R02_Table'[Category]
        )
    RETURN
        IF(__Category IN __Table,BLANK(),1)
```

2. On a **Report** page, create a **Slicer** visualization and place the `Category` column from the `R02_Categories` table into the **Field** area of the visualization.

3. On the same **Report** page, create a **Table** visualization and place the `Category`, `Department`, and `ProductID` columns from the `R02_Categories` table into the **Values** area of the visualization.

4. In this **Table** visualization, set the `ProductID` column to `Don't summarize`.

5. On the same **Report** page, copy and paste the table visualization.

6. In the second **Table** visualization, add the `Inverse Selector` measure to the **Values** area of the visualization.

How it works...

This recipe takes advantage of Power BI's behavior of filtering out rows in a **Table** or **Matrix** visualization where numeric values are included in the visualization but numeric values are blank (`BLANK`).

We start by simply getting the value of the `Category` column within the current context and storing this value in the `__Category` variable. Next, we get all of the values in the `Category` column that are currently selected in the slicer using the `VALUES` function and store these values in the `__Categories` table variable.

Next, we create the `__Table` table variable. We begin by using `ALL` to return all of the rows in our data table, `R02_Table`. Then, we use `FILTER` to only include rows where the `Category` column is included in our `__Categories` table variable (`IN`). Finally, we use `SELECTCOLUMNS` to return a single column table of the filtered values in the `Category` column.

Now, we can determine if our `__Category` is included in the `__Table` variable. If so, we return `BLANK` as this is an undesired row. Otherwise, we return `1`.

> If you are using a **Table** or **Matrix** visualization that includes numeric values that are not blank and force undesired rows to display, or if you're using visualizations other than the **Table** or **Matrix** visualizations, you can still use the `Inverse Slicer` measure to filter out undesired rows. Simply use the **Filter** pane and set the filter for the `Inverse Slicer` measure so that it only includes rows where the `Inverse Slicer` measure equals 1.

See also

For more details regarding the functions that were used in this recipe, please refer to the following links:

- DAX Operators: https://docs.microsoft.com/en-us/dax/dax-operator-reference
- SELECTCOLUMNS: https://docs.microsoft.com/en-us/dax/selectcolumns-function-dax
- FILTER: https://docs.microsoft.com/en-us/dax/filter-function-dax
- MAX: https://docs.microsoft.com/en-us/dax/max-function-dax
- VALUES: https://docs.microsoft.com/en-us/dax/values-function-dax
- ALL: https://docs.microsoft.com/en-us/dax/all-function-dax
- IF: https://docs.microsoft.com/en-us/dax/if-function-dax
- BLANK: https://docs.microsoft.com/en-us/dax/blank-function-dax

Unpivoting columns in DAX

Unpivoting columns means that the unpivoted column values become new rows in a table. Unpivoting columns is generally handled in Power Query. However, there are documented cases where unpivoting columns in Power Query causes performance issues, particularly when unpivoting columns coming from a SharePoint list.

This recipe demonstrates how to unpivot columns using DAX instead of Power Query.

Getting ready

To prepare for this recipe, do the following:

1. Open Power BI Desktop.
2. Use an **Enter Data** query to create a table called R03_Table that contains the following data:

Date	Column1	Colum2	Column3	Column4	Column5	Column6	Item
1/1/2018	Greg	Jason					Meeting 1
1/5/2018	Jason	Frank	George	Battina			Meeting 2
1/10/2018	John	Greg	Jason	Battina	George	Frank	Meeting 3

We wish to unpivot the Column1, Column2, Column3, Column4, Column5, and Column6 columns.

How to do it...

To implement this recipe, do the following:

1. Create the following table, that is, R03_Unpivot:

```
R03_Unpivot =
    VAR __Table = 'R03_Table'
RETURN
    SELECTCOLUMNS (
        FILTER (
            UNION (
                SELECTCOLUMNS (
                    __Table,
                    "Item", [Item],
                    "Date", [Date],
                    "Column1", [Column1]
                ),
                SELECTCOLUMNS (
                    __Table,
                    "Item", [Item],
                    "Date", [Date],
                    "Column1", [Column2]
                ),
                SELECTCOLUMNS (
                    __Table,
                    "Item", [Item],
                    "Date", [Date],
                    "Column1", [Column3]
                ),
                SELECTCOLUMNS (
                    __Table,
                    "Item", [Item],
                    "Date", [Date],
                    "Column1", [Column4]
                ),
                SELECTCOLUMNS (
                    __Table,
                    "Item", [Item],
                    "Date", [Date],
                    "Column1", [Column5]
                ),
                SELECTCOLUMNS (
```

```
                __Table,
                "Item", [Item],
                "Date", [Date],
                "Column1", [Column6]
            )
        ),
        [Column1] <> ""
    ),
    "Item", [Item],
    "Date", [Date],
    "Attendees", [Column1]
)
```

How it works...

While the code looks fairly long, this recipe is relatively straightforward. Reading the DAX from the inside out, we start by using SELECTCOLUMNS statements to return all of the rows in each of the columns we wish to unpivot, that is, Column1, Column2, Column3, Column4, Column5 and Column6, along with the Item column and the Date column, which are the two columns that we do not wish to unpivot. Crucially, for this technique to work, each SELECTCOLUMNS statement must include the same number of columns. In addition, the column names must be the same between all of the SELECTCOLUMNS statements.

Because all of the unpivoted columns have been given the same column name coming out of the SELECTCOLUMNS statements, Column1, when we UNION all of the tables resulting from the SELECTCOLUMNS statements, all of the values from the unpivoted columns become row values within the same column, Column1. Because we have included our Item and Date columns in every SELECTCOLUMNS statement, those columns are not unpivoted.

Now, we can use FILTER to filter out rows where the values from the unpivoted columns are empty and then use one last SELECTCOLUMNS statement to return friendly column names.

See also

For more details regarding the functions that were used in this recipe, please refer to the following links:

- SELECTCOLUMNS: https://docs.microsoft.com/en-us/dax/selectcolumns-function-dax

- FILTER: https://docs.microsoft.com/en-us/dax/filter-function-dax
- UNION: https://docs.microsoft.com/en-us/dax/union-function-dax

Transposing tables

Transposing tables means that the columns in a table become rows and the rows in a table become columns. Transposing tables is necessary for certain mathematical operations such as matrix multiplication. Excel has a handy function called TRANSPOSE that performs such an operation in a single function statement. In addition, Power Query can also be used to transpose a table in a single operation. Unfortunately, DAX has no equivalent TRANSPOSE function.

This recipe implements a table transpose using DAX.

Getting ready

To prepare for this recipe, do the following:

1. Open Power BI Desktop.
2. Use an **Enter Data** query to create a table called R04_Table that contains the following data:

Column1	Column2	Column3	Index
A	B	C	1
D	E	F	2

How to do it...

To implement this recipe, do the following:

1. Create the following table, that is, R04_Transpose:

```
R04_Transpose =
    VAR __Table = 'R04_Table'
    VAR __Transpose =
        SELECTCOLUMNS (
            {
                (
                    SELECTCOLUMNS (
                        FILTER (
```

```
                    __Table,
                    [Index]=1
                ),
                "Row",[Column1]
            ),
            SELECTCOLUMNS(
                FILTER(
                    __Table,
                    [Index]=2
                ),
                "Row",[Column1]
            ),
            "1"
        ),
        (
            SELECTCOLUMNS(
                FILTER(
                    __Table,
                    [Index]=1
                ),
                "Row",[Column2]
            ),
            SELECTCOLUMNS(
                FILTER(
                    __Table,
                    [Index]=2
                ),
                "Row",[Column2]
            ),
            "2"
        ),
        (
            SELECTCOLUMNS(
                FILTER(
                    __Table,
                    [Index]=1
                ),
                "Row",[Column3]
            ),
            SELECTCOLUMNS(
                FILTER(
                    __Table,
                    [Index]=2
                ),
                "Row",[Column3]
            ),
            "3"
        )
    )
```

```
                },
                "Row",[Value3],
                "1",[Value1],
                "2",[Value2]
            )
        RETURN
            __Transpose
```

How it works...

The technique here is, unfortunately, but necessarily, brute force. We use a table constructor to reconstruct our table by picking individual column values out of our base data table, R04_Table, and placing these values into the *correct* position for transposing the table. We do this by using a combination of the table constructor syntax coupled with the SELECTCOLUMNS and FILTER functions.

Since we begin with a two-row and three-column table in our base data table, R04_Table, the transpose of this table should result in a table with three rows and two columns. Thus, our table constructor for transposing R04_Table consists of three row sets. Each row set includes two columns, which are the values, and a third column, which we use for identification purposes. Technically, we would not need this additional third column (Row) unless we were to use the transposed table in further transformation or mathematical operations.

Each row set includes two SELECTCOLUMNS statements that form our first two columns, plus a hardcoded row identifier, that is, 1, 2, or 3. Within the first row set, for our first value, we use the FILTER function within the SELECTCOLUMNS function to filter down to only the row where the Index column equals 1. Then, we use SELECTCOLUMNS to get the value within the Column1 column. For our second value, we use the FILTER function within the SELECTCOLUMNS function to filter down to only the row where the Index column equals 2. Next, we use SELECTCOLUMNS to again get the value within the Column1 column. Our third value is hardcoded to 1.

The next two row sets repeat the same pattern as the first row set, except that we get Column2 values in the second row set and Column3 values in the third row set. In addition, our hardcoded row identifiers are 2 and X, respectively. Now, we can use a final SELECTCOLUMNS statement to return friendly names for columns from our table constructor.

See also

For more details regarding the functions that were used in this recipe, please refer to the following links:

- Table Constructor: `https://docs.microsoft.com/en-us/dax/table-constructor`
- SELECTCOLUMNS: `https://docs.microsoft.com/en-us/dax/selectcolumns-function-dax`
- FILTER: `https://docs.microsoft.com/en-us/dax/filter-function-dax`

Repeating counter with criteria

When it comes to data analysis, counting things is fundamental. DAX includes a default count aggregation, as well as the `COUNT`, `COUNTA`, `COUNTX`, and `COUNTAX` functions. However, there will be situations where you'll desire a counter that operates differently from normal count operations. In these circumstances, you'll wish to have more of an index that starts over when you're given specific criteria. A good example of this is consecutive wins. Your consecutive wins count increments by one for every game that you win. However, once you lose a game, your consecutive wins count starts over. Thus, you can imagine a dataset that holds a historical record of wins and losses. A counter that keeps track of consecutive wins but starts over once there is a loss would be necessary to determine the longest streak.

This recipe implements a counter that repeats or starts over when it's provided with specific criteria.

Getting ready

To prepare for this recipe, do the following:

1. Open Power BI Desktop.
2. Use an **Enter Data** query to create a table called `R05_Table` that contains the following data:

Animal	Index
Tiger	1
Tiger	2
Tiger	3

Tiger	4
Tiger	5
Lion	6
Lion	7
Lion	8
Tiger	9
Tiger	10
Elephant	11
Elephant	12
Elephant	13
Tiger	14
Tiger	15
Tiger	16

We wish to implement a counter that increments by one for each consecutive row in which there is the same Animal. However, when the Animal changes, we want the counter to start over.

How to do it...

To implement this recipe, do the following:

Create the following column in the R05_Table table:

```
Counter =
    VAR __Table =
        ADDCOLUMNS (
            FILTER (
                'R05_Table',
                'R05_Table'[Animal] = EARLIER('R05_Table'[Animal]) &&
                    'R05_Table'[Index] < EARLIER('R05_Table'[Index])
            ),
            "__diff",
            [Index] -
                MAXX (
                    FILTER (
                        ALL('R05_Table'),
                        'R05_Table'[Index]<EARLIER('R05_Table'[Index]) &&
'R05_Table'[Animal]=EARLIER('R05_Table'[Animal])
                    ),
                    [Index]
```

```
                    )
                )
        VAR __Max = MAXX(__Table,[Index])
        VAR __MaxStart =
            MAXX(
                FILTER(__Table,[__diff]>1),
                [Index]
            )
        VAR __Table2 = FILTER(__Table,[Index]>=__MaxStart)
    RETURN
        IF(
            ISBLANK(__Max),
            1,
            IF(
                __Max=[Index]-1,
                COUNTROWS(__Table2)+1,
                1
            )
        )
```

How it works...

For this recipe to work, you must have a unique index column for your dataset. We start by creating the table variable, __Table. This table variable uses the FILTER function to return all the rows in our base data table, R05_Table, that have the same group key column (Animal) value as the current row's value for the group key (Animal) column and have a value for the Index column that is less than our current row's value for the Index column. Then, we use ADDCOLUMNS to add the __diff column. The calculation for the __diff column determines the difference between the current row's value for the Index column and the maximum Index value for all the preceding rows with the same group key column (Animal) as the current row. We do this by essentially repeating the same table calculation that is used to create the __Table table variable and then using MAXX to find the maximum value within this table. The end result is that for rows where the group key column (Animal) is in sequence (one row in the same group right after another row in the same group), the value of __diff is 1. For rows that are not in sequence, the value of __diff will be greater than 1.

Now, we can calculate the overall maximum Index value within __Table using the MAXX function and store this in the __Max variable. Next, we calculate the __MaxStart variable. This variable holds the maximum value for the Index column after the latest *skip* between different values in the group key column (Animal). In order to account for these skips in the grouping, we figure out the maximum Index value of the latest skip (the row right after the skip where the group starts again). This Index value is the greatest value for the Index column where the difference from the previous rows' values for the Index column in the same group is greater than 1. Thus, we use FILTER to filter the rows in __Table where the __diff column is greater than 1 and then use MAXX to find the maximum value for the Index column within that filtered set. Then, we create a second table variable, __Table2, which uses FILTER to return only the rows in __Table where the value of the Index column is greater than the value of the Index for the last skip between groups, __MaxStart. Thus, __Table2 only contains rows after the latest skip in the group key column (Animal).

Now, we can return a value for our Counter. The first IF statement checks if the __Max variable is blank (ISBLANK). The __Max variable holds the maximum value for the Index column from __Table. __Table holds all the rows in the same group key column (Animal) that are in the same group and have an Index lower than the current row's Index. Thus, __Max will be blank at the first occurrence of a unique group value, in other words, at the start of the very first sequence for a group. In this situation, the correct value for our Counter is 1, that is, the start of a sequence for a group.

If we are not at the start of the first sequence for a group and __Max is not blank, then we perform a second check using an IF statement. In this case, we check if __Max is equal to the current row's value for Index, minus 1. If __Max is equal to the current row's value for Index, minus 1, then we know that this row is part of a sequence and that the value for Counter becomes the count of the rows in __Table2, plus 1. Recall that __Table2 holds all of the rows in the base data table, R05_Table, that have an Index less than the current row's Index and are after the latest skip between the current row's value for the group key column (Animal). If __Max is not equal to the current row's value for Index, minus 1, then we know that this row is the first row where the value in the group key column (Animal) has changed; that is, it's the start of another sequence. Thus, we assign the value of 1.

My sincere hope is that this explanation is clear. If the logic that's been employed to arrive at this solution makes your head hurt, do not fear. I originally called this solution *Cthulhu* because solving this riddle nearly drove me insane.

There's more...

The measure version of Counter is as follows:

```
Repeating Counter =
    VAR __Index = MAX('R05_Table'[Index])
    VAR __Group = MAX('R05_Table'[Animal])
    VAR __Table =
        ADDCOLUMNS(
            FILTER(
                ALL('R05_Table'),
                'R05_Table'[Animal] = __Group && 'R05_Table'[Index]<__Index
            ),
            "__diff",
            [Index] -
                MAXX(
                    FILTER(
                        ALL('R05_Table'),
                        'R05_Table'[Index] < EARLIER('R05_Table'[Index]) &&
                            'R05_Table'[Animal] =
EARLIER('R05_Table'[Animal])
                    ),
                    [Index]
                )
        )
    VAR __Max = MAXX(__Table,[Index])
    VAR __MaxStart =
        MAXX(
            FILTER(__Table,[__diff]>1),
            [Index]
        )
    VAR __Table2 = FILTER(__Table,[Index]>=__MaxStart)
RETURN
    IF(
        ISBLANK(__Max),
        1,
        IF(__Max=__Index-1,
            COUNTROWS(__Table2)+1,
            1
        )
    )
```

The DAX code for the Repeating Counter measure is extremely similar to the DAX code for the Counter column, but with only minor modifications.

See also

For more details regarding the functions that were used in this recipe, please refer to the following links:

- ADDCOLUMNS: https://docs.microsoft.com/en-us/dax/addcolumns-function-dax
- FILTER: https://docs.microsoft.com/en-us/dax/filter-function-dax
- ALL: https://docs.microsoft.com/en-us/dax/all-function-dax
- EARLIER: https://docs.microsoft.com/en-us/dax/earlier-function-dax
- MAXX: https://docs.microsoft.com/en-us/dax/maxx-function-dax
- COUNTROWS: https://docs.microsoft.com/en-us/dax/countrows-function-dax
- IF: https://docs.microsoft.com/en-us/dax/if-function-dax
- ISBLANK: https://docs.microsoft.com/en-us/dax/isblank-function-dax

Using across then down

Normally, when displaying a table of information and providing total rows and columns, the rows in the table total into a totals column and the columns in the table total into a totals row. Essentially, each row aggregates across the columns, while each column aggregates down the rows. However, there are certain analytical packages that include what is referred to as **across then down** and **down then across** aggregation.

In across then down aggregation, the first row aggregates normally across the columns of the table. However, in the second and subsequent rows, the total value from the previous row becomes the starting value for the first column in the next row. Similarly, in down then across aggregation, the first column aggregates normally down the rows of the table but, in the second and subsequent columns, the total value from the previous column becomes the starting value for the first row in the next column.

Power BI does not include any native functionality to perform across then down or down then across aggregation within a table. This recipe implements across then down and down then across aggregation within DAX using measures.

Getting ready

To prepare for this recipe, do the following:

1. Open Power BI Desktop.
2. Use an **Enter Data** query to create a table called `R06_Table` that contains the following data:

Col A	Col B	Value
A	a	5
A	b	6
B	a	-4
B	b	3
C	a	-9
C	b	0
C	c	14
D	d	5
E	e	5
F	f	5
G	g	5
H	h	5
I	i	5
J	j	5
K	k	5
L	l	5

How to do it...

To implement this recipe, do the following:

1. Create the following measure:

```
AcrossThenDown =
    VAR __Table = ALL('R06_Table')
    VAR __ColA = MAX('R06_Table'[Col A])
    VAR __ColB = MAX('R06_Table'[Col B])
    VAR __Count = COUNTX(FILTER(__Table,[Col A] < __ColA),[Col A])
+ 1
    VAR __PreviousRows =
```

```
            SUMX (
                 FILTER (__Table, [Col A] <__ColA),
                 [Value]
            )
        VAR __CurrentRow =
            SUMX (
                 FILTER (__Table, [Col A] =__ColA && [Col B] <=__ColB),
                 [Value]
            )
    RETURN
        IF (ISINSCOPE ('R06_Table' [Col A]),
            IF (__Count = 1,
                __CurrentRow,
                __PreviousRows + __CurrentRow
            ),
            IF (ISINSCOPE ('R06_Table' [Col B]),
                SUMX (
                     FILTER (__Table, [Col B] <= __ColB),
                     [Value]
                ),
                SUMX (__Table, [Value])
            )
        )
```

2. On a **Report** page, create a **Matrix** visualization.
3. In the **Matrix** visualization, place the Col A column from the R06_Table table into the **Rows** area of the visualization.
4. In the same **Matrix** visualization, place the Col B column from the R06_Table table into the **Columns** area of the visualization.
5. In the same **Matrix** visualization, place the AcrossThenDown measure into the **Values** area of the visualization.

How it works...

We start by creating the table variable, __Table, and setting the value for __Table equal to all (ALL) of the rows in our base data table, R06_Table. We use ALL here to remove the filter context from the matrix visualization. Next, we get the values of Col A and Col B within the current context and store these values in the __ColA and __ColB variables, respectively. Then, we calculate the __Count variable and set __Count equal to the number of rows in __Table that have a value for Col A that is less than our current row's value for Col A, __ColA, and add 1. We do this using COUNTX and FILTER.

If you're modifying this recipe so that it fits your own data, it is important to keep in mind that this recipe has been set up so that Col A is placed in the rows of the matrix and Col B is placed in the columns of the matrix.

Now, we create the __PreviousRows variable in order to store the sum of any rows that are prior to the current row. Previous rows are rows where the value of Col A is less than the current row's value for Col A, __ColA. We do this using SUMX and FILTER. Similarly, we create the __CurrentRow variable in order to store the sum of the current row. Since we are going across, the value for the current row is the sum of the rows in __Table where Col A equals the current value for Col A, __ColA, and the value for Col B is less than or equal to the current value for Col B, __ColB.

For our RETURN statement to assign the correct value for AcrossThenDown, we must determine if we are in the first row of the matrix, in a subsequent row of the matrix, or in a total row, a total column, or in the grand total cell (the intersection of our total row and total column). We do this by using ISINSCOPE to check if Col A is within the current scope. If Col A is within the current scope, then we know that we are not in a total row. Then, we check to see if our __Count variable is equal to 1. If __Count equals 1, then we know that we are in the first row of the matrix and thus return __CurrentRow. Otherwise, if __Count is not equal to 1, then we know that we are in a subsequent row of the matrix and return the sum of __PreviousRow and __CurrentRow. Conveniently, this math takes care of the total columns as well as all of the individual cells within the matrix.

Now, we must take care of the case where we are in a total row or the grand total cell. To determine if we are in a total row cell or a grand total cell, we use ISINSCOPE to check if Col B is within the current scope. If Col B is within the current scope, then we know that we are not in the grand total cell. If we are not in the grand total cell, then we want the cumulative column sums of all of the rows within the matrix. Thus, we use FILTER on __Table for all the values of Col B that are less than the current value for Col B, __ColB. Then, we use SUMX to sum the Value column of this filtered set. Finally, if Col B is not within the current scope, then we know that we are in the grand total cell and simply return the sum of the Value column in __Table using SUMX.

There's more...

You can also create a *down then across* measure. This operates the same as AcrossThenDown except that we sum down the first column first and then the first row in the second column gets the total from the first column and so on.

To implement down then across, create the following measure:

```
DownThenAcross =
    VAR __Table = ALL('R06_Table')
    VAR __ColA = MAX('R06_Table'[Col A])
    VAR __ColB = MAX('R06_Table'[Col B])
    VAR __Count = COUNTX(FILTER(__Table,[Col B] < __ColB),[Col B]) + 1
    VAR __PreviousColumns =
        SUMX(
            FILTER(__Table,[Col B]<__ColB),
            [Value]
        )
    VAR __CurrentColumn =
        SUMX(
            FILTER(__Table,[Col B]=__ColB && [Col A]<=__ColA),
            [Value]
        )
RETURN
    IF(ISINSCOPE('R06_Table'[Col B]),
        IF(__Count = 1,
            __CurrentColumn,
            __PreviousColumns + __CurrentColumn
        ),
        IF(ISINSCOPE('R06_Table'[Col A]),
            SUMX(
                FILTER(__Table,[Col A] <= __ColA),
                [Value]
            ),
            SUMX(__Table,[Value])
        )
    )
```

See also

For more details regarding the functions that were used in this recipe, please refer to the following links:

- ALL: https://docs.microsoft.com/en-us/dax/all-function-dax
- MAX: https://docs.microsoft.com/en-us/dax/max-function-dax
- COUNTX: https://docs.microsoft.com/en-us/dax/countx-function-dax
- SUMX: https://docs.microsoft.com/en-us/dax/sumx-function-dax
- FILTER: https://docs.microsoft.com/en-us/dax/filter-function-dax

- HASONEVALUE: https://docs.microsoft.com/en-us/dax/hasonevalue-function-dax
- SUM: https://docs.microsoft.com/en-us/dax/sum-function-dax
- IF: https://docs.microsoft.com/en-us/dax/if-function-dax

Using matrix multiplication

Multiplying matrices or tables is a fairly common mathematical operation, particularly in the field of matrix algebra. There are certain statistical calculations, such as Krippendorff's Alpha, that require matrix multiplication. Excel has a handy function called MMULT that performs matrix multiplication in a single function. Unfortunately, DAX has no equivalent MMULT function.

This recipe demonstrates how to perform matrix multiplication using DAX.

Getting ready

To prepare for this recipe, do the following:

1. Open Power BI Desktop.
2. Use an **Enter Data** query to create a table called R07_Table3x4 that contains the following data:

Column1	Column2	Column3	Column4	Index
-4	1	4	-2	1
-3	-1	2	5	2
3	0	6	7	3

3. Use an **Enter Data** query to create a second table called R07_Table4x2 that contains the following data:

Column1	Column2	Index
8	1	1
9	10	2
11	3	3
-1	0	4

How to do it...

To implement this recipe, do the following:

1. Create the following table, that is, `R07_Table`:

```
R07_Table =
    VAR __Table1 = 'R07_Table3x4'
    VAR __Table2 = 'R07_Table4x2'
    VAR __Table2a =
        SELECTCOLUMNS (
            {
                (
SELECTCOLUMNS (FILTER (__Table2, [Index]=1), "Row", [Column1]),
SELECTCOLUMNS (FILTER (__Table2, [Index]=2), "Row", [Column1]),
SELECTCOLUMNS (FILTER (__Table2, [Index]=3), "Row", [Column1]),
SELECTCOLUMNS (FILTER (__Table2, [Index]=4), "Row", [Column1]),
                    "1"
                ),
                (
SELECTCOLUMNS (FILTER (__Table2, [Index]=1), "Row", [Column2]),
SELECTCOLUMNS (FILTER (__Table2, [Index]=2), "Row", [Column2]),
SELECTCOLUMNS (FILTER (__Table2, [Index]=3), "Row", [Column2]),
SELECTCOLUMNS (FILTER (__Table2, [Index]=4), "Row", [Column2]),
                    "2"
                )
            },
            "Row", [Value5],
            "1", [Value1],
            "2", [Value2],
            "3", [Value3],
            "4", [Value4]
        )
    VAR __Table3 =
        ADDCOLUMNS (
            GENERATE (
                SELECTCOLUMNS (
                    __Table1,
                    "Row", [Index],
                    "Column1", [Column1],
                    "Column2", [Column2],
                    "Column3", [Column3],
                    "Column4", [Column4]),
                SELECTCOLUMNS (
                    __Table2a,
                    "Column", [Row],
                    "1", [1],
                    "2", [2],
```

```
                            "3",[3],
                            "4",[4])
                ),
                "Value",[Column1]*[1] + [Column2]*[2] + [Column3]*[3] +
[Column4]*[4]
            )
    VAR __Table3a =
        SELECTCOLUMNS(
            {
                (
                    SELECTCOLUMNS(FILTER(__Table3,[Row]=1 &&
[Column]="1"),"Value",[Value]),
                    SELECTCOLUMNS(FILTER(__Table3,[Row]=1 &&
[Column]="2"),"Value",[Value]),
                    1
                ),
                (
                    SELECTCOLUMNS(FILTER(__Table3,[Row]=2 &&
[Column]="1"),"Value",[Value]),
                    SELECTCOLUMNS(FILTER(__Table3,[Row]=2 &&
[Column]="2"),"Value",[Value]),
                    2
                ),
                (
                    SELECTCOLUMNS(FILTER(__Table3,[Row]=3 &&
[Column]="1"),"Value",[Value]),
                    SELECTCOLUMNS(FILTER(__Table3,[Row]=3 &&
[Column]="2"),"Value",[Value]),
                    3
                )
            },
            "Row",[Value3],
            "1",[Value1],
            "2",[Value2]
        )
RETURN
    __Table3a
```

How it works...

We start by setting the __Table1 and __Table2 variables so that they're equal to our base data tables of R07_Table3x4 and R07_Table4x2, respectively.

To understand what comes next, we must understand a bit about matrix algebra. When multiplying two matrices, we multiply the elements of each row of the first matrix by the elements of each column in the second matrix. We could brute force our way to victory here, but we also know from matrix algebra that the transpose of a matrix is equivalent to the original matrix. Thus, if we transpose our second matrix, we can generate a Cartesian product of the two matrices and make the mathematical work much simpler and less brute force.

We transpose our second matrix in the __Table2a table. The technique here is unfortunately, but necessarily, brute force. We use a table constructor to reconstruct our table by picking individual column values out of our second table, __Table2, and placing these values into the correct position for transposing the table. We do this by using a combination of the table constructor syntax coupled with the SELECTCOLUMNS and FILTER functions.

Since we begin with four rows and two columns in __Table2, the transpose of this table should result in a table with two rows and four columns. Thus, our table constructor for transposing __Table2 consists of two row sets. Each row set includes four columns, which are the values, and a fifth column that we use for identification purposes.

Each row set includes four SELECTCOLUMNS statements that form our first four columns, plus a hardcoded row identifier, 1, 2. Within the first row set, for our first value, we use the FILTER function within the SELECTCOLUMNS function to filter down to only the row where the Index column equals 1. Then, we use SELECTCOLUMNS to get the value within the Column1 column. For our second value, we use the FILTER function within the SELECTCOLUMNS function to filter down to only the row where the Index column equals 2. Then, we use SELECTCOLUMNS to again get the value within the Column1 column. Our values for the third and fourth columns follow the same pattern. Our fifth value is hardcoded to 1.

The next row set repeats the same pattern as the first row set, except that we get `Column2` values in the second row set. In addition, our hardcoded row identifier is 2. Now, we can use a final `SELECTCOLUMNS` statement to return friendly names for the columns from our table constructor.

Now that we have transposed the second table, we can implement our Cartesian product using `GENERATE`. This is done in `__Table3`. We use `SELECTCOLUMNS` to select the various columns within our `__Table1` table and our transposed `__Table2` table, `__Table2a`. We use `GENERATE` to create our Cartesian product. Then, we use `ADDCOLUMNS` to add the `Value` column. The calculation for `Value` implements our matrix multiplication by multiplying the correct elements together and adding the products together. This part is made far easier because we used our transposed table, `__Table2a`, when generating our Cartesian product. For each row in our Cartesian product, we simply need to multiply the corresponding columns from the two tables that generated the Cartesian product.

Since we transposed our second table, we must now transpose `__Table3`. This is done in `__Table3a` using the same transposing technique we used previously. `__Table3a` is now our final table and thus we simply return `__Table3a` as the output of our table calculation.

See also

For more details regarding the functions that were used in this recipe, please refer to the following links:

- Table Constructor: https://docs.microsoft.com/en-us/dax/table-constructor
- SELECTCOLUMNS: https://docs.microsoft.com/en-us/dax/selectcolumns-function-dax
- FILTER: https://docs.microsoft.com/en-us/dax/filter-function-dax
- ADDCOLUMNS: https://docs.microsoft.com/en-us/dax/addcolumns-function-dax
- GENERATE: https://docs.microsoft.com/en-us/dax/generate-function-dax

Forecasting with a de-seasonalized correlation coefficient

Calculating correlation coefficients is a method of determining whether or not two sets of data are related to one another. In addition, correlation coefficients can tell you whether the datasets are positively or negatively (inversely) related. Positive relationships exist when the values in the data change in the same direction, either going down or up at the same time. Inverse relationships exist when values in the datasets go up and down contrary to one another. Both positively and inversely related datasets can be useful forecasting indicators as long as the correlation coefficient between the two datasets is strong. If we know that two datasets are related, then we can potentially use the known values in one dataset to estimate the unknown values in the other dataset.

A typical formula for calculating a correlation coefficient is Pearson's Correlation Coefficient, which returns a value between -1 and 1. Values closer to -1 and 1 are deemed to indicate a strong correlation (not causation!), while values closer to zero indicate a weak or no correlation. Negative values indicate an inverse relationship, while positive values indicate a positive relationship. Pearson's Correlation Coefficient is given by the following formula:

$$r = \frac{n \sum_i^n x_i y_i - \sum_i^n x \sum_i^n y}{\sqrt{\left[n \sum_i^n x_i^2 - \left(\sum_i^n x_i\right)^2\right]\left[n \sum_i^n y_i^2 - \left(\sum_i^n y_i\right)^2\right]}}$$

Here, n represents the count of dataset pairs, x represents one set of data points, and y represents the corresponding set of data points. r is the correlation coefficient.

However, when comparing two sets of data, you must be aware that one or both of the sets of data may exhibit what is called seasonality. In short, seasonality refers to regular, predictable patterns that occur within time series data. These patterns occur on a frequency that is less than a year, such as monthly or quarterly. There are many factors that might cause these patterns, such as vacations, holidays, and so on. The classic example of seasonality is retail sales in the United States, which predictably spike (peak) between Thanksgiving and Christmas. The problem with seasonality and calculating correlation coefficients is that, unless both sets of data exhibit the same seasonality, the calculation of the correlation coefficient will turn out to be weaker than it actually is. Thus, if you're dealing with time series data that exhibits seasonality, it is imperative that you de-seasonalize the data prior to calculating the correlation coefficient.

Years ago, I wrote one of the first – if not the first – implementations of using DAX to de-seasonalize data in order to calculate a correlation coefficient and forecast a future value. The article I wrote appeared on the venerable TechNet. Being fairly new to DAX, the process was very column-centric. Years later, Power BI community member Daniil published an excellent DAX correlation coefficient calculation as a measure. However, Daniil's formula did not include de-seasonalization. Microsoft then created, in my opinion, a deficient, Power BI Quick Measure based on Daniil's formula that is now included in Power BI Desktop. Somehow, the whole forecasting aspect of the correlation coefficient was lost over the years. But what good is having a correlation coefficient if you cannot forecast values with it? This recipe attempts to combine the entire history of calculating correlation coefficients in DAX and demonstrate how to de-seasonalize data before calculating a correlation coefficient and then, most importantly, forecasting future values.

Getting ready

To prepare for this recipe, do the following:

1. Open Power BI Desktop.
2. Use an **Enter Data** query to create a table called `R08_Sales` that contains the following data:

Quarter	Year	Sales
1	2013	47
2	2013	49
3	2013	53
4	2013	44
1	2014	43
2	2014	55
3	2014	58
4	2014	48
1	2015	44
2	2015	43
3	2015	58
4	2015	49

3. Use an **Enter Data** query to create a second table called `R08_Wages` that contains the following data:

Quarter	Year	Wages
4	2012	19.25
1	2013	18.5
2	2013	17.75
3	2013	17.7
4	2013	18
1	2014	20
2	2014	18.75
3	2014	18.7
4	2014	18.25
1	2015	17
2	2015	18.75
3	2015	19
4	2015	20.25
1	2016	19

4. Use an **Enter Data** query to create a third table called `R08_Estimates` that contains the following data:

Quarter	Year
1	2013
2	2013
3	2013
4	2013
1	2014
2	2014
3	2014
4	2014
1	2015
2	2015
3	2015
4	2015

1	2016
2	2016

5. Create the following column in the R08_Sales table:

```
YearQuarter = 'R08_Sales'[Year] & 'R08_Sales'[Quarter]
```

6. Create the following columns in the R08_Wages table:

```
YearQuarter = 'R08_Wages'[Year] & 'R08_Wages'[Quarter]

YearQuarterFuture =
    IF('R08_Wages'[Quarter] = 4,
        'R08_Wages'[Year]+1 & "1",
        'R08_Wages'[Year] & 'R08_Wages'[Quarter]+1
    )
```

7. Create the following columns in the R08_Estimates table:

```
YearQuarter = 'R08_Estimates'[Year] & 'R08_Estimates'[Quarter]

YearQuarterPrevious =
    IF (
        'R08_Estimates'[Quarter] = 1,
        'R08_Estimates'[Year]-1 & "4",
        'R08_Estimates'[Year] & 'R08_Estimates'[Quarter]-1
    )

YearQuarter2Previous =
    SWITCH(TRUE(),
        'R08_Estimates'[Quarter] = 1,'R08_Estimates'[Year]-1 & "3",
        'R08_Estimates'[Quarter] = 2,'R08_Estimates'[Year]-1 & "4",
        'R08_Estimates'[Year] & 'R08_Estimates'[Quarter]-2
    )
```

8. Create a relationship between the YearQuarter column in the R08_Sales table and the YearQuarterFuture column in the R08_Wages table. The relationship should be 1:1 and have a Cross filter direction of Both. Ensure that there are no relationships between the R08_Sales table and any other table. Ensure that there are no relationships between the R08_Wages table and any other table.

9. Ensure that there are no relationships between the R08_Estimates table and any other table.

10. Create the following measure:

```
Power BI's Correlation =
VAR __CORRELATION_TABLE = VALUES('R08_Sales'[YearQuarter])
VAR __COUNT =
 COUNTX(
  KEEPFILTERS(__CORRELATION_TABLE),
  CALCULATE(SUM('R08_Sales'[Sales]) * SUM('R08_Wages'[Wages]))
 )
VAR __SUM_X =
 SUMX(
  KEEPFILTERS(__CORRELATION_TABLE),
  CALCULATE(SUM('R08_Sales'[Sales]))
 )
VAR __SUM_Y =
 SUMX(
  KEEPFILTERS(__CORRELATION_TABLE),
  CALCULATE(SUM('R08_Wages'[Wages]))
 )
VAR __SUM_XY =
 SUMX(
  KEEPFILTERS(__CORRELATION_TABLE),
  CALCULATE(SUM('R08_Sales'[Sales]) * SUM('R08_Wages'[Wages]) * 1.)
 )
VAR __SUM_X2 =
 SUMX(
  KEEPFILTERS(__CORRELATION_TABLE),
  CALCULATE(SUM('R08_Sales'[Sales]) ^ 2)
 )
VAR __SUM_Y2 =
 SUMX(
  KEEPFILTERS(__CORRELATION_TABLE),
  CALCULATE(SUM('R08_Wages'[Wages]) ^ 2)
 )
RETURN
 DIVIDE(
  __COUNT * __SUM_XY - __SUM_X * __SUM_Y * 1.,
  SQRT(
   (__COUNT * __SUM_X2 - __SUM_X ^ 2)
    * (__COUNT * __SUM_Y2 - __SUM_Y ^ 2)
  )
 )
```

11. Create the following additional measure:

```
Daniil's Correlation Coefficient =
    VAR Correlation_Table =
        FILTER (
```

```
ADDCOLUMNS (
    VALUES ( 'R08_Sales'[YearQuarter]),
    "Value_X", CALCULATE ( SUM('R08_Sales'[Sales]) ),
    "Value_Y", CALCULATE ( SUM('R08_Wages'[Wages]) )
),
AND (
    NOT ( ISBLANK ( [Value_X] ) ),
    NOT ( ISBLANK ( [Value_Y] ) )
)
)
VAR Count_Items = COUNTROWS ( Correlation_Table )
VAR Sum_X = SUMX ( Correlation_Table, [Value_X] )
VAR Sum_X2 = SUMX ( Correlation_Table, [Value_X] ^ 2 )
VAR Sum_Y = SUMX ( Correlation_Table, [Value_Y] )
VAR Sum_Y2 = SUMX ( Correlation_Table, [Value_Y] ^ 2 )
VAR Sum_XY = SUMX ( Correlation_Table, [Value_X] * [Value_Y] )
VAR Pearson_Numerator = Count_Items * Sum_XY - Sum_X * Sum_Y
VAR Pearson_Denominator_X = Count_Items * Sum_X2 - Sum_X ^ 2
VAR Pearson_Denominator_Y = Count_Items * Sum_Y2 - Sum_Y ^ 2
VAR Pearson_Denominator = SQRT ( Pearson_Denominator_X *
Pearson_Denominator_Y )
RETURN
    DIVIDE ( Pearson_Numerator, Pearson_Denominator )
```

12. On a **Report** page, create a **Card** visualization and place the `Power BI's Correlation` measure into the **Fields** area of the visualization. Notice that the visualization is broken or provides a nonsensical number that's not between -1 and 1.

13. On the same **Report** page, create a second **Card** visualization and place the `Daniil's Correlation Coefficient` measure into the **Fields** area of the visualization. You should get a result of about **.54** (**.5362**). If you get a value of **1**, make sure that you have the measure set to the data type of a `Decimal` number and not a `Whole` number.

Here, we can see the issue with Power BI's built-in implementation of Pearson's Correlation Coefficient (`Power BI's Correlation`): it does not handle correlations between unbalanced tables (tables with different numbers of rows). Also, we can see that by using Daniil's implementation of Pearson's Correlation Coefficient (`Daniil's Correlation Coefficient`), the relationship between the `Sales` column in the `R08_Sales` table and the `Wages` column in the `R08_Wages` table does not appear to be very strong (.54).

The data and its setup presents a scenario. The scenario is that a retail business believes that the real, hourly average wage (represented by the `R08_Wages` table) is a 3-month leading indicator for their sales (represented by the `R08_Sales` table). A 3-month leading indicator means that when wages go up, the businesses' sales go up 3 months later. The business wishes to test if there is a correlation between real, hourly average wages and their sales. Furthermore, the business wishes to use this correlation, if it exists, to forecast sales for one quarter in the future.

Because we believe that wages are a 3-month leading indicator for sales, we linked the `YearQuarter` column in the `R08_Sales` table with the `YearQuarterFuture` column in the `R08_Wages` table. This relationship effectively means that we are comparing a particular quarter's sales with the previous quarter's wages.

How to do it...

To implement this recipe, do the following:

1. Create the following measure:

```
DeSeasonal Correlation Coefficient =
    VAR __SeasonalTable =
        FILTER (
            ADDCOLUMNS (
                SELECTCOLUMNS (
                    ALL ('R08_Sales'),
                    "YearQuarter", 'R08_Sales'[YearQuarter],
                    "Quarter", 'R08_Sales'[Quarter],
                    "X", 'R08_Sales'[Sales]
                ),
        "Y", SUMX (RELATEDTABLE ('R08_Wages'), 'R08_Wages'[Wages])
            ),
            NOT (ISBLANK ([YearQuarter]))
        )
    VAR __SeasonQ1Avg =
AVERAGEX (FILTER (__SeasonalTable, [Quarter]=1), [X])
    VAR __SeasonQ2Avg =
AVERAGEX (FILTER (__SeasonalTable, [Quarter]=2), [X])
    VAR __SeasonQ3Avg =
AVERAGEX (FILTER (__SeasonalTable, [Quarter]=3), [X])
    VAR __SeasonQ4Avg =
AVERAGEX (FILTER (__SeasonalTable, [Quarter]=4), [X])
    VAR __SeasonAverage = AVERAGEX (__SeasonalTable, [X])
    VAR __SeasonQ1SI = __SeasonQ1Avg/__SeasonAverage
    VAR __SeasonQ2SI = __SeasonQ2Avg/__SeasonAverage
```

```
VAR __SeasonQ3SI = __SeasonQ3Avg/__SeasonAverage
VAR __SeasonQ4SI = __SeasonQ4Avg/__SeasonAverage
VAR __CorrelationTable =
        ADDCOLUMNS (
            __SeasonalTable,
            "Deseasonal_X",
            SWITCH([Quarter],
                1,[X]/__SeasonQ1SI,
                2,[X]/__SeasonQ2SI,
                3,[X]/__SeasonQ3SI,
                4,[X]/__SeasonQ4SI
            )
        )
VAR __Count = COUNTROWS ( __CorrelationTable )
VAR __SumX = SUMX ( __CorrelationTable, [Deseasonal_X] )
VAR __SumX2 = SUMX ( __CorrelationTable, [Deseasonal_X] ^ 2 )
VAR __SumY = SUMX ( __CorrelationTable, [Y] )
VAR __SumY2 = SUMX ( __CorrelationTable, [Y] ^ 2 )
VAR __SumXY = SUMX ( __CorrelationTable, [Deseasonal_X] * [Y] )
VAR __r =
    DIVIDE (
        __Count * __SumXY - __SumX * __SumY * 1.,
        SQRT (
            (__Count * __SumX2 - __SumX ^ 2)
                * (__Count * __SumY2 - __SumY ^ 2)
        )
    )
RETURN
    __r
```

2. Create the following additional measure:

```
DeSeasonal Sales =
    VAR __YearQuarter =
MAXX(RELATEDTABLE('R08_Sales'),'R08_Sales'[YearQuarter])
    VAR __SeasonalTable =
        FILTER (
            ADDCOLUMNS (
                SELECTCOLUMNS (
                    ALL('R08_Sales'),
                    "YearQuarter",'R08_Sales'[YearQuarter],
                    "Quarter",'R08_Sales'[Quarter],
                    "X",'R08_Sales'[Sales]),
    "Y",SUMX(RELATEDTABLE('R08_Wages'),'R08_Wages'[Wages]
                )
            ),
            NOT(ISBLANK([YearQuarter]))
        )
```

```
        VAR __SeasonQ1Avg =
AVERAGEX(FILTER(__SeasonalTable,[Quarter]=1),[X])
        VAR __SeasonQ2Avg =
AVERAGEX(FILTER(__SeasonalTable,[Quarter]=2),[X])
        VAR __SeasonQ3Avg =
AVERAGEX(FILTER(__SeasonalTable,[Quarter]=3),[X])
        VAR __SeasonQ4Avg =
AVERAGEX(FILTER(__SeasonalTable,[Quarter]=4),[X])
        VAR __SeasonAverage = AVERAGEX(__SeasonalTable,[X])
        VAR __SeasonQ1SI = __SeasonQ1Avg/__SeasonAverage
        VAR __SeasonQ2SI = __SeasonQ2Avg/__SeasonAverage
        VAR __SeasonQ3SI = __SeasonQ3Avg/__SeasonAverage
        VAR __SeasonQ4SI = __SeasonQ4Avg/__SeasonAverage
        VAR __CorrelationTable =
            ADDCOLUMNS(
                __SeasonalTable,
                "Deseasonal_X",
                SWITCH([Quarter],
                    1,[X]/__SeasonQ1SI,
                    2,[X]/__SeasonQ2SI,
                    3,[X]/__SeasonQ3SI,
                    4,[X]/__SeasonQ4SI
                )
            )
RETURN
    MAXX(FILTER(__CorrelationTable,[YearQuarter] =
__YearQuarter),[Deseasonal_X])
```

3. On the same **Report** page we used previously, create a **Card** visualization and place the `DeSeasonal Correlation Coefficient` measure in the **Fields** area of the visualization.

4. On the same **Report** page, create a **Line chart** visualization and place the `YearQuarter` column from the `R08_Sales` table into the **Axis** area of the visualization.

5. In the same **Line chart** visualization, place the `Sales` column from the `R08_Sales` table, the `Wages` column from the `R08_Wages` table, and the `DeSeasonal Sales` measure into the **Values** area of the visualization.

6. Sort the **Line chart** visualization ascending by `YearQuarter`.

Your `DeSeasonal Correlation Coefficient` in the **Card** visual should be **1.00**, that is, a perfect correlation. In addition, you should be able to visually see the correlation in the **Line chart** visualization. When `Wages` go up, so do `DeSeasonal Sales`. When `Wages` go down, so do `DeSeasonal Sales`.

How it works...

To calculate the `DeSeasonal Correlation Coefficient` measure, we start by creating the table variable, `__SeasonalTable`. This is the table that we will use to compute our seasonality. We get `ALL` of the rows in the `R08_Sales` table using `SELECTCOLUMNS` to rename our `Sales` column `X`. Then, we use `ADDCOLUMNS` to add our `Y` column, which is the sum of all the related rows in `R08_Wages`. Finally, we use `FILTER` to filter out any rows where `YearQuarter` is blank. This accounts for having more unbalanced tables.

Now, we start accounting for seasonality. We do this by computing the average of sales for each quarter (`__SeasonQ1Avg`, `__SeasonQ2Avg`, `__SeasonQ3Avg`, and `__SeasonQ4Avg`), as well as the overall average (`__SeasonAverage`). Then, we divide each quarter's average by `__SeasonAverage` and store these values in the seasonal index variables, that is, `__SeasonQ1SI`, `__SeasonQ2SI`, `__SeasonQ3SI`, and `__SeasonQ4SI`.

Now, we can calculate `__CorrelationTable` by adding the `Deseasonal_X` column to `__SeasonalTable` using `ADDCOLUMNS`. The calculation for the `Deseasonal_X` column simply checks the value of the `Quarter` column for each row and, depending on the value of the `Quarter` column, it divides the `X` column by either `__SeasonQ1SI`, `__SeasonQ2SI`, `__SeasonQ3SI`, or `__SeasonQ4SI`. The `Deseasonal_X` column now contains the de-seasonalized values for our sales.

Now, we can calculate the parts of `Pearson's Correlation Coefficient`, `__Count`, `__SumX`, `__SumX2`, `__SumY`, `__SumY2`, and `__SumXY`. However, when computing our values for `__SumX`, `__SumX2`, and `__SumXY`, instead of using our `X` column, we substitute our `Deseasonal_X` column. By doing this, we can simply plug `__Count`, `__SumX`, `__SumX2`, `__SumY`, `__SumY2`, and `__SumXY` into the formula for `Pearson's Correlation Coefficient` to compute `__r` and then return `__r` as the value for our measure, that is, `DeSeasonal Correlation Coefficient`.

The calculation for the `DeSeasonal Sales` measure is nearly identical to the one for the `DeSeasonal Correlation Coefficient` measure, except we return our `Deseasonal_X` values. This measure is present simply for display purposes within the **Line chart** visualization.

There's more...

Now, we know that there is a strong correlation between Wages and Sales when Wages is viewed as a 3-month leading indicator and we deseasonalize the sales data. Our next task is to determine how to estimate future quarter sales and regression test our estimation formula. To accomplish this, do the following:

1. Create the following measures:

```
Sales4Est =
    VAR __YearQuarter = MAX('R08_Estimates'[YearQuarter])
RETURN
SUMX(FILTER('R08_Sales','R08_Sales'[YearQuarter]=__YearQuarter),'R0
8_Sales'[Sales])

Slope =
    VAR __YearQuarter = MAX('R08_Sales'[YearQuarter])
    VAR __SeasonalTable =
        FILTER(
            ADDCOLUMNS(
                SELECTCOLUMNS(
                    ALL('R08_Sales'),
                    "YearQuarter",'R08_Sales'[YearQuarter],
                    "Quarter",'R08_Sales'[Quarter],
                    "X",'R08_Sales'[Sales]),
"Y",SUMX(RELATEDTABLE('R08_Wages'),'R08_Wages'[Wages]
                    )
                ),
                NOT(ISBLANK([YearQuarter]))
        )
    VAR __SeasonQ1Avg =
AVERAGEX(FILTER(__SeasonalTable,[Quarter]=1),[X])
    VAR __SeasonQ2Avg =
AVERAGEX(FILTER(__SeasonalTable,[Quarter]=2),[X])
    VAR __SeasonQ3Avg =
AVERAGEX(FILTER(__SeasonalTable,[Quarter]=3),[X])
    VAR __SeasonQ4Avg =
AVERAGEX(FILTER(__SeasonalTable,[Quarter]=4),[X])
    VAR __SeasonAverage = AVERAGEX(__SeasonalTable,[X])
    VAR __SeasonQ1SI = __SeasonQ1Avg/__SeasonAverage
    VAR __SeasonQ2SI = __SeasonQ2Avg/__SeasonAverage
    VAR __SeasonQ3SI = __SeasonQ3Avg/__SeasonAverage
    VAR __SeasonQ4SI = __SeasonQ4Avg/__SeasonAverage
    VAR __CorrelationTable =
        ADDCOLUMNS(
            __SeasonalTable,
            "Deseasonal_X",
```

```
                              SWITCH([Quarter],
                                  1,[X]/__SeasonQ1SI,
                                  2,[X]/__SeasonQ2SI,
                                  3,[X]/__SeasonQ3SI,
                                  4,[X]/__SeasonQ4SI
                              )
                          )
            VAR __Count = COUNTROWS ( __CorrelationTable )
            VAR __SumX = SUMX ( __CorrelationTable, [Deseasonal_X] )
            VAR __SumX2 = SUMX ( __CorrelationTable, [Deseasonal_X] ^ 2 )
            VAR __SumY = SUMX ( __CorrelationTable, [Y] )
            VAR __SumY2 = SUMX ( __CorrelationTable, [Y] ^ 2 )
            VAR __SumXY = SUMX ( __CorrelationTable, [Deseasonal_X] * [Y] )
            VAR __Slope =
                DIVIDE (
                    __Count * __SumXY - __SumX * __SumY * 1.,
                        __Count * __SumX2 - __SumX ^ 2
                )
    RETURN
        __Slope
```

2. Create the following additional measure:

```
SalesEstimate =
    VAR __SeasonalTable =
        FILTER (
            ADDCOLUMNS (
                SELECTCOLUMNS (
                    ALL('R08_Sales'),
                    "YearQuarter",'R08_Sales'[YearQuarter],
                    "Quarter",'R08_Sales'[Quarter],
                    "X",'R08_Sales'[Sales]),
    "Y",SUMX(RELATEDTABLE('R08_Wages'),'R08_Wages'[Wages]
                )
            ),
            NOT(ISBLANK([YearQuarter]))
        )
    VAR __SeasonQ1Avg =
AVERAGEX(FILTER(__SeasonalTable,[Quarter]=1),[X])
    VAR __SeasonQ2Avg =
AVERAGEX(FILTER(__SeasonalTable,[Quarter]=2),[X])
    VAR __SeasonQ3Avg =
AVERAGEX(FILTER(__SeasonalTable,[Quarter]=3),[X])
    VAR __SeasonQ4Avg =
AVERAGEX(FILTER(__SeasonalTable,[Quarter]=4),[X])
    VAR __SeasonAverage = AVERAGEX(__SeasonalTable,[X])
    VAR __SeasonQ1SI = __SeasonQ1Avg/__SeasonAverage
    VAR __SeasonQ2SI = __SeasonQ2Avg/__SeasonAverage
```

```
    VAR __SeasonQ3SI = __SeasonQ3Avg/__SeasonAverage
    VAR __SeasonQ4SI = __SeasonQ4Avg/__SeasonAverage

    VAR __Quarter = MAX('R08_Estimates'[Quarter])
    VAR __YearQuarter = MAX('R08_Estimates'[YearQuarter])
    VAR __PreviousQuarter =
MAX('R08_Estimates'[YearQuarterPrevious])
    VAR __Previous2Quarter =
MAX('R08_Estimates'[YearQuarter2Previous])
    VAR __PreviousWages =
        MAXX(
            FILTER(
                'R08_Wages',
                'R08_Wages'[YearQuarter]=__PreviousQuarter
            ),
            'R08_Wages'[Wages]
        )
    VAR __2PreviousWages =
        MAXX(
            FILTER(
                'R08_Wages',
                'R08_Wages'[YearQuarter]=__Previous2Quarter
            ),
            'R08_Wages'[Wages]
        )
    VAR __PreviousSales =
        MAXX(
            FILTER(
                'R08_Sales',
                'R08_Sales'[YearQuarter]=__PreviousQuarter),
                'R08_Sales'[Sales]
        )
    VAR __X = ( (__PreviousWages - __2PreviousWages) / [Slope]) +
__PreviousSales
RETURN
    SWITCH(TRUE(),
        ISBLANK(__PreviousWages),BLANK(),
        ISBLANK(__2PreviousWages),BLANK(),
        ISBLANK(__PreviousSales),BLANK(),
        __Quarter = 1,__X * __SeasonQ1SI,
        __Quarter = 2,__X * __SeasonQ2SI,
        __Quarter = 3,__X * __SeasonQ3SI,
        __X * __SeasonQ4SI
    )
```

3. On the same **Report** page we used previously, create a second **Line chart** visualization and place the `YearQuarter` column from the `R08_Estimates` table into the **Axis** area of the visualization.

4. In the same **Line chart** visualization, place the `Sales4Est` and `SalesEstimate` measures into the **Values** area of the visualization.

5. Sort the **Line chart** visualization ascending by `YearQuarter`.

Here, we can see that our `SalesEstimate` tracks fairly closely with our actual sales (`Sales4Est`) and that, on the right-hand side of our second **Line chart** visual, we can see our estimate for quarter 1 of 2016 (`20161`).

The `Sales4Est` measure simply gets the value for `Sales` in `R08_Sales` for the given `YearQuarter` from `R08_Estimates`.

The `Slope` measure is largely identical to the `Deseasonal Correlation Coefficient` measure, except that instead of calculating the correlation coefficient, we calculate the slope of the correlation line. The slope of the line is given by the following formula:

$$m = \frac{n \sum_{i}^{n} x_i y_i - \sum_{i}^{n} x \sum_{i}^{n} y}{n \sum_{i}^{n} x_i^2 - \left(\sum_{i}^{n} x_i \right)^2}$$

Finally, `SalesEstimate` is again largely identical to the `Deseasonal Correlation Coefficient` measure, except that instead of calculating the correlation coefficient, we use the slope to solve the estimated current value of sales (`__X`) using the standard line slope formula:

$$m = \frac{y_2 - y_1}{x_2 - x_1}$$

Since we know the slope of the line (*m* in the formulas), we can simply solve the slope formula for *m* and then plug in our `Slope` value for *m*, the previous quarter's wages for y_2 (`__PreviousWages`), the wages two previous quarters ago for y_1 (`__2PreviousWages`), and the previous quarter's sales for x_1 (`__PreviousSales`). However, since we deseasonalized the data when computing our correlation, we must now re-seasonalize our estimate. We do this by checking the current quarter and then multiplying by either `__SeasonQ1SI`, `__SeasonQ2SI`, `__SeasonQ3SI`, or `__SeasonQ4SI` as appropriate.

See also

For more details regarding the functions that were used in this recipe, please refer to the following links:

- Daniil's correlation coefficient: https://community.powerbi.com/t5/Quick-Measures-Gallery/Correlation-coefficient/m-p/196274
- Pearson's correlation coefficient: https://en.wikipedia.org/wiki/Pearson_correlation_coefficient
- SELECTCOLUMNS: https://docs.microsoft.com/en-us/dax/selectcolumns-function-dax
- FILTER: https://docs.microsoft.com/en-us/dax/filter-function-dax
- ADDCOLUMNS: https://docs.microsoft.com/en-us/dax/addcolumns-function-dax
- ALL: https://docs.microsoft.com/en-us/dax/all-function-dax
- RELATEDTABLE: https://docs.microsoft.com/en-us/dax/relatedtable-function-dax
- SUMX: https://docs.microsoft.com/en-us/dax/sumx-function-dax
- NOT: https://docs.microsoft.com/en-us/dax/not-function-dax
- ISBLANK: https://docs.microsoft.com/en-us/dax/isblank-function-dax
- BLANK: https://docs.microsoft.com/en-us/dax/blank-function-dax
- AVERAGEX: https://docs.microsoft.com/en-us/dax/averagex-function-dax
- SWITCH: https://docs.microsoft.com/en-us/dax/switch-function-dax
- COUNTROWS: https://docs.microsoft.com/en-us/dax/countrows-function-dax
- DIVIDE: https://docs.microsoft.com/en-us/dax/divide-function-dax
- SQRT: https://docs.microsoft.com/en-us/dax/sqrt-function-dax
- KEEPFILTERS: https://docs.microsoft.com/en-us/dax/keepfilters-function-dax
- CALCULATE: https://docs.microsoft.com/en-us/dax/calculate-function-dax
- MAX: https://docs.microsoft.com/en-us/dax/max-function-dax
- MAXX: https://docs.microsoft.com/en-us/dax/maxx-function-dax

Creating an SVG graphic

Power BI supports SVG. SVG is an open standard created by the **World Wide Web Consortium (W3C)** as a way to specify the rendering of two-dimensional images within **Extensible Markup Language (XML)**. In other words, you can use the same basic text formatting that you use to code web pages to display images in a web browser. Power BI supports SVG graphics. SVG graphics can be created using DAX code and displayed on report pages within Power BI. This can come in very handy as it allows us to present entirely new visualizations of data, as well as the flexibility to use custom shapes and not be constrained by Unicode characters or font symbols.

This recipe demonstrates how to create an SVG graphic using DAX.

Getting ready

To prepare for this recipe, do the following:

1. Open Power BI Desktop.
2. Use an **Enter Data** query to create a table called R09_Table that contains the following data:

Name	Value
Greg	200
Julie	75
Pam	100
Mike	50

How to do it...

To implement this recipe, do the following:

1. Create the following measures:

```
Target = IF(MAX('R09_Table'[Value])>=100,TRUE,FALSE)

Heart =
    VAR __header = "data:image/svg+xml;utf8," &
            "<svg
                xmlns:dc='http://purl.org/dc/elements/1.1/'
                xmlns:cc='http://creativecommons.org/ns#'
                xmlns:svg='http://www.w3.org/2000/svg'
```

```
                        xmlns='http://www.w3.org/2000/svg'
                        viewBox='0 0 150 150' version='1.1'>"
    VAR __footer = "</svg>"
    VAR __shapeTextCircle = "
        <g>
            <circle cx='30' cy='50' r='30' stroke='Red'
fill='Red'/>
            <circle cx='70' cy='50' r='30' stroke='Red'
fill='Red'/>
            <path stroke-width='2' stroke='Red' fill='Red' d='M7
70, L50 112, L93 70'/>
        </g>
        "
RETURN
    IF([Target],"",__header & __shapeTextCircle & __footer)
```

2. Set the `Data` category for the `Heart` measure to an `Image Url`.

3. On a **Report** page, create a **Table** visualization and place the `Name` column from the `R09_Table` table into the **Values** area of the visualization.

4. In the same **Table** visualization, place the `Heart` measure into the **Values** area.

How it works...

A full treatment of SVG is beyond the scope of this book. However, every SVG graphic must start with the text defined in the `__header` variable. In addition, every SVG graphic must end with the text defined in the `__footer` variable. SVG, like other XML, consists of a series of code tags that begin with a tag such as `<tag>` that must be matched with a corresponding ending tag, `</tag>`.

The `__shapeText` variable defines the actual heart graphic. Within the `__shapeText` string, the first element is the `g` tag. This is the grouping element within the SVG specification. This means that all the elements within the `g` tag should be treated as a group. The next tag is a `circle`. These `circle` tags define the top of the heart. The next tag, `path`, draws a triangle that starts at the bottom of the circles and forms the bottom point of the heart. Then, we end the `g` tag.

Now, we can simply concatenate our `__header`, `__shapeText`, and `__footer` together to return the full SVG image. However, since SVG code is just text, we must tell Power BI to treat the text that's returned by the `Heart` measure as a web graphic. This is the reason we need to set the `Data` category for the measure to an `Image Url`.

See also

For more details regarding this recipe, please refer to the following links:

- *Use SVG in Power BI: Part 1*: https://dataveld.com/2018/01/13/use-svg-images-in-power-bi-part-1/
- *Creating SVG Images in Power BI*: https://visualbi.com/blogs/microsoft/creating-svg-images-in-power-bi/
- *Using SVG to Create Microcharts in Power BI*: https://www.minceddata.info/2018/08/12/using-svg-graphics-to-create-microcharts-in-power-bi/

Creating an SVG animation

Power BI supports SVG. SVG is an open standard created by W3C as a way to specify the rendering of two-dimensional images within XML. In other words, you can use the same basic text formatting that you use to code web pages to display images in a web browser. Part of the SVG specification includes the ability to animate graphics. Power BI supports SVG graphics. SVG graphics can be created using DAX code and displayed on report pages within Power BI.

This recipe demonstrates how to create an animated SVG graphic using DAX.

Getting ready

To prepare for this recipe, do the following:

1. Open Power BI Desktop.
2. Use an **Enter Data** query to create a table called `R10_Table` that contains the following data:

Name	Value
Greg	200
Julie	75
Pam	100
Mike	50

How to do it...

To implement this recipe, do the following:

1. Create the following measures:

```
Flag = IF(MAX('R10_Table'[Value])<100,TRUE,FALSE)

BeatingHeart =
    VAR __header = "data:image/svg+xml;utf8," &
                "<svg
                    xmlns:dc='http://purl.org/dc/elements/1.1/'
                    xmlns:cc='http://creativecommons.org/ns#'
                    xmlns:svg='http://www.w3.org/2000/svg'
                    xmlns='http://www.w3.org/2000/svg'
                    viewBox='0 0 150 150' version='1.1'>"
    VAR __footer = "</svg>"
    VAR __shapeText = "
    <g>
        <circle cx='30' cy='50' r='30' stroke='Red' fill='Red'/>
        <circle cx='70' cy='50' r='30' stroke='Red' fill='Red'/>
        <path stroke-width='2' stroke='Red' fill='Red' d='M7 70,
L50 112, L93 70'/>
        <animateTransform
            attributeName='transform'
            attributeType='XML'
            type='scale'
            from='1'
            to='1.1'
            dur='1s'
            begin='0s'
            repeatCount='indefinite'
            />
        </g>
        "
    RETURN
        IF([Flag],"",__header & __shapeText & __footer)
```

2. Set the `Data` category for the `BeatingHeart` measure to an `Image Url`.
3. On a **Report** page, create a **Table** visualization and place the `Name` column from the `R10_Table` table into the **Values** area of the visualization.
4. In this same **Table** visualization, place the `BeatingHeart` measure into the **Values** area.

How it works...

A full treatment of SVG is beyond the scope of this book. However, every SVG graphic must start with the text defined in the __header variable. In addition, every SVG graphic must end with the text defined in the __footer variable. SVG, like other XML, consists of a series of code tags that begin with a tag such as `<tag>` that must be matched with a corresponding ending tag, `</tag>`.

The __shapeText variable defines the actual heart graphic. Within the __shapeText string, the first element is the g tag. This is the grouping element within the SVG specification. This means that all the elements within the g tag should be treated as a group. The next tag is a `circle`. These `circle` tags define the top of the heart. The next tag, `path`, draws a triangle that starts at the bottom of the circles and forms the bottom point of the heart. The next tag, `animateTransform`, is what performs the animation. The type of transform being performed is a scale transform (bigger and smaller) and this is specified in the `type` property. The initial scale is provided in the `from` property. The transition scale is provided in the `to` property. The duration of the animation is provided in the `dur` property and is set to `1s` (zero seconds). Thus, to make the heart beat faster or slower, simply adjust the `dur` property. A `repeatCount` property of indefinite means that the animation will continually repeat. Then, we end the g tag.

Now, we can simply concatenate our __header, __shapeText, and __footer together to return the full SVG image. However, since SVG code is just text, we must tell Power BI to treat the text that's returned by the `BeatingHeart` measure as a web graphic. This is the reason we need to set the `Data` category for the measure to an `Image Url`.

There's more...

Try these additional animated SVG measures:

```
Blink =
    VAR __header = "data:image/svg+xml;utf8," &
            "<svg
                xmlns:dc='http://purl.org/dc/elements/1.1/'
                xmlns:cc='http://creativecommons.org/ns#'
                xmlns:svg='http://www.w3.org/2000/svg'
                xmlns='http://www.w3.org/2000/svg'
                width='100%' height='100%'>"
    VAR __footer = "</svg>"
    VAR __shapeText =
        "<circle cx='10' cy='30' r='9' fill='Red' fill-opacity='1'
stroke='Black' stroke-width='1'>"
```

```
                <animate
                    attributeName='opacity'
                    from='1'
                    to='0'
                    dur='1s'
                    begin='0s'
                    repeatCount='indefinite'
                    />
            </circle>"
    RETURN
        IF([Flag],__header & __shapeText & __footer,"")

Bounce =
    VAR __header = "data:image/svg+xml;utf8," &
                "<svg
                    xmlns:dc='http://purl.org/dc/elements/1.1/'
                    xmlns:cc='http://creativecommons.org/ns#'
                    xmlns:svg='http://www.w3.org/2000/svg'
                    xmlns='http://www.w3.org/2000/svg'
                    width='100%' height='100%'>"
    VAR __footer = "</svg>"
    VAR __shapeText =
        "<circle cx='10' cy='30' r='9' fill='Red' fill-opacity='1'
stroke='Black' stroke-width='1'>
            <animate
                attributeName='cy'
                from='30'
                to='9'
                dur='.5s'
                begin='0s'
                repeatCount='indefinite'
            />
        </circle>"
    RETURN
        IF([Flag],__header & __shapeText & __footer,"")

Spinner =
    VAR __header = "data:image/svg+xml;utf8," &
                "<svg
                    xmlns:dc='http://purl.org/dc/elements/1.1/'
                    xmlns:cc='http://creativecommons.org/ns#'
                    xmlns:svg='http://www.w3.org/2000/svg'
                    xmlns='http://www.w3.org/2000/svg'
                    width='100' height='100'>"
    VAR __footer = "</svg>"
    VAR __shapeText = "
        <rect stroke='Black' width='50' height='50' x='25' y='25'
fill='Red'>
```

```
                <animateTransform
                attributeName='transform'
                attributeType='XML'
                type='rotate'
                from='0 50 50'
                to='360 50 50'
                dur='2s'
                begin='0s'
                repeatCount='indefinite'
                />
            </rect>"
    RETURN
        IF([Flag],__header & __shapeText & __footer,"")
```

See also

For more details regarding this recipe, please refer to the following links:

- *Use SVG in Power BI: Part 1*: https://dataveld.com/2018/01/13/use-svg-images-in-power-bi-part-1/
- *Creating SVG Images in Power BI*: https://visualbi.com/blogs/microsoft/creating-svg-images-in-power-bi/
- *Using SVG to Create Microcharts in Power BI*: https://www.minceddata.info/2018/08/12/using-svg-graphics-to-create-microcharts-in-power-bi/

Making things anonymous

Many datasets can include sensitive data. While proper security, such as the use of row-level security, should always be implemented in production situations, there are other times where things are less formal, such as providing a presentation at a conference where you simply wish to obfuscate the data displayed versus implementing full-on security practices and protocols.

This recipe implements a simple pattern that's intended to obfuscate data that's displayed in a report. This recipe should never be mistaken for anything resembling actual security – it is simply intended to obscure sensitive information during a display or presentation.

Getting ready

To prepare for this recipe, do the following:

1. Open Power BI Desktop.
2. Use an **Enter Data** query to create a table called `R11_Table` that contains the following data:

Name	Salary
Greg	90,000
Mike	100,000
John	85,000
Julie	110,000
Pam	95,000
George	65,000

How to do it...

To implement this recipe, do the following:

1. Create the following column in the `R11_Table` table:

```
Anonymous =
    VAR __Table =
        {
            UNICODE(MID('R11_Table'[Name],1,1)),
            UNICODE(MID('R11_Table'[Name],2,1)),
            UNICODE(MID('R11_Table'[Name],3,1)),
            UNICODE(MID('R11_Table'[Name],4,1)),
            UNICODE(MID('R11_Table'[Name],5,1)),
            UNICODE(MID('R11_Table'[Name],6,1)),
            UNICODE(MID('R11_Table'[Name],7,1)),
            UNICODE(MID('R11_Table'[Name],8,1)),
            UNICODE(MID('R11_Table'[Name],9,1)),
            UNICODE(MID('R11_Table'[Name],10,1))
        }
    RETURN
        CONCATENATEX(__Table,[Value])
```

2. On a **Report** page, create a **Table** visualization and place the `Anonymous` and `Salary` columns into the **Values** area of the visualization.

How it works...

The technique here is perhaps a bit brute force. We use a table constructor to create the __Table table variable. Within the table constructor, we create a row for every character in the Name column. Because there is no looping in DAX, we must use a reasonable maximum approach. The table constructor that's used in this example creates 10 rows, but this technique could be extended to include 25, 50, or even 100 or more rows. Each row in the table constructor uses MID to get the value of a single character within the Name column. Then, we use UNICODE to return the numeric code point for the character; for example, the Unicode number for a capital A is 66.

The __Table variable essentially deconstructs the string in the Name column one character at a time with each character becoming a row within __Table and then being converted into a Unicode number. Once we have our __Table constructed, we can simply use CONCATENATEX to reconstruct the rows of Unicode numbers back into a string.

See also

For more details regarding the functions that were used in this recipe, please refer to the following links:

- Table Constructor: https://docs.microsoft.com/en-us/dax/table-constructor
- MID: https://docs.microsoft.com/en-us/dax/mid-function-dax
- CONCATENATEX: https://docs.microsoft.com/en-us/dax/concatenatex-function-dax
- UNICODE: https://docs.microsoft.com/en-us/dax/unicode-function-dax
- UNICODE: https://dax.guide/unicode/

Debugging and Optimizing DAX 13

Previous chapters have focused on how to perform common and uncommon DAX calculations for a wide variety of purposes. However, these DAX recipes did not magically spring into existence fully formed. Significant time and effort went into the creation of these DAX recipes. And you must not discount the loss of more than a few previously well-connected hairs from the top of my head. Any reasonably complex DAX calculations inevitably require a certain amount of troubleshooting and debugging in order to make the calculation work correctly and account for any and all boundary cases that might occur. This chapter provides numerous tools and techniques that I used in the creation of the DAX recipes within this book, including recipes for troubleshooting, debugging, optimizing, and handling various errors. You can use these same tools and techniques when troubleshooting, debugging and optimizing your own DAX calculations.

The following is a list of recipes that we will be covering in this chapter:

- Handling errors with ERROR, ISERROR, and IFERROR
- Handling errors with other DAX functions
- Debugging with variables
- Debugging with CONCATENATEX
- Debugging with COUNTROWS
- Debugging with FIRSTNONBLANK and LASTNONBLANK
- Debugging with tables
- Debugging context
- Dealing with circular dependencies
- Optimizing the data model
- Optimizing DAX calculations

Technical requirements

The following are required to complete all of the recipes in this chapter:

- Power BI Desktop
- A GitHub repository: `https://github.com/PacktPublishing/DAX-Cookbook/tree/master/Chapter13`

Handling errors with ERROR, ISERROR, and IFERROR

As with any programming language, coding DAX calculations will inevitably result in an error being generated. While error handling in DAX is perhaps not quite as mature and robust as some other programming languages, DAX does provide some basic capabilities for handling errors within DAX code. This recipe demonstrates how to use three special DAX functions, `ERROR`, `ISERROR`, and `IFERROR`, in order to perform basic error checking within DAX calculations.

Getting ready

To prepare for this recipe, perform the following steps:

1. Open Power BI Desktop.
2. Use an **Enter Data** query to create a table called `R01_Table` with the following data:

Color	Value
Red	0
Green	1
Blue	2

How to do it...

To implement this recipe, perform the following steps:

1. Create the following measures:

```
Red Error =
    VAR __Color = MAX('R01_Table'[Color])
RETURN
    IF(
        __Color = "Red",
        ERROR("Error: Red encountered"),
        __Color
    )

Red IsError =
    VAR __Color = MAX('R01_Table'[Color])
RETURN
    IF(
        ISERROR(
            IF(
                __Color = "Red",
                ERROR(""),
                FALSE
            )
        ),
        "Error: Red encountered",
        __Color
    )

Red IfError =
    VAR __Color = MAX('R01_Table'[Color])
RETURN
    IFERROR(
        IF(
            __Color = "Red",
            ERROR(""),
            __Color
        ),
        "Error: Red encountered"
    )
```

2. On a **Report** page, create a **Slicer** visualization and place the `Color` column from table `R01_Table` into the **Field** area of the visualization.

3. On the same **Report** page, create a **Table** visualization and place the `Color` column from table `R01_Table` and the measure `Red Error` into the **Values** area of the visualization.

4. On the same **Report** page, create a second **Table** visualization and place the `Color` column from table `R01_Table` and the measure `Red IsError` into the **Values** area of the visualization.

5. On the same **Report** page, create a third **Table** visualization and place the `Color` column from table `R01_Table` and the measure `Red IfError` into the **Values** area of the visualization.

Note that if the color `Red` is selected in the slicer, then the first **Table** visualization with the measure `Red Error` shows an error saying that the visual cannot be displayed. Clicking on the **See details** link provides an error description that includes the error message `Error: Red encountered`. Conversely, the other two table visualizations with the measures `Red IsError` and `Red IfError` continue to display the visualizations and include the error message `Error: Red encountered` as the value for the measures `Red IsError` and `Red IfError` respectively.

How it works...

With the `Red Error` measure, we use the `ERROR` function to return an error when the color `Red` is selected in the **Slicer** visualization. The `ERROR` function throws a DAX error exactly as if a DAX function threw an error during calculation.

With the `Red IsError` measure, we wrap an `IF` statement checking for the color `Red` with the `ISERROR` function. When an error is thrown by our `ERROR` statement, the `ISERROR` function returns `TRUE`. Otherwise, if the color `Red` is not present, the `ISERROR` function returns `FALSE`. We can use the `TRUE/FALSE` output of the `ISERROR` function within a second `IF` statement to return values based on the error condition returned. In this case, if `ISERROR` returns `TRUE`, we return the text `Error: Red encountered`. Otherwise, we return the variable `__Color`.

With the `Red IfError` measure, we wrap an `IF` statement checking for the color `Red` with the `IFERROR` function. The entire code block of our `IF` statement is the first parameter of our `IFERROR` function. The second parameter of our `IFERROR` function is what to return if an error is encountered. In our case, if an error is encountered we return `Error: Red encountered`. When an error is thrown by our `ERROR` statement, the `IFERROR` function returns the second parameter. If no error is thrown, `IFERROR` simply returns the result of the calculation within the `IFERROR` function's first parameter (our `IF` code block).

It should be obvious from this simple example that the `IFERROR` function is more syntactically efficient than using `ISERROR` coupled with an `IF` statement. In fact, `IFERROR` is more efficient in terms of its overall calculation speed as well. What's more, the `IFERROR` function operates like a more traditional programming language's `try`/`catch` block. In other words, entire complex sections of code can be wrapped with an `IFERROR` statement where multiple, different errors might occur. Thus, `IFERROR` is the preferred method of performing error checking in DAX.

 Using `ISERROR` and `IFERROR` can cause performance degradation in DAX calculations. Thus, `ISERROR` and `IFERROR` should be used primarily when debugging and troubleshooting code and only used sparingly in production calculations.

See also

For more details regarding the functions in this recipe, refer to the following links:

- ERROR: https://docs.microsoft.com/en-us/dax/error-function-dax
- ISERROR: https://docs.microsoft.com/en-us/dax/iserror-function-dax
- IFERROR: https://docs.microsoft.com/en-us/dax/iferror-function-dax

Handling errors with other DAX functions

As with any programming language, coding DAX calculations will inevitably result in an error being generated. While error handling in DAX is perhaps not quite as mature and robust as some other programming languages, DAX does provide some basic capabilities for handling errors within DAX code. A certain, limited number of DAX functions include internal error checking, and this recipe demonstrates using the built-in error checking provided by these special DAX functions.

Getting ready

To prepare for this recipe, perform the following steps:

1. Open Power BI Desktop.
2. Use an **Enter Data** query to create a table called R02_Table with the following data:

Color	Value
Red	0
Green	1
Blue	2

How to do it...

To implement this recipe, perform the following steps:

1. Create the following measures:

```
Selected Color =
    SELECTEDVALUE(
        'R02_Table'[Color],
        "Select a single value"
    )

Lookup Value =
    LOOKUPVALUE(
        'R02_Table'[Value],
        'R02_Table'[Color],
        [Selected Color],
        "Select a single value"
    )

Divided =
    DIVIDE(
        SUMX(ALL('R02_Table'[Value]),[Value]),
        SUM('R02_Table'[Value]),
        -1
    )

Find =
    VAR __Text = CONCATENATEX(DISTINCT('R02_Table'[Color]),[Color])
RETURN
    FIND("u",__Text,,-1)
```

```
Search =
    VAR __Text = CONCATENATEX(DISTINCT('R02_Table'[Color]),[Color])
RETURN
    SEARCH("u",__Text,,-1)
```

2. On a **Report** page, create a **Slicer** visualization and place the `Color` column from `R02_Table` in the **Field** area of the visualization.

3. On the same **Report** page, create a **Card** visualization and place the `Selected Color` measure in the **Fields** area of the visualization.

4. On the same **Report** page, create a second **Card** visualization and place the `Lookup Value` measure in the **Fields** area of the visualization.

5. On the same **Report** page, create a third **Card** visualization and place the `Divided` measure in the **Fields** area of the visualization.

6. On the same **Report** page, create a fourth **Card** visualization and place the `Find` measure in the **Fields** area of the visualization.

7. On the same **Report** page, create a fifth **Card** visualization and place the `Search` measure in the **Fields** area of the visualization.

Note that if nothing is selected in the slicer, the card visualizations for `Selected Color` and `Lookup Value` both display **Select a single value**. If only the color `Red` is selected in the slicer, then the **Card** visualizations for `Divided`, `Find`, and `Search` all display **-1**.

How it works...

The last parameter for the `LOOKUPVALUE`, `DIVIDE`, `FIND`, and `SEARCH` functions is an optional parameter that specifies the value to return in the event that an error is generated by the function. In the case of the `SELECTEDVALUE` function, if there is no single value for the specified column, `SELECTEDVALUE` defaults to returning `BLANK` and so will never throw an error. This default return value can be overridden by specifying a second parameter for the `SELECTEDVALUE` function.

The internal error checking of the `LOOKUPVALUE`, `DIVIDE`, `FIND`, `SEARCH`, and `SELECTEDVALUE` functions is more efficient and therefore preferred over other methods of performing error checking in DAX, such as `ISERROR`, `IFERROR`, or `HASONEVALUE`.

See also

For more details regarding the functions in this recipe, refer to the following links:

- SELECTEDVALUE: https://docs.microsoft.com/en-us/dax/selectedvalue-function-dax
- LOOKUPVALUE: https://docs.microsoft.com/en-us/dax/lookupvalue-function-dax
- DIVIDE: https://docs.microsoft.com/en-us/dax/divide-function-dax
- FIND: https://docs.microsoft.com/en-us/dax/find-function-dax
- SEARCH: https://docs.microsoft.com/en-us/dax/search-function-dax

Debugging with variables

Debugging DAX is not nearly as advanced or user-friendly in Power BI, Excel, and SQL as debugging in the **integrated development environments (IDEs)** for many other programming languages. While IDEs for other languages include the ability to set code execution breakpoints, step through code, and watch variable values change during code execution, the environments in which DAX is written do not provide similar capabilities. Hence, debugging DAX is unquestionably more *old school* when it comes to trying to figure out what is wrong with a particular calculation. This recipe provides a technique to assist in troubleshooting efforts that leverages DAX's ability to create variables. Variables can be used to break down complex DAX calculations into manageable pieces that can be debugged individually.

Getting ready

To prepare for this recipe, perform the following steps:

1. Open Power BI Desktop.
2. Use an **Enter Data** query to create a table called R03_Table with the following data:

Color	Value
Red	0
Green	1
Blue	2

How to do it...

To implement this recipe, perform the following steps:

1. Create the following measures:

```
My Calc =
    SUM('R03_Table'[Value]) *
        AVERAGE('R03_Table'[Value]) *
            STDEV.P('R03_Table'[Value]) *
                MEDIAN('R03_Table'[Value]) *
                    VAR.P('R03_Table'[Value])

My Calc Debug =
    VAR __Sum = SUM('R03_Table'[Value])
    VAR __Average = AVERAGE('R03_Table'[Value])
    VAR __StDev = STDEV.P('R03_Table'[Value])
    VAR __Median = MEDIAN('R03_Table'[Value])
    VAR __Variance = VAR.P('R03_Table'[Value])
RETURN
    __Variance //__Sum * __Average * __StDev * __Median *
__Variance
```

2. On a **Report** page, create a **Slicer** visualization and place the `Color` column from `R03_Table` in the **Field** area of the visualization.

3. On the same **Report** page, create a **Card** visualization and place the `My Calc` measure in the **Fields** area of the visualization.

4. On the same **Report** page, create a second **Card** visualization and place the `My Calc Debug` measure in the **Fields** area of the visualization.

How it works...

In our `My Calc Debug` measure, we simply take the individual calculation components present in our `My Calc` measure and separate each part of the calculation into its own variable using VAR. Thus, when debugging our measure, we can comment out the normal RETURN line using `//` or even `/* */` and return any of our variables. In this way, we can check parts of the entire calculation in order to determine where there might be a problem.

See also

For more details regarding the functions in this recipe, refer to the following link:

- VAR: https://docs.microsoft.com/en-us/dax/var-dax

Debugging with CONCATENATEX

Debugging DAX is not nearly as advanced or user-friendly in Power BI, Excel, and SQL as debugging in the IDEs for many other programming languages. While IDEs for other languages include the ability to set code execution breakpoints, step through code, and watch variable values change during code execution, the environments in which DAX is written do not provide similar capabilities. Hence, debugging DAX is unquestionably more *old school* when it comes to trying to figure out what is wrong with a particular calculation. This recipe provides a technique to assist in troubleshooting efforts that leverages the CONCATENATEX function.

Getting ready

To prepare for this recipe, perform the following steps:

1. Open Power BI Desktop.
2. Use an **Enter Data** query to create a table called R04_Table with the following data:

Color	Value
Red	0
Green	1
Blue	2

How to do it...

To implement this recipe, perform the following steps:

1. Create the following measures:

```
My Sum =
    VAR __Table = ALLSELECTED('R04_Table')
RETURN
```

```
        SUMX(__Table,[Value])

My Sum Debug =
    VAR __Table = ALLSELECTED('R04_Table')
RETURN
    CONCATENATEX(__Table,[Value],",") //SUMX(__Table,[Value])
```

2. On a **Report** page, create a **Slicer** visualization and place the `Color` column from `R04_Table` in the **Field** area of the visualization.

3. On the same **Report** page, create a **Card** visualization and place the `My Sum` measure in the **Fields** area of the visualization.

4. On the same **Report** page, create a second **Card** visualization and place the `My Sum Debug` measure in the **Fields** area of the visualization.

How it works...

In our `My Sum Debug` measure, we simply substitute the `CONCATENATEX` function for the `SUMX` function present in the `My Sum` measure. Thus, when debugging our measure, we can essentially take a peek inside the table that `SUMX` is iterating over in order to see the individual values that make up our calculation since our `My Sum Debug` measure now returns the individual values that comprise the calculation.

This technique can be used with any of the iterator functions, such as `SUMX`, `AVERAGEX`, `COUNTX`, and `MEDIANX`. In addition, this technique can also be used with any table created within a DAX expression. Seeing the individual values that comprise otherwise hidden, internal DAX tables can greatly aid in the troubleshooting and debugging of measure and column calculations.

See also

For more details regarding the functions in this recipe, refer to the following link:

- CONCATENATEX: https://docs.microsoft.com/en-us/dax/concatenatex-function-dax

Debugging with COUNTROWS

Debugging DAX is not nearly as advanced or user-friendly in Power BI, Excel, and SQL as debugging in the IDEs for many other programming languages. While IDEs for other languages include the ability to set code execution breakpoints, step through code, and watch variable values change during code execution, the environments in which DAX is written do not provide similar capabilities. Hence, debugging DAX is unquestionably more *old school* when it comes to trying to figure out what is wrong with a particular calculation. This recipe provides a technique to assist in troubleshooting efforts that leverages DAX's COUNTROWS function.

Getting ready

To prepare for this recipe, perform the following steps:

1. Open Power BI Desktop.
2. Use an **Enter Data** query to create a table called R05_Table with the following data:

Color	Value
Red	0
Green	1
Blue	2

How to do it...

To implement this recipe, perform the following steps:

1. Create the following measures:

```
My Average =
    VAR __Table = ALLSELECTED('R04_Table')
RETURN
    AVERAGEX(__Table,[Value])

My Average Debug =
    VAR __Table = ALLSELECTED('R04_Table')
RETURN
    COUNTROWS(__Table) //AVERAGEX(__Table,[Value])
```

2. On a **Report** page, create a **Slicer** visualization and place the `Color` column from `R05_Table` in the **Field** area of the visualization.

3. On the same **Report** page, create a **Card** visualization and place the `My Average` measure in the **Fields** area of the visualization.

4. On the same **Report** page, create a second **Card** visualization and place the `My Average Debug` measure in the **Fields** area of the visualization.

How it works...

In our `My Average Debug` measure, we simply substitute the `COUNTROWS` function for the `AVERAGEX` function present in the `My Average` measure. Hence, when debugging our measure, we can essentially get information about the table that `AVERAGEX` is iterating over in order to understand whether the expected number of rows is being processed or not.

This technique can be used with any of the iterator functions, such as `SUMX`, `AVERAGEX`, `COUNTX`, and `MEDIANX`. In addition, this technique can also be used with any table created within a DAX expression. Understanding the properties of otherwise hidden, internal DAX tables can greatly aid in the troubleshooting and debugging of measure and column calculations.

See also

For more details regarding the functions in this recipe, refer to the following link:

- `CONCATENATEX`: https://docs.microsoft.com/en-us/dax/concatenatex-function-dax

Debugging with FIRSTNONBLANK and LASTNONBLANK

Debugging DAX is not nearly as advanced or user-friendly in Power BI, Excel, and SQL as debugging in the IDEs for many other programming languages. While IDEs for other languages include the ability to set code execution breakpoints, step through code, and watch variable values change during code execution, the environments in which DAX is written do not provide similar capabilities.

Hence, debugging DAX is unquestionably more *old school* when it comes to trying to figure out what is wrong with a particular calculation. This recipe provides a technique to assist in troubleshooting efforts that leverages DAX's FIRSTNONBLANK and LASTNONBLANK functions.

Getting ready

To prepare for this recipe, perform the following steps:

1. Open Power BI Desktop.
2. Use an **Enter Data** query to create a table called R06_Table with the following data:

Color	Value
Red	0
Green	1
Blue	2

How to do it...

To implement this recipe, perform the following steps:

1. Create the following measures:

```
My Standard Deviation =
    VAR __Table = ALLSELECTED('R04_Table')
RETURN
    STDEVX.P(__Table,[Value])

My Standard Deviation Debug =
    VAR __Table = ALLSELECTED('R04_Table')
RETURN
    //STDEVX.P(__Table,[Value])
    FIRSTNONBLANK(
        SELECTCOLUMNS(
            __Table,
            "__Value",[Value]
        ),
        [__Value]
    )
    & "," &
    LASTNONBLANK(
        SELECTCOLUMNS(
```

```
        __Table,
        "__Value",[Value]
    ),
    [__Value]
)
```

2. On a **Report** page, create a **Slicer** visualization and place the `Color` column from `R06_Table` in the **Field** area of the visualization.

3. On the same **Report** page, create a **Card** visualization and place the `My Standard Deviation` measure in the **Fields** area of the visualization.

4. On the same **Report** page, create a second **Card** visualization and place the `My Standard Deviation Debug` measure in the **Fields** area of the visualization.

How it works...

In our `My Standard Deviation Debug` measure, we comment out the normal `RETURN` value for our `My Standard Deviation` measure and instead use `FIRSTNONBLANK` and `LASTNONBLANK` to return the minimum and maximum values from our `__Table` variable. Hence, when debugging our measure, we can essentially get information about the table that `STDEVX.P` is iterating over in order to understand whether the table adheres to the expected range of our calculation.

This technique can be used with any of the iterator functions, such as `SUMX`, `AVERAGEX`, `COUNTX`, and `MEDIANX`. In addition, this technique can also be used with any table created within a DAX expression. Understanding the properties of otherwise hidden, internal DAX tables can greatly aid in the troubleshooting and debugging of measure and column calculations.

See also

For more details regarding the functions in this recipe, refer to the following links:

- `FIRSTNONBLANK`: https://docs.microsoft.com/en-us/dax/firstnonblank-function-dax
- `LASTNONBLANK`: https://docs.microsoft.com/en-us/dax/lastnonblank-function-dax

Debugging with tables

Debugging DAX is not nearly as advanced or user-friendly in Power BI, Excel, and SQL as debugging in the IDEs for many other programming languages. While IDEs for other languages include the ability to set code execution breakpoints, step through code, and watch variable values change during code execution, the environments in which DAX is written do not provide similar capabilities. Hence, debugging DAX is unquestionably more *old school* when it comes to trying to figure out what is wrong with a particular calculation. This recipe provides a technique to assist in troubleshooting efforts that leverages DAX's ability to create tables.

Getting ready

To prepare for this recipe, perform the following steps:

1. Open Power BI Desktop.
2. Use an **Enter Data** query to create a table called `R07_Table` with the following data:

Color	Value
Red	0
Green	1
Blue	2

How to do it...

To implement this recipe, perform the following steps:

1. Create the following measures:

```
My Calculation =
    VAR __Calculation =
        CALCULATE (
            SUM('R07_Table'[Value]),
            'R07_Table'[Color] <> "Blue"
        )
    RETURN
        __Calculation
```

2. Create the following table:

```
R07_Debug =
    VAR __Table =
        FILTER (
            'R07_Table',
            'R07_Table'[Color] <> "Blue"
        )
    VAR __Calculation =
        CALCULATE (
            SUM('R07_Table'[Value]),
            'R07_Table'[Color] <> "Blue"
        )
RETURN
    __Table
```

3. On a **Report** page, create a **Card** visualization and place the `My Calculation` measure in the **Fields** area of the visualization.

How it works...

In our calculated table, `R07_Debug`, we create a table variable, `__Table`, with the same `FILTER` function as that used in our `My Calculation` measure. We can then return `__Table` as the output of our calculated table to peek inside the table that `CALCULATE` is using within the DAX calculation for the `__Calculation` variable in order to see the individual table rows that make up our calculation.

This technique can be used with any table created within a DAX expression. Seeing the individual rows of otherwise hidden, internal DAX tables can greatly aid in the troubleshooting and debugging of measure and column calculations.

See also

For more details regarding the functions in this recipe, refer to the following link:

- `FILTER`: https://docs.microsoft.com/en-us/dax/filter-function-dax

Debugging context

The concept of context is a huge strength of the DAX language. The ability to create a single calculation whose value changes based upon contextual filters is fundamental to the proper operation of Power BI reports and dashboards. However, troubleshooting and debugging context can prove challenging as it is sometimes difficult to know exactly what context filters might be operating on a particular DAX calculation. This recipe provides techniques to assist in troubleshooting and debugging context issues by leveraging three special DAX functions: FILTERS, ISFILTERED, and ISCROSSFILTERED.

Getting ready

To prepare for this recipe, perform the following steps:

1. Open Power BI Desktop.
2. Use an **Enter Data** query to create a table called R08_Table with the following data:

Color	Value
Red	0
Green	1
Blue	2

How to do it...

To implement this recipe, perform the following steps:

1. Create the following measures:

```
Filters =
CONCATENATEX(FILTERS('R08_Table'[Color]),'R08_Table'[Color],",")
```

2. On a **Report** page, create a **Slicer** visualization and place the `Color` column from `R08_Table` in the **Field** area of the visualization.

3. On the same **Report** page, create a **Card** visualization and place the `Filters` measure in the **Fields** area of the visualization.

How it works...

In our `Filters` measure, we use the `FILTERS` function to return the filter values that are active on the `Color` column of our table, `R08_Table`. We then use `CONCATENATEX` to concatenate these values for display purposes within our visualization. Understanding how columns are being filtered internally within DAX calculations can be invaluable when debugging measures.

There's more...

The `FILTERS` function is not the only DAX function that can be used to debug and troubleshoot context issues within measures. Two other DAX functions, `ISFILTERED` and `ISCROSSFILTERED`, can also be used to help debug context. To see how these two functions work, perform the following steps:

1. Create the following measures:

```
Is Filtered = ISFILTERED('R08_Table'[Color])

Is Cross Filtered = ISCROSSFILTERED('R08_Table'[Color])
```

2. On the same **Report** page used previously in this recipe, create a second **Slicer** visualization and place the `Value` column from `R08_Table` in the **Field** area of the visualization.

3. On the same **Report** page, create a second **Card** visualization and place the `Is Filtered` measure in the **Fields** area of the visualization.

4. On the same **Report** page, create a third **Card** visualization and place the `Is Cross Filtered` measure in the **Fields** area of the visualization.

When selecting a value in the first **Slicer** visualization that uses the `Color` column from `R08_Table`, both `Is Filtered` and `Is Cross Filtered` return `True`. However, when selecting a value in the second **Slicer** visualization that uses the `Value` column from `R08_Table`, `Is Filtered` returns `False` while `Is Cross Filtered` returns `True`. This is because the `ISFILTERED` function returns `True` only when the specified column is being filtered directly. However, `ISCROSSFILTERED` returns `True` if the specified column is being filtered by any column within the table or because of filters applied to any related table that cause filtering on the specified column.

See also

For more details regarding the functions in this recipe, refer to the following links:

- FILTERS: https://docs.microsoft.com/en-us/dax/filters-function-dax
- CONCATENATEX: https://docs.microsoft.com/en-us/dax/concatenatex-function-dax
- ISFILTERED: https://docs.microsoft.com/en-us/dax/isfiltered-function-dax
- ISCROSSFILTERED: https://docs.microsoft.com/en-us/dax/iscrossfiltered-function-dax

Dealing with circular dependencies

Circular dependency errors in DAX are perhaps the most feared of all DAX errors. In short, a circular dependency is essentially a loop where a value, *A*, depends on another value, *B*, which depends on the original value, *A*. The reason that circular dependencies tend to be feared is that people do not necessarily understand where circular dependencies come from, and so circular dependencies can be complex and time-consuming to troubleshoot and resolve, especially in complex data models and complex DAX calculations. This recipe provides techniques to help you understand how circular dependencies get created as well as techniques to avoid circular dependencies.

Getting ready

To prepare for this recipe, perform the following steps:

1. Open Power BI Desktop.
2. Use an **Enter Data** query to create a table called R09_Table with the following data:

Item	Value
One	1
Two	2
Three	3
Four	4
One	1
Two	2
Three	3

3. Use an **Enter Data** query to create a table called R09_Items with the following data:

Item
One
Two
Three

4. Create a relationship between the Item columns in the R09_Table and R09_Items tables.

How to do it...

To implement this recipe, observe the following steps:

1. Create the following tables:

```
R09_ItemDistinct = DISTINCT('R09_Items'[Item])

R09_ItemValues = VALUES('R09_Items'[Item])
```

2. Create a relationship between the Item columns in the R09_Items and R09_ItemDistinct tables. The creation of the relationship is successful.

3. Attempt to create a relationship between the Item columns in the R09_Items and R09_ItemValues tables. The creation of the relationship results in an error stating that a circular dependency has been detected.

How it works...

The reason why relating R09_ItemDistinct to R09_Items works, while relating R09_ItemValues to R09_Items does not work, comes down to a subtle but important difference between the DISTINCT function and the VALUES function. If you inspect the R09_ItemValues table, you will notice that there is a row with a blank value. This blank value comes from the relationship between the R09_Items table and the R09_Table table. Because there is a row in the R09_Table table (Item = Four) that does not match any row value in R09_Items, when VALUES evaluates the unique values in the Item column of R09_Items, VALUES adds this blank value. This means that the R09_ItemValues table created by the VALUES function is dependent upon the relationship between the R09_Items and R09_Table tables. Hence, when attempting to create a relationship between R09_ItemValues and R09_Items, a circular dependency is created between R09_ItemValues and R09_Table. This is likely highly unexpected.

Conversely, when using DISTINCT, only the actual values within R09_Items are considered, and not any relationships. Therefore, no circular dependency is present when creating the relationship between the R09_ItemsDistinct and R09_Items tables. Thus, if creating calculated tables within a data model, it is safest to use DISTINCT rather than VALUES.

The same subtle difference between VALUES and DISTINCT also exists between ALL and ALLNOBLANKROW.

There's more...

It is possible for columns and measures to also exhibit circular dependencies. To demonstrate, follow these steps:

1. In `R09_Table`, create the following columns:

   ```
   Column = 'R09_Table'[Value] * 100

   Column 2 = 'R09_Table'[Value] * 'R09_Table'[Column]
   ```

2. Now, change the formula for `Column` as shown:

   ```
   Column = 'R09_Table'[Value] * 'R09_Table'[Column 2]
   ```

Note that a circular dependency error is displayed and that both `Column` and `Column 2` are blanked out.

The fix in this case is obvious; simply create a single column with the following formula:

```
Column = 'R09_Table'[Value] * 100 * 'R09_Table'[Value]
```

However, there are instances where DAX's precise detection of a circular reference can be maddeningly obscure.

See also

For more details regarding the functions in this recipe, refer to the following links:

- Understanding circular dependencies in Tabular and Power Pivot: https://www.sqlbi.com/articles/understanding-circular-dependencies/
- VALUES: https://docs.microsoft.com/en-us/dax/values-function-dax
- DISTINCT: https://docs.microsoft.com/en-us/dax/distinct-function-dax
- ALL: https://docs.microsoft.com/en-us/dax/all-function-dax
- ALLNOBLANKROW: https://docs.microsoft.com/en-us/dax/allnoblankrow-function-dax

Optimizing the data model

The underlying data model used for DAX is the in-memory tabular cube. Since this data model is designed to be used in memory, the overall size of the data model is an important performance consideration since, after all, computers only have a finite amount of memory. Understanding the underlying workings of the tabular data model is imperative to building efficient data models that fit into available memory and optimize the speed and performance of DAX calculations. This recipe provides guidance on how to optimize your data model for peak efficiency.

Getting ready

To prepare for this recipe, perform the following steps:

1. Open Power BI Desktop.
2. Create a new file using **File** and then **New** from the ribbon.
3. Save this file with the name `Chapter13R10Step1.pbix`.
4. Observe that the file size of `Chapter13R10Step1.pbix` is **12 KB.**

How to do it...

To implement this recipe, perform the following steps:

1. Use **File** and then **Save As** to save `Chapter13R10Step1.pbix` as `Chapter13R10Step2.pbix`.
2. Create the following table:

```
R10_Table =
    VAR __Table =
        ADDCOLUMNS (
            GENERATESERIES(1,1000000,1),
            "TimeStamp",NOW()+[Value]/24/60/60
        )
RETURN
    SELECTCOLUMNS(__Table,"TimeStamp",[TimeStamp])
```

3. Save the file using **File** and then **Save**.

4. Observe that the file size of `Chapter13R10Step2.pbix` is **11,912 KB**.

5. Use **File** and then **Save As** to save `Chapter13R10Step2.pbix` as `Chapter13R10Step3.pbix`.

6. Create the following table:

```
R10_Table2 =
    VAR __Table =
        ADDCOLUMNS (
            ADDCOLUMNS (
                GENERATESERIES(1,1000000,1),
                "TimeStamp",NOW()+[Value]/24/60/60
            ),
    "Date",DATE(YEAR([TimeStamp]),MONTH([TimeStamp]),DAY([TimeStamp])),
            "Hour",HOUR([TimeStamp]),
            "Minute",MINUTE([TimeStamp]),
            "Second",SECOND([TimeStamp])
        )
RETURN
    SELECTCOLUMNS (
        __Table,
        "Date",[Date],
        "Hour",[Hour],
        "Minute",[Minute],
        "Second",[Second]
    )
```

7. Delete the `R10_Table` table.

8. Save the file using **File** and then **Save**.

9. Observe that the file size of `Chapter13R10Step3.pbix` is **51 KB**.

How it works...

In `R10_Table`, we create the table variable, `__Table`. The `__Table` variable creates a 1 million row table with each row having a unique index value and unique date and time stamp using `GENERATESERIES` and `ADDCOLUMNS`. We then use `SELECTCOLUMNS` to only select our `TimeStamp` column from `__Table`.

In `R10_Table2`, we also create the table variable, `__Table`. `__Table` starts out with the same calculation as used in `R10_Table`. However, we use `ADDCOLUMNS` to add four columns, `Date`, `Hour`, `Minute`, and `Second`. We then use `SELECTCOLUMNS` to only select our `Date`, `Hour`, `Minute`, and `Second` columns from `__Table`.

Although we have exactly the same information within both tables, R10_Table and R10_Table2, storing R10_Table requires nearly **12 MB** of disk space (which equates to required memory storage space as well), while table R10_Table2 only requires **39 KB** (51 KB-12 KB) of disk space. This means that R10_Table requires over *300 times* the amount of storage as R10_Table2. What is going on?

At issue here is the underlying data model behind DAX, the in-memory tabular cube. The tabular data model utilizes columnar compression to compress data to a fraction of its original size under the right set of circumstances. To understand how this works, consider the simple scenario of a dataset that includes the following values in a column:

111
111
222
222
333
333

Without delving into the gory details of how column compression actually operates, you can essentially visualize the compression process by understanding that in the circumstance provided by the example table, the optimization implemented by the tabular data model is to only store unique values within the column, 111, 222, and 333, instead of storing each value within each row. In the example provided, this effectively cuts the amount of data required to be stored in order to express the data model in half.

Thus, the problem with the first table, R10_Table, is that each row value is unique, and so compression cannot occur. However, in the second table, R10_Table2, by splitting out the information in the single column into four different columns, there are lots of repeating values within the columns of R10_Table2, so columnar compression has a huge impact on the amount of storage required to express the data.

There's more...

Additional optimization techniques include reducing unnecessary precision in decimal numbers (which tends to reduce the uniqueness of values) as well as using integers versus text whenever possible. Finally, implement the table in this recipe as shown in the following manner:

```
R10_Table3 =
    VAR __Table =
        ADDCOLUMNS (
```

```
        ADDCOLUMNS (
            GENERATESERIES(1,1000000,1),
            "TimeStamp",NOW()+[Value]/24/60/60
        ),
        "Year",YEAR([TimeStamp]),
        "Month",MONTH([TimeStamp]),
        "Day",DAY([TimeStamp]),
        "Hour",HOUR([TimeStamp]),
        "Minute",MINUTE([TimeStamp]),
        "Second",SECOND([TimeStamp])
    )
RETURN
    SELECTCOLUMNS (
        __Table,
        "Year",[Year],
        "Month",[Month],
        "Day",[Day],
        "Hour",[Hour],
        "Minute",[Minute],
        "Second",[Second]
    )
```

You will see that this version of the table only takes 34 KB of storage within the model.

See also

For more details regarding this recipe, refer to the following link:

- Power BI performance best practices: `https://docs.microsoft.com/en-us/power-bi/power-bi-reports-performance`

Optimizing DAX calculations

Optimizing DAX calculations for performance is hugely complicated and a vast subject that arguably deserves its own book. This recipe introduces the subject of how to analyze DAX calculations for performance and provides a number of techniques for optimizing the performance of DAX calculations.

Getting ready

To prepare for this recipe, perform the following steps:

1. Open Power BI Desktop.

2. Create a new table, R11_Table, using the following formula:

```
R11_Table =
    ADDCOLUMNS (
        SELECTCOLUMNS (
            GENERATESERIES(1,1000000),
            "ID",[Value]
        ),
        "Value",100
    )
```

3. Create the following measures:

```
Sum 1 = 1000000 * 100

Sum 2 = COUNTROWS('R11_Table') * MAX('R11_Table'[Value])

Sum 3 = SUMX('R11_Table','R11_Table'[Value])

Sum 4 =
MAXX(SUMMARIZE('R11_Table','R11_Table'[Value],"__Sum",SUM('R11_Tabl
e'[Value])),[__Sum])

Sum 5 =
    SUMX (
        ADDCOLUMNS (
            SELECTCOLUMNS (
                GENERATESERIES(1,1000000),
                "ID",[Value]
            ),
            "Value",100
        ),
        [Value]
    )
```

4. Create a **Card** visualization and place the Sum 1 measure in the **Fields** area of the visualization.

5. Create a second **Card** visualization and place the Sum 2 measure in the **Fields** area of the visualization.

6. Create a third **Card** visualization and place the Sum 3 measure in the **Fields** area of the visualization.

7. Create a fourth **Card** visualization and place the Sum 4 measure in the **Fields** area of the visualization.

8. Create a fifth **Card** visualization and place the Sum 5 measure in the **Fields** area of the visualization.

How to do it...

To implement this recipe, perform the following steps:

1. In the ribbon, click on the **View** tab.
2. Click on **Performance analyzer**.
3. In the **Performance analyzer** pane, click on **Start recording**.
4. In the **Performance analyzer** pane, click on **Refresh visuals**.
5. In the **Performance analyzer** pane, click on **Stop**.
6. In the **Performance analyzer** pane, click on the individual visualization rows to highlight the visual on the page that corresponds to the performance analyzer result.

How it works...

The **Performance analyzer** records the duration in milliseconds for visuals to calculate their display values and write their results to the screen. The results for each visual are broken down into three elements:

- DAX query
- Visual display
- Other

Here, the DAX query portion represents the amount of time between the visual sending the DAX query and Analysis Services returning a result. The Visual display portion consists of the amount of time required for the visual to draw on the screen. The Visual display component also includes any time required to retrieve web images and perform geocoding. The Other component includes the time required to prepare the query, the time spent waiting on other visuals to complete, and the time spent on background processing.

There's more...

To demonstrate the efficiency of using VAR statements, perform the following steps:

1. Create the following measures:

```
Sum 6 =
 IF(
 SUMX('R11_Table','R11_Table'[Value]) = 0,
 0,
 SUMX('R11_Table','R11_Table'[Value])
 )

Sum 7 =
 VAR __Sum = SUMX('R11_Table','R11_Table'[Value])
 RETURN
 IF(__Sum = 0,
 0,
 SUMX('R11_Table','R11_Table'[Value])
 )
```

2. Create a **Card** visualization and place the Sum 6 measure in the **Fields** area of the visualization.
3. Create a second **Card** visualization and place the Sum 7 measure in the **Fields** area of the visualization.
4. Analyze the **Card** visualizations for Sum 6 and Sum 7 using Performance Analyzer.

You should see that Sum 7 consistently takes a shorter amount of time to complete than Sum 6. This is because Sum 6 performs the SUMX calculation twice, while Sum 7 only performs the SUMX calculation once.

See also

For more details regarding this recipe, refer to the following link:

- Using Performance Analyzer to examine report element performance: `https://docs.microsoft.com/en-us/power-bi/desktop-performance-analyzer`

Other Books You May Enjoy

If you enjoyed this book, you may be interested in these other books by Packt:

Learn Power BI
Greg Deckler

ISBN: 978-1-83864-448-2

- Explore the different features of Power BI to create interactive dashboards
- Use the Query Editor to import and transform data
- Perform simple and complex DAX calculations to enhance analysis
- Discover business insights and tell a story with your data using Power BI
- Explore data and learn to manage datasets, dataflows, and data gateways
- Use workspaces to collaborate with others and publish your reports

Hands-On Business Intelligence with DAX
Ian Horne

ISBN: 978-1-83882-430-3

- Understand DAX, from the basics through to advanced topics, and learn to build effective data models
- Write and use DAX functions and expressions with the help of hands-on examples
- Discover how to handle errors in your DAX code, and avoid unwanted results
- Load data into a data model using Power BI, Excel Power Pivot, and SSAS Tabular
- Cover DAX functions such as date, time, and time intelligence using code examples
- Gain insights into data by using DAX to create new information
- Understand the DAX VertiPaq engine and how it can help you optimize data models

Leave a review - let other readers know what you think

Please share your thoughts on this book with others by leaving a review on the site that you bought it from. If you purchased the book from Amazon, please leave us an honest review on this book's Amazon page. This is vital so that other potential readers can see and use your unbiased opinion to make purchasing decisions, we can understand what our customers think about our products, and our authors can see your feedback on the title that they have worked with Packt to create. It will only take a few minutes of your time, but is valuable to other potential customers, our authors, and Packt. Thank you!

Index

Runge-Kutta (RK4)
about 397
reference link 400
using 398, 399, 400

S

sample size
determining 429, 431, 432
Scalable Vector Graphics (SVG) 433
sensitive information
obscuring 483, 485
sequential day numbers, year
determining 55, 57, 59
sequential week number
constructing 70
sequential week
constructing 72, 73
sequential working day numbers, year
determining 55, 57, 58
Shannon entropy
calculating 388, 390, 391
shifts
calculating 108, 110
calculating, reference links 110
simple interest
versus compound interest 175
skewness, set of values
calculating 414, 416, 417
skewness
reference link 418
SQL Server Analysis Services (SSAS) 10
SQL Server
DAX, using 11
SVG animation
creating 479, 481, 483
SVG graphic
creating 477, 478

T

Table Constructor
reference link 264
tables
transposing 444, 446, 447
used, for debugging DAX 502, 503

text
extracting 152, 154
time intelligence
using 46, 47, 49
time tables
constructing 92, 93, 94
reference links 95
time zones
tinkering with 116, 118
time
adding 101, 103, 104
subtracting 101, 103, 104
transitive closure
calculating 354, 355, 356, 357
concept and technique 358, 359, 360

U

unfiltering 27, 29, 31, 33
Unit Market Share column
using 172
Unix
converting, into UTC 100, 101
utilization
calculating 266, 267, 268
working 268
Utrecht Work Engagement Scale (UWES) 242

V

variables
used, for debugging DAX 494
using 15, 17, 19

W

week end dates
finding 61, 63, 64, 65
week start dates
finding 61, 63, 64, 65
working days
for months, finding 65, 67, 69
for quarters, finding 65, 68
for weeks, finding 65, 67, 69
for years, finding 65, 68, 69
World Wide Web Consortium (W3C) 477